Imperial City

SUSAN VANDIVER NICASSIO

Imperial City

ROME UNDER NAPOLEON

Preface by
Professor Claudio Rendina

THE UNIVERSITY OF CHICAGO PRESS
Chicago & London

TO ALEXANDRA ELISE RICHARDSON NICASSIO
AND COLIN JOSEPH MAXIMUS NICASSIO

The University of Chicago Press, Chicago 60637
Chicago and London

© 2005 by Susan Vandiver Nicassio
All rights reserved
Originally published in England in 2005 by Ravenhall Books,
an imprint of Linden Publishing Ltd.
University of Chicago Press edition, 2009

Printed in the United States of America

18 17 16 15 14 13 12 11 10 09   1 2 3 4 5

ISBN: 978-0-226-57973-3 (paper)
ISBN: 0-226-57973-5 (paper)

Library of Congress Cataloging-in-Publication Data

Nicassio, Susan Vandiver.
Imperial city : Rome under Napoleon / Susan Vandiver Nicassio ;
preface by Claudio Rendina.
p. cm.
ISBN-13: 978-0-226-57973-3 (alk. paper)
ISBN-10: 0-226-57973-5 (alk. paper)
1. Rome (Italy)—History—1798–1870. 2. Rome (Italy)--Social life and customs—19th
century. 3. Rome (Italy)—Politics and government—19th century. 4. Rome (Italy)—Social
life and customs—18th century. 5. Rome (Italy)—Politics and government—18th century.
6. Rome (Italy)—History—Revolution, 1798–1799. I. Title.
DG812.7.N53 2009
945'.632082—dc22
                                                2009013437

♾ The paper used in this publication meets the minimum requirements of the American
National Standard for Information Sciences—Permanence of Paper for Printed Library
Materials, ANSI Z39.48-1992.

CONTENTS

A view of Tivoli by Ingres, a French resident in Napoleonic Rome.

It is the Rome of Napoleon's dreams - an imperial city to be all of his own making, worthy of the great Corsican's majesty, but a city destined for the most part to remain on paper, or in his mind. It was a city of struggles and of changes: Jacobin-style between 1796 and 1800, and Napoleonic between 1808 and 1813, with a postscript in 1815. Napoleon's attachment to the conquered city was always ambiguous: now coaxing flattery, now threats of retribution, now plans for vengeance, now tokens of love. He decreed that Rome should be his second Capitol, and planned to make it the most beautiful city of the empire; he gave his son the title of King of Rome, and projected a future radiant with glory for the city.

So the orders to carry out archaeological excavations, to free the ancient monuments from the filth that suffocated them, were simply an extension of his desire to see Rome returned to the greatness of her past. The same was true of the project for the Pincio gardens and the Piazza del Popolo that stood below them, creating an imperial square in the French style. This last project was actually carried out, and remains almost the sole witness of the Napoleonic dream. Everything else was in vain, as we know, and yet the shadow of Napoleon remains. He never came to Rome: perhaps he intended to go there once he had won his great gamble; perhaps Rome was to be the prize for his own personal glory.

It is the story of this Napoleonic Rome that Susan Nicassio relates for us. She is an American scholar who has undertaken to bring to light particular periods of the history of Rome through literary, artistic and social documentation, documentation which she uses to present a political reality. Nicassio has a profound understanding of the historic period which she brings to life in this book, something shown in her preceding work, *Tosca's Rome*, which holds up a mirror to the Jacobin republic. From this understanding has emerged a book of notable depth, a study that ranges from the world of the nobility, with the great families and their homes, to the artists, to the world of the common folk and the precincts of the Church, from the journals to the pasquinades, from doctors and hospitals to crimes and the law, from merchants to bandits and to saints.

Citations of archival collections and from printed works add to the value of the text, which acknowledges its debt to the scientific labours of contemporary Roman scholars. The writer leads us with the hand of an authentic *romanista*, allowing us to relive from the inside episodes from the chronicles of daily life that seem to be tangential to the official history, but which in fact provide a vivid interpretation of events in close-up. From this technique flows a sort of double-entry account, one the mirror of the other. The document makes history, the poetry tells the story, the miraculous sacred image generates apocalyptic visions, the work of art hints at the description of the city. In this way everything contributes to recreate the dream of an imperial Rome, which we can visit again in the pages of this book. On the surface, the Rome of today offers little of that vanished dream: the Piazza del Popolo; some relics in the Napoleonic Museum; an inscription on a stone tablet at the Palazzo della Cancelleria that recalls that the palace was the seat of the imperial tribunal; the rooms of the Quirinal rebuilt for the arrival of the emperor who never came to see them. A few mementos are also scattered in the Villa Paolina, pictures of the Egyptian countryside that recall Napoleon's Egyptian campaign. Napoleonic Rome vanished like the dream that it was. But it is a dream that Nicassio's book magically brings back for us.

Professor Claudio Rendina
Rome, 2005

CAST OF CHARACTERS

The Main Contenders
Napoleon, the genius who never came to Rome; ardent and sometimes enraged lover of a city that refused to return his affection
Pius VI (Braschi), pious, amiable, vain and an enthusiastic practitioner of nepotism, he managed at the end to ascend to the dignity of virtual martyrdom
Pius VII (Chiaramonti), seemingly pliant but unbending Benedictine monk and patriarch of Venice, a much more daunting papal adversary

The Napoleonide
Madame Mère, who took refuge in Rome – sometimes from her beloved son, sometimes from his enemies – and died there, a tragic heroine, in 1835
Cardinal Fesch, her half-brother, appointed by his imperial nephew to deal with a pope who could not be dealt with, he too died in Rome, pious but credulous in old age
Joseph (Giuseppe), the eldest Bonaparte son, who did as he was told as ambassador to Rome, King of Naples and King of Spain
Lucien (Luciano), a republican at heart, he married against the imperial will and defiantly betook himself to Rome, to establish a Roman branch of the family
Pauline (Maria Paola), the pretty one and most sympathetic of the Bonaparte sisters, patron of the arts, she might have regretted her marriage to Camillo Borghese had she felt compelled to spend much time with him
Camillo Borghese, scion of a great Roman house, collector of art, handsome and much-maligned husband of Pauline
Caroline (Maria Annunziata), Queen of Naples, one of the sensible ones except where it came to her husband …
Joachim Murat, brother-in-law to Napoleon, Marshal of France and King of Naples, the word 'dashing' was coined to describe him; unfortunately, the words 'successful conspirator' were not ›
Elise (Maria Anna), the most sensible one, her brother made her Princess of Lucca and Piombino and Grandduchess of Tuscany, while her husband made her the mother of the little princess Napoleona

Madame Mère.   Pauline Bonaparte.   Joseph Bonaparte.

Felice Baciocchi, Elise's husband, a boy from back home in Corsica, who gave his brother-in-law little help and less trouble
Louis (Luigi), the onetime King of Holland who went into exile for a while in Rome with Madame Mère and Lucien, but soon quarrelled with them
Jerome (Girolamo), the baby of the family who caused everyone a great deal of trouble by loving not wisely but too well

The French and their Friends
Camille de Tournon, the 'youngest and best' of the imperial prefects, amateur painter and author of a statistical study of the city he loved and tried to guide
General Radet, a flamboyant soldier and head of the Roman gendarmerie, to his chagrin best remembered for scaling the walls of the Quirinal and kidnapping Pope Pius VII
General Count Sextius Alexandre François Miollis, a *bon vivant,* dependable soldier, head of the Special Council (*Consulta Straordinaria,* hereafter simply the *Consulta*), a poet who loved Italy and gave great parties, he found himself acting governor-general of the Roman States
Baron Joseph-Marie de Gérando, the always-smiling polymath, philosopher, and friend of Madame de Staël, he was the popular number two man on the *Consulta*
Baron Laurent-Marie Janet, the money man on the *Consulta,* unloved and unlovable, he was talented with numbers but made people nervous
Fernando del Pozzo, a 'foreigner' from Piedmont, he was in charge of setting up the new judicial system in Rome, he and Janet were birds of a feather who flocked together
future Italian patriot; he found that his scruples made it hard for him to enjoy his job

Lucien Bonaparte.   Caroline Bonaparte.   Joachim Murat.

Antoine Salicetti, Murat's Corsican chief of police and agent in Rome, he acted as a member of the *Consulta* and played all sides of the field, until someone (probably) poisoned him

Martial Daru, an intendant who arrived in Rome in March 1811, and something of a writer. Stendhal remarked that he died from an overdose of aphrodisiacs

Jean-Baptiste Wicar, a competent artist and a highly skilled confiscator of art

Juliette Récamier, the beautiful one, out of favour with the emperor she held court in Rome and was adored

François Chateaubriand, one of those who adored her, along with …

Henri Beyle (Stendhal), *Alfonse de Lamartine* and other young Frenchmen of literary inclinations, who would later become famous Romantics

The Romans

Liborio Angelucci, political radical, physician, translator of Dante, Consul of the 1798–99 Roman Republic (and a likely model for Angelotti in Puccini's *Tosca*)

Giuseppe Barberi, aka *Tissifonte,* architect, political radical, caricaturist, unhappy husband and father of a large and demanding family

Giuseppe Valadier, Roman architect with a French name, he worked for the popes and for the French, but mostly he worked for Rome

Giuseppe Camporese, worked with Valadier on revealing and restoring Rome's architectural heritage

Carlo Fea, the papal antiquarian and lover of academic feuds

Pietro Piranesi, artist and son of the great engraver, he did his best for the new regime, but it wasn't always good enough

Francesco Fortunati, cleric and diarist, he kept a journal from 1775 until 1828, and gleefully noted down anything that made the French look bad

Antonio Galimberti, a lawyer and another diarist who recorded anything that made the French look worse

Abbate Benedetti, who may have been a diarist

Marchese Giovanni Naro Patrizi, a Roman of very blue blood who went to the Chateau d'If rather than agree to turn his sons over to Napoleon

… *Saverio and Filippo,* the two sons who were sent to France anyway, and

… *Cunegonde,* their mother, the Saxon princess, who went with them

Father Canali, a deportee with a sense of humour

Father Gaspare del Bufalo, another deportee, too young to have a sense of humour

Anna Maria Taigi, a servant with a reputation for sanctity, wife of a servant and mother of a numerous and impoverished family

Elisabetta Canori-Mora, a saint, and a respectable Roman matron with a bad husband

Nicolo Zingarelli, an opera composer admired by the emperor, and director of music who refused to play ball

Antonio Canova, undisputedly the greatest sculptor of his day, who played ball but not with any enthusiasm

Bartolomeo Pinelli, a very fine artist from the bottom of society, too much of an individualist to play ball with any great success

Vincenzo Camuccini, a successful landscape painter and head of the mosaic factory, and a much more sensible man, if not nearly so good an artist

Cardinal Consalvi, Chamberlain to Pius VII and a skilled diplomat

Cardinal Pacca, bull-necked and uncompromising, closest advisor to Pius VII

Felice Battaglia, a liberal cleric with a flexible view of vows, he made a premature and completely unsuccessful attempt at creating Italy out of the shambles that followed the fall of Napoleon

CHAPTER ONE
URBE ET ORBE: THE CITY AND THE WORLD
࿇

In July of 1796, a strange phenomenon was reported in the popular districts of Rome.

Romans traditionally prayed that the Madonna might 'turn her eyes towards them', and now it seemed as if their prayers had been answered in a notably literal way. Marian miracles, already reported in the provincial towns of Ancona and in the Marches, began to occur in Rome itself: in the street-side shrines, the eyes of the madonnas seemed to come alive, moving in their painted faces to look up in supplication, down in grief, or side to side to take in with love and pity the people who clustered around. At the bedside of an elderly nun, it was reported, the radical physician Liborio Angelucci cried out in alarm and fled from the room as the icon above the sick woman looked at him with reproach and gentle disdain.[1] As French invasion seemed to grow ever more inevitable carnival was cancelled in favour of barefoot penitential processions led by cardinals and bishops, and the exposition of relics. None of this would be of any use. Nor would diplomacy, or barely disguised bribery. By 1798 Rome would fall to the armies of revolutionary France; in 1809, Rome would be absorbed into the empire as an imperial city, and ruled directly as if it were part of France. The French in one guise or another would dominate the city until 1814.

In the summer of 1796 Rome stood, as she always had, on the banks of the Tiber, enclosing within her walls the battered glories of the ancient empire of the West, the heart of Catholic Christendom, and a population who considered themselves citizens of the capital of the world. She was a little shabby, more than a little down at the heels. Her theocratic government was hopelessly old-fashioned even before the French Revolution; her economy was a shambling wreck despite the intermittent efforts at reform by a string of popes; her prisons and her hospitals were shining examples of the best that Europe could produce while her universities were outdated, her law courts were strangled in overlapping jurisdictions, and the most charitable thing to say about her police and army is to say nothing at all.

---

1   Fortunati, 22 July 1796.

Italy in 1796.

Late eighteenth-century Rome was ruled by the pope, an elected monarch who, in addition to being head of the universal Church, was also the king of the Papal States. These states ran, or straggled, from Terracina and Gaëta in the south, on the edge of the Kingdom of Naples, across central Italy north and east to the borders of Modena and the Republic of Venice. They were a hodgepodge of territories, states and cities including the Legations of the Romagna, Ferrara and Bologna, the Marches, the ports of Ancona and Civitavecchia, and decrepit but once great Renaissance cities like Perugia, Orvieto and Urbino. The pope, usually elderly, ruled along with his often elderly cardinals who served as heads of government departments; the cardinals in turn depended on a semi-clerical body of middle-rank administrators called prelates; and working for the prelates were the secretaries. The whole structure creaked along, increasingly outmoded but apparently eternal. The system was the object of universal scorn among international observers; it was maddening for the few Romans who had an eye for progress; but it was surprisingly popular with the people as a whole.

Eighteenth-century popes had been mild and benevolent rulers. Most had at least attempted to be good shepherds to their city and their world. But while their city remained much the same, by the last decades of the century the world had changed dramatically. The defences of Rome had for a long time been more spiritual than physical, and by 1796 they were clearly on the point of crumbling.

France has a long history, going back to Clovis and then to Charlemagne, of 'protecting' the papacy, with or without the papacy's cooperation. By the Renaissance, Italy was an irresistible prize – rich and virtually undefended, consisting of dozens of small, often mutually hostile, states. The French, the Spanish, and various combinations of German-speakers dominated or outright snatched convenient pieces, and Italy was the treasure chest from which victors were rewarded in European wars. When the balance of peace in Europe was disturbed, the Italian states were inevitably troubled. But what began in France with the fall of the Bastille and continued, changing but not stopping, for the next 25 years until the fall of Napoleon, was far more than a disturbance. A new world was being born, a world that would be the antithesis of everything that Rome represented.

The new world would be much concerned with reason and progress; in Rome, reason would only be valued as a means to faith, while the right to remain unchanged was sacred.

In the new world the state spoke in the name of the people, and in that name claimed the right to change itself and its prerogatives profoundly; in Rome, the state spoke in the name of God, and in that Name the people claimed the right to change not at all, and bitterly resisted any attempts to make them do so.

The new world dissolved the corporations that stood guard between man and the state, be they guilds or extended families; Rome *was* a corporation and, in the pre-modern sense, a family.[2]

The new world was led by the iron will of a genius whose prerogatives were in theory limited by the will of the people but whose powers were curtailed hardly at all; Rome was governed by a geriatric collection of vaguely benevolent amateurs headed by an elected sovereign whose prerogatives were, in theory, absolute but whose powers were severely curtailed by an entrenched bureaucracy (the *curia*) and a crushing weight of inertia.

In the new world wealth was exalted and poverty was crime; in Rome, one revelled in the display of wealth, but poverty bore the mark of the Most Holy, a fact that gave the poor an annoying attitude of self-contained superiority.

Most fatally, the new world would be much concerned with military might; for at least a century, Rome's army had been a running joke. It was small, ineffectual, top-heavy with superannuated officers, and existed primarily for parades and to provide guards for theatres and troops for policing the carnival.

Inevitably, the meeting between Rome and the new world was a monstrously bad match, and for 20 years or so, Rome would suffer. In what appeared to be the end, she would triumph, but she would never be the same, and after a half century of twilight,

---

2   The Latin term for family included not only blood relations, but also the entire household of employees, clients and dependants.

the Rome that had been would disappear forever – the *Roma sparita* long remembered only in old watercolours and faded memoirs, despised by patriots and apologised for by the pious.

The story of Rome between the outbreak of revolution in France and the triumph of counter-revolution in 1814 and 1815 is the story of a series of more or less cataclysmic military, political, and cultural convulsions, with more than a dozen major changes of governing power and multiple mini-spasms within the convulsions.

Shockwaves from France began to strike Rome almost immediately after 1789, in the form of refugees. After the refugees came the invasions. The pretexts for the first invasion of the city were the violent but mostly accidental deaths of two more or less official French representatives, Nicholas Hugon de Basseville, a sort-of diplomat, and Léonard Duphot, a young general who was there to combine a little rabble rousing with his honeymoon. It is impossible to tell the players or events without a score card, and difficult enough to do so with one. But we shall try. Each number indicates a major change in the governing of Rome.

Despite unmistakable rumblings (which included the deaths of Basseville and Duphot, the Napoleonic conquest of northern Italy, and papal acceptance of the treaty of Tolentino), the first major governmental change in Rome came in February 1798 (1) when the avenging if businesslike General Berthier arrived in response to Duphot's death and, with minimal enthusiasm on either his part or that of almost all Romans, overthrew the tyranny of the popes (Pius VI was summarily deported and soon died) and re-created the classical republic (or such was the plan). This Roman Republic of 1798–99 (2), known by its enemies as the *repubblica per ridere*, or Ridiculous Republic, was a papier-mâché construct that lasted as long as the French were there to defend it. When their protective hand was briefly withdrawn in November 1798 (General Bonaparte had gone to Egypt with grander geo-political designs), Ferdinand IV of Naples marched up to occupy the city (3); when French troops reappeared a few days later, Ferdinand wisely scampered back home (inspiring one of Pasquino's best: *veni, vidi, e fuggi* – he came, he saw, he fled). The moribund republic staggered back (4), but as French military control in Italy dissolved, Romans waited for the coalition Allies to move into the city, which they finally did at the end of September, 1799 (5). There they remained, despite the fact that a new pope, Pius VII, was elected in Venice in March 1800; they left only reluctantly after Bonaparte, abandoning his troops in Egypt, returned to Italy and won the battle of Marengo in June 1800. Thereafter, though Bonaparte allowed the newly elected Pius VII to assume the rule of his city – the First Restoration (6) – it was clearly on French terms. The Concordat in 1801 returned the Church to France, and Pius participated more or less enthusiastically in the imperial coronation in 1804. But when Pius proved to be less accommodating than the emperor wished, he was encouraged to obedience by the gradual but inexorable encroachment of French forces. Finally, in February 1808, General Miollis moved into the Castel Sant'Angelo to herald a new French occupation (7). On 10 June 1809 Rome was declared a 'free, imperial city' (8), with an extraordinary committee or *Consulta* to whip it into shape, and a prefect, the appealing Count Camille de Tournon, to rule in the emperor's name. The intransigent pope immediately excommunicated anyone associated with the new government, starting with the emperor; the pope was then kidnapped (it is not clear if Napoleon ordered it) and forcibly removed from the city and sent under close guard to Savona, where he would remain for the next three years. The *Consulta* finished its work and was disbanded on the last day of 1810, and Rome was annexed to the empire (9). Although Napoleon declared his intention of ruling benevolently in Rome, and probably meant it, by the spring of 1810 some ugly aspects of coercion were visible: religious orders were suppressed, clerics who refused to sign an oath of allegiance were arrested, and conscription was introduced into a city which had felt itself immune. Romans were unenthusiastic about the birth of Napoleon's son, the King of Rome, in May 1811. While 1812 and 1813 were eventful, including the disastrous Russian campaign and the threat of a march on Rome by an insurgent cleric, nothing substantial changed in Rome until January 1814 (10) when Joachim (Gioachino) Murat, Napoleon's brother-in-law and King of Naples, arrived to declare himself head of an amorphous and premature Italian state, allied with Napoleon's enemies, Austria and Prussia. Murat's new Italy received scant support, and five months later Pius VII returned in triumph to his city – the Second Restoration (11). This, one might reasonably assume, was the end of the story; but there was to be a bizarre postscript. During Napoleon's One Hundred Days, Murat again changed sides to join him; the pope fled Rome (12) in March 1815 but returned (13) three months later. There he would remain until his death in 1823. Some 25 years after that, another Roman republic would be declared, but that is no part of our story.

Thus, the chronological outline. But there were, of course, wheels within wheels. While the major part of our story lies with the Roman republic of 1798–99 and the direct rule instituted unofficially in 1808 and officially in 1809, it is difficult to understand those events without a closer look at events that preceded them (the deaths of Basseville and Duphot), and followed them (papal rule between 1800 and 1808, and the doomed attempts by both Napoleon and the pope to come to mutually acceptable arrangements).

Prelude: Hugon de Basseville, Léonard Duphot, and General Bonaparte
When France began her rapid slide into revolution in 1789, it did not take Rome long to notice that something potentially unpleasant was going on beyond the Alps. Almost from the start, for a whole complex of reasons, revolutionary France had been antiChristian in general and anti-Roman in particular. By the summer of 1789, Europeans who read newspapers, or heard them read, were nervous; future events did nothing to calm their fears. By 1790, when the Civil Constitution of the Clergy brought the property and personnel of the Church in France under the direct control of the government and demanded an oath of loyalty to the state, the bitter clash between Rome and her disobedient daughter France was unavoidable. Pius VI, elderly and never terribly decisive at the best of times, vacillated while the Church in France dissolved into hostile camps: on one side, accused of greed, those who accepted the loyalty oath; on the other side, accused of intransigence, those who refused.

As the wars began refugees from France flooded into Rome, from the aunts of the king to half-starved *curés* from the provinces. Revolution arrived in Rome in the urbane person of Nicholas Hugon de Basseville, amateur poet, physician, faithful

Pope Pius VI.

servant of the regime in Paris and emissary of the republic via the French ambassador at Naples.[3] Among the problems he was instructed to solve was the fact that the court of Rome would receive no such ambassador, and refused to allow the consul – a banker named Mont, or Mutte – the right to change the lilies of France over the ambassadorial door to the revolutionary tricolour.

Basseville wisely left the lilies in place, but undiplomatically encouraged the revolutionary ardour of the young men at the French Academy (who hardly needed encouragement), and cultivated the company of Romans thought to be open to new ideas – among them *haute bourgeois* like the banker Torlonia and more modest members of the middle class like the intellectual obstetrician Liborio Angelucci, as well as potentially radical nobles like Santa Croce and the intellectual Sigismondo Chigi.

While Bassville found some receptive ears, he also aroused the less amiable interest of two groups: one, relatively harmless – the Roman curia; the other, much more dangerous – the people of Rome, always liable to casual violence. Romans murdered one another at an astonishing rate [see chapter 6], but rarely threatened foreigners. They would be happy to make an exception in the case of Basseville.

Nothing much happened until the catalyst arrived, in the person of Charles de la Flotte, in November 1792. When his official diplomatic request for permission to place the arms of the republic over the ambassadorial residence was diplomatically refused, de la Flotte took the offensive. After a January 1793 banquet at which tricolour cockades featured prominently, Basseville ordered the change in emblems and the artists of the Academy leapt into the breach, cobbling one together in an overnight work session. It was promptly put up and even more promptly torn down and trampled underfoot by a group of angry Romans of the popular class. From that point on, matters deteriorated rapidly, until that afternoon when Basseville, his wife and de la Flotte made the fatal error of sallying forth in a carriage decked out with revolutionary insignia and escorted by servants flaunting the offensive red, white and blue.

If the papacy was timid and conciliatory (the elderly pope and his curia knew perfectly well how vulnerable they were), the people of the Roman street were cocksure and ready to defend their prerogatives, which in their opinion included an absolute right not to be publicly offended. The French promenaded in their carriage along the Corso; the Romans made obscene gestures and flung insults; the French sneered; the Romans responded with a hail of rocks; the French fled to the courtyard of a nearby palace; the Romans followed with blood in their eyes and knives in their

---

3   Andrieux, *Les françaises à Rome*, pp. 198-201.

The assassination of Hugon de Basseville.

hands. In fact, the blow that fatally injured Basseville came, not from the typical Roman dagger, but from the razor that a barber, called from his craft by the excitement, used to cut the hapless poet-revolutionary's throat.

Basseville's death not only had profound consequences over the coming years, it also had echoes in the propaganda war that inevitably followed. Rome issued a statement that, before his death, the misguided radical had made his peace with the Church and received the sacraments; the French indignantly issued their own statement that, surrounded by priests, he had 'turned his face to the wall and announced that he died "faithful to my country, having done my duty". The government in Paris declared Nicolas Hugon de Basseville a revolutionary martyr, with all rights and privileges appertaining thereunto.

Romans were ecstatic about their triumph over revolution and irreligion, and celebrated the event in *pasquinades*, songs, impromptu recitations, and published epics.[4] Paris was outraged, and took the event as an official defiance by the papal government (nothing could have been further from the truth). But, while they issued proclamations and denunciations, for the time being the defenders of Reason and Light were forced to hold fire. Their armies were busy elsewhere and the very survival of the republic was by no means certain. Three years later a young general from Corsica assumed command of the threadbare Army of Italy, and everything changed. Under his command, the French revolution exploded across the Alps and down into the fertile plains of Austrian-dominated Lombardy. When they came to enter the Papal States, the military forces of the pope dissolved.

---

4   The prolific poet Vincenzo Monti quickly published a celebratory epic he called the *Bassviliade*.

Although Bonaparte summoned up the martyrdom of Basseville to rouse his troops ('Your mission is not completed while the ashes of those who defeated the Tarquins are still fouled by the assassins of Basseville'), the future emperor, after roundly defeating the papal troops, stopped short of Rome at Foligno and allowed himself, Attila-like, to be bought off by the treaty of Tolentino [19 February 1797]. Pope Pius VI swallowed what was left of his pride, recognised the Directory as the legitimate government of France, and agreed to appoint representatives acceptable to the French. He also agreed to pay 30 million *livres* in silver and goods, to surrender Ancona, Bologna, Ferrara and the province of Romagna, and to hand over 100 paintings, statues and works of art, and 500 manuscripts, to be selected by the commissioners who had already been appointed for the job. In all, the cost of Tolentino was, as General Bonaparte commented, 'ten times more than Rome is worth'. When the Paris Directory urged him to take the city and depose the pope, he confidently assured them that 'the old machine will fall apart by itself'.

While the agreement at Tolentino was harsh enough, it only opened the door. As part of the treaty, Rome was forced to accept an ambassador of the French republic. At the end of August Joseph Bonaparte arrived in that role to take up residence in the Corsini palace, with instructions from his younger brother to do everything possible to stop the election of a new pope when Pius VI died. The new ambassador brought with him a retinue that included Napoleon's stepson Eugene de Beauharnais (later Viceroy of the Kingdom of Italy); Joseph's wife, Julie; her sister and Napoleon's former fiancée, Desirée Clary; and Desirée's current fiancé, the enthusiastic young general Léonard Duphot, who was to become the next sacrificial victim on the altar of Roman liberation.

Duphot, two days away from his wedding, was apparently under orders to revolutionise the city. If so, he must have been discouraged to find so few interested in the project, but he soldiered on, and by December 1797 there had been several noisy if inconsequential disturbances. The fracas of 28 December seemed like just one more of the same. A tiny group of patriots or Jacobins (as revolutionary sympathisers continued to be called) gathered to demand Liberty, Equality, and whatever else the French might bring along. But this time, they attracted the attention of a much larger group of angry men from Trastevere (the Trans-Tiber district of Rome). They fled for their lives to the Corsini palace and the protective arms of Joseph Bonaparte, closely pursued by the Roman *bulli* [5] in full cry. Joseph was having dinner, but he dutifully got up and went out to his courtyard to try to calm things down, and here the story becomes murky. The Jacobins, rather like dogs who have reached the safety of their own yard, turned to confront their enemies, who rejoiced at the opportunity to have some fun while defending religion and home. Meanwhile, a detachment of papal troops under the command of a certain Corporal Martinelli, who had been posted to defend the embassy, took up arms and joined the fracas, no doubt uncertain about who was who. Joseph, Eugene, and Léonard also waded in — perhaps to calm things down, perhaps to egg on the protesters – and the result was that someone fired a shot and General Duphot, much to his own and everyone else's astonishment, was fatally

5   Dashing and violent young men of the Roman *popolo*, see chapter 3.

Proclaiming the republic at the Campidoglio in February 1798.

wounded. French blood had once again flowed in the streets (well, courtyards) of Rome! The iron fist of tyranny had again crushed the flower of Liberty!

In Rome, carnival was cancelled and the pope and his cardinals led prayers and processions for the salvation of the city. In the popular quarters, the street-side madonnas who had astonished and comforted the people by moving their eyes and weeping in 1796, moved their eyes and wept again.

General Berthier, nearby at Ancona, moved on Rome, prepared (according to orders from Bonaparte in Milan) to 'use all [his] influence to organise the Roman Republic'. It was perfectly obvious that very few Romans had any interest in a republic, but duty is duty, and Berthier did his. Supporters were recruited from other parts of Italy, and an agent provocateur named Bassal spread money and rumours through Rome (one of the more original was the story that the French were merely acting for the pope). On 15 February 1798, while a *Te Deum* was being sung at St Peter's marking the 23rd anniversary of the pope's election, a handful of men planted a Liberty Tree at the Forum (known to Romans as the cow field), appointed seven consuls (five more than required by the ancient constitution), and demanded a republic. The news was sent to Berthier, who sighed, unpacked the laurel wreath provided for the occasion, and next day marched his liberating troops along the Flaminian road into the city, through the Porta del Popolo, along the Corso, and up the Capitol steps where he made a speech full of references to Cato, Cicero, Brutus, and the sons of the Gauls. The Ridiculous Republic was born. Historians debate its pros and cons, but one thing is certain: if it was a joke, it wasn't a very funny one.

As soon as the republic was established (the usual French-style affair, with antique Roman trappings) the octogenarian Pope Pius VI was bundled into a carriage with a handful of attendants and sent on his travels. To his plea that he be allowed to die in Rome, Commissioner Haller, the Calvinist in charge of the operation, is said to have replied, 'one can die anywhere'.

The French carting away Roman art.

When Rome fell to General Berthier the commissioners, generals, staff officers and agents stole everything they could cart away. Some of this was more or less official. The general was under orders to raise 'contributions' from the richest families, and confiscate all the property of the pope and the families most closely associated with him (including the Braschi and the Albani) and to take whatever 'paintings, books, manuscripts, statues and works of art' he and the commissioners thought 'worthy of being transported to France'. If effect, loot was limited only by their ability to ship it.

By the time the commissioners got to Rome, however, the looting party was already well under way. General Berthier, short of cash to pay his troops (officers and men were dressed in rags and hadn't been paid for five months), had begun to strip the silver from the churches. This was (according to General Thiebault's memoirs) quickly followed by 'diamonds, pictures, statues, works of art, articles of gold and silver' and virtually anything belonging to anyone who might be considered not firmly in the French camp.[6] The 40,000-volume private library of Pius VI was stripped while he watched, with the 1,000 choicest items sent to Paris while the rest were sold. Dealers from France, plus Italian and Roman supporters of the republic, set up impromptu auctions, on their own terms, and sold priceless treasures to one another at bargain basement prices (the famous Raphael tapestries from the Vatican went for some 1,200 *piastres* each, according to Duppa).[7] Cloths, cameos, medallions, liturgical chalices and patens, monstrances and ciboria, jewellery, and sacred relics – or rather the ornate containers that held relics – were fair game. Probably the single most beloved image in Rome, the miraculous olive-wood *bambino* of Ara Coeli was, according to reports, stolen, stripped of his valuable robes and jewels, and then tossed aside to be burned as fuel (the image of the holy infant survived, found refuge with a convent of nuns and was returned in glory once the storm had passed). Gold and

6   Thiebault, quoted by Turner, 'Art Confiscations', p. 94 fn 17.
7   Duppa, *A Journal*, fn 22.

Pierre-Alexandre Berthier.   André Massena.

silver bars, hundreds of diamonds, emeralds, rubies, sapphires and pearls (many of them prized off papal tiaras) were pocketed or sent to Paris. Not content with taking valuables from homes and churches, someone had the bright idea of opening tombs and taking the lead caskets. A project for breaking into the tombs of the popes and relieving the corpses of their jewels was reluctantly shelved because it would take too much time.

When General Berthier, a relatively moderate man, was replaced by General André Massena, it got worse. Massena (the word usually used to describe him is 'harsh') was already famous as the 'greatest plunderer in the Army of Italy'. When the army's greatest plunderer arrived in Italy's most plunderable city, the results were spectacular. Even the army couldn't stand him. Finally, the junior officers, supported by the commissioners, went into open mutiny in protest. While the officers felt they were upholding the honour of France, they also hated and feared Massena and wanted to get rid of him; and the commissioners were unable to go about their official looting with so much dedicated competition.

While the junior officers protested, the men of Trastevere took up arms and crossed the bridges into the city. For a few hours it looked as if the French would be driven out. But angry men armed with knives, rocks and passion, were no match for the army. The next day, the executions began in the Piazza del Popolo and in the Piazza of Santa Maria in Trastevere. They would continue as opponents of the regime were silenced.

Meanwhile the Ridiculous Republic proceeded, attended by what Andrieux has called 'all the stale bric-a-brac of the civic celebrations of the Year II' – republican processions, altars to the Nation, spectacles, secular hymns, nothing was lacking. Unfortunately they were attempting the tricks that had dazzled the Paris mob in Rome, the home of spectacles and the mistress of carnival. Romans attended only to heckle and critique the shows – and shows like the burning of the records of the Inquisition were particularly hilarious, when the mostly naked boys with little wings stuck to their shoulders, and the totally naked young women representing Truth and

A republican festival at the Forum.

other virtues, had to flee from a hail storm.[8] Undeterred, the adherents of the republic went along their bombastic and bloody way, creating institutions and traditions *ex nihilo* and making tidy fortunes from the sale of Church property.

From late 1798 into the new year, the price of a loaf of bread rose while the weight of the loaf was cut from 8 ounces to 4, and the flour used to bake it was adulterated with non-wheat additives. The republicans tried to continue the traditional free distributions of bread, but these were limited to those who could prove their destitution. Even so, there was less and less available for distribution or for sale at any price. Romans, for centuries accustomed to the papal dole, were outraged. Bread riots become commonplace; bakeries became impromptu meeting places for opponents of the republic; quarrels, riots, and even murders threatened the government.

Bread is no longer among the things sold here. Everyone keeps what he can for himself, at the peril of his life. No man who is not a commissioner, or a general, or a servant or courtier of one, can eat an egg.[9]

'One can die anywhere', as Haller had truthfully if brutally pointed out: and on 29 August 1799, Giovanni Angelo Braschi, Pope Pius VI, exiled from his city more than a year before and dragged through Italy and northern France, died in Valence, whither he had been carried on a litter. When the news of his death reached Rome, the city plunged into mourning, as befitted orphans. The Roman Republic was also

---

8   Andrieux, *op. cit.*, p. 212.
9   Andrieux, *op. cit.*, p. 214, quoting Paul-Louis Courier de Méré, a captain of artillery who was one of the young officers of the Pantheon revolt.

an orphan, though few mourned its long drawn out death agony. Doomed from the moment French power in Italy began to crumble, it would not officially die until the Allies took the city at the end of September 1799. No sooner had General Bonaparte ordered its creation than he had gone on to further adventures in Egypt, leaving Rome and the other puppet Italian republics – the Cispadane, the Cisalpine, and soon, the Parthenopean – to flounder. In his absence, the French began to lose their grip on Italy. When his Egyptian experiment came to a disastrous end, thanks to the English fleet under Nelson, King Ferdinand IV of Naples was encouraged to follow his own dream and marched up to seize Rome for himself (22 November 1798). But while Nelson could rule the waves, his fleet was of limited value against even a weakened French land army. Ferdinand was forced to flee (some said, disguised as his own equerry) not only to Naples but all the way to Palermo, while the French even without Napoleon re-took Rome, barely paused to dust off the republic, and proceeded south to revolutionise Naples – a bloody and dramatic episode that does not concern us here. However, by September 1799, the French had lost Naples and were forced to retreat from Rome. The victorious Allies – who included Austria, Prussia, England, Naples, Russia and the Ottoman sultan (strange bedfellows indeed!) – marched in and set up a government that was in theory only a temporary stopgap until a new pope could be elected and returned to the city.[10] It was an open secret that the Neapolitans were as eager as Napoleon for that day never to arrive, so that Rome could be permanently absorbed into the Kingdom of Naples (15 years later, King Murat of Naples would dream the same dream, with as little success).

As far as anyone knew, the French episode was over. The dangerous young General Bonaparte had over-reached himself and returned from Egypt, empty-handed. He had overthrown the weak Directory in a coup,[11] but it seemed likely that the entire revolutionary experiment was dissolving. It was under these circumstances that, on 30 November 1799, a conclave opened in Venice to elect a successor to the now-martyred Pius VI (thanks to Napoleon's 1797 treaty of Campoformio, Venice was now under the control of Catholic Austria). The conclave proceeded, and on 14 March 1800 a diminutive, scholarly Benedictine monk with the reputation for accommodating faith with democracy was elected pope. Symbolically, Barnaba Chiaramonti chose the name Pius VII – he would not turn his back on his predecessor, but would continue along his path.

Napoleon was nothing if not flexible in his plans. After overthrowing the Directory and making himself First Consul (with the invaluable assistance of his brother Lucien), he set out, evoking images of Hannibal and Charlemagne, to bring a new army across the Alps (a passage later immortalised, with considerable artistic licence, in the painting by Jacques-Louis David). His re-conquest of Italy was rapid and decisive, and culminated with the June 1800 battle of Marengo. Whether or not Marengo sealed the future of Italy, for the next 14 years France would decide who ruled in Rome.[12]

---

10 This is the point in history in which Victorien Sardou chose to set his 1887 melodrama, *La Tosca*.

11 The coup of Brumaire, 9 November 1799, made Bonaparte First Consul.

12 Historians argue about the battle's actual effect, see Laird Kleine-Ahlbrandt, 'Victorien Sardou and the Legend of Marengo', in *Tosca's Prism*.

Napoleon's victory made him *de facto* ruler of Italy, but he did not interfere with Pius taking possession of Rome in July 1800. He hoped to make peace with the pope, and to incorporate the Church as an active part of his reign. In June, he had ordered a *Te Deum* at Milan (in direct defiance of the 'atheists in Paris'), and then announced to a group of 200 astonished bishops and priests that he was the sincere friend and protector of the Catholic religion. In fact, he had no intention of continuing the revolutionary war against Christianity, which he considered to be counter-productive and a waste of time. All in all, at this point in his plans, a cooperative pope would be much more useful than no pope at all. And Chiaramonti, though younger and psychologically tougher than the Braschi pope, had a reputation as a man who could be dealt with.

Unfortunately for any hopes of compromise, there were problems that would prove impossible to solve. One of these was the temporal sovereignty of the popes. This Pius absolutely would not give up: he believed that his independence as a religious leader depended on his independence as a sovereign. While he was willing to compromise on some of the outlying territories of the papal domains, he would not entertain the idea of giving up his claim to the temporal rule of the city of Rome. From Napoleon's point of view, temporal sovereignty was an absurd medieval relic that merely distracted from the pope's role as religious leader. Worse, this medieval relic threatened to interfere with important aspects of Napoleonic policy.

Through a string of French ambassadors at Rome (including his uncle, Cardinal Fesch), Napoleon tried to find a way to live with the papacy.[13] These ambassadors were, from the French point of view, loyal Catholics and favourable to the Church, but they represented the interests of France and of a ruler who saw the Church as an institution whose function was to maintain order in society. It became increasingly apparent that this was a classic case of the Irresistible Force and the Immovable Object.

Interlude: The First Restoration, 1800–1808, Concord, Coronation and Conflict
In 1801, Napoleon won Pius' undying gratitude and respect by proposing a concordat that would resolve a dozen years of conflict between France and the Church.[14] They had been bitter and difficult years. The vast properties of the Church in France had been confiscated to support the new state. Hundreds of clerics had been executed as enemies of the revolution (which, indeed, they were); many more had been lynched, or died in prison; thousands had been driven into exile; churches had been converted to stables, or temples to the revolutionary faith, or simply looted and closed.

After Napoleon was exiled to St Helena, Pius praised the emperor's 'pious and courageous initiative of 1801', and wrote to his secretary of state, Cardinal Consalvi, asking him to intervene with the English on the emperor's behalf because '...we ought both to remember that, after God, it is to him chiefly that is due the reestablishment of religion in the great kingdom of France.'

---

13 Napoleon's mother's half brother, Fesch, was reminded of his clerical status (more or less forgotten in the dangerous days of the revolution), and consecrated bishop and then cardinal, and sent to Rome as ambassador, to take up his residence at the Corsini palace.

14 A concordat is a treaty between the papacy and a sovereign state, with regard to religion.

Napoleon's uncle, Cardinal Fesch.   Pius VII and cardinals Consalvi and Pacca.

Seen in the context of Bonaparte's overall policy, the concordat was neither quite so surprising, nor quite so Christian and heroic. In 1802, after a decade of war, general peace seemed at least a possibility. In February, the treaty of Lunéville ended war between France and the Holy Roman Empire. In March the treaty of Amiens brought a cessation of hostilities between France and her most implacable opponent, England (it would not last long). At home, the First Consul wanted to put a stop to the long-running war in the Vendée, where opponents of the revolution gathered around the standard of religion to oppose rule from Paris.[15] Peace with the Church would encourage rebels to lay down their arms, and allow Bonaparte to consolidate his gains at home and abroad.

In his usual abrupt fashion, he wanted the treaty negotiated and signed immediately. But despite whatever gratitude he felt, Pius was in no such hurry, and it took a year before both parties were satisfied that they had gained as much as they could by the agreement.

The document that the First Consul signed in September 1801 was an imperfect one, but it did allow the Church in France to climb out from under the rubble and begin to rebuild. In it, the Church agreed to accept – only in France – a number of revolutionary innovations, including a vague police authority over certain public aspects of religious activity. Nothing was said about the huge potential problems that would loom if and when Napoleon unilaterally chose to expand the concordat to the

15 Connolly, *French Revolution. Napoleonic Era*, pp. 216–8.

traditional Catholic states of Europe, most especially Italy, and specifically, Rome. It was a hornets' nest waiting to be disturbed [see chapters 8 and 9].

By the summer of 1803, news reached the papal court that Napoleon Bonaparte, First Consul for Life, had responded to the pleas of his grateful nation and agreed to accept a crown. Pius agreed to play his part, over the protests of many of his cardinals, and the criticism of Pasquino:[16]

To save his faith, one Pius lost his throne [an obvious reference to Pius VI].
To save his throne, one Pius lost his faith [an unflattering reference to Pius VII].

Pius, however, was convinced that Napoleon was at least a potential friend of the Church. Finally, on 2 November 1804, the papal retinue set out on the long road to Paris, where the anointing and coronation of the new emperor was set for 2 December.[17] The pope travelled with an entourage of more than 100, including six cardinals. One, the elderly Cardinal Borgia, fell ill and died at Lyons. Napoleon had wanted an even dozen cardinals, partly for the pleasure of the display, partly for the neat, biblical symmetry of the number, but perhaps also because he was already considering having the entire papal court move lock stock and barrel to Paris. The papal court declined to cooperate. Pius VI had been kidnapped and dragged, dying, across the Alps to France. Would Pius VII, summoned with an invitation, be allowed to leave France? The court planned to stay where it was, or in any case not to be lured out by a ruse.

Why did Napoleon want the pope at his coronation? Was it only to demonstrate his equality with sovereigns who claimed their authority from God, somehow hedging his bet on an authority that came (as his clearly did) from the will of the people? He certainly valued the effect of ceremony, as any master of public relations must. And no ceremonies were older, or more impressive to the people, than the ceremonies of the Church. Like Clovis and Charlemagne, he had won his crown with his sword; like them, he wanted that crown blessed with the authority of whatever God might have the power to bless it.

Napoleon's secretary, with a perfectly straight face, reports the *accident* of the meeting between the pope and the emperor-elect in the forest of Fontainebleau. As the pope's entourage made its way through the forest on the way to Paris, they encountered a hunting party. To everyone's surprise, it was Napoleon himself, in hunting garb. He got down from his horse, the pope stepped out onto the muddy road in his white slippers, and they greeted one another like old friends. They turned aside to spend the night at the hunting lodge, where most of the court just happened to be waiting. It was, of course, all carefully planned. When the party finally

---

16 One of the 'talking statues' of Rome, Pasquino served as a sort of mail box for complaints, and an outlet for the sometimes amazing freedom of speech in the papal city, so long as it remained anonymous

17 15 August would have been preferable; it was a date he had already laid claim to, with the nearby feast of the (unfortunately rather dubious) St Napoleon, plus the added advantage that the feast was associated with the Bourbons, whom he was replacing. And he was wise enough to know that piggy-backing on an established festival could be used to amplify a new one. Another auspicious date would have been 9 November, the anniversary of the 1799 coup that had made him First Consul.

proceeded on into Paris they arrived at night, so that the population would not be treated to the sight of their ruler deferring to a foreign monarch.

The ceremony was Napoleon's own invention, an impressive – but not too priest-ridden – mixture of Catholic, Gallican, and Napoleonic elements, with a strong symbolic overlay of largely imaginary medieval rites. The idea was to evoke but improve on the coronation of Charlemagne, complete with pseudo-Carolingian replicas (the last Holy Roman Emperor still had the originals and was hardly likely to lend them). One element of Charlemagne's coronation Napoleon would most definitely not copy: Leo III had placed the crown on the head of the Frankish king, making him emperor in the name of the Church. Pius VII would be allowed to bless the crown, but the placement would be in the hands of the self-made titan himself. In another symbolic gesture of independence from the authority of Rome, neither the emperor nor the empress would take communion. The sacrament would have had to be preceded by confession and absolution, neither of which Napoleon was willing to undergo.

There was one sacrament, however, that the emperor was unable to avoid, and that was probably the empress' idea. She let it slip that she and the ambitious young general, who had married in 1796 during the revolutionary reinvention of tradition, had had only one of the new civil marriages, never a religious ceremony. This went to the heart of the social order that Pius was determined to preserve: the inviolability of marriage was a rock on which imperial-papal negotiations would often founder. The otherwise compliant pope absolutely refused to preside over the joint coronation of a technically unmarried couple, and on the day before the coronation Uncle-Cardinal Fesch married them in a secret ceremony. If this was all Josephine's doing, she probably hoped that it would help keep her husband bound to their childless marriage. And it might have done so, but by the time the issue came to a head in 1809, the pope was a prisoner at Savona and unable to interfere one way or the other.

The coronation went well, despite potential hazards. Josephine's sisters-in-law despised her, and did their best to make her trip on her train, but she remained erect; Napoleon's sense of dignity showed only occasional lapses, as when he prodded Uncle Fesch in the back with his sceptre; and the pope was left sitting alone on his throne for the best part of two hours when the coronation party was late. Perhaps most irksome of all, the emperor's mother never showed up. Angry with Napoleon for having quarrelled with, and exiled, his brother Lucien, she had taken herself to Rome to show her displeasure. She agreed to attend the coronation but delayed on the road and did not arrive until 19 December, more than two weeks too late. At one point during the ceremony, Napoleon leaned over to his brother Joseph and said, 'If only father could see me now!' If he mentioned mother, Joseph did not report it. Father had been dead since 1785 and whilst mother was absent one of the advantages of being emperor, and a master of propaganda, is the ability to shape history closer to one's own desires. When Jacques-Louis David presented his much-reproduced canvas of the great event, Madame Mère was among the onlookers.

Pius lingered on after the coronation, and found himself unexpectedly popular in France, where he set about mending fences with a people whose ties with Rome had been shattered by events of the revolutionary years. While some remained devoted to the Roman Church, many French men and women were hostile, or had drifted away, replacing religious fervour with love of nation, or not at all. Now, the image of the pope as a blood-thirsty foreign tyrant was being replaced with the image of a simple and benevolent elderly priest. He even managed to charm the Jacobin regicide and 'pageant master to the republic', the great painter Jacques-Louis David, who painted his portrait while the pontiff was in Paris.[18]

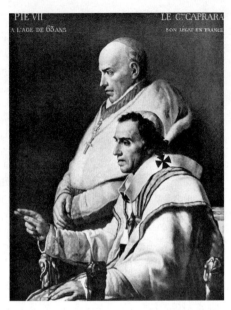

Emperor and pope apparently parted on the warmest of terms. Napoleon promised suitably imperial gifts: he would send an altar, two heavily ornate ceremonial coaches, and a jewel-encrusted tiara worthy of both a pope and an emperor. It was not a good sign for the future that

David's portrait of Pius VII with Cardinal Caprara.

neither the coaches nor the altar ever arrived. Worse, the tiara, which did arrive eventually, featured a magnificent jewel. But it was the jewel that Pius VI had been forced to take from his own crown in order to pay the 1797 extortions.[19]

In March 1805, four months after his Paris coronation, Napoleon I placed another crown – the iron crown of the Lombards – on his brow and made himself King of Italy in Milan (his stepson Eugene de Beauharnais would serve as viceroy). The concordat, which the pope had accepted for France, was extended without papal approval to Italy. Soon, Napoleon began to secularise the law, among other things making divorce legal within the empire (like Henry VIII, he had his reasons, and like Henry VIII he considered it a point on which he must overrule the Church). An open rift widened, and by 1807 Napoleon wrote to his stepson, 'Perhaps the day is not far off when I shall recognise the pope merely as bishop of Rome'.

This did not mean that Napoleon was moving away from the Church as a support for his reign. The Imperial Catechism of 1806, which Pius never approved, included a commentary on the fourth commandment to the effect that the emperor held his empire by the will of Providence and that the faithful were obliged to obey him in the same way as they were bound to obey God 'whose image he is on earth'. But the Church that sustained the emperor was to be a Church obedient to the emperor.

---

18 David was charmed by his self-deprecating humour, as when Pius commented with a smile that he shuddered to think what a man who had killed his king might do to 'a poor, papier-mâché pope'.

19 Hales, *The Emperor and the Pope*, pp.70-1

CHAPTER TWO
THE CITY

For people who didn't live there, Rome at the time of Napoleon was the stuff of dreams and epic poetry and opera and nursery stories, not a place where real life was lived. Every eighteenth-century schoolboy, and not a few girls, knew about Brutus and Lucretia and Tarquin the Proud, and about Horatius Cocles and his companions who broke down the bridge and swam the Tiber to save their city from the Etruscan tyrants. Enlightened and revolutionary heads were full of Marius and Sulla, and Scipio Africanus and his daughter Cornelia and her jewels, her sons Gaius and Tiberius Gracchus; for them Rome was a place where Julius Caesar and Marc Antony and Cato and Cicero walked about in togas and thought high and noble thoughts.

Maybe all of that dreaming explains why, when they got there as tourists or as conquerors, they were so uniformly outraged by the real garlic and salt cod of the disappointing people who dared call themselves Romans. And maybe that helps to explain why Napoleon, who was a great deal more intelligent than most men, never set foot in the real city. If he had, perhaps he would have loved it less, and hated it less.

'I am of the race of the Caesars, and of the best of their kind, the founders', he told Canova.[1] This was the city that Napoleon had loved since he had been a small, lonely and soaringly ambitious boy, a stranger in a strange land at the military school of Brienne, a boy convinced (as all boys are) of his own uniqueness and raised (as many boys of the time were) on the classical stories of Rome. By 1811 that boy was 42 years old, Emperor of the French, King of Italy, and Protector of the Confederation of the Rhine. If he saw himself as the second Augustus, the heir of Charlemagne, it was no longer a childish fantasy but a tantalising possibility. And he still dreamed of Rome.

In the summer of 1811, after the birth of the King of Rome, an architect and hydraulic engineer named Scipione Perosini submitted an impossibly grandiose and destructive plan for an imperial palace that would span the Capitoline Hill and the Forum, and dominate the Palatine. It was far too expensive to build, and it would

---

1 Driault, *Rome et Napoléon*, p. 8. 'Je suis de la race des Cesars, et de la meilleure, de ceux qui fondent.'

Napoleon as Mars the Peacemaker.

have required a destruction of ancient monuments that would have outdone the barbarians. But it was a dream worthy of the new great Caesar.[2]

Look down in a dream, as Napoleon might have done in 1811. He sees a world at peace, under the benevolent rule of the emperor of the West. The longed-for son and heir, the infant King of Rome who will ensure the limitless future of the House of Bonaparte, is sleeping in his cradle. Paris, the adopted home, the city of light, powerful and rational, has long been subservient; now is the time for Rome, beloved but unloving, to resume her ancient prerogatives. Heirs might be crowned there, at St Peter's basilica, by an obedient pope. A palace of the new Caesars might rise in the moonlight, more vast than any ancient ruler had ever dared to dream.[3] It could cover an area from the Palazzo Venezia and the Gesù, to the Coliseum and the Circus Maximus.

It could flow over the Capitoline hill, swallowing Michelangelo's great piazza and the medieval pile of the church of Santa Maria in Ara Coeli. The Campidoglio and the Ara Coeli could be enclosed in a pentagon, with its outer edges made up of barracks for the Imperial Guard. Then, connected by stairs and passageways, the palace would extend down into a huge, oblong complex enclosing the ancient Forum in a sort of interior courtyard. The complex would be dedicated to the imperial offices and some 20 ministries – a court of appeals, a prefecture, customs officials, theatres, the all-important minutiae that ensure the prosperity and security of a great state. The facade would be the grandest that imperial architects can design, yet recalling the chaste classical simplicity of the ancients. The lower facade would be supported by austere Doric columns; the upper one by Ionic columns; and at the very top, the ornate Corinthian. Festooned with stone garlands, studded lavishly with great classical and pseudo-classical statuary, balconied and terraced, arched and ceremonial-entranced, the palace would rise up to 10 or more monumental stories in five window-studded facades and topped by a great dome. More a collection of palaces than a single palace, it would include the emperor's residence as well as the meeting places for the constitutional assemblies, and surrounding these, the barracks

---

2   The Perosini palace would have been a worthy heir to Nero's Golden House, then under excavation. The Capitoline and Palatine areas are prime real estate for imperial dreams. Cola di Rienzo could lay some claim to the medieval Ara Coeli steps and church. Napoleon's palace would have dwarfed the monument to Victor Emanuel that would be tacked on to the end of the area after Rome was subsumed yet again, this time into the Kingdom of Italy. There is another imperial project that parallels Napoleon's grandiose dreams, and that of course is the Fori Imperiali project of Mussolini, a triumphal processional avenue that cut through some ruins of ancient Rome, but hardly on the Napoleonic scale.

3   There were several plans proposed for the imperial palace, but the most ambitious was this one by 'Scipione Perosini, Architetto e Hydraulico Pensionato della Spagna', presented in 1810 – the plans are in the Archives Nationales de Paris, N III Rome. It was, inevitably, shelved in favour of an expansion of the existing papal Quirinal palace, which at least had the advantage of elbowing the pope firmly aside.

of the Imperial Guard. From the Capitoline edifice a broad terrace would descend gently by means of ramps to the Forum, where the ancient monuments might be replaced by new ones worthy of the new Great Caesar. From the Forum, footpaths would lead up to the imperial residence on the Palatine, and, behind that, splendid new gardens would absorb the remains of the palaces of the ancient caesars and cascade down to the Circus Maximus. Bas reliefs and inscriptions line the ramps and corridors, while the whole area will be ornamented by busts and statues, some on horseback like Marcus Aurelius astride his golden horse, some on foot, many of their founding emperor Napoleon the Great (perhaps crowned by Canova's Mars the Peacemaker?), some of worthy descendants, some representing the heroes of the new empire, others fanciful evocations of ideals of the past and the future. Great avenues leading to the city would be introduced by triumphal arches. The greatest of these will take the traveller to the Corso, and from that to the Porta del Popolo, and from there to the Flaminian road, and the north. The pope? Surely in the light of Reason Christianity will shrink to a collection of quaint, colourful cults, tolerated but controlled. If some of them wish to be led by a bishop of Rome, that too will be useful. But his primary residence could be moved to Paris or Avignon, leaving Rome for the emperors.

But these were dreams and plans. Let us instead look at Napoleon's second imperial city as it was, not as it might have been in a future that never came. In 1811, a multi-century, multi-continental rule of the House of Bonaparte seemed entirely possible; within two years the Napoleonic rule in Europe had begun to crumble, and before 1815 it was gone.

If the Perosini megastructure was an impossible dream – and Napoleon must have realised that it was – there were other possible uses for the area. As Mrs Eaton would note a few years later, the Forum and Coliseum were 'exactly where you would wish [them] to stand – far from modern Rome, her streets, her churches, her palaces, and her population, alone in its solitary grandeur, and surrounded only with the ruins of the imperial city.'[4] One could easily make this district a sort of Antique theme park where archaeologists would uncover classical ruins and get rid of the surrounding bits of living city. 'Pilgrims' could admire the glories of ancient paganism in an outdoor temple, open to the clean air of nature and far removed from the stuffy, dark, medieval temples of Christianity, and equally free of the annoying presence of Romans. As the imperial city, Rome would have to be rebuilt to more nearly reflect her great destiny, and if that involved more demolition than construction, so be it.

Architecture is a tool of cultural revolution. By the late eighteenth century the Baroque style was seen as the style of absolute monarchy (now passé), while the Rococo reflected the mind-set and life-style of the aristocracy (in the process of becoming dangerously unfashionable). A new style, the Neo-Classical, was already stepping forward to be recognised, proclaiming itself the pure, clean, virile style with the manly vigour required to remake the world in its own, more bourgeois, image. Like most new things, the Neo-Classical already had a long history, rooted as it was in the eighteenth-century desire for efficiency. Enlightenment engineers and rulers

---

4   The confident and opinionated Mrs Charlotte Eaton lived in Rome immediately after the Napoleonic period, in 1817 and 1818, and published her letters describing the city.

The project for the gardens on the Pincian hill.

worked away like beavers, building centralised markets and slaughter-houses, out-of-town cemeteries, new roads and bridges, reinforcing river banks, and generally remaking the world in a shiny new image. Romans, of course, were used to this sort of thing. Reforming or self-aggrandising popes (and the two were by no means mutually exclusive) often tried to re-make the city, with greater or lesser success.

When the whirlwind of revolution struck, then, it was inevitable that the new rulers would attempt to scrape away what they regarded as the excrescences of later ages and return Rome to its Greco-Roman origins. It was the vigorous 'scraping away' that caused much of the trouble. The Roman architects – Valadier and Camporese – knew better, but the keen men from the Paris *Conseil des Bâtiments Civils* understood what their imperial sovereign wanted. It was, perhaps, equally inevitable that this effort would fail, given the short time available to them (less than five years) and their profound misunderstanding of the city, its history, and its people.

None of this, of course, in the least prevented their trying.

The planners in Paris and their Roman representatives, following the lead of their emperor, had the distinct advantage of not having to concern themselves too much about the needs and wants of the living city, or about money. An imperial decree of July 1811 set aside (or at least, promised to set aside) an annual fund of one million *francs* a year to embellish Rome (the idea is rather astonishing). [5]

Early French redevelopment plans called for an area on the right bank of the Tiber between the Milvian bridge and the city walls to be converted to gardens and places of amusement, to be called the Villa Napoleon. The area outside the Porta del Popolo had long been a popular gathering place – the fry-feasts on St John's Day traditionally took place there – and the papal government had already asked for plans for improving the area. In 1805, Valadier had provided an ambitions design for a huge garden (to be called the New Campo Marzio), crossed by roads for carriages and pedestrians, with shops, restaurants, cafés, a race track, baths, a swimming pool, halls for billiards and tennis, and an *arcadia* with a place for performances. Other plans called for permanent buildings that would host biannual fairs. There would be two wide, tree-lined porticoes, with a triumphal column in the centre.

---

5   These figures are drawn from the French plans for the city of Rome, as detailed in a decree published in July 1811.

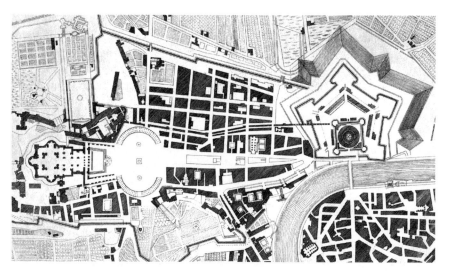

Plan to demolish the island of houses in the Borgo, between the Bridge of the Angels and St Peter's.

Unfortunately, neither the papal government, nor the French, managed to do much with these plans, but some of them were recycled for the Garden of the Great Caesar. This new plan was for a garden (not unlike the one proposed for the Villa Napoleon) to extend from the Pincian hill to the Tiber, with great tree-lined avenues and open fields.

The idea of organising and beautifying the area immediately around the Piazza del Popolo was not new (Raphael had had a go at it under Sixtus V). Valadier had proposed a plan to Pius VI, in 1793, before anyone had dreamed of a new great Caesar. It is appropriate then that one of the remaining delights of the whole construction project is the Valadier Casino, a charming little eighteenth-century style summer-house that was designed as a restaurant in 1813.

The gardens would be one of the most important, and successful, works undertaken during the French occupation. As de Tournon noted early in his stay, Rome lacked a public promenade within the city, where people could go to enjoy the shade and the open fields. They had only the 'laurels of the villa Borghese' and 'the pines of the Pamphili villa'.[6]   Now, as Stendhal noted a few years later, Rome had gardens to match or even surpass those of Paris:

The Pincio gardens are not buried like the Tuileries gardens, they dominate 80 or 100 feet of the Tiber and the surrounding countryside. The view from them is superb.

As the Garden of the Great Caesar was to beautify the entry into the city from the north, the Campidoglio *passaggiata* was to benefit the southern entry, from Naples. It was to include the archaeological area of the Coliseum, the Forum, the Palatine with its ruins, and the area along the Tiber that had been the site of the Boario forum, the oldest of Rome's marketplaces and site of the Temple of Fortuna and the *Bocca della Verità*.

6   LaPadula, *Roma e la Regione*, p. 112 et seq.

On 9 August 1811 a further imperial decree ordered the demolition of what was called the island of houses in the Borgo, between the two streets that led from Bridge of the Angels to St Peter's, and some of the houses that surrounded the Palazzo Venezia and the Corso. Other projects were to include clearing the clutter that obscured the view of great monuments like Trajan's column (hidden behind two convents), the Pantheon (strangled by markets and shops that leaned up against the ancient structure), and the Trevi fountain, where the piazza was and remains so small that one could not get a good view of the astonishing wall of marble and water.

The Tiber was to be made navigable for heavy traffic from Perugia to the sea, and plans would be made to enclose it within banks, to put an end to flooding like that in 1806. There were only three working bridges across the Tiber – much of the traffic had to be carried by ferries. In order to remedy this situation, a new bridge would be erected where the ancient bridge of Horatius Cocles had stood, and the narrow Ponte Sisto would be repaired and renovated.

A central market and two slaughter houses were badly needed. In 1811, cattle were driven in from the countryside (Romans made a dangerous game of it) and held in pens and stalls around the Coliseum – pens and stalls created by irreverently blocking up some of the arches of that venerable structure. From there, they were purchased by butchers and killed in the streets.

If killing animals in the streets were not unsanitary enough, Romans persisted in dying and being buried in the churchyards, and sometimes inside the very churches, of their neighbourhoods. This must, of course, end. Two new civic cemeteries would be built, one near San Lorenzo fuori le mura, and one to the west near the town of Sacchetti.

Further plans included theatres. It was determined that there were enough of those, but Valadier proposed an extensive plan to enlarge the mausoleum of Augustus. The Chancellery would be converted into imperial courts; the Monticitorio palace would become the Prefecture. Continuing another papal initiative, one often overseen by the argumentative papal antiquarian Carlo Fea, programmes were restarted for excavating and preserving ancient monuments and buildings, including the Pantheon and the Coliseum, along with the temple of Vesta, the baths of Diocletian and of Nero, the triumphal arches of Constantine and of Septimus Severus. By the time the *Consulta* started its work (immediately after the February 1809 incorporation of the city into the empire), projects were already being carried out on the Coliseum, the Via Flaminia, and the Forum. Rome was being re-fashioned closer to the emperor's heart.[7]

The Real Rome
Rome encouraged illusion, or at any rate she encouraged dreams and visions. The city was a medieval jumble of churches, ruins, shops and homes dotted with open spaces (large and small), intersected by long, straight roads, and hemmed in on all sides by marshes and wasteland. She had been consciously designed as the stage-set for a sacred drama, where the physical existed to point the way to the spiritual, and

---

7   For the magesterial study of archaeology in Napoleonic Rome, see Ridley, *The Eagle and the Spade.*

the spiritual redefined the physical. Even more than most great cities, Rome was and remains a city of layers, an organic living thing. Part of being eternal is being timeless, so all of western history seemed to bustle along together in Rome in much the same way that all social classes, languages and world-views rubbed shoulders in her long streets and her oddly-shaped piazzas (no one speaking Italian could possibly call them *quadri* or squares).

The result was often anything but ethereal. Romans, from cardinals and princes to beggars and vagrants, considered the streets as extensions of their homes. This may help to explain their attitude towards street lighting: one did not have to be a criminal to resent strangers shining lights where God intended there should be darkness. In addition to being their dining rooms and parlours, and sometimes bedrooms, streets were also amenities and Romans of all descriptions tended to carry out their functions of elimination wherever the need took them. The more delicate foreigners were horrified, and looked on this as a disgusting sort of exhibitionism. Madame de Staël apparently considered this possibility, but rejected it: 'It is not being looked at that makes them do this, nor will they refrain when nobody is looking.' This behaviour, coupled with the fact that there was virtually no organised street cleaning (at least none that was either effective or regular: 'the broom of Rome is the rain'), should have made the city a death trap of cholera and such diseases, but in fact it was relatively healthy for a city of its size. The most famous, and dreaded, of diseases was the fever caused by bad air, the infamous *mal aria*. But this rarely struck in Rome, and confined itself – like brigands and wolves – to the band of swampy rural land of the Campagna, where the Pontine marshes lay. No Roman not bent on suicide would venture beyond the populated areas after dark. If one had to go to the hill towns, one made a dash across this insalubrious land in full daylight. Wine carters were an exception to this rule, but they were a hardy and daring breed, looked upon with awe by their fellow citizens.

The city was surrounded by two green rings, one outside and one inside the Aurelian walls (with the loop completed by the Tiber).[8] Just outside the walls lay a band of parks and gardens. These green spaces were normally available to the people, sometimes by formal permission, sometimes by custom, and sometimes simply because they were empty: in the summer the great families went to their summer homes in the hills above the city.

At the Porta del Popolo[9] the Borghese gardens extended to the Porta Salaria, where they met the Albani gardens, and these continued on around the city until they met the great park of the Patrizi. Then there were orchards, vineyards, and villas to Porta San Giovanni, from there to the Tiber. On the right bank of the river, outside Trastevere and the Janiculum (itself a wooded, nearly deserted hill) lay the gardens of the Villa Pamphilj, beyond them the Vascello, descending to the Porta Angelica (the angelic gate) and the fields around the Castel Sant'Angelo (the *prati del castello*) and the wooded Tiber banks that sloped down to the river and the Porta Flaminia.

On the inside of the walls was another circle of green, starting with the Pincian hill (where French administrators planned their great public promenade and garden)

8   As pointed out by Diego Angeli, in *Roma Romantica*.
9   The name probably means Gate of the Poplars, not gate of the people.

and the gardens of the Villa Medici (where the French Academy moved in 1803). Circling around inside the walls from the Villa Medici were a series of villas, orchards and gardens: the Villa Malta and the Villa Ludovisi, the orchards of Salluste and the Villa Paolina, from the Villa Torlonia and the orchards of the Holy Cross in Jerusalem, the gardens of the Lateran to the little villa of the Orsini, then the wide fields and hillside of Testaccio, where the *popolo* traditionally went for their October feasts. Inside the walls on the far side of the Tiber lay the Villa Sciara, and the villas and gardens of the Corsini and the Barberini, ending with the Vatican gardens, after which the ring was completed with the smaller villas of the Patrizi and the Barberini families.

Even within the populated areas of the city that clustered in the bend of the Tiber, the princely families had their parks and gardens, their courtyards full of trees and flowers; almost every house, even the most humble, had its little garden, its pergola, its courtyard covered by leaves; and as it flowed through the city, the Tiber was overlooked by hanging gardens and terraces.

Charlotte Eaton, with an Englishwoman's eye for gardens, described the vegetation around the city as she saw it in 1817. She was amazed by

> ... *the variety and prodigality of beauty which paint the hills, the woods, and the plains around Rome ... Fields covered over with patches of purple annemonies; others blue with hyacinths; others yellow with a pretty species of ranunculus; others white with little bulbous-rooted plants, like crocuses. The cliffs and rocky hills abound in shrubs similar to the laburnum but of a different species, and with Daphnes, Passerinas, and Euphorbiums; the woods with primulas, verbascums and cyclamens. The common daisy is generally found twice as large as in our cottage gardens, and its 'crimson tips' are infinitely more brilliant. ... excepting the plains of Granada there is no other equal to the Campagna of Rome; indeed, the fine luxuriant leaves of the plants that cover it, as well as the rich tints of the flowers, seem to afford the strongest proof of the excellence of the soil.*[10] *So great is the variety of plants that have rooted themselves in the ancient walls of the Coliseum alone that Sebastiani, the professor of botany at Rome, published a work in quarto entitled* Flora Colisea, *in which he describes 260 different kinds that are found there. But I am informed this does not nearly include the whole, which, with the various sorts of mosses and lichens, amount to upwards of 300 species. Nearly one quarter of these are papilionaceous; and there are three sorts of hyacinths (one very beautiful) peculiar to the vicinity of Rome. ...*

Within the walls, Romans lived in somewhere between a quarter and a fifth of the space, mostly pressed up against the river and in the area defined by the Tiber where it swings west to the Castel Sant'Angelo, then meanders back to the Tiber island and then swings west again. The city proper lay on the east bank between the Porta del Popolo in the north and Ponte Sisto to the south. Two populated areas lay within the city walls on the west bank, separated by the long, steep, and heavily wooded bulk of the Janiculum hill: they were the Vatican and the Borgo district to the north, and Trastevere (or Trans-Tiber), to the south. On the east bank, the population reached

---

10 A typical Eaton-esque dig at the Romans, who did not cultivate this area to her satisfaction.

The Forum.

out eastwards as far as Santa Maria Maggiore and the baths of Diocletian (not far from where the modern Termini railway station is located), separated by the Viminal and Quirinal hills. The rest was vineyards, open land and hillsides, sprinkled with ancient ruins and the occasional villa. To the south, what had once been the Roman Forum was now a field for holding cattle and a venue for rock-fighting matches. To the east, there was little between the great basilica of San Giovanni in Laterno and Santa Maria Maggiore. To the north, halfway between the Porta del Popolo and the Quirinal hill, was a district that during the eighteenth century had built up around the powerful Spanish ambassador's residence. This was the foreigner's base in Rome, because it was near the main entrance to the city, and because here Roman clerical law was tempered by international law, which extended from the embassy personnel to the other residents of the district. A guide published in 1800 noted that the area around the Spanish Steps 'is inhabited principally by foreigners, for whose accommodation it contains many good lodging-houses, while antiquaries and guides, or *ciceroni*, flock around it.'[11]

The large Piazza di Spagna, in the usual irregular Roman fashion, is made up of two intersecting triangles joined by the astonishing baroque triumph of the eight-terraced Spanish Steps (built between 1723 and 1726). The discriminating President de Brosses called it 'the largest and grandest staircase in Europe, interrupted by eight terraces'. These sweep up the steep hillside to the site of the famous classical gardens of Lucullus (who gave his name to the sensual delights of the table). By the time of the Renaissance, these gardens had become the property of the Medici family of Florence, who tamed them in the usual Renaissance fashion by turning them into a quirky sort of outdoor/indoor space, with hedge-lined walks, floral carpets, fountains, arbours, and secret gardens. In 1803, Napoleon took the property for the new site of the French Academy.

---

11 Salmon, *An Historical Description of Ancient and Modern Rome.*

The Piazza di Spagna and the Spanish Steps.

Like all cities, the shape and life of Rome was determined in large part by its history. After a thousand years or so as the seat of empire, Rome had had a bad Dark Ages, when the papacy, along with Western civilisation, clung to life in the face of barbarian onslaughts; then had come a brilliant if violent medieval period culminating in the High Middle Ages when the papacy defined the West, and the papal capital was at or near the prosperous centre of the religious, political, and economic life of Europe. With the failure of the crusades to re-capture the Holy Land, Rome became the undisputed centre of Christian life in Europe and the focus of pilgrimage, especially during the Holy Years when tens of thousands of more or less pious tourists descended on what was still a rather small city. This in turn led to an organised city planning that was ahead of its time in Europe, as popes built bridges, hospitals and shelters to deal with the overflow that might be expected every quarter century.

All of that came crashing down with the Babylonian Captivity during the catastrophic fourteenth century when the popes moved to Avignon, and Rome again clung to a precarious life until the popes returned and the Renaissance began. When Martin V came back to Rome in 1420, he and his successors found a devastated city – a village, really, whose population may have been as small as 17,000 souls or even fewer. But it was this devastation, coupled with the burst of wealth and power of the Renaissance, which allowed them to rebuild the city almost from scratch. They rebuilt it as a city of marble and clear water, churches, palaces and fountains, commandeering the talents of the greatest artists and architects of the succeeding centuries – Michelangelo, Da Vinci, Bramante, Bernini, Borromini, Maderno.

Each phase of history, each generation of artists, added its own layer to the great onion that was Rome. But it was the Renaissance and the Baroque that made it, physically, the city it was by the end of the eighteenth century. On their return, the popes resumed their city planning, and the practice of cutting direct routes between major sites (primarily, but not exclusively, churches). So long, straight roads led from the major gates into the city, most notably from the Porta del Popolo. Another set of roads connected the Coliseum with San Giovanni in Laterno, and San Giovanni in Laterno with Santa Maria Maggiore, while another went from the Castrense Amphiteatre at the city walls to Santa Maria Maggiore, and then on to the Four Fountains at the foot of the Quirinal hill, where it became a cross roads, with vistas extending to the obelisks on the Quirinal, the Esquiline, and the Pincian hills, and continuing straight ahead to the Spanish Steps. Part of this was an act of Christian charity, blended with the economic impetus for encouraging a very ancient form of tourism: foreigners coming into Rome needed to be able to get from one place of devotion to another, and back to their places of residence, without wandering helplessly through back streets. It was also an act of civic control: confused foreigners wandering about were an invitation to crime, and tangled back streets could be impenetrable to the forces of law and order.

Along the east bank of the Tiber the Via Giulia cut directly from the Ponte Sisto to the Castel Sant'Angelo; on the west bank, the Via della Lungara took pedestrians and vehicles from the Vatican into Trastevere, and then connected with another straight road leading though Trastevere to the Ponte Sisto.

It was not until the middle of the eighteenth century that a pope finally published an official list of names for the streets. In 1744, Benedict XIV's list identified 271 streets and 185 piazzas. Most of the piazza names were the names of the nearest church, institution or major palace, while the great bulk of the streets either took their names from same source, or from nearby landmarks, or the occupations of the people who worked there, or simply from where they went from and to (as in 'the road that runs from the church of Santa Catarina of the Rota to the river'). Even after the streets got names, there was nothing in the nature of signs until 1803, when Pius VII had boundary stones placed giving the name, number and distinct badge of the *rione* or district which one was entering or leaving.

Beyond the city of the avenues, pilgrims and processions lay the city of the people, which consisted of the normal human warren of tangled backstreets and jumbles of buildings public and private, tucked in beside, between, and on top of one another. Many of the smaller dwellings were attached to, or built into, ancient ruins (like the theatre of Marcellus) or towers. House numbers were neither assigned nor missed until the organising French arrived in 1808. Instead, people made do with the sort of addresses that had served primitive man. As Maurice Andrieux reports, the eighteenth-century lawyer Dominico Sisto's address was in 'the Via dei Serpenti, the house with the doorway adjoining the butcher's shop, nearly next to the Corsican guardhouse'.[12]

While there were the occasional individual shops and houses, most of the buildings of Rome were large edifices which rejoiced in the name of *palazzi*, or palaces. The French, for whom the word palace suggests a royal residence, found this particularly amusing. Some of these great buildings still served, in whole or in part, as housing for the noble or otherwise distinguished families that gave them their

---

12 Andrieux, *Daily Life in Papal Rome*, p. 16.

The interior of San Giovanni in Laterno.

names, though by the end of the French occupation most of these people would be irretrievably ruined. As homes, the *palazzi* reflected the makeup and role of the noble families who built them. The *famiglia* consisted not only, or even primarily, of people related by blood or marriage, but also included their employees, hangers-on and clients, all of whom found living space in some corner or other of the huge, ornate, and very uncomfortable edifices. This was made even more complicated by the fact that living nobly meant that one's home was open on all days of the year and all hours of the day to anyone who might happen to want to wander through it, in search of influence or amusement or edification, or simply out of curiosity.

It was not such a great stretch of the imagination that buildings put to this sort of use should turn into apartment houses. We can let the opinionated Mrs Eaton describe them, as she had extensive experience with them:

The people here live in flats and have a common stairs … Though by no means conductive to cleanliness or comfort, it is highly favourable to grandeur of appearance, and architectural effect; for by this means the houses are built upon so much larger a scale, that their exterior is susceptible of fine design and ornament; and even when plain, or in bad taste, it is scarcely possible that they should not have a more noble air than the mean, paltry little rows of houses in England and Holland, where every body must have one of their own. …

There is one peculiarity of the flats of Rome, which (thank heaven!) we have not in Edinburgh. As you go up a common stair here, you observe a square grating in every door. Knock at one of them – somebody comes, uncloses the wooden shutter that covers it, and eyes you suspiciously thorough the bars before he ventures to open it – and this at noonday! Wherever you live in Rome, you must be content to live on a common stair. If your abode be a palace, it will be the same thing. The most you can hope for is a primo

Piazza Navona.

or secondo piano *to yourself. Lodgings for single gentlemen, or for small families abound; upon a larger scale, it is more difficult to find accommodation.*

The great families whose *palazzi* in town were virtually public property also generally maintained a villa in the open land within the city walls, or just outside them. These villas were somewhat more private, if only because they were in less populated areas, but even they were open to passers-by or picnickers, at least at designated times. Even the great parks and gardens of the Borghese family were regularly opened to the populace of Rome. These villas were surrounded by Italian renaissance gardens, made less to recall the idealised Nature beloved of the Enlightenment (and the English), and more as in token of an ordered Garden of Eden, complete with stately halls, carpets of grass and flowers, hedge walls, the secret delights of little houses, or *casinos,* and the delicious jokes of pools and fountains (though few if any were as elaborate as the Cardinal d'Este's famous retreat in the hills near Frascati).

In addition to the classical Seven Hills – the Palatine, Capitoline, Aventine, Viminal, Esquiline, Quirinal, and Celian – there were others, notably the Pincian, to the north, site of the Borghese gardens; the Vatican (all but levelled at the time of Constantine to accommodate the basilica), and the Janiculum.

In the populated districts of the city, neighbourhoods were punctuated by irregularly shaped piazzas, some large and others barely qualifying as wide places at the interchange of alleys. Most of the parish churches and many of the conventual churches of the city had their own homonymous piazzas. Few of these were as theatrically effective as the piazza of the church of Sant' Ignazio, where the visitor steps out of the church dedicated to the soldier-saint who founded the Jesuit order, only to find himself in an operatic stage set. But each of them, large or small, had its own familiar character, and it was largely these eccentric spaces that gave the city its human scale and its warmth.

The largest of the piazzas was, predictably enough, enclosed in the circling arms of the Bernini colonnade outside St Peter's basilica. This was closely rivalled or even surpassed by the group of piazzas around the city's second church, San Giovanni in Laterno, one of which also served as the open space within the Porta San Giovanni. Each of the 16 city gates opened onto a large or small piazza, with the largest after that of San Giovanni being at the Porta del Popolo that opened onto the Corso.

The Piazza Navona was built over a racecourse, the Circo Agonale of Nero's time. At the end of the eighteenth century this was a great public space for puppet shows and preaching and *ciarlitani* selling medicines and toothache remedies and snake oils, printers and book-sellers' shops, stands peddling fritters and dried cod and watermelons, and, at special times of celebration, the great wood and *papier maché macchine* for fireworks and the distribution of free wine. The great events of the Piazza Navona were replicated on a smaller scale in the smaller piazzas of the city.

The other of the older commercial centres was the Campo dei Fiori. This market and meeting space was sometimes the site of the scaffold for executions. Capital executions were rare by now, but corporal punishment was freely, and publicly, meted out to carriage drivers who raced in the city streets, or bakers who sold bread that didn't meet government guidelines for weight and content, or common criminals of any other description. These corporal punishments were usually of two sorts: the *tratti di corda*, or the *cavaletto* [see chapter 6]. There was no fixed site or timetable for such events, but they tended to float depending on circumstances: sometimes in the Piazza Sant'Angelo opposite the castello; sometimes in the Campo Vaccino or Forum, or the piazza in front of the Pantheon, or, at carnival time, as a great show in the Piazza del Popolo, upstaging even the horse racing.

Most piazzas had their own fountains, which could be stately (like the Aqua Paola on the Janiculum), or playful (like the *Barcaccia* in the Piazza di Spagna, designed to look like a stranded boat), or astonishing (like that great white Baroque theatre of the Trevi). There is something North African in the love of water and fountains in Rome. These were the most beloved gifts the popes gave to their city, and the hydraulic engineers made the waters dance and sparkle in a hot and dirty world.

Even in the greatest of the piazzas or the grandest of the *palazzi*, the smells and noises of the countryside were never far away, and the lush animal life added their own layers of ordure to the public spaces. People raised chickens in their courtyards and streets and sometimes even in their rooms. Dogs and cats were everywhere, while food was provided for them by their own caterers, the *carnaccioli* who distributed scraps of otherwise inedible meat. Working horses pulled carriages and carts, and once a year for a few riotous days during carnival, the main street of the city became a racecourse. Milk was delivered on the hoof, by means of goats and cattle that were brought to the customers' doors and milked on the spot. Cattle to be butchered were driven into town by cowherds who brought them in by the Porta del Popolo and drove them at breakneck speed down the Corso, while the tough young men of the city dodged and tried to outrun them in a sort of weekly running of the bulls (or steers).

Romans' prelapsarian relationship with nature extended to the telling of time. This was a complex affair, based on the rhythm of the days and years, not arbitrarily imposed by clocks. Roman clocks politely adapted themselves to nature (when you

Ponte Milvio – the famous Milvian bridge.

bought one, it included a chart telling you how to reset it, by the week, as the seasons changed). French time, for instance, might insist that it was six in the morning whether the sun had just come up, or had been up for two hours, or wouldn't appear for another two hours; and 12 hours later, come light or come dark, it would be six again, this time in the evening. In Roman time, the first hour of the day came half an hour after sunset (according to the ancient custom of starting the day with nightfall, as in the Biblical 'and evening and morning came, the first day'. Most Romans simply listened for the sound of the Angelus bells that called the faithful to prayer at dawn, mid-day and sunset.

The Tiber
The river was usually sluggish and brown, but occasionally turned angry, overflowing its shallow banks to flood most of the city. In 1806 a flood reached as far as the Pantheon. Romans used the Tiber for bathing, for drinking (when filtered through sand, the water was more or less potable), for fishing and for commerce at the city's two ports, the Ripa Grande, or big port, on the bank across from the Aventine, and the Ripetta (small port) near the Porta del Popolo. It was navigable only for small vessels and part of the great French plan was to secure the banks of the Tiber and open it to navigation from the sea as far inland as Perugia.

The Bridges
There were only three bridges crossing the Tiber within the city walls. These were Ponte Sant' Angelo, from the Castel Sant'Angelo to the city; the Ponte Sisto, or Janiculum bridge; and the Tiber island, connected to the west, or Trastevere, bank by the short Ponte San Bartolomeo, and to the city on the east bank by the Ponte Quattro Capi (Four Heads bridge).

To the North, three miles beyond the Porta del Popolo, stood the most historic of Rome's existing bridges, the Milvian, where Constantine defeated Maxentius and made Rome Christian. Between the Milvian and the bridge of the Angels there were only ferry crossings, and the small port, or Ripetta. At more or less regular intervals, there was a system of ropes to bring ferries across the river.

Around the bend, and moving south, there was an ancient vestige of the Ponte Trionfale, more ferry crossings and then, on the road leading from the Porta di San Pancrazio to the Via Giulia, the Ponte Sisto, built first by Caracalla, then rebuilt in the 1470s and renamed for Pope Sixtus IV. The great 'eye' of the bridge served Romans for a flood warning: when the water rose to the top of the arches, but not to the 'eye', there was no danger; if it reached the eye, it was time to move upstairs and hope for the best.

Where the river bends to the west, the Tiber island with its ancient hospital is connected to the west by the short Ponte San Bartolomeo, and to the east by the oldest working bridge in the city, the Ponte Quattro Capi.

Just below, at the point where the water tends again to the east, Scipio Africanus built a bridge that now reaches almost halfway to the western bank before it stops abruptly, cut off by the great flood of 1598, and there it remains, Ponte Rotto – the (eternally?) Broken Bridge. Here, to all intents and purposes, the populated city of 1811 ended. Below that stood the ruins of the Ponte Sublicio, said to have been the site of the ancient wooden bridge of Horatius Cocles.

The *Rioni*

The city within the walls, tucked around the hills, and more or less served by the ferries and the river, was divided into 14 districts (French administration would change that), each with its history and its more or less passionately held identity.

There were between 300 and 400 churches, chapels, and shrines in the city, ranging in size from the vastness of St Peter's or the Pantheon or San Giovanni in Laterno, down to private chapels designed to hold a handful of worshippers or none at all. There were far too many for any rational purposes, put up by regular orders extant and extinct, by families, by confraternities, in fulfillment of vows or for favours (worldly and otherwise) granted, to serve neighbourhoods of a few houses, in honour of patron saints, for hospitals and hospices, schools or universities, to mark pilgrim routes or miraculous events, for and by the members of guilds or craft organisations, or to serve national congregations (Swedish or Florentine, Venetian or French).

When the French arrived in Rome in 1798, they found a city divided, as it had been since the rule of Augustus Caesar, into 14 *rioni*, or districts.[13] The district where one lived was usually the district in which one had been born, and it was as key an element in one's identity as family or parish. Each district had its own distinct character, and its own distinct emblems, its own administrative structure, and its own government officials who wore traditional costumes. As part of their on-going work of tearing down the Old in order to replace it with the New, the republicans

---

13 Augustus authorised 14 districts, but the eighteenth century *rioni* did not coincide with the ancient ones. Friz, *Consumi, Tenore di vita, e prezzi*, p. 14; Maes, *Curiosità Romane*, III, pp. 131-6.

dismembered and renamed the old wards.[14] The diarist Benedetti, who like most Romans resented all the chopping and changing, noted on 8 March 1798 that '[i]n less than 24 hours they have removed all the stones which marked the boundaries of the old districts. Now one does not know where one is!'[15]

The *rioni* varied widely in area: the smallest (Sant'Angelo in Pescheria) consisting of 12 ha, while the largest (Monti) enclosed some 142 ha. They also varied in density of population: the central districts of Sant'Eustachio and Pigna had buildings on 70% of their land, while the large Monti district and Campitelli (also on the periphery) were 85% open country, park or farmland. The Ripa district, between the Tiber and the Aventine hill, was 95% unbuilt.[16]

Monti (Rione I): This was an enormous district that went from the extreme south-east of the city, around the Porta Maggiore, north to the Porta Pia and the great ruins of the baths of Diocletian. It was sparsely populated, and included important ruins like the baths, the arches of Titus and Septimus Severus, and Trajan's column. It was also the site of the Protestant cemetery. The men of the Monti district were traditional rivals of the men of Trastevere, and regularly met them for ritual rock fights in the neutral area of the Forum. On ceremonial occasions, their *caporione,* district chief, wore a colour described as 'changing' (perhaps shot silk). The republicans divided it into two parts, to be called the Terme (baths) and Suburra districts.

Trevi (Rione II): A much smaller area in the heart of the city, bordering on the Corso and including, in addition to the famous Trevi fountain and palace, the even grander palace of the popes on the Quirinal hill, and the little church of Santa Maria della Vittoria with the famous (or infamous) Bernini scene of St Theresa in Ecstasy. The *caporione* wore the costume of a pilgrim, with staff and cockle shell. Under the Ridiculous Republic this was known as the Quirinal.

Colonna (Rione III): Included the Pincian hill and three important colleges – the Nazarene, the Capranica, and the Roman Seminary – as well as the palaces of the Chigi, Spada, Ludovisi and Capranica families, plus the theatre run by the Capranica. The *caporione* of the Colonna district wore grey (Maes suggests this was meant to recall the colour of marble). It was called the Pincio under the republic.

Campo Marzo (Rione IV): Named after the military parade ground (the field of Mars), Campo Marzo was the heart of the old city. It stretched from the Spanish Steps and the Villa Medici (after 1803 the French Academy) to the Porta del Popolo, and on to the smaller of the two ports on the Tiber, the Ripetta. The district was dark and dirty, but it included the most elegant of the city theatres, the Aliberti, as well as the Pallacorda and the Corea amphitheatre, the site for bullfights and balloon ascensions and fireworks displays. Since the name already had classical allusions, the republicans merely changed the spelling to Marte (Mars).

Ponte (Rione V): Site of the Sant' Angelo bridge ('*ponte*') and the remnants of the Ponte Trionfale; its main street was the elegant Via Giulia that ran along the Tiber from the Castel Sant'Angelo to Ponte Sisto. Its most important church was the church

14 Maes, *op. cit.,* II, p. 26, and Nolli, *Roma al tempo di Benedetto XIV, La pianta di Roma.* The numbers vary in different listings, we have adopted those used by Nolli.

15 Silvagni, *La Corte Pontificia,* I, p. 299.

16 Friz, *op. cit.,* p. 14, note 4.

of San Giovanni de' Fiorentini, on the river across from the Castello but it also included a chapel in which those condemned to death spent their last night, comforted and exhorted to repentance by the confraternity dedicated to that work (the piazza at the Ponte Sant' Angelo was one of the traditional places of execution). Its *caporione* wore sky blue. The republicans re-named it the Brutus district.

Parione (Rione VI): Another of the central districts, it included the two great market spaces of the city, the Piazza Navona and the piazza of the Campo dei Fiori, as well as the Braschi palace, the Granari and Pace theatres and the remnants of the ancient theatre of Pompey. The Street of the Lutemakers was there, as was the palace of the Cancelleria (chancellery) and the new church of Santa Maria in Vallicelliana, the church of St Philip Neri's Oratorians. The *caporione* wore a tawny yellow, the colour of the lion. Under the republic, Parione was combined with Regola (VII) and the new district was named Pompey.

Regola (Rione VII): This was rather grim site of the New Prison, the palace of the tragic Cenci family and the church of Santa Maria dell'Orazione e Morte, decorated with human bones and extremely popular during the Octave of the Dead in November. The tanners carried out their bloody trade here. The English College and the Farnese palace (embassy of the Neapolitans and then of the French) were both located in this district. Regola also included the Ponte Sisto, and bordered on Rione V, Ponte. Regola's *caporione* wore one of the more peculiar outfits, described as the costume of a Moor, with multi-coloured stockings.

San Eustachio (Rione VIII): One of the most densely populated of the central districts, San Eustachio was the site of the newest and largest of Rome's theatres, the Argentina (where Sardou's Floria Tosca sang) and also of the church of Sant'Andrea della Valle (where Puccini set the first act of his *Tosca*). The Sapienza, the university of Rome, was there, along with its collegial church, the elegantly bizarre St Ivo, the Valle theatre, and the lane where one of Rome's famous 'talking statues', Abbate Luigi, was found. The *caporione* was even more distinctive than Regola's: he was accompanied by two singing nymphs. Under the republic, this became the Flaminian district.

Pigna (Rione IX): Another of the densely-populated central districts, it ranged from the Piazza Venezia to the piazza of Minerva with its famous elephant and obelisk, and from the Pantheon to the church of Sant' Ignazio, with its theatrical little piazza and *trompe l'oeil* cupola. It was also home to the other famous Jesuit churches, the Gesù (where the great silver statue of St Ignatius was melted down to pay part of the tribute of Tolentino). The district *caporione* wore flesh-colour. Under the republic, Pigna was united with Sant'Angelo in Pescheria as the Pantheon district.

Campitelli (Rione X): Consisting mostly of open country and ruins, the Capitoline and Palatine hills were at the heart of this district. It was home to the Forum, the palaces of the Caesars and the Coliseum, as well as the Campidoglio, the palace of the Conservators, the residence of the Senator of Rome and the church of Santa Maria in Ara Coeli. Since the Forum was the venue of choice for the rock fights between men from Trastevere and from Monti, it was fortunate that Campitelli also included the hospital of the Consolation which specialised in accidents and wounds. The colour of the *caporione* was green. Under the republic, Campitelli was united with Ripa, as the Campidoglio district.

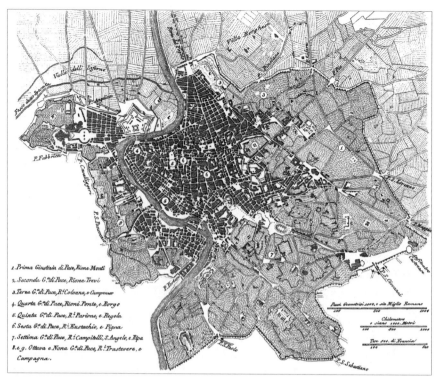

1. *Prima Giustizia di Pace, Rione Monti*
2. *Seconda G.ᵃ di Pace, Rione Trevi*
3. *Terza G.ᵃ di Pace, R.ᵗ Colonna, e Campomar*
4. *Quarta G.ᵃ di Pace, Rioni Ponte, e Borgo*
5. *Quinta G.ᵃ di Pace, R.ᵗ Parione, e Regola*
6. *Sesta G.ᵃ di Pace, R.ᵗ Eustachio, e Pigna*
7. *Settima G.ᵃ di Pace, R.ᵗ Campitelli, S. Angelo, e Ripa*
8. e 9. *Ottava e Nona G.ᵃ di Pace, R.ᵗ Trastevere, e Campagna.*

The *Rioni* in 1812.

Sant'Angelo (Rione XI): This was the district where the ghetto was located. It also included, among others, the palaces of the Patrizi and the Altieri families. Appropriately for a district that included a great fish market, the Sant'Angelo *caporione* wore a colour described as *diverso*, or the colour of the eyes of a dying fish. The republic abolished the ghetto, united Sant'Angelo with the Pigna district, and called it the Pantheon district.

Ripa (Rione XII): Between the Aventine hill and the Tiber, it consisted almost entirely of ruins, churches and cemeteries, and only 5% of it was inhabited. It included the old Greek district with the church of the 'Mouth of Truth' (*bocca della verità*), ancient ruins like the baths of Trajan and Antoninus, aqueducts, and cemeteries, including those for Protestants and for Jews. The church of 'St John the Beheaded' was there, home of the confraternity whose members were dedicated to comforting, exhorting, and burying executed convicts (the cemetery of the executed was near their church). Its *caporione* wore white, the colour of marble. Ripa was united with Campitelli under the republic, as part of the Campidoglio district.

Trastevere (Rione XIII): This was and remains perhaps the most distinctive and the most characteristic Roman district, an area set apart since the days when it was the Etruscan neighbourhood across the Tiber from Rome. The clothing of the Trastevere *caporione* was yellow. Under the republic, the district was re-named for the hill in whose shadow it lies, as the Janiculum district.

Borgo (Rione XIV): The Borgo was the other of the two trans-Tiber districts, separated from Trastevere by the Janiculum hill. This was the neighbourhood of St Peter's and of the Castel Sant'Angelo, with the raised and fortified corridor running between them. National churches of the Germans and the Hungarians were located here, along with a number of hospices and hospitals, the most famous being the hospital of Santo Spirito. The colour of the Borgo *caporione* was violet, or purple, the colour of bishops and emperors. The republic re-named this the Vatican section.

If Napoleon dreamed of the Forum and the Campidoglio, other men dreamed less powerful, but no less passionately held, dreams. One of them was an artist named Bartolomeo Pinelli, who worked for a time as an illustrator for the French archaeological projects. Whatever else he was, Pinelli was a man of Trastevere – the dialect poet Belli, who knew him, gave him the title of *er pittor di Trastevere* – the painter of Trastevere. He was a highly skilled, hugely talented, mostly successful wild man who earned his living in the middle ranks of the artists of Rome. He sometimes aspired to, but never reached, the rarified ranks of a Canova or a Camuccini, not because his talent was lacking but because he simply would not or could not reconcile himself to a regular life of being dependable and courteous to his clients and employers.

Rome for a Roman was made up of concentric circles – a family, a parish, a neighbourhood, a district and a city. Pinelli was born 20 November 1781, near the Gallicano hospital in San Crisogono parish, the heart of Trastevere. His birthplace was demolished long ago, in one of the projects for improving the area – that is, for making it easier for outsiders to penetrate that tangled, medieval district. There was little loss in the destruction of his birthplace, as it has been commonly described as a *casupola*, a slum hovel. His mother was Francesca Gianfarani and his father, Giovanni Battista Pinelli, made a precarious living decorating household jars and vases and making little terracotta figurines in a pottery shop near his home.

When discussing artists in Rome, it would be well to remember that, in addition to the great and the famous who make the art history books, there was a whole subculture of Romans who made their living (more or less) by art of some sort or other. These included the tapestry workers, the miniaturists, the employees of the mosaic factory and the drapers and painters and decorators who formed the army in charge of the hundreds of festivals, large and small, that made up the pattern of Roman life. Among the most humble of these were men like Bartolomeo Pinelli's father. The things he made almost never survived long enough to become collectable – little *bas-relief* as Raggi calls them, imaginary scenes, animals, curley-ques and patterns on vases and jars, and little terracotta figures of Christ, or the Virgin, or the saints, for devotional objects in the homes of people who couldn't afford paintings; and, most piquant and ephemeral of all, little figures and animals for the presepios, the manger scenes that appeared in churches, palaces, and the homes of the *popolani* during Christmas.

It was said that Bartolomeo Pinelli couldn't cross the Ponte Mollo (that is, the Milvian bridge leading out of Rome) 'without being struck by a profound sadness, and feeling short of breath.'[17] So what was the *rione* that Pinelli called home like?

---

17 Raggi, *Vita di Bartolomeo Pinelli*, p. 2.

Self-portrait of Bartolomeo Pinelli with his beloved dogs below the reminder that 'everything ends'.

Trastevere is less a part of Rome than a separate riverport town. Before ancient Rome was a republic, the district across the Tiber was an Etruscan military outpost. Horatius Cocles and his two companions hacked down a wooden bridge that crossed from here to the Aventine, and saved the young city. In imperial Rome (the first and rather more successful one), the Trastevere was the home of the sailors who worked the river trade, and were on call to rig the great awning that could cover the Coliseum. Merchants and bargemen, exotic foreigners and assorted river-rats, clustered here. This was the original home of the Jewish colony of Rome, before they moved across the river to what became the ghetto. Out of this fertile mix came a people who are considered, and consider themselves, the most Roman of the Romans. They were a people set apart – handsome, erect, touchy, insular and prone to act before they thought.

While all Romans tended to be independent minded and not much inclined to gainful employment, *Trasteverini* were famous even among Romans for working only at occupations that allowed them to retain their liberty – carters, porters, vendors and small tradesmen. *Trasteverini* considered themselves, and were considered, the purest Romans of them all, older than Romans, descended from the ancient race of Etruscans. They held themselves to be a caste apart and rarely married outside their district. They carried on fierce rivalries, especially with their arch-rivals from Monti. Proud, appallingly ignorant, violent, chivalrous and devout, they carried both knives and rosaries and were quick to use either... or both.

The tangled maze of unnamed alleys where most people in Trastevere lived were typical of the ungovernable mess that the French were determined to fix. Among the earliest and most lasting of the reforms would be giving official names to streets, and assigning numbers to identify each house or building on each street. This was not, of course, for the benefit of the people who lived there, who knew where they were. It was rather for the benefit of the government representatives who might want a quick way of finding people who lived (or hid out) in such places.

Indoors and Outdoors

The very poor lived in broken-down hovels like the one in which Bartolomeo Pinelli was born. The homes of Rome were often not only dark, but also damp, even when the Tiber was not in flood. Fortunately, as in most Mediterranean places, Romans of the popular class did most of their living in the streets and squares, not indoors. It is hardly accidental that, of the hundreds of images and pictures of daily life that an artist like Bartolomeo Pinelli made, barely a handful show any sort of indoor scene, and that is usually a tavern.

Trastevere is, appropriately enough, the site of the great port, or Ripa Grande. The Ripa lay at the far south-western extreme of the city, just inside the Porta Portese. Its wharves and flights of steps were under construction in the early years of the eighteenth century when an earthquake brought down part of the Coliseum and gave the builders a convenient pile of rubble to use for the port. The ancient port of Rome had been in this area – broken amphora used as packing crates piled up on the opposite bank of the Tiber into Mount Testaccio (shards).

Hospitals and Hospices, Prisons and the Cemetery

There were four hospitals in Trastevere. Two of these – one for men and one for women – made up the San Gallicano complex in the heart of the district. The other two were part of San Michele, an enormous complex of buildings deliberately located beyond the last houses of Trastevere, past the Ripa Grande. San Michele consisted of a series of courtyards and wings that included institutions for orphans and abandoned children, and for juvenile offenders. Boys 20 and under were kept in separate cells – an innovation at the time – and taught a trade, or at least worked, during the day in the courtyards and communal halls. There was a wing for prostitutes (traviate, 'women who lost their way or took the wrong road') and another for poor but respectable unmarried women and girls. The complex also included an old-age home for men and for women, and wool and tapestry factories that employed as many as 200 women.

The San Gallicano hospital was a masterpiece of sanitary engineering, and a lovely and elegant piece of architecture, constructed by the master mason Raguzzini for a rather grim purpose: to care for suffers from skin and venereal diseases. Spacious and airy, the San Gallicano hospital had 50 beds and boasted an amazing cure rate of between 80% and 90% of the 4,200 patients it treated each year, while only 6% to 7% died.[18]

If care for venereal disease and skin diseases was notably progressive and successful, the same cannot be said for care of the mentally impaired. Trastevere was the site of the madhouse, Santa Maria della Pietà for the insane poor, located on the Lungara road along the river. While the late eighteenth and early nineteenth centuries

---

18 Gross, *Rome in the Age of Enlightenment*, p. 207.

saw some notable humanitarian improvements in care for the mentally ill, Santa Maria della Pietà was not one of the places where this was evident. Run of the mill poor people with mental or apparent mental problems of any sort – from drunks to epileptics – were crowded into this hospital that was always too small for the numbers it housed. It was crowded despite the fact that dangerous madmen were usually sent to prisons. Trastevere had two prisons, one for boys and one for women (these were part of the San Michele complex).

Trastevere had 44 churches, chapels and oratories, including Bramante's Tempietto (the famous little jewel of a chapel built over the place where St Peter was believed to have been crucified) and the hilltop hollow where the fathers of the Oratorio gave their picnic sermons. Of these 44, only six were parish churches, including the church of Santa Cecilia, martyr and patroness of music, and San Crisogono, or Grisogono, or Crisogonus (near the hospital of San Gallicano).

Santa Maria in Trastevere, the ancient basilica that was the primary church of the district, stood in its own square deep in the tangle of alleys and lanes. Much of the wonderful mosaic facade is worked in gold that glowed and glittered when the church and piazza were lit up for festivals. The rectangular piazza is one of the largest in the district, and its great fountain, one of the oldest in the city, is raised on a square platform with steps leading up to it. The fountain stands in a spot where, according to tradition, a spring of pure oil broke out when Jesus was born. Like an open glade in a forest of masonry and stone, this was the principal gathering place of the district. In February 1798, after the men of Trastevere had flooded across the Ponte Sisto to attack the French troops, some of them were brought back here and shot by French firing squads, to 'encourage the others'.

Quite near the piazza of Santa Maria in Trastevere is another church dedicated to the Virgin, Santa Maria della Scala (built to house one of the street-side shrines that had the reputation for miracles). More prosaic miracles were performed in the pharmacy there, run by the Carmelite monks. This was the home of the Carmelite herbalist, Fra Basilio, who died there in 1802. He was famous as the inventor of several medicines – Aqua Antipestilenziale, a remedy for plague, or at least for stomach aches; and a headache cure, Aqua Antisterica (since many headaches were thought to be the result of some malfunction of the womb). His second floor shop has been preserved, with its great marble urns and majolica jars, its carved walnut cupboards and glass cases filled with vials, and its painted cupboards decorated with portraits of famous physicians of Greece and Rome. Fra Basilio's 1755 herbal directory contains 230 varieties of herbs, dried, pressed and beautifully mounted.[19]

Half of the remaining 38 churches were associated with convents and monasteries (the terms were almost interchangeable and had nothing to do with the gender of the inhabitants). These institutions sheltered regular orders like the white-robed Carthusians, Augustinians, Benedictines, several communities of Discalced Carmelites and Franciscans, along with less familiar orders like the Hermits of St Peter of Pisa.

---

19 Kolega 'Speziali, spagirici, droghieri e ciarlatani'. The square is also the site of the Museo di Roma Trastevere.

Some of these monastic churches were open to the public, some were not, but virtually all of the convents and monasteries were part of what we would call the social welfare network: some took in the sick, some taught the children, some offered shelter to abused wives and girls from the street, and almost all of them dispensed bread and soup to the hungry.

The district was cut at irregular intervals by 16 broad ways dignified by the name of *strade*, or streets, including the one that ran alongside the river (Lungara) and the long street that led from the steep stairs going up the wooded Janiculum hill. Most people lived in the maze of alleys and lanes (there were 25 named on the Nolli map), off the 14 *piazze* that ranged from the tiny open spot in the road called the Piazza Renzi to the spacious piazza outside of the Gallican hospital or the oblong piazza with its raised fountain outside the basilica of Santa Maria in Trastevere.

There were seven buildings called palaces in Trastevere. They included such gems as the Farnese palace and gardens (now called the Farnesina), and the elegant Corsini palace that served as home and headquarters for Ambassador Joseph Bonaparte, and later (for a time) the prefect Camille de Tournon. Several, like many Roman palaces, had long been converted into flats and apartments.

Trastevere, important as it was, was only one district in 14. But it was, perhaps quintessentially, the Rome of the people.

CHAPTER THREE
THE PEOPLE

On the eve of the French occupation Romans were young – the largest single age group was between 21 and 30, and the average age was between 28 and 31.[1] They lived in small households (the average had about four people in it, and some 12% of households consisted of only one person), and there were considerably more men than women – in 1795 there were 100 men for every 81 women. The percentage of women gradually rose until, by the end of the French period, there were 93.96 females to 100 males. Young men were either conscripted, or fled the city to avoid military service; and as the welfare state closed down, Rome became a much less attractive place for young men from the countryside and surrounding areas. At the same time large numbers of clerics (most of them male) were deported or ordered out of the city, and this meant a fall in the masculine population, while the feminine population remained static.[2]

The excess of males does not seem to have been simply the result of the relatively large number of celibate clerics in the city; that did play a part in distorting the balance, although not nearly so great a part as most visitors assumed.[3] Tourists reported that half the men in Rome seemed to be clerics; in fact, in 1798–99, slightly more than 3.5% of the men in Rome were clerics; by 1815, that had fallen to about 3%. The percentage of female religious was even lower, at about 2%.

Other factors in the preponderance of men included the large floating population of unattached male pilgrims and tourists, along with the fact that Romans who owned property were reluctant to marry.[4] At the same time, the city had a relatively

---

1 Statistics on the population of Rome are taken largely from Friz and from Gross pp 55–86.
2 Studies of birth records indicate that 80.7% of mothers were native Romans, while only 66.7% of fathers were born in the city, showing a very old pattern of men moving to Rome.
3 As we shall see below, visitors were often misled by the large numbers of men who wore clerical dress, many of whom were in fact lay, and some of whom were married.
4 This was not just a Roman phenomenon: in Milan, for instance, during the first half of the century, patricians had married late and half of the well-to-do never married at all. The custom of allowing only one of the brothers in a propertied family to marry and have legitimate children was a common early modern strategy for preserving and increasing family wealth.

low birth rate and a death rate that was higher than that in most Italian cities. What this meant, of course, was that any increase in population had to come from immigration – either people coming into the city from nearby towns and countryside, or from other states within or beyond Italy. And most of these immigrants were men.

Roman women, especially the women of the people, and of those most especially the women of Trastevere, had a reputation for beauty and independence. Chateaubriand wrote of them that 'you would think, to see them, that antique statues of Juno or Pallas had come down from their pedestals to walk about the temples.' Painters were fascinated by them, by their classical profiles and erect carriage, by their natural beauty unembellished by rouge, and by their unnerving habit of looking men straight in the eye.

On the other hand, most cultivated Grand Tourists, whether they were French, German, British, American, Danish or Russian, devoted at least a part of their journals to lamenting the fact that their lovely imaginary Rome was clogged up with people who ate garlic, rarely bathed, never swept their streets and used any convenient corner as a latrine. It is virtually certain that, could the tourist have been transported back to ancient Rome, he would have been at least as disappointed with his first impressions of ancient Romans as he was with modern ones.

Like most European societies of the day, Roman society was legally divided into inherently unequal orders, or estates, as they had been in the Middle Ages: the first, those who pray (the church); the second, those who defend (the nobility); the third, those who work (everybody else). But, in the West at least, this system no longer described reality. Reality was an emerging world of classes rather than estates. The idea of social orders based on function was being challenged by the new reality of townsmen, rich merchants, and the rise of a large group of non-noble, non-clerical professionals, plus a tiny but growing group of industrial workers. But Rome remained substantially as it had been: urban, hierarchical, ruled by the Church, resolutely non-modern, an economic and political basket case – and incongruously happy.

The vitality and independence of ordinary Romans alarmed foreigners, especially when it resulted (as it often did) in violence. But foreigners did not speak the language (even those who had some Italian knew nothing about the Roman dialect) and they had little contact with people outside their own class. They tended to miss the fact that Romans were also generous, good humoured, not given to brooding over the past, and while their fatalism did not lead to progress and ambition, it no doubt made it possible for them to live relatively serene and happy lives.[5] These characteristics were pretty generally true of all Romans, not just of the popular classes. English visitors like Mrs Eaton were appalled to see that Romans of all classes didn't *do* much of anything – they seem to have perfected the Italian art of *dolce far niente*.

Romans as a group were relatively healthy. Their diet was adequate despite their poverty. Those who worked regularly (and many if not most did not) normally had jobs that required physical labour, but jobs where they could choose when and where they worked, and when they stopped working – fishermen, porters, carters, butchers

5 Friz, *op. cit.*, p. 21.

and cow herds, gatherers and vendors of doughnuts, aquavit, greens, shells, snails or salt. And those who did fall ill had an extensive and, for the time, effective system of health care and pharmaceuticals available to them whether or not they could pay for it.

Population

Imperial Rome at its height had seen a city population of as many as one and a half million (1,200,000 to 1,600,000) within the area of the Aurelian walls. During the darkest days of the Dark Ages, Procopius says that the population fell to 500 men. While that is unlikely, the total population may well have fallen to somewhere around 17,000 (around 1% of imperial numbers) during the Avignon papacy. Nothing like accurate census figures began until the first quarter of the sixteenth century (in 1527, just before the disastrous siege, there were 55,000 people in Rome, after a century of prosperity), but by the eighteenth century the civic officials of Rome (like all European rulers) were counting noses with some accuracy. By the end of the 1770s, the number of noses was approaching 160,000 (or 10% of the imperial maximum), making Rome the second largest city in Italy (after Naples). In the early years of the revolutionary cataclysm, the population swelled with refugees as tens of thousands of French priests refused the oath of revolutionary loyalty, and many of those fled to Rome.

When Napoleon made Rome his imperial city in 1809, the population was 134,973 (with births narrowly outnumbering deaths at 5,186 to 4,821). Three years later, at the height of the French period (by 1813, the decline had begun) the population hit a low of 123,023 (with deaths outnumbering births by 3,804 to 3,138). In 1815, the year that the pope returned for good and Napoleon, defeated at Waterloo, was sent to die on the island of St Helena, the population had risen very slightly to 123,384 though the number of births was once again slightly higher than the number of deaths (4,362 to 4,094).

Marriage and Morals

Many of the thousands of tourists who descended on Rome during the eighteenth century and the first part of the nineteenth century wrote memoirs or travel tales. Most of these accounts had the following in common: Rome was astonishingly dirty; Roman people were wretchedly poor, beggars were everywhere, and yet most of the people were amiable and apparently happy; religion in Rome was spectacular, all pervasive, and not too burdensome in terms of private conduct; and Roman husbands of all classes were permissive and their wives all had lovers.

How much of this last observation was wishful thinking or the desire to find a striking anecdote is hard to say. It is also difficult to know how much their perception that 'everybody is doing it' can be explained by the fact that people given to promiscuity like to associate with others of similar inclinations. Casanova's extravagant and much cited memoirs paint a picture of libertinage triumphant all over the peninsula, and Rome seething with entertaining vice. It may be worth noting that Casanova wrote these recollections as an old man in France, looking back with nostalgia at a lost world, and a world far enough in the past to bow to imagination.

Arranged marriages often left little room for personal choice, and this would have been an invitation to infidelity, especially in a world where fashion encouraged such activities. The upper classes in Italy, like the upper classes everywhere, suffered from an epidemic of Gallomania. They tended to copy French fashions slavishly, and French fashion in the eighteenth century did not encourage domestic fidelity. To judge by the popular novels, polite society was prone to languor, sentiment, and a taste for the more amusing passions.

The French General Marmont visited Rome in 1790 and wrote:

Roman society, I found, was very gay and devoted exclusively to amusement. The freedom of the women passes all belief and their husbands permit it, speaking cheerfully and without embarrassment of their wives' lovers.

Tourists were especially fascinated by the institution of the *cigisbeo*, or *cavaliere servante* (which seems to have been a Spanish idea, not a French one). Their impression that all ladies had lovers might have been in part a misunderstanding of this institution. By tradition, a lady of the propertied classes, and especially of the nobility, had a gentleman attendant who was not her husband, and whose job was to accompany her when she went out of the home and generally to dance attendance on her. Mrs Eaton was convinced that the institution held true for Romans of all classes. Roman women, she observed,

… encourage liberties of speech, which would offend and disgust our countrywomen; and the strain of uniform gallantry, hyperbolical flattery, and unadulterated nonsense of the worst description, in which the men usually address them and which they seem to like and expect, is a very decisive proof of the difference between the female character here and in England.[6]

But then, Mrs Eaton disapproved of almost everything about Romans.

Italian women, and Roman women in particular, were generally conceded to be attractive, their hair glossy and dark, their complexions clear and generally unimproved by artificial means. In Florence, Montesquieu noted that:

The majority of them look as fresh and as youthful at 40 as at 20. You see women who have had 10 or 12 children and are as pretty, fresh, and attractive as ever. I think that their regular life, simple diet, and something special in the air keeps them like this.[7]

In noble families, the age difference between husband and wife was often (though not always) wide, and generally speaking there was little or no idea of the companionate marriage. Reformers, taking their cue from Rousseau, made the call for family sentiment one of their major themes. On the other hand the Roman lower classes had a habit of marrying as they liked. The reason for both of these situations was the same: dowries. In aristocratic and propertied families, the marriage was a merger of property, and a major instrument of distribution was the girl's dowry. It ensured that

---

6   Eaton, *Rome in the Nineteenth Century,* II, p. 307.
7   Quoted in Vaussard, *Daily Life in Eighteenth-Century Italy,* p. 95.

Courtship among the popular classes included the ever-popular serenade.

daughters brought a share of the family property to their new households, even if the father or brother had to go into debt for it. But it also was a settlement that precluded any later claim on inheritance. For daughters of artisans, labourers and peasants the dowry allowed the new family to set up a home – bed, pots and pans, clothing. These small dowries were freely available in Italy. The lottery in Rome and in Tuscany, for instance, provided five dowries a week. Other charitable institutions distributed dowries to orphans of impoverished aristocratic families, to the daughters of poor state employees (like the military), to orphans and foundlings, or to the daughters of poor families. In the opinion of foreign observers (who disapproved), this free availability of dowries undermined the work ethic of the poor.

Gender roles in Rome were strictly defined. Young women guarded their virtue before marriage, married young, bore many children, and nursed them to the age of three or four. But at the same time, travellers observed (and usually disapproved of) what they regarded as the unseemly freedom of Roman women of every class. Women of the popular classes were famous drinkers, and tavern scenes show them seated with the men on what appear to be shockingly equal terms. Women of the upper classes conversed, flirted and fended off or accepted men with an easy good humour that the French in particular found disconcerting (Dupaty reported that 'you cannot make them drop their eyes before yours, they have the boldest way of looking at men.'). Roman women, like women throughout the early modern west, worked outside the home, and not just as domestic servants. For example, the painters and decorators of Rome included a large number of women, from the famous foreigners (like Angelica Kauffmann and Elizabeth Vigée-Lebrun) to hardworking local miniaturists, and down to and including the anonymous tapestry makers of San Michele.

While liberty was the rallying cry of the revolution, in fact women lost many rights in the revolutionary period, especially when the Napoleonic Code was promulgated in the Kingdom of Italy and later extended to all Italy including Rome. Propertied women in Lombardy and Tuscany lost the right to vote in local elections and to control their property; in Lombardy as in Rome they lost the right to free, compulsory primary schooling, the right to be trained as teachers in the same secondary schools with the same curricula as male teachers; married women were placed under their husband's authority, a law that would not be changed until 1919.[8]

Italian women were certainly not independent before the revolutionary period. The ancient tradition of *pater potestas* put women (no matter what their age) and younger sons under the authority of the male head of the family. This was ended with the Napoleonic Code. But the new law gave every father the absolute power that had once been vested in the *pater familius*. The result was that there was little or no control over the father of each nuclear family, not even that exercised by his own father or older brother.

Infant Mortality

When the French occupied Rome for the second time in 1809 they began to keep precise records, so we have good statistics for births and deaths in 1810 and succeeding years.[9] In 1810 there were 5,110 births registered, including 141 children born dead. Of those born alive, 762 babies were abandoned, mostly at the Santo Spirito hospital. These children were placed in the wheel, or *ruota*, in the hospital wall. A bell rang automatically when someone turned the crank to move the opening from the street side to the hospital side, and the baby was immediately taken to one of the wet-nurses who lived at the hospital.

Within a few days of arriving at the hospital, abandoned babies were handed over to families who lived in the countryside within the walls or near the city. These families, who were paid a small amount for each child, cared for them to the age of 10, when they went back to institutions where they received some training for work, and (in the case of girls) dowries to allow them to marry.

About half of the babies were abandoned within 24 hours of birth, and these had a good chance of surviving their first two years (about 17% died). The other half, those who didn't reach the hospital until they were one day to two weeks old, almost all died before reaching their second birthdays. Babies born into intact families, then as now, were much more likely to thrive. They had a mortality rate of about 212 deaths per 1,000, a number that compared well with statistics for London and Brussels at the time, and was considerably better than most places in Italy (where 250 or more deaths per 1,000 was about as good as it got).

The average age of mothers at birth was 29.5 years, the average age of fathers was 35.9. The younger the mother, the higher the danger to the child; first-born children of younger mothers were especially at risk. The other overwhelming risk factor was, of

---

8   Saraceno 'Women, Family, and the Law, 1750–1942', pp. 427-442.
9   Sonnino and Brasiello have produced a study of infant mortality in Rome, 'La mortalita infantile a Roma', pp. 326-337.

Country women in traditional dress pause for a chat.

course, poverty. The highest survival rate was among the children of landowners, followed by merchants and the upper bourgeoisie. Children born to families where the father worked for wages had the next lowest mortality rates, and the sons and daughters of butchers, bakers and innkeepers – people involved in the food business – did especially well, probably because the mothers had a better diet. The picture was darker for the children of artisans, vendors, artists, soldiers and servants, and darkest of all for agricultural workers, who not only had very little money and poor diets, they also tended to live in the periphery of the city where malaria was endemic.

The Ghetto
The Jewish population of Rome was small – the first official census was taken in 1809, when it came to 3,076 or 2.5% of the Christian population – but this was a very ancient community, which pre-dated Christianity. Indeed, Rome was home to one of the oldest Jewish communities in Europe. In the time of the ancient republic and empire they lived on the far side of the Tiber from the city in Trastevere, but during the Renaissance they were forced to move across the river to the ghetto, a small, damp section of the city next to the Tiber and near the theatre of Marcellus and the Portico d'Ottavia. Their economic situation as a corporate body was not enviable, and in 1755 the community as a whole declared bankruptcy when its debt reached a total of 279,425.20 *scudi*.

Individual Jews could, of course, be prosperous, and some were. There is a law of history that says that whenever you find laws being passed against something, this suggests that people are doing a great deal of whatever it is. So in 1661 we find a law being passed against feasts and celebrations in the ghetto that featured music, singing, and dancing, and to which all comers were invited. Such events were only to be legal for betrothals, weddings and circumcisions. Considering the size of ghetto families, such events would happen frequently enough, but it seems that there were enough other big feasts and celebrations being thrown to catch the eye of some lawyer in the curia. The law also stated that musicians at parties and balls all had to be Jewish and could only be paid three *paoli* each for the evening.

The ghetto was walled, and there were five gates that were normally closed at night and during carnival time (when the purpose was as much to keep Christians out as to keep the Jews in). Conditions for Roman Jews varied depending on the policy of the popes and the mood of the populace. But, despite the unquestionably wretched living conditions in the ghetto and the usual hostility of the lower classes, the popes by and large ruled their Jewish population with a degree of benevolence that was uncommon in early modern Europe and extended a correspondingly broad freedom of conscience. Every effort was made to convert them to Christianity, but forced baptisms were not a policy, and no one was burned at the stake. Five or six times a year there would be a convert, and it was always considered an occasion for public celebration. Great nobles, and even the pope himself, vied to stand as godparents.

Even though Rome offered Jews the most favourable living conditions in Europe (outside of Florence), they were hardly ideal, and Jewish numbers were depleted by disease and by emigration, although the popes, who liked to keep a close eye on their Jewish subjects, imposed heavy fines on any who wished to leave. The population losses were offset somewhat by immigration, but mostly by a high fertility rate. Jewish girls married before they reached the age of 20, younger than their Christian counterparts. Their youth, and the poverty and unhealthy conditions of the ghetto, probably help explain why only one in four Jewish babies reached the age of six.

Estates and Classes
About 6–7% of the general population, and about 2% of the Jewish community, could be considered wealthy. These included much (but by no means all) of the nobility, along with the upper clergy and holders of major benefices. The rich owned most of the property in the city, and virtually all of the farmland around Rome (the *agro romano*) belonged to 64 religious houses and 113 rich laymen. The remaining 90% or so of the population were in the popular or plebian classes. There were great variations within the *popolo*, from absolute misery to the relative wealth of the big merchants, but even these came nowhere near the wealth of the great families, and in reality, there was not much middle ground in wealth and power between the lower class and the upper class. The few exceptions – superstar artists like Canova, and bankers like Torlonia – eventually gained titles and merged with the aristocracy (as did both Canova and Torlonia).

Madelin describes the Roman population as divided into six categories: clergy (very diverse, ranging from begging brothers to the pope and his cardinals); patricians (the great Roman families, divisible into ancient, papal, and the recently ennobled); 'innumerable' lower nobility (most in the provinces, not in the city, where the great nobles congregated); a very low bourgeoisie (merchants, and men and women in the service industries); artisans; and the populace.[10] Charles de Brosses was more blunt,

10 Madelin, *La Rome de Napoléon*, chapter 3 of Book I.

if less accurate: he asked his readers to '[i]magine a populace one third of whom are priests, one third doing very little, and the other third nothing at all.'

Clergy
In 1808 there were 85 parishes and 250 churches in Rome, serving a population of 136,268. The parishes were served by the secular clergy. In addition, there was a large group of regular clerics.[11] In the city of Rome, there were 1,463 monks and 1,121 nuns in 43 religious houses (confusingly for the non-Italian speaker, houses of both monks and nuns were called *conventi* or convents). Despite the myth of enormous wealth, in fact neither the monks nor the nuns were particularly rich, although they certainly owned a lot of land. They were the largest employers of craftsmen, artisans and artists, even greater than the patriciate. Their property enabled them to provide food for all comers, and when they were removed from the equation (as they would be in the imperial city) the result was havoc – hungry, angry Romans, and thousands of dispossessed religious thrown out on the streets to join them. Dispossessing the regular clergy in Rome was arguably one of Napoleon's worst ideas, and de Tournon did his best to mitigate the effects. As Fouché's agents reported in 1808, the clergy was represented in virtually the whole of Roman society, from the begging brothers to the canons of San Giovanni in Laterno and St Peter's, and there was as much a difference among them as one would expect to find between a beggar and a duchess. There were 30 different regular orders, as different as the jovial Capuchin who won over the lower classes with their jokes, to the austere Dominican confessors to the aristocracy, to the scholarly Benedictines.[12] Everyone, at every level of society, had some family member in some order or other. It was an authoritative, disciplined network embedded in every level of Roman society, so powerful that not even the most energetic pope could begin to compete with its influence. The new regime attempted to oppose that influence by imposing loyalty oaths, and arresting, imprisoning or deporting any they suspected of not fully supporting the new order. The attempt was not notably successful, and created bitter resentment among the people.

The Church had a monopoly on education, which was like most education under the Old Regime – there were a lot of schools, but not much learning below the university level. The Sapienza, the Roman university, was about as old as the Sorbonne in Paris. It had five faculties, with six masters in theology, six in law, nine in the sciences, 11 in letters; they also maintained collections in physics and natural history, and had excellent libraries [see chapter 7].

Clerical nobility
Cardinals lived as great lords and kept households and courts appropriate to that rank. All government was in the hands of the Church hierarchy, and Rome was ruled by the

---

11 The term regular cleric refers to members of religious orders, who tended to live in community and had their own command structure; secular clerics, so called because they worked in the world, were under the direction of the bishops and made up the staffs of parishes. The Enlightenment in general disapproved of regular clergy, considering them old-fashioned and of little practical use.

12 Madelin, *op. cit.*.

cardinals, as appointed by the pope. This meant that the great families could play no real role except through an ordained member of the family. It was therefore vital for the great families to have at least one member in orders in each generation, an exigency that led to any number of dubious vocations. By no means all cardinals were from the great Roman families, and not all were from the nobility (though it certainly didn't hurt). Their number included the Cardinal Duke of York, last of the Stuarts.

When a man was elevated to the scarlet, he was expected to entertain royally – that is, he was expected to entertain the entire city of Rome. This meant, at the very least, free food and free wine for all comers. When the French removed the pope, the only man who could create cardinals, they also removed a major source of public joy. Cardinals, like most clerics, were also expected to dispense charity on demand. Along with the ambassadors of major states (Spain, France, Venice, the Empire and such), cardinals had the power of pardon, which they could exercise at any point during a criminal trial or punishment up to the point when the lash or the trap door actually fell. This was the sort of thing that drove reformers like the Lombard Cesare Beccaria wild with frustration. It could be a particular problem with public punishments – and virtually all punishments in Rome were public until after the second restoration. It was said that processions leading to execution of sentences (whether it be whipping, the *tratti di corda*, the pillory, or a formal capital execution) had to be very careful not to cross the path of a cardinal or an ambassador out for a drive. If the criminal caught sight of one of these, he would set up a cry for *gratia* (mercy), and the crowd that had gathered for the fun of watching his punishment might very well take it into its collective head that it would be even more entertaining to see the story of the Prodigal Son re-enacted. In any case, the eminent personage could and often did bring the whole thing to a screeching halt by forgiving the star of the proceedings, who would then be escorted on his way to liberty by a cheering mob (except, perhaps, for the victims of the crime, who probably felt rather differently about the event, and by the jurists, foiled again). But it was all part of the great Roman love for games of chance – even to the foot of the scaffold, even to the point of death, there was always the chance that fate would intervene and raise one from despair to triumph.

Secular Nobility
The Second Estate in the city of Rome meant the great nobles. There were few minor nobles in Rome, though the countryside was full of them, where some lived in great rambling villas, others in crumbling or well-repaired medieval piles in the towns, according to their income. Most had considerable landed property, but few had much ready cash.

There were fewer than a hundred of the great families. Some were of the feudal nobility; some claimed descent from the ancient patriciate (though few of these genealogies held up to close examination). Most of them were descendants of papal nephews. These families could be very old, but most dated from the late Middle Ages or the Renaissance. The French carefully divided them up into three categories: the first, the patrician families; the second, papal families; and the third, recently ennobled families.

Many of the great Roman nobles were virtual sovereigns, holding large estates throughout the peninsula. The Gaëtani were counts of Caserta and princes of Teano;

the Boncompagni were dukes of Sora and princes of Venosa; the Doria were dukes of Melfi; the Orsini were dukes of Gravina; the Borghese, who held vast estates in Tuscany, Rome (including their famous villa, gallery and gardens) and Naples, were princes of Sulmona.[13]

Great papal families included the Farnese, the Boncompagni, the Ludovisi, the Borghese, the Barberini, the Pamphilj; also the Chigi, Rospigliosi, the Altieri, the Ottoboni. Among the greatest were the Colonna, who included among their titles the Duke of Paliano, Grand Constable of the Kingdom of Naples, and grandee of Spain.

Last of the great papal families before the revolution were the Albani (the family of Clement XI) and the Braschi. The Albani claimed descent from the famous fifteenth-century Albanian warrior, Skanderbeg. The Braschi, or Onesti-Braschi, were nephews of Pius VI, who gave them the title of duke and built the last great palace of Rome, the Palazzo Braschi, for one of them. After the French arrived, Duke Braschi accepted the post of Governor of Rome and was one of the leading noble collaborators.

The usual form of entertaining in the great houses was the *conversazione*, which almost always included cards. Like the *popolo*, the Roman nobility were wild about gambling, and indulged in games with names like *basetta, faraone, zecchinetta*, 'thirty-forty', 'break the bank' and 'twenty-one', on which it was said that they bet fortunes so large that only primogeniture and entails prevented them from losing their entire estates. While that may have been true at one time, by the late eighteenth century most of the noble houses were on short rations, and by the turn of the nineteenth century wars, revolutions, confiscations, forced contributions and economic disruption in general had reduced most of them to relative, or even absolute, poverty. The Borghese, with their Napoleonic marriage, were of course an exception to this general rule, but even the Borghese had their lean times: these were not helped when Prince Camillo was all but forced to sell his fabled art collection to his imperial brother-in-law at a fraction of its value.

Roman noble families, whose first duty was survival, had over the centuries perfected techniques for weathering the not infrequent storms to which Rome was subject. Like biological specimens, they specialised in protective colouring. The Borghese family was particularly adept, though by no means singular. When revolution came, Prince Marcantonio Borghese was a Patriot. He took to the 1798–99 republic with such enthusiasm that he became a senator in July of 1798, and put on a red liberty cap and starred in one of the republican spectacles, tossing his titles of nobility (but not, Madelin notes, the titles to his property) into a fire provided for the occasion. His brother was a royalist and devoted to the cause of the pope. Prince Borghese's elder son Camillo was a royalist (though, as he married Napoleon's sister Pauline, he doesn't seem to have much minded which monarch he supported), while Checco, the younger son, was a Patriot, and took an enthusiastic part in the newly formed National Guard.

In 1798 Duke Altemps held a constitutional circle of Jacobin admirers in his palace; Prince Sforza-Cesarini, who owned the Argentina theatre, accepted an appointment as senator of the republic; Duke Pio-Bonelli was so enthusiastic a

13 Silvagni, *op. cit.*, I, p. 46.

participant in the new regime that he earned a death sentence from the returned Allies (it was suspended and later reversed by the pope, who understood the danger of making martyrs of his enemies). In all, the *abbate* Benedetti – whose supposed diary formed the basis of one of the major books on the period – says that 10 of the great nobility participated in the republic, and another 20 went along for the ride.[14] Prince Agostino Chigi, he commented on 16 March 1798, 'seems as if he were mad. He is acting the Jacobin at the Farnese. Does he also wish to be a consul?' On 30 September, reporting on the guests at a republican-sponsored ball, Benedetti notes sarcastically that 'Signor Torlonia, Marchese of Old Rome, was there of course. He used to make his money out of the pope, and now he makes it out of the French.' Also present were 'princes Altinori, Altemps, Cesarini, Borghese, and some other nobles.' There was a shortage of ladies, which deficiency was overcome with 'women of bad character'.

When one group fell from power, family members on the winning side protected the relatives who supported the losing party. So when the Ridiculous Republic fell in Rome in 1799, the plan swung into effect. Patriots in Naples in 1799 were butchered, either formally by the Nelson-backed monarchy or informally by the more enthusiastic *lazzaroni*, the Neapolitan lower classes; in Rome, there was little or none of this. Checco, the Patriot Borghese, was required to go to Vienna to apologise personally to the Holy Roman Emperor, and then retired for a while to the Borghese country estates before returning to Rome.

No Roman group came unscathed out of the French experience – the clergy were persecuted and dispersed, the poor cut off from their accustomed means of support, and even the middle classes generally found that the opportunities that opened up to them did not match their hopes or make up for the dislocations. The nobility also suffered, losing much of their property and influence, and not (for the most part) gaining what they might have hoped for in compensation as being part of the new order. Mrs Eaton when she visited in 1817 found them in pitiful straits. She reported that they had no social life, didn't ride to hounds, didn't entertain, and on the rare occasions when they had people in for a *conversazione* served nothing in the way of refreshments, not even *eux sucré*. They rented out their palaces to strangers, or opened them as shops or cafes, and lived wretchedly in the attics, 'among obscurity, dirt, pride, penury and wretchedness'.[15] The occupation had reduced some of the greatest families to 'complete beggary' (she was horrified to be approached by counts and marquises and asked for charity), 'and almost all to comparative indigence'[16].

The ladies 'never walk, never ride, never move but in a carriage'; and the men rarely walk or ride, either: 'the only time I ever remember seeing a Roman nobleman on horseback, he tumbled off'. All they seemed to her to do was to 'meander up and down the Corso', an activity that may have been pleasant enough

---

14 David Silvagni based *La corte pontificia e la societa Romana*, his anti-clerical look at late eighteenth-century Rome, on what he claimed to be the diaries of Benedetti (which are no longer available). Scholars have cast some doubt on the authenticity of the diaries.

15 Eaton, *op. cit.*, II, p. 302.

16 Eaton, *op. cit.*, II, p. 313: 'Counts, in full dress, often come to you a-begging; and Marquises, with lace veils and splendid necklaces, will thankfully accept half-a-crowns. A woman dressed very expensively, begged of us the other day in the streets …'

in the summer, but they seemed obliged to do it whatever the weather. In fact, she notes, 'nothing can be conceived more unsocial or more gloomily domestic than the habits of the nobility of Rome'.

The Clerical Middle Orders

Secular clerics were usually assigned to one of the numerous parishes or non-parish churches in the city. There they might be the chief administrator (the parish priest) or one of his assistants (in a large parish there would be several), or they might work at specialised jobs such as confessor or preacher. Rooms or (in the case of senior priests) a house often came with the job. Father Canali, for instance, worked as a confessor [see chapter 9]. He lived with his aunts and his sister who acted as his housekeepers and were supported by him. When he was taken off to prison, one of his major worries was what would become of his female relatives who were left without support.

Regular clerics, that is, members of orders (Dominicans, Franciscans, Trinitarians, or such) lived in community. Rome was often the site of the mother house of the order, that is, the central administration of a world-wide organisation. Most orders had representatives in towns and cities throughout the Catholic world, while many also maintained missionary representatives elsewhere. In addition to the mother house, there would be a number of separate institutions where the monks or nuns lived, scattered around the city and especially in the 'green belt' where the gardens and vineyards were located. Life in these convents could vary widely, but it was by and large at least comfortable, and in some cases, luxurious. Nuns in particular were known for their pleasant life-styles, ample meals, and for their fondness for pet cats. The houses of the regular clergy were the central dispensers of charity, and especially of food, for the indigent.

Women convicted of crimes, especially women of the respectable classes, could be sentenced to serve their time in one of the convents. The artist Giuseppe Barberi, whose home life was volcanic, on at least one occasion had his wife confined to a convent (during one of his absences she had brought a lover and some of his friends to live in their home, along with the numerous Barberi progeny). Barberi called her place of confinement 'the convent of vipers', but he could not afford to keep her there indefinitely so she came back home.[17]

Abbati

Eighteenth-century Rome was home to a large group of men who were neither clearly clerical nor obviously lay. These were the *abbati*, or in French, *abbés*. Among these was one gentleman about whom we know a good deal, since his diaries reportedly formed the basis for a famous book by David Silvagni, translated into English as *The Papal Court and Roman Society in the Eighteenth and Nineteenth Centuries*. Luca Antonio Benedetti was the son of a land-owner in Gennazzano, a small town in the Alban hills. At the age of 12, his father secured a post for him as a page in the noble Colonna household (the Colonna were the feudal lords of Gennazzano). His education was first in the seminary at Palestrina near his home and then, as a dependant of the Colonna,

---

17 See Nicassio, 'The Unfortunate Giuseppe Barberi'.

he was sent to the College of the Propaganda Fide in Rome, where he studied law. As a lawyer, he adopted the simple, severe clerical clothing of the *abbati*, though he was never in clerical orders. There were many different kinds of *abbati*. Some were in clerical orders, either secular (that is, working in the saecula, or world, under the direction of a bishop, or actually holding the rank of bishop themselves, with or without any episcopal jurisdiction); other clerical *abbati* were regular and were attached to convents or monasteries. Many *abbati* were laymen, but dressed as clerics as part of their work. Benedetti was one of these lay *abbati* , so he was free to marry. He did so at the age of about 30, and became the father of three daughters.

This practice of wearing clerical clothing was so common at the end of the eighteenth century that many tourists assumed that most men in Rome were priests, when in fact fewer than 5% were clerics at any time during the century. The rest, as the visiting Casanova quickly discovered, dressed like clerics in order to fit in – on his first formal evening out, Casanova found that he was the only man at the dinner table who wasn't dressed like a cleric. He soon took a friend's advice, and put on simple black clothing himself. Benedetti was a lawyer for the curia, and so had a right to present himself as an *abbate*, unlike hundreds of other men who simply adopted the title and the dress with no right to it whatsoever.

Benedetti was, it was said, one of the last men who wore the old-fashioned formal dress of the papal court – knee breeches, shoes with large silver buckles, two watches (presumably one with Roman time, one with French time, like the city's twin clocks), and a long pigtail. This last is doubtful. When Benedetti mentions in his diary that men have stopped wearing pigtails with the arrival of the French, he comments that a number of amputated pigtails have been stuck up on the city walls, and notes that he is lucky because he never wore one. Maybe he took up wearing one later, as a conservative political statement. On official business he wore his full lawyer's costume – a long cassock, a four-cornered hat, and a silk cloak, attended by a servant carrying his documents in a bag made of violet-coloured silk.

Benedetti loathed the French, but tolerated their presence during the Ridiculous Republic. In fact, when they were driven out by the Neapolitans, he got in trouble with the Neapolitans and was thrown into prison until the French returned. He was delighted when the new pope, Pius VII, arrived in the city in 1800, but when the French began to occupy the city again in 1808, the *abbate* was said to have been part of a conspiracy against them. He refused to take the loyalty oath in 1810, was arrested, sent to the Castel Sant'Angelo, and then deported to Corsica along with the most determined and dangerous enemies of the regime.

According to Silvagni, the *abbate* was a witty and sociable man, and had a keen eye for the ladies. He regarded Marianna d'Este Colonna, the wife of his patron, with the sort of platonic passion that was said to characterise the medieval troubadours, and arranged the other famous charmers of the day in a sort of hierarchy: the Most Beautiful (Pauline Bonaparte Borghese); the Most Cultivated (the Duchess of Albany), the Cleverest (the Princess Altieri), the Most Witty (the Princess Santacroce), the Most Fascinating (the Princess Rezzonico).

The Benedetti family (like many if not most in Rome) lived in an apartment in a palazzo that had been converted into flats. Silvagni later described the home as 'serious, dark, cold, and restrained'. The floors were bare and even in this prosperous household, the furniture was scant, old, and very heavy – only a few chairs set against the walls, and the occasional table, and enormous beds with curtains.[18] There was an entry hall with tables and an alcove where a servant slept; a room with a few chairs and a little table. Off of this entry way there were three doors, one leading to a studio, a second led to the salon, and a third to a dining room.

It may be of interest to look in some detail at Silvagni's description of the home of the Abbate Benedetti, as he recalled it many years later.

The study was lined with bookcases where heavy, dark books stood in cabinets with grillwork rather than glass doors. There were leather-covered chairs and a huge oak table on which stood three inkwells, with a portrait of the Madonna and a bust of the pope. There was no fireplace, a portable charcoal heater was used in the winter (but never before St Catherine's Day, 25 November).

The salon furniture was covered in yellow silk and the wooden chairs were white with gilded backs. There were two large mirrors and two large tables, and gaming tables set against the wall. Light was provided by candles in lamps and candelabras. The clock was an old one, enclosed in a wooden case. There was a little equestrian statue of Prince Eugene of Savoy, and a small spinet, some landscape paintings, and a little Venetian crystal lamp embellished with coloured glass flowers.

The bedroom was large, with two large windows covered in white cotton curtains, pulled back and tied with a fabric like silk, that also covered the furniture in the room, including the canopy over the bed, supported by four twisted wooden columns. On the sides of the bed were two *prie-dieus*, with small drawers, and over one of them there was a little reliquary enclosing the bones of various saints and martyrs, authenticated by the pope. There were two commodes each about four feet high, made of some kind of dark wood inlaid with red and green stone enclosed in bronze, that ran down the legs of the commode and became lion's feet. There was also a cabinet with a mirror in the same style. On one of the commodes there was a sort of altar with an image of the Madonna where a little lamp was always lit, and on the other, a dark wooden cross with an ivory figure of Christ. Beside the bed was a painting of the Madonna nursing the Christ-child, a silver crucifix, two holy water fonts, a blessed candle with ribbons, and a woven blessed palm.

The fireplace in the dining room was large enough for a child to stand upright, with brass-trimmed andirons. The fire was rarely lit, and when it was, it tended to make more smoke than heat. A black cabinet stood against the wall, and the tableware were kept there behind glass doors. There were black and white majolica-ware cruets for vinegar and oil, and containers for seasonings, made in shapes like angels or animals. On the wall there was a bronze basin and a bronze shell, operated with a key. Turning the key released water for washing one's hands before and after a meal. A tall, convent-style clock stood in another corner, with a barometer shaped like a little monk, his head covered with a hood when it was humid or rainy.

The kitchen had another huge fireplace, and two animals. There was a talking blackbird that recited the Our Father (Silvagni reports that this terrified him, as the

---

18 Silvagni, *op. cit.*, I, pp. 81-88

servant girl told him this was a witch who had been punished by being turned into a blackbird and forced to say the Our Father constantly). In another corner was a fat, sleek and hostile black cat.

From the kitchen, a little stairway led to a courtyard where there was running water and a washroom with large tubs for laundry.

Family relationships were as formal as their living accommodations. A wife called her husband 'Signor Pietro' or 'Signor Paolo', the children referred to their parents as 'Signor Padre' and 'Signora Madre', and a husband used the formal *voi* in speaking with his wife or children. Children kissed their parents' hands as a gesture of respect, spoke when spoken to, and spent most of their time at school or outdoors. Small children were bound tightly in swaddling clothes or kept in a sort of basket, like a basket for fruit.

Another example of the genus *abbate* was the Cavaliere Levizzari, who for a brief time was the patron of the unruly young Trastevere artist, Bartolomeo Pinelli. Levizzari was, like many of his kind, a well-born gentleman from outside the city, in his case, from the Duchy of Modena in the north. An *abbate*, he thrived in the hothouse society of the Roman upper classes. He was a gallant cavalier of the ladies – he was the gentleman companion or *cigisbeo* of Princess Marianna d'Este Colonna (the wife of Benedetti's employer). A man of the world, he was a charming guest at the *conversazioni*, a *raconteur* and *viveur* in the French manner, and an eater of ices. He was courteous, generous and kind, and Pinelli treated him with utter contempt, abused his hospitality and cheated him by palming off a cheap print as a piece of original art. Their relationship gives us an intriguing insight into the relationships among the social orders in the Rome of their day.

The Third Estate, or Everyone Else

At the top of the everyone else estate some people could be very rich indeed. These people, the bankers and the most successful artists, generally made their way into the second estate, or nobility. Even in Rome, some members of the third estate could be very wealthy. Men who made it up from the bottom were rare, but not completely unknown. The most famous of these in the Napoleonic period was Giovanni Torlonia, a mercer and linen draper who got into the banking business and managed to prosper even when winds of war and of revolution were chilling the prospects of most.[19] When the popes ruled Rome, he served them well (both Pius VI and Pius VII trusted him); when the French ruled Rome, he went to their parties and processed their loans. With consummate skill which made him rich if not beloved, he even survived not one but two papal restorations. He married his eldest son, Marino, to Anna Sforza Cesarini; his two daughters married well: one to Prince Orsini, the other to Count Marescotti. His second-born son, Alessandro, inherited the fortune and married the sister of a Colonna duke, while another son became a Knight of Malta. Alessandro Torlonia built a family mortuary chapel in the pope's own basilica of San Giovanni in Laterno; perhaps even more impressive, he bought and continued to improve the fabulous Villa Albani, one of the greatest private store houses of artistic

19 Silvagni, *op. cit.*, I, pp. 56-7.

and archaeological masterpieces in the world. Torlonia, as one would expect of a man who did well in Rome, was ennobled and became Duke of Bracciano in 1809. He went, with a delegation of important men, to Paris to offer the 'homage, fidelity and submission' of the Roman people at the foot of the throne; before he was ennobled, Torlonia was one of the few non-noble members of the imperial Roman senate, along with Canova, a few businessmen and scholars, and 30 nobles. Mrs Eaton mentions Torlonia as an example of the unfortunate continental custom of allowing anyone into the nobility who could pay for it. She also mentions his parties, which were among the few good parties in Rome in 1817-18 when she was there.

Torlonia, a tireless speculator, was involved in the unsuccessful cotton project at the baths of Diocletian [see chapter 7] and, although he (like everyone else) only reluctantly sent his son to the military academy at La Flèche during the Golden Levy [see chapter 9], he joined General Miollis in holding splendid receptions. His wife, dripping with enough diamonds to rival her husband's famous diamond shirt studs, shone at French parties in 1809 and 1810. On the other hand, when Napoleon fell and Murat claimed Rome, Torlonia was there to cut a deal for the Prefect de Tournon's furniture as he left town.[20]

Torlonia was not the only banker to prosper in this period. In November 1809, Benedetti reported that the banker Lavaggi had bought the Salviati palace for a ridiculously low price (he later sold it at a profit and bought another). Another at least potentially rich group of non-nobles included successful artists like Antonio Canova (a Venetian) and Elizabeth Vigée-Lebrun (a French refugee), as well as musicians like the popular composer Zingarelli and some of the singers in the opera. The most successful of these singers could be quite wealthy. Few of these were Roman; most came for the short season and went on to other cities or courts. Except for a handful of great stars, few singers were independent contractors; most were court employees, working for cardinals, dukes, princes and nobles in the other cities and states of Italy.

The middle class included lawyers, scholars, librarians and secretaries – most of them attached to the great families as hangers-on – along with employees of the various public institutions. Except for a few famous physicians, most doctors were considered to be 'purgers and blood-letters' and were little more than the upper rank of the servant class. The pharmacists and herbalists were more successful and more respected.

There was a large foreign population, some of them refugees and others long-term residents: artists, sculptors, writers, important exiles like the Stuarts and humble people like the Giannetti family, who went broke in Siena and came to Rome for anonymity and a fresh start. And, of course there were the pilgrims, rich and poor, driven by love or by private demons, pious or merely curious. In normal times people paused on the Grand Tour to soak up the atmosphere and take advantage of the low cost of living. Most of these foreigners lived in self-contained communities – German, French, Danish, Spanish or what have you.

Everyone dabbled in literature and poetry. Lawyers, priests, and nobles wrote bad poetry and tomes on archaeological topics (the craze for archaeology had spread

20 Madelin, *op. cit.*, pp. 484, 563, 573 and 647.

from Naples); illiterate men and women of the popular class improvised poetry and ballads. There were several societies and academies dedicated to poetry, the most famous of these being the Arcadians.

Far below the artists and bankers, and below the lawyers and herbalists in status if not in income, were the successful artisans, shopkeepers, innkeepers, bakers and craftsmen, a group known as the *minenti*.[21] These were people who not only made a little money, but were able to hold on to it. They lived in the same areas as the popular classes, but their homes were better furnished and a bit larger. Their wives and daughters wore fashionable dresses 'of one colour' – that is, made of matched fabric in a current style, not the traditional clothing of the women of the city, with different fabrics and mixed colours. Mrs Eaton, an incurable snob, opined that 'the women of this shopkeeper class are sometimes dressed most ludicrously fine; satin gowns of all colours, and often white, trailing about in the dirty streets, and thin pink, or yellow slippers, sticking fast in the mud …'[22]

Businesses were generally carried out by people who were not Roman. According to Silvagni, 'innkeepers are often from Genoa or from Abruzzi; pork butchers, cheese mongers and delicatessens are from Norcia and Cascia; bakers are from Friuli; the pharmacists and pastry makers are Swiss (usually from the province of Grisons and so called *Grici*); *patturini* from Abruzzi; charcoal sellers from Genoa; masons, sailors, and hat-makers from the Marches.'[23] Romans could be found as ironworkers, carpenters, wood turners and cabinet makers, and as carters and carriage drivers. They were also servants, which was a major occupation, although statistics show that it was not as common as anecdotal evidence suggests. However, even a family as humble as the Taigi had one (a girl for general work) and, when Anna Maria fell ill, two [see chapter 4]. Anna Maria, as one might expect from a saint, treated her servant girl like one of the family. But servants in general seem to have expected to be treated that way. Like the poor (and financially at least, servants were close to absolute poverty) they felt that they were particular favourites of Jesus, with something of an edge over their employers.

The Third Estate, even in Rome, included a lot of very different people, though not so many as one might have found elsewhere. By and large, members of the small middle class, like most Romans, had little in the way of cash income. Money salaries tended to be quite small and most were less than a family could live on. However, there was another element to income in Rome, as elsewhere at this time. These were perquisites and tips, some of which were formally listed but many of which were not.

That incurable gossip and cynic, the president de Brosses, recounts an episode when he saw the perquisite system in full swing. Roman nobles rarely gave dinner parties. They seemed to regard it as a French or English eccentricity, and an odd and somewhat demeaning thing to do (as in many Mediterranean cultures, the Roman tradition was to entertain outside of the home).[24] The French ambassador, on the

---

21 The word may have come from *eminente*, but its derivation is unclear.

22 Eaton, *op. cit.*, II, p. 301.

23 Friz, *op. cit.*, p. 22, fn 3, citing Silvagni, *op. cit.*, I, p. 60.

24 Eaton, *op. cit.*, II, p. 305: 'However intimate you may be with an Italian, however warm the regard he professes for you, however often, if he has been a traveller, he may have been entertained at your table in England, he never dreams of asking you to his.'

other hand, in the golden days before the revolution, entertained regularly, most notably on each 13 December, when he gave a dinner for 150 to celebrate Henry IV's conversion to Catholicism.

De Brosses left an extensive description of this occasion. He describes crowds of footmen and servants who had no connection to the ambassador, who flocked in and appropriated turkeys, chickens, slabs of sturgeon, venison, tongue, ham, partridges, fruit, sweetmeats and anything else that was not nailed down, including the plates and cutlery (the ambassador reported losing 25 to 30 pieces of his dinner service every year):

The more restrained lackeys were vying with each other in the amount they could cram into their pockets, even wrapping the truffled poultry in napkins to keep their fingers clean, for the linen was worth taking too. The cleverest ones were whisking the dishes away, you could see them filing out of the room and taking them home under their ferraiuoli, *the big cloaks they wear. The better-organised, to avoid having to go to their own houses … had wives and children posted on the staircases as intermediaries …*[25]

Tips were an unavoidable institution. Foreign visitors who attended *conversazioni* reported that all the lackeys lined up and gave the newcomer very polite bows, then called by the next day for a tip. Once a tip was given, Romans assumed that a patron-client relationship had been established, and they would then return on feast days and special occasions of all sorts. De Brosses (as usual) has a description, which is as usual amusing, and as usual may or may not be dependable:

If their employer has a cold, and even if you know nothing about it and care less, round they come when she is better, so you may rejoice together. They rejoice continually, in fact – the happiest band you could meet, and all at your expense.

Homes of the Popolo
In 1817–18, the French artist Antoine Jean-Baptiste Thomas spent a year in the city and returned home to Paris to tell his fellow countrymen all about it in a number of charming watercolours, with descriptive text.[26] Thomas' picture of a typical home of the common people shows a single room with large window or dutch door, out of which a woman looks, holding a pot. To her right, a tambourine decorated with a heart and arrow hangs on the wall; a *calascione* (a gourd-shaped mandolin-type stringed instrument) rests against a chair. To her left, a broom, a stand with ewer and bowl, a cabinet with a large flask wrapped in straw cord, above that a shelf with a brass water jar. At the angle is an alcove for the bed, curtained and trimmed with matching cloth, with an image of the Madonna lit by a candle in the alcove. Before that, a table with a large and elaborate lamp and plate; there are drawers in the table; on the floor, which is of patterned bricks, a cat sits beside a *focone*. In the homes of the common people, he writes:

---

25 Cited in Andrieux, *op. cit.*, pp. 150-1.
26 Thomas, *Un an à Rome.*

... one does not usually warm oneself with fires in chimneys, and one almost never uses poeles. In general, in Italy, one usually uses only a focone *against the cold. This* focone *is a container of terracotta or leather filled with ashes and hot coals; the shape and the material vary with the wealth of the people using them; the origins of the* focone *go back to ancient times. Romans often carry a hand-warming pot, similar to those in Paris ... In Rome, it is called a* scaldino *or* il marito *[the husband]; among the common people it is of terracotta, among the bourgeoisie it is made of faience decorated in a fashionable style.*

We have not examined everything that makes up the interior of a house of the people. One often finds a guitar or a tambourine, used above all in the country dance, the saltarello. *The lamp is a required piece of furniture; since the people, to light the house, ordinarily use the oil of Italy, rich in olives, supplied at a good price. The rich use candles. As for the image of the Madonna, one finds it everywhere.*

The Poor

Beggars were everywhere, and most foreign visitors complained bitterly about their omnipresence. Even more, they resented or were amused by the fact that beggars expected to be treated with respect as well as with generosity. The beggar-saint Benedict Joseph Labbré was a popular hero,[27] and begging was a profession with biblical origins in a society where the ruling class' very reason for being was to exercise biblical charity.

Superior, multi-lingual beggars operated in the area of the Spanish Steps. Street-corner scribes earned a very good living writing begging letters for clients who had every expectation that the letters would generate a favourable response. The recipients were not just the clerics and nobles whose own respectability hung on their reputation for open-handed charity. The letters went to anyone with any property at all, and people were expected to respond with generosity, and usually did. It went without saying that it was regarded as the duty of any cleric, and most especially rich clerics and monastics, to succour the needy on demand.

The Charity of Beggars

Maddalena Patrizi, in her account of the adventures of Cunegonde and Giovanni Patrizi [see chapter 9], includes a curious little story she heard from an old servant, about a relative who lived in Siena, the family seat. In the early nineteenth century he was a powerful and important man, the acting Grand Master of the Knights of Malta; and he was also an elderly man of fixed habits. One of these was to go every day to pay his respects to the sanctuary of the Madonna of Provenzano, and then to give alms to at least one beggar on the road. On one especially bitter winter day he ploughed through the snow to the church, then headed back towards home. Unfortunately for him, not a single one of the usual beggars had braved the storm, which by then had turned into something of a blizzard. Sighing, he trudged on past his home and headed into town. Just as the wind blew the hat off his head, he saw an old woman making her way towards him, with her hand out. Delighted, he dropped a silver piece in her palm. 'May God reward you for your alms', the old woman

---

27 Labbré, a pious young French pilgrim, died in Rome in the 1780s, probably of voluntary malnutrition and exposure.

An elaborate system of social welfare included the distribution of food.

croaked. 'May God reward you for asking!' he shouted over his shoulder as he dashed off after his hat. 'If you hadn't, Heaven knows how far I might have had to go!'

The word 'paternalism' fails in the face of this example of why beggars in Rome, as in Siena, believed that they filled an important, not to say vital, role in their society.

One didn't have to be an outright beggar to earn a living by asking for it (not that there was anything shameful in begging – the shame would be on anyone who failed to respond in a quick and generous manner). There were entire classes of Romans who earned the nickname of *cavalieri dei denti* – knights of the teeth – because they lived by flattery and by odd jobs, by making themselves amiable and useful to people who could provide dinner, shelter or support. Some of them, in the ancient Roman tradition of clienthood, simply moved in with their patrons. Others were content with a tip. They 'rented apartments, hunted for relics, dealt in cameos, organised concerts.' They held horses or provided chairs or gave directions to lost foreigners. They hired porters or found friendly women or opened doors or carried lanterns. A decent living might be made by getting to ceremonies and processions early, securing a good post, and then giving it up with a smile in return for a tip. Or one could tell stories or sing pious or satirical, or obscene, songs, or sell trinkets or give impromptu sermons and speeches, and then pass a hat.

In addition to private and ecclesiastical charity, there were the confraternities and the great families, who would cease to be considered great families if they stopped giving to anyone who asked them. Then there were the charitable institutions: the hospitals, the orphan asylums, the shelters for abandoned or abused women or repentant women of the streets, as well as institutions that provided a bed and a meal for the destitute, and dowries for girls who wished to marry or enter a convent (it was her choice, and most reportedly chose to marry).

Almost every district had a hospital; Trastevere had four. Some hospitals specialised: San Gallicano in skin diseases, Santa Trinità in convalescent care, Santa Maria della Pietà in mental illness, San Teodoro in children's diseases. Santa Maria dells Consolazione cared for accident victims, and was especially busy during carnival and after rock fights. The Fatebene fratelli, a confraternity dedicated to medical assistance, provided home visits for the sick. The Santo Spirito hospital in the Borgo district had beds for 1,600 and offered organ concerts for patients and visitors.

There were 20 institutions for the care of orphans and the old. Two confraternities, the Santi Apostoli and the Pietà Divina, gave home assistance to those known as the 'embarrassed poor' – people of middle or noble estate who had fallen on hard times. The confraternities of Sant'Ivo and San Girolamo paid for legal assistance for those who could not afford lawyers, and where that did not do the job, the Pietà dei Carcerati took care of the needs of prisoners (this was still an age where convicts were responsible for their own keep). If you were condemned to death, you could count on the moral support of the Confraternity of St John the Beheaded, whose members accompanied you from the time the sentence came down all the way to the scaffold, consoling, encouraging and exhorting. If anyone threatened to die without repenting and consigning his soul to God, everyone concerned became seriously distressed. Confraternity members would also provide financial support for your dependants if they were needy. The confraternity associated with the church of Santa Maria dell'Orazione e Morte provided decent funerals at no cost to anonymous people who had died in the *campagna*, victims of disease or wolves or bandits.

When the French arrived to organise things in 1808, they introduced a very different attitude towards the poor, one designed to control, confine and punish them. It was an attempt to eradicate poverty by a combination of economic programmes, and by making it very unpleasant to be poor. One of their first steps was to make a statistical survey. They reported finding an astonishing 70,000 unemployed and able-bodied Romans. One of their first, and most resented, acts was to close down the dole and the Monti di Pietà (which provided loans on pawned goods) and set the able-bodied poor to working on public projects. It was not a popular policy.

In July 1808 came an even less popular move, when Napoleon issued a decree establishing *dépots de mendicité* where men and women arrested for vagrancy were to be held.[28] Although this was French policy wherever they held sway, it possibly received added impetus from the Spanish insurgency with the fear that poor people wandering around free might cause trouble for the army. The *dépots de mendicité* were not put into effect in Rome until 1811. In September of that year, de Tournon reported that there were more than 900 beggars to be enclosed. He proposed to put 600 men in the Lateran palace, and to put 300 to 400 women in the Santa Croce in Gerusalemme convent.

Class and Clothing
Clothing speaks. Even in the twenty-first century, it gives anyone who can see it information about its wearer's attitudes, traditions, financial condition and the

---

28 Piccialuti, 'Istituzioni napoleoniche a Roma: i *dépots de mendicité*' pp. 95-119.

image he or she chooses to project. This was even more true in the early nineteenth century in a place like Rome, where clothing was a semi-official (and sometimes official) statement about a man or woman's station, origins, work, social relationships and age.

One could also tell much about a person's politics or spiritual state from their clothing – or at least, one could tell what they wanted you to think about their politics or spiritual state. For men, queue and powdered hair were old fashioned and conservative; short hair or military-style braids were daring and radical. For women, traditional bodices tight to the waist and full skirts were conservative; light, loose dresses *à la grec* gathered under the bust and clinging to the body and legs were radical (and, from time to time, illegal). There was the usual panorama of clerical wear, as easy for a Roman to read as street signs would have been if Rome had had such things (which it didn't). There were the obvious brown-robed, sandled, tonsured Franciscans; the black and white robed Dominicans, severe and rather elegant; white robe and slippers for the pope, scarlet for cardinals and purple for bishops, with scarlet trim for *monsignori*. But spiritual signposts were not confined to the religious. Women who had made vows attached long ribbons to their waists, falling down to the hem of their skirts – the colour showed to whom the vow had been made: black for St Anne, white for Vincent de Paul, sky-blue for the Virgin, violet for Our Lady of Sorrows, or red for Jesus himself. It was possible to commission someone else – usually a 'woman of the people' – to fulfill one's vows, and wear the appropriate ribbon. This was considered a form of charity rather like paying to have a Mass said.[29]

Rome was full of day-labourers who came in from the country before dawn, and lay about in squares like the Piazza Montanara waiting to be hired. The basic work clothing of the country people around Rome consisted of a short, double-breasted jacket, ample shirt, a waistcoat, and short pants, to the knees. Like everyone in this pre-modern society, the various workers could be identified at a glance by their clothing. Shepherds wore cone-shaped hats made of hide, a hide cape or coat over their jackets and hide over-trousers to protect their legs. Cattle herders wore a large, dark coloured mantle, a linen hood or cap under their hats, leather leggings rather like the chaps of the American cowboys, and carried a long wooden pole to control the cattle.

Carters, whose work took them out of the city at night to the Castelli Romani (the string of hill towns famous for their wine), wore large capes (*feraiuoli*) made of rough wool (*borgonzone*) and a characteristic wide hat with a tall, cut-off crown and 'good-luck' ribbons with a jaunty cock feather. Their legs were protected with buckled leather leggings, and they were protected against cold or boredom by the small barrel of wine they slung over their shoulders or hung by a chain to the cart.

Country women wore wide shirts confined with a *bustière*, full skirts and long aprons; they wore white headscarves, sometimes pleated and starched stiff. Famous among them were the *ciociare*, who got their name from their rough leather shoes, tied on with crossed bands of leather.

---

29 Thomas, *op. cit.*, plate LII, p. 37.

Country women known as *ciociare* from their stle of footwear.

Dowry lists almost always mention the specific fabric that an item of clothing has been made from, even when they don't mention the colour.[30] They describe the style, and whether or not the item is embroidered or decorated with ribbon or lace, and sometimes even the pattern of the decoration. The dowry of Smerelda Anselmi mentions a short wool cloak (*cappotino*), flea-coloured (puce); a turquoise dress made of *stoffetto*; one of red *borgonzo* (a tough woollen fabric) and another of blue *borgonzo;* a outfit made from white *doboletto* (a French-style fabric of linen and cotton wool), another of embroidered white muslin and another of orange *galangà* (calico cotton).[31]

The clothing in Mariano Petruccia's will include black and yellow silk suits and two suits made of cambric, one stripped; six white muslin handkerchiefs and seven coloured handkerchiefs, 'very used'; a large muslin handkerchief with a woollen fringe; and a grey ('lead-colour') corset.[32]

For men of the popular classes, clothing seems to have been inspired by old Spanish styles – the short velvet or woollen jacket, worn casually thrown over the shoulder (handy to be wrapped quickly around the left arm as an impromptu shield, in case of a knife or rock fight); the white shirt with wide sleeves folded back to the forearm; the scarf around the neck; the solid-coloured waistcoat (velvet or woollen) and short trousers of the same fabric, buttoned or buckled below the knee; white, blue or coloured stockings (the striped stockings in art and in the theatre were not in fact common). Shoes were square toed and decorated with silver buckles so large they clanked against the street

---

30 Donatella Occhuizzi includes a fascinating list of fabrics, from the bright yellow *anchenne* (named after Nanking in China); the rough *borgonzo*, used in capes and men's trousers; *corame* or *coranne*, used for sheets and pillowcases; to *giaconetta*, a fine, almost transparent weave of cotton. Ochiuzzi, 'L'abito popolare', p. 15.

31 Archivio di Stato Capitolino [ASC], Archivio urbano, 1803-1805, Sez. IX, vol 54.

32 ASC, Archivio urbano, 1819–1820, Sez. XXIX, vol 92.

when their wearer walked, 'as if they were wearing spurs' says Zanazzo.[33] They wore wide, multi-coloured silk sashes with fringes and broad-brimmed felt hats (they called them *fungi*, mushrooms) decorated with large cock feathers.

Men and women both wore their hair long, caught up in a silk or linen net bag that tied on top of the head. Over this, both men and women wore top hats made of muskrat (they called them *ramoschè*, from the French *rat-musqué*) – in the early years of the nineteenth century, there were at least 30 hat manufacturers in Rome, and the hats they made were considered the best in Italy. Women wore their *ramoschè* with bright coloured ribbons, flowers and cock feathers, set raffishly to one side. Men too liked to decorate their hats with cock feathers or plumes, but usually wore them flat on top of their heads.

Men as well as women wore jewellery – four or five gold rings on each finger, heavy gold chains for their watches, and small gold earrings.

The wives of the *minenti* often worked outside the home, usually at some job associated with textiles, or perhaps in the tobacco factory in Trastevere. This contribution to the family income gave them a higher status, one which they flaunted with their more fashionable clothes and their gold and coral jewellery.

Traditional clothing remained an important part of dress in Rome for a long time, characterised by a combination of colours, styles and accoutrements. Ordinary women's work clothes or daily clothes consisted of the usual skirt and corset-style bodice, but on festive occasions they wore the short velvet jacket with lapels and long sleeves called the *carmagnole* (it was named after the region in Piedmont called Carmagnola, but later took on overtones connected with the famous French revolutionary song and dance). The skirt was velvet and ankle-length, with a long embroidered silk apron, white stockings and low shoes with the same sort of enormous buckles favoured by their men. Young women wore bright ribbons braided in their hair, with large ornate tortoise-shell combs. The method with which they held their long, braided hair was rich with symbolism, wonderful (and potentially dangerous) long pins, some with heads shaped like flowers or ears of corn; others shaped like a fist with the thumb stuck out between the index and middle finger in the classic (and obscene) 'fig' gesture. (In Dante's Hell, the unrepentant Farinata makes the 'fig' at God, who presumably shrugs it off: what else might you expect from the damned?) One wonders what message the girls of Rome wished to convey. Married women wore pins like trembling roses on fine spiral stems that shook when the wearer moved her head. Old ladies wore their hair in a green silk *sac* with long tassels. Men also wore their long hair in similar bags, under their hats or worn alone tied at the top of the head. *Minenti* finished off the look with as much jewellery as they could afford: three or four gold necklaces with discs ornamented with precious or semi-precious stones; pendant pearl ear rings, and as many rings on each finger as it could take.

This look appalled visitors like Mrs Eaton, who considered the women of the *popolo* to be 'slovenly and dirty' at home, and 'tawdry' when they dressed up to go out. But it was typical of the Roman tendency to enjoy life and not save for the future, on the assumption that the paternalistic state would be standing by to take care of them in the inevitable event that they needed it.

---

33 Zanazzo, *Tradizioni popolari romane*, p. 83.

Bagpipes provide music for a country wedding.

As the eighteenth century came into its last decade, Romans were happy. This was reported by most tourists, though most tourists (who didn't think the primary function of government was to make people happy) considered them to be deluded. The historian Madelin went so far as to suggest why Romans were happy: they liked their government, they didn't work much, and they were never bored. As the saying goes, '*Chi se contenta, gode*' (the contented man enjoys himself).

One may, perhaps even should, take this Roman happiness with a grain of salt. Romans took full advantage of the *jus mormorara*, the right to complain, either through the mouth of Pasquino or in the streets. It is certainly true that most Romans believed themselves lucky to be living in what was still, in their eyes at least, the First City of the world. No one forced them to work hard, living was cheap and heavily subsidised by public and private charity, taxes were low, and there was plenty of free entertainment. But it is equally true that 90 to 95% of the people were remarkably poor even by the not-very-demanding standards of the day; that their city was remarkably dirty by the same undemanding standards (several of Pinelli's genre scenes show families picking lice out of one another's hair) and located in the middle of a malarial swamp. Also that there was an astonishingly high rate of casual (and often fatal) interpersonal violence; and that, while their hospital and prison systems were among the best in the world, their police and justice systems were among the worst.

Maybe they were happy because they had hope – not only one of the three great theological virtues, but also a virtue indispensable for gamblers. In an age when, elsewhere, almost everyone but those born to the nobility were excluded from playing any effective role in their government, Romans could look to Sixtus V, pope from 1585 to 1590, who had begun his life herding swine. Or on a more modest and attainable scale, they could look to young men living among them, men like Gaspare del Bufalo, son of a servant of the Chigi family. He became not only an ordained priest – an office that came with built-in authority and real power – but would end his life as an important and influential man in the Church, founder of an order and a man deferred to by the highest powers (it was on his advice that an entire town, destined to be destroyed to control the scourge of banditry, was spared). The very fact of being ordained a cleric raised a man to the First Estate, no matter what his status at birth. And ordination was, in theory and often in fact, open to any capable man.

We should also remember that the contempt for money that most Romans showed was not just the result of their not having any, but had a sound philosophical base in the Christian ideal of poverty.[1] As in the medieval world, power and influence in Rome were not yet inextricably tied to wealth, and even the rich and the powerful paid poverty the sincere if facile homage of pretending to be poor when they died. It is not surprising, then, that the poor, who had the most to gain in terms of self-respect by believing that poverty was a noble state, in fact believed it.

Romans were by and large healthy. They lived most of their lives outdoors, and they normally had jobs that required physical labour, but offered relative independence, jobs where they could choose when and where they worked, and when they stopped working. Roman women traditionally worked in the vineyards at harvest and at pruning time, in much the way that northern Italian women later worked the rice harvests. It was a bacchanalian, anything-goes time that didn't last long, but that provided welcome extra money and independence.

Dowries, Weddings and Christenings

Dowries

Whatever the status of the family of the bride or the groom, the bride had to bring to the marriage at least enough money to purchase a bed, along with her clothing and essential household equipment.[2] The dowry served several vital social purposes. In propertied families it ensured the daughters some share in the inheritance; it also gave the wife a degree of independence – if the marriage failed, the dowry money sometimes returned to her, and if she died it could go to her children, not to her husband. Marriage without a dowry was a flat impossibility in the early modern world. If the bride were poor, or an orphan, the dowry was provided by some charitable institution, and Rome was full of these.

More than one critical traveller pointed to the free availability of dowries as the cause for two deplorable lower class customs: young women chose their own mates, and young couples married when the urge struck them, not waiting to build up a suitable financial base. It is difficult to say how many dowries were available in Rome, distributed by the lottery, confraternities, and institutions. And if all else failed, one could always appeal to the parish priest, or a cardinal, or some wealthy patron or patroness.

Italian dowries were given on condition that the recipient could either *maritarsi o monacarsi* – become a wife, or a nun. Despite the fact that, in Rome, a larger amount was often given if the girl decided on the convent, the vast majority chose marriage (of course, when the girl became a nun, the money went to the convent).

---

1   The nobility were particularly contemptuous of money and did their best to gamble it away; the quality of being acquisitive was regarded as contemptible.
2   See Sonnino, pp. 428-29, and Woolf, *A History of Italy*, pp. 23, 32 and 128.

Dowering a Nun

Charitable organisations, parishes and, for that matter, the Roman lottery were all sources for dowries for the poor. The lottery offered over 200 each year, and as many as 150 dowries were awarded every year by the Confraternity of the Most Holy Annunciation. On 1 October, the feast of the Virgin of the Rosary, the lucky girls processed through the city, on the arms of their gentlemen escorts:[3]

The girls were dressed entirely in white, and covered with long white veils which fell to their feet, with their faces veiled in the Turkish fashion, and both veil and dress were pinned into a regular pattern of folds by multitudes of pins. Each girl carried a lighted candle in her hand and wore a belt from which hung a purse containing her dowry. Girls who had chosen to become nuns also marched in the procession, wearing crowns.

Daughters of the nobility were often sent to convents to be educated, from which they emerged for their weddings or, if they so chose, for their profession as nuns. Just as it was not possible to marry without a dowry, it was equally impossible for a woman to enter on the other main career path open to her – that of the nun – without bringing some sort of dowry with her. As we have noted, only about 2% of the women of Rome were in religious orders, but that still represented a sizeable number, and the many convents of the city were not short of personnel.

Protestant visitors to the city, most notably the English, felt a delicious thrill of horror at the idea of a young girl choosing what they regarded as the living death of the convent. By the end of the century, sceptical or anticlerical Frenchmen and Italians shared their opinion. They would have been shocked and insulted to hear the argument that nineteenth-century liberalism reduced rather than expanded freedom for women, or that the convent represented the one Western institution where women could exercise official authority.

When a girl entered a convent to take her vows as a nun, it was customary to take her on a round of formal visits, and give her a great procession through the city, dressed in her finest. Noble ladies, acting as godmothers, took charge of such events. So, shortly after her own marriage, Cunegonde Patrizi sponsored two young women, one, Serafina Albani, noble, the other, Dorotea Papini, a commoner, both of whom entered the convent of Santa Chiara. As was the custom, the girls were brought to their homes while a sumptuous reception was prepared, with all the delicacies usual to a wedding feast, while the church at which their reception was to take place was draped and lighted with the customary splendour. The street between their home and the church was strewn with yellow sand and sprigs of myrtle, and Swiss guards served as escorts of honour. A cardinal presided, in full ceremonial panoply. The whole affair was part of the theatricality of life and faith, and was admired and critiqued like a theatre performance, but with rather more charity.

---

3 Silvagni, *op. cit.*, III, p. 115.

Weddings
In a normal year there were between eight and a half and nine marriages per 1,000 people, but there was a marriage boom during the republic of 1798–99 (when numbers rose to over 11 per 1,000), another in 1805 (during the first papal restoration) and yet another in 1808 (when the French returned). War and dramatic changes of fortune, for good or for ill, tend to produce weddings, sometimes as an expression of defiant hope, sometimes as a hasty effort to regularise messy relationships, and sometimes, as in 1810, to help the husband avoid conscription.

Mrs Eaton dismisses the whole question of Roman weddings by saying that, except for 'a few signs of the cross and sprinklings of holy water', they were unremarkable and exactly like weddings in England. People got dressed up in their best clothes, mothers cried, friends and relatives offered congratulations and everybody ate too much.

Like everything else, weddings varied depending on the status and the wealth of the family. The marriages of the Saxon princesses – Marianna, Beatrice, Cunegonde, and Cristina – approached the ultimate limits of luxury in the last years before the French occupation of Rome.[4] Marianna was the first of the Saxon princesses to marry in Rome. Her oldest sister, Elizabeth, had been married in 1787 at Versailles, in the presence of her cousin, Louis XVI, and his wife, Marie Antoinette. The four younger girls had been brought to Rome by their father and placed for safe-keeping in the convent at the Torre dei Specchi, to await suitable grooms. A contract was quickly arranged for Marianna to form an alliance with the Paluzzi-Altieri, one of the great papal families, by marrying their son, the Duke of Monterano, in 1793. The next year Beatrice was married to Prince Riario Sforza of Naples, whose sister Princess Gabrielli lived in Rome. In January of 1796, Cunegonde married the young heir of the Patrizi family, and finally, Cristina married Camillo Massimi in 1798.[5]

Weddings were family business, not the private affair of two people. The greater the family, the less likely that the bride or groom would have much say in deciding whom to marry or when. Neither the wedding day nor the wedding night, nor the honeymoon (if there was one) provided much in the way of privacy for the happy couple. After the ceremony, friends and relations had to be fed and entertained, and their curiosity and congratulations endured. When the time came to retire for the evening, the bride was brought to her bedroom by her mother-in-law, followed by all the guests. The bed was blessed and a great deal of cheerful practical advice was given to the couple. Very early next morning, the mother-in-law and mother of the bride arrived with a meal designed to revive the couple after what was hopefully presumed to have been a strenuous night – egg yolk beaten in broth, a generous chunk of meat, and a bottle of wine, all supposed to fortify and encourage fertility. Then the entire wedding party and guests piled into the room to help the bride dress, along with more good advice and gales of laughter at jokes that she was now supposed to understand and share. When the time came to depart for the wedding trip, the entire family and their retainers trooped along for the outing.

---

4   The Saxon princesses, the daughters of Prince Xavier, son of the King of Saxony, were brought to Rome after the death of their mother, the Countess Chiara Spinelli of Fermo.
5   Silvagni, *op. cit.*, II, appendix 3, gives the bridal contract for Marianna of Saxony on the occasion of her marriage to Prince Paluzzi-Altieri, Duke of Monterano.

The gifts that the groom gave to the bride were on public display: her husband gave Marianna a wedding purse of gold rings joined by tiny bars of emerald, and filled with freshly minted coins; clothing and household goods, jewels set and unset; and a portrait of the bride's recently deceased mother. Duke Strozzi gave the couple a pianoforte, made in England (the pianoforte was just beginning to replace the clavichord); the Altieri family gave them deeds to land, and jewels, and cash; the Princess Borghese gave Marianna two gowns of Genoa velvet and the Princess of Palestrina provided a dress made of Brussels lace.

Cunegonde, Princess of Saxony, married the Marchese Giovanni Naro Patrizi on 7 January 1796. The bride was 16, the groom was 19. On 3 January, Cardinal Braschi, the nephew of Pius VI, had given a great banquet for 30 guests whose number included Duke Braschi, brother of the cardinal and nephew of the pope, for whom His Holinesss had built what would be the last of the great Roman palaces, the Palazzo Braschi.[6] The two princes of Saxony, her father and her brother, were there, along with the noble parents of the groom – the Patrizi, as befitted their name, were among the oldest and most noble, if not the richest, of the Roman patriciate.[7]

The wedding of the lady's maid Anna Maria Gianetti to Domenico Taigi, a porter in the kitchen of the Chigi palace, was a great deal simpler, but it was just as important to the families concerned.[8] Anna Maria was 21 (her husband thought she was 18); Domenico was 28. While the Saxon princesses waited in their convent for a marriage contract to be arranged, the lady's maid and the porter arranged things for themselves. They met when he was sent to bring meals to Anna Maria's employer. Anna Maria was pretty, and charming, and well-spoken; he was handsome and fun-loving and distinctly rough around the edges. Soon after they met, he decided that she was the wife he wanted; she decided, for reasons of her own, to accept him. As a pretty servant in a noble household, she was flattered and pursued and courted, and she liked it. But she saw a pit opening up at her feet, and decided that marriage would be her salvation. So she chose to marry. What we know about the marriages of Marianna and Beatrice and Cunegonde and Cristina we know because the newspapers reported it, the distinguished guests described the splendour and excitement, and the family left the usual stack of documentation that a consequential organisation generates and leaves behind. What we know about the Taigi-Gianetti wedding we know because Anna Maria later lived a spectacularly holy life and, many years after the wedding, the Church held a series of inquiries to discover the details of that life. One of the witnesses was her aged widower, Domenico. Domenico didn't remember anything about gifts or parties; he remembered that he fell in love with her, that she agreed to marry him, and that he went to her parents – servants themselves – to make the necessary arrangements.

---

6 Patrizi, *Memorie di Famiglia*, pp. 7-8.

7 According to Silvagni, the original Patrizi line had died out in 1735 when Virginia, daughter of the last Patrizi prince, married Giovanni Chigi Montoro. The descendants of their daughter assumed the Patrizi name.

8 It was a matter of life or death: Anna Maria's parents were servants, and their only daughter's marriage was their insurance for their old age. By all reports, her mother was a dragon, but when she needed shelter, they took her in and she lived with the young couple until her death.

Marriages among the lower classes, like those of their betters, were not always voluntary. If extended families had a strong interest in marriage alliances, the state too played a role in ensuring domestic regularity. If a young man was accused of compromising a girl (and this by no means always meant pregnancy), she or her parents, or the priest, or indeed anyone who took notice, might inform the city officials, who would have the swain thrown into the prison of the Carcere Nuove.[9] There were only two ways for him to get out: if she were willing, he could provide her with an acceptable dowry so someone else would marry her; or he could marry her himself. If the couple chose the latter alternative, a priest brought the bride to the prison and the knot was tied before the cell door was opened. Everyone then went home and, as the saying went, 'ate treats' [dei confetti], the traditional wedding pastries and sweets. The arrangement was a useful one. Impatient girls could take advantage of it to bring reluctant grooms to the altar; and couples facing parental opposition could do an end run around them by having recourse to the law.

Under the Ridiculous Republic there was a piquant variation added to the marriage mix: the introduction of the so-called democratic marriages – civil unions without the benefit of clergy. Francesco Fortunati, who certainly did not approve, recounts one such marriage.[10] A radical physician, Giacomo Chinozzi, wanted his daughter to marry in the new, democratic style, and beat the girl when she refused. Her fiancé intervened and took her away – but he left her at a third house, 'in good custody, without the least hanky-panky' (un minimo scherzo) until they could be married in church. And thus, Fortunati says, 'her wicked father looked like a fool'.

Folk-ways and Finding a Mate

If a girl wanted to get married, but didn't know whom to choose, there were ways of finding out. One way would be to make a novena to San Pasquale Baylonne, who would then show you your bridegroom in a dream. Or a girl could wait until St John's Day in mid-summer, and melt a bit of lead, then throw it into a pot of cold water. The lead might tell her what she wanted to know, by taking on forms that suggested the tools of the trade of her future mate. Failing that, she could throw the water out of her window. The first of her suitors who stepped over the water was the lucky one.

Daisies were a reliable way of telling just how much any given man loved a girl. While Anglo-Saxon daisies confined themselves to saying whether he did or did not love, Roman daisies were more specific. As the petals were plucked, you learned if he loves … Not much … A little … A lot … or, he's mad about me.[11]

Girls wanting husbands, or wives wanting children, were advised to climb the steps to St Peter's basilica on their knees, holding a lighted candle. This was unlikely, however, to help wives who smoked; according to folk tradition, they would have no children. On the other hand, if a child came near the bride and groom while they were standing at the altar, then the marriage would be fruitful.

If you want to know who will die first, the husband or the wife, watch to see which one blows out the light on the wedding night – that one will die first.

---

9   Zanazzo, *op. cit.*, Part II, pp. 125-6.

10 Fortunati, *op. cit.*, 30 June 1798.

11 Zanazzo, *op. cit.*

May and September were considered to be unlucky months for marrying, as were all Tuesdays and Fridays. And it was against the law to marry during Lent.

To see the character of the man she might marry during the year, on 1 January a girl could take three fava beans and peel the first one completely, take half the peel off the second, and leave the hull intact on the third. The beans were then wrapped in bits of paper and placed under her pillow. Immediately on waking the next morning, she was to put her hand under her pillow and select one at random. If she chose the unpeeled bean, she would marry a rich man; if she chose the second bean, she would marry a dandy; but if she picked the peeled bean, her husband would be *migragnoso migragnoso!*

A way of foretelling whether or not one would marry had to do with needles and thread. You took three needles and threaded them, one with white thread, one with red, and one with black. The girl then closed her eyes and chose one of the three. If she picked the white, she would remain an old maid; if she picked the red, marriage was in her future; and if she found herself holding the needle threaded with black thread, there was nothing to be done: she would die within the year.

Christenings

After the wedding came the baby, and the christening. Babies were normally born at home, with the assistance of a midwife. In Rome after 1699, midwives or *mammane* were supposed to be licensed by the priest in charge of the parish where they practised, but this system never seemed to work very well. Towards the end of the century, in the years just before the French invasion and occupation, courses in obstetrics were set up at the university, and at the main hospital of Santo Spirito, as well as at San Rocco, the lying-in hospital. Midwives were supposed to qualify at one of these courses before being licensed, but again, there is not much evidence that many of them did. There were physicians who specialised in delivering babies – one of them was Liborio Angelucci, a consul of the Roman republic and likely pattern for Angelotti in the opera *Tosca* – but physicians in general were not highly regarded, and most families chose to call in a midwife, officially qualified or not. The great majority of babies were born at home. There were fewer than 20 hospital beds available for the purpose.

No matter what one's social status, the birth of a baby was an important event. In Rome, the event was traditionally marked by sending gifts to the new mother, in the form of a *padiglione,* or 'pavilion'. The idea was relatively simple. This was a gift of food, to celebrate fertility. It usually consisted of various types of pasta and a chicken. In the case of wealthy gift-givers these pavilions could be astonishing and elaborate, delivered in a sort of festive *macchina* constructed in fantastic shapes, as *macchine* were, of *papier mâché* and wood or canvas. The edifice was filled with containers of pasta and chickens and capons were attached to it. Then the whole construction was carried through the streets to the home of the new mother. If the giver were particularly eminent, he would see to it that the procession included liveried servants, trumpeters and ushers in black ceremonial dress to hold back the crowds attracted by the show. The parade stopped from time to time so that one of the attendants could step forward and announce the name and titles of the lady, and of the donor.

The giving of 'pavilions' was not limited to the rich, although of course they were expected to put on the best show. Most neighbourhoods had shops that specialised in concocting appropriately magnificent gifts, which were carried through the streets with as much ceremony as possible, and loudly proclaimed.

If the survival of a baby seemed doubtful, it was the duty of the midwife to baptise it immediately. If the baby were healthy a formal date was set for christening, usually very soon after the birth. The parents chose the godparents carefully. Sometimes they were peers, but very often they were of dramatically different status. Popes and great nobles might be asked to stand godparent to quite a humble baby. At the other extreme, Roman nobles often asked a beggar or a destitute pilgrim to stand sponsor. Babies rejoicing in names like Barbarini, Santacroce and Cesarini found themselves held at the baptismal font by the poorest of the poor, and their parents counted them lucky to thus secure the spiritual assistance that could only be obtained through the poor, those most beloved by God. Silvagni reports the case of the Prince Francesco Ruspoli, who selected as godfather to his son a miserable cripple named Giuseppe Mochi. Mochi graciously agreed to accept the post, and was given a handsome gift, free quarters in the Ruspoli palace for the rest of his life, along with a pension and free medical care.

The Joys of Devotion

Religion was Rome's reason for being, and religious devotions permeated everyday life as well as the great annual festivals [see chapter 5]. It was rare to find a day that was not marked by some religious celebration – days dedicated to the Virgin under any of her many titles; days dedicated to patron saints, whether the patron of a church or parish, or the personal patron after which the individual took one of his names (and everyone had at least two, plus a family name – one under which he or she was baptised, one for confirmation). Then there were the celebrations specific to a particular confraternity or religious order – anniversaries of founding, or of saints who had belonged to or had specially favoured the group in question. Most popes celebrated at least a few beatifications (ceremonies recognising that a candidate has reached the next to last hurdle on the road to official sainthood) or canonisations (the formal declaration of sainthood). These were occasions for great (and very expensive) celebration for anyone who had any tie with the new *Beato* or *Santo*'s family or place of origin, or order, or station in life.

For the feast of St Philip Neri in 1795, Fortunati reports the Chiesa Nuova was draped and illuminated and filled with music, while throughout the neighbourhood windows were hung with tapestries and damasks, every shop was lit up, and there were 'numerous orchestras of instruments' in all the streets. The celebrations continued for 'two really beautiful evenings'.[12]

In November and December 1797, the Oratory of the Caravita held a three-day celebration (a *tridium*) in honour of the Blessed Leonardo of Porto Maurizio. The façade of the church was illuminated for three successive evenings, while paintings draped with velvet showed the *Beato* and his miraculous deeds. Events like this were a bonanza for painters, who were commissioned to provide suitable canvases for the life and work of the holy person in question. In the case of the Blessed Leonardo, the

---

12 Fortunati, *op. cit.*, 20 May 1795.

committee arranged for a number of paintings showing his miracles and his childhood, while *festaioli* prepared a great *macchina* complete with stairs and gradations leading up to a representation of the Blessed Leonardo in Glory.

Rome, a city that specialised in public spectacle, had a large class of professionals, called *festaioli* or *festaroli* who worked on such productions.[13] Like designers of theatrical sets or carnival floats – both of which were profitable lines of work in Rome – the *festaioli* had an elaborate and traditional stock in trade. This consisted primarily in fireworks, and silver *crepe de chine* or scarlet or black silk draperies (the colour depending on the occasion), with gold fringes and embroidery; and candles and torches in gilt holders, for illumination, and the long ladders to use for hanging the decoration.[14] Celebratory *macchine* resembled carnival floats, and could be used to transform the interior of a church or a palace. Funeral machines, with black drapery, were more sombre but just as elaborate, whether they were displayed indoors or outdoors. Fireworks were carried out under the direction of experts from the bombardier's guild. Their repertoire included stars, fountains, spinning tops and 'chestnuts' or firecrackers, attached to the elaborate *macchine*. These *macchine* were, in effect, stage sets that could tower as much as 100 feet into the air. They represented castles, mountains on which gods dwelled or wild animals prowled, obelisks and pyramids, warships, or theatres where live dancers and musicians performed – the shapes were limited only by the imagination of the artists who designed them. At the climax of the show, the machine seemed to explode in a burst of fireworks, but in fact they were not burned. The structures were built of massive timber frames, covered with canvas panels painted in *trompe l'oeil* style, and given an architectural look with stucco and *carta pesta* (a sort of *papier mâché*), often painted to look like polychrome marble. After the show they were dismantled and the component parts used for other spectacles.

Whenever a prelate was raised to the rank of cardinal (and every pope created at least a few cardinals), the fortunate man was obliged to hold a party for the entire city and most especially for the poor. Some of these became extremely elaborate, and even the more modest parties had to involve free wine, musical entertainments and something in the way of theatrical display.

If the elevation of a cardinal was an occasion for celebration, the election of a pope ignited a fuse that caused the entire city to explode in unruly exultation. Among the traditional privileges of the common people at such a time was the right to sack the apartments of the new pontiff, and cart off anything of value they could find. This might have been a gesture towards an ideal of apostolic poverty – surely anyone holy enough to be pope would want to distribute all of his goods to the poor? – or simply a rite of passage, but it was a prerogative that the *popolo* guarded jealously and only gave up with the greatest reluctance.

Births and deaths among the great and famous could also be entertaining. See, for example the funeral *macchina* designed by the architect Benedetto Piernicoli in honour of Victor Amadeus III of Savoy. The ceremonies took place at the church of

---

13 Nicassio, *Tosca's Rome*, pp. 177–8.
14 Two *festaioli* found themselves conscripted to help with the kidnapping of Pius VII in 1809, because their ladders were needed for the assault. See chapter 9.

the Most Holy Shroud of the Piedmontese in September 1797 (on the eve of the French occupation). As usual, the church was draped in rich black fabric. In the centre was a great porphery urn, covered with a pall made of velvet heavy with gold fringe and bearing the royal coat of arms. A cushion held the dead king's crown, sceptre and sword.[15] All of this, with the singing of the choirs, incense, and the light of hundreds of wax candles, made an appropriately impressive display, even for people who hadn't the slightest interest in Savoy or its dead ruler.

Celestial Patronage

For Romans, the world of God and His saints was very much like their everyday world with its system of patrons and clients. It therefore seemed to them perfectly reasonable to take their problems directly to whichever heavenly patron they trusted most. This attitude often shocked visitors, especially Protestant ones. The Madonna, of course, was a great favourite, as she was presumed to take a motherly interest in the well-being of her children. Romans appealed to these heavenly patrons for help in all sorts of circumstances, some more theologically appropriate than others.

Altars and shrines were hung with *ex votos*, gifts given in thanksgiving for favours received. These could include weaponry – usually knives, but also represented were the long sharp hair pins favoured by Roman women of all classes. Some of the weapons were no doubt hung there in repentance; others were perhaps dedicated in thanksgiving for a successful bit of violence undertaken for what the perpetrator considered the best of motives. More usually *ex votos* commemorated a miraculous escape of some sort – a man falling off a ladder was preserved from serious injury, so he or his family presented a little painting of the event, to be hung near the altar of the Virgin, or the saint considered responsible for the rescue. A child plagued with asthma recovered, so the mother or grandmother commissioned a silversmith to make a tiny silver throat as an *ex voto*; or a leg was broken and healed well, so a little silver leg joined the collection of trophies offered to the heavenly patron.

There were many religious observances that were not limited to particular days or seasons. St Philip Neri's followers, the Oratorians, held musical picnics cum prayer meetings, sometimes in church but often out of doors. These all-day outings often ended up at a sunny hollow near the top of the Janiculum hill with short sermons, food and drink, and musical plays on biblical themes (the original 'oratorios').

Around the middle of the eighteenth century, the tradition of following the Stations of the Cross in the Coliseum became popular, inspired by the belief that the early Christians had met their deaths there (it now seems likely that most martyrs died in the Circus Maximus or the circus of Nero). The Stations marked the events in Jesus' arrest, trial, scourging and crucifixion, and they were especially popular during Lent and carnival time, as it was hoped that they helped make up for the misdeeds of the season. During the French occupation, Romans wanted to continue to make the Stations, much to the annoyance of the archaeologists whose work was interrupted. The archaeologists won a temporary victory, but at the fall of Napoleon the Stations resumed with greater enthusiasm than ever, led by none other than Cardinal Fesch, the fallen emperor's uncle.

---

15 Gori Sassoli, *Catalogo delle Feste* p. 255, Chracas 1797 n. 2372, 23 September, pp. 17–19.

Shrines and Madonelle

Before the French occupation, the only street lights in Rome were the flickering candles or oil lamps that were set before the shrines – some on corners, some in niches in the walls of palaces, some merely painted onto the surface of more humble buildings. In 1853, while Rome was still *vecchia Roma* under the rule of the popes, a scholar counted 2,739 shrines in and on the walls of Rome; 1,421 were dedicated to the Madonna. These *madonelle* (little Madonnas) or *altarini* (little altars) were found throughout the city, and many still remain, some faded and neglected but others regularly decorated with flowers and candles. It was these *madonelle* that comforted or warned the people as the invaders drew near in 1798. The rougher the neighbourhood, the more numerous the *madonelle*, either because the people there had more trouble and so more reason to appeal for immediate divine aid, or because those in charge of the city believed they would have a calming effect on the dangerous classes.

The Lottery, or Running the Numbers

Romans loved every sort of gambling, from *morro* to the great lottery. In its way, the lottery symbolised Rome, the place where everything was at least possible: after all, this was the only state where virtually every man had at least the remote chance of being elected absolute ruler. Had not Sixtus V herded pigs? Every conclave was a great lottery. No one knew which way the Spirit would blow, bringing unimaginable power and wealth not just to an individual, but (thanks to the patronage system) to every member of his family and all of his associated hangers-on, and on down through their families and associated hangers-on, and so on as the ripple effects spread through the city. If the grand prize was the papal triple crown, there were plenty of consolation prizes like small jobs, modest sinecures, licences, permits and gifts.[16]

It is ironic, then, that the Church never really approved of the lottery. Neither did tourists, but that is hardly surprising. Tourists rarely approved of Romans, and Romans were addicted to the lottery:

The infatuation of the lower orders for the never-ceasing lotteries which go on here is inconceivably pernicious to their industry and morals and brings misery and ruin upon thousands. Too often the last necessary of life, taken from a starving family, is pawned at the Monte di Pietà to purchase a lottery ticket. The scene at the drawing of the lotteries here may be a study for the painter or the philosopher, but it is a heart-sickening sight for a man.[17]

Certainly, it took money out of circulation. And certainly, the lottery was just one more reason for Romans to trust in an unpredictable fate rather than in work and thrift. Gambling, hope, trust in fortune, or in the mysterious ways of God, were fundamental to the Roman way of life. So was violence. And it is worth noting that the term *riffa*, which means both lottery and raffle, also means violence or riot.

---

16 Friz, *op. cit.*
17 Eaton, *op. cit.*, II, p. 360.

The Church had tried to stamp out private lotteries, where entrepreneurs pocketed the profit and cheated on the distribution of prizes (Clement X went so far as to threaten to excommunicate gamblers). But lottery remained a popular passion, and by 1732, on the theory that if you can't beat them, join them, the pope made the lottery a state-directed monopoly. At first, the treasurer was determined that the state should derive no profit from this venture, and that all income should be distributed as prizes. But the amounts that rolled in were substantial – in the first six years, the Roman lottery made 1,980,897.60 *scudi*. It was decided that, after prizes, the profits should be distributed for state expenses. A substantial amount went for public works like restoring archaeological sites and treasures, building new roads and fixing old ones, and repairing aqueducts: in the first six years of operation, the project for building the famous Trevi fountain benefited to the tune of 94,435.26 *scudi*. Building and embellishing churches was another use for the money; and charitable institutions like hospitals, hospices and refuges for poor children, endangered women and girls, and the elderly all benefited.[18]

The lottery was a universal obsession that absorbed much of the attention, and the cash, of virtually all Romans. Drawings took place every Saturday except for Holy Week, Christmas, the feast of the Assumption in mid-August, and the last weekend of October.[19] In Rome, the drawings were an occasion for spectacle, passion, and multi-class elbow-rubbing in much the same way that the elevation of cardinals, the running of the wild horses, carnival, or public executions were. Like these occasions, the lottery drawing epitomised that tangy combination of the spiritual, the carnal, the violent, and the beautiful that contributed to the unique savour of life in the ancient city.

The minimum bet was half a *bajocco*. Five tickets were drawn, out of 90 possible tickets, each of which was associated with a particular respectable unmarried woman. If her ticket were drawn, she received a dowry of seven and a half *scudi*, while people who bet on that number won money. It is all reminiscent of the Irish Sweepstakes, with girls instead of horses.

One could bet in various ways – on a random draw, on some combination of the numbers, or on a 'tern', which was a bet that your sequence of three numbers would appear in the same order in all five numbers drawn. If your long-shot paid off, you received 5,000 to 1 odds. Winning too much too regularly could be counted upon to attract the attention of the authorities, who could ask awkward questions. Of course, the person doing the excessive winning very probably *was* employing some arcane and shady system – who didn't? – so investigations naturally found what they were looking for.

How to choose a number
The popes had reason to be ambivalent about the lottery, which smacked of the occult. According to Belli, people decided on the right number on the basis of consultations with a wide array of potential advisors – Capuchins, astrologers, *comari* (godmothers), magicians, cabalists, and ticket sellers – and an equally bizarre

---

18 Gross, *op. cit.*, pp. 128–9.
19 The lottery was shared between the Papal States and the Grand Duchy of Tuscany. The 46 draws were held thus: 24 in Rome; 1 each in Pistoia and Massa; 2 in Arezzo, Pisa; 6 each in Livorno, Pisa and Florence.

collection of possible guides – hunches, prayers and interpretation of events and images in dreams and in everyday life.[20]

For those who wished to try the scientific approach to divining winning lottery numbers, there were guidebooks. One of the most popular was attributed to an astrologer whose pseudonym was Fortunato Indovino, or 'lucky guess'.[21] Fortunato gave reassuringly complicated rules for 'knowing the right, and precise, number not only for *ambos* and *ternos*, which make up the numbers that will be played, but please God, of all 90 numbers on the list.'

The method for choosing numbers has been described as cabalistic and it is a good word. One technique was to select a number, then multiply it by its nearest inferior; then take half of the product of this multiplication, and that half gave the number you want for the *ambo*. For example, you may decide (from a dream, or from seeing one, or having something unusual to do with one, or just a hunch that one may be important) that the appropriate symbol for you this week is a dog. The number for a dog, in the Roman lottery, is 17. You multiply 17 by 16, its nearest inferior, and arrive at 272. Half of 272 is 136. So the number you want for the *ambo* is 136.

All of this calls for some relatively complicated mathematics for people who were often illiterate despite the availability of free schools. The process has something of the charm that memorising statistics for football games or opera singers offers, an eternal charm that finds its roots both in manipulating something as magical as numbers (Pythagoras knew a thing or two), and in trying to outguess and control destiny (a Roman preoccupation since before the ancient republic). Romans loved complexity and interlocking factors, to be weighed, discussed, decided upon, and held *in petto* until an advantage might be gained.

Dream books were in great demand for deciding the numerical meaning of dreams (a drowned man translated to 88). Events in everyday life had numbers. If a child in your family were ill with a fever, you would bet 18-28-48; if you had an unhappy or one-sided love affair, your number was 90. For a long time, Jews were restricted in the numbers they could back – they had to choose low numbers, and numbers in sequence (30-31-32 etc). This was because Jews were considered to be especially clever at using arcane and cabalistic knowledge, and the limitations were designed to prevent such manipulations. Ironically, these numbers were as likely as any to be successful, and for generations Jewish people traditionally chose low numbers, and numbers in sequence, long after the restrictions had been forgotten.

Since for Romans the world of God and His saints overlapped substantially with their everyday world, each lottery was the subject of prayers, novenas, and other petitions to heavenly patrons. The Virgin, considered to be especially amiable about worldly problems, was a favourite. Another was the *bambino* in the church of Ara Coeli – a rather plain olive wood image of the infant Jesus that was considered miraculous. Taking a petition to the *bambino* had the added benefit of involving an arduous physical effort as one had to climb the narrow, steep and very long flight of steps that lead up from the Campidoglio.

---

20 Friz, *op. cit.*, pp. 306-7
21 Fortuno Indovino, *Il vero mezzo di vincere al lotto*. Recently reprinted in an edition edited by Carla Ferrario.

The 1798–99 republic allowed the lottery to continue sporadically, and at one point they had a property lottery in which the prizes were confiscated Church properties. After the first restoration (1800–1809), the lottery returned but private games of chance (as always) were banned on severe penalties; annual edicts were issued against them (always a good sign that the activity being prohibited is widespread).[22] When, in 1809, the people heard that Napoleon had ordered the *Consulta* to suppress the lottery, there was a mini-revolution. Public protests were intense enough to make the authorities change their minds, for the time being, about their proposed action. Later, in 1811, the government did suppress the game, with a surprisingly mild reaction from the Romans. The only real result was the addition of a few hundred lottery employees to the thousands of other unemployed.

Street Theatre and Commercial Entertainment

Romans were mad about theatre of any sort, which had something of the appeal of forbidden fruit. Tickets were expensive, and until the French arrived theatres were open only for a few weeks of the year, during carnival and sometimes for a short spring or summer season. In 1805, the cheapest seats at the Corea amphitheatre cost 10 and 20 *bajocchi* (the daily wages of a labourer) respectively, both for the daytime jousts and the evening festivals. A subscription for 10 shows in 1808 cost between 10 and 30 *scudi*[23] for the boxes, from two to 43 *scudi* for the palcattone, and 1.20 to 1.50 *scudi* for the cheap seats in the gradinate. 'Real' theatres were even more expensive than the Corea and prices went up during carnival: in 1795, a box seat at the stylish Argentina cost 20 *scudi*; in 1805, a third tier box at the Alibert cost 15 *scudi*; other boxes cost between 15 and 35, and after 1809, in the Napoleonic period, they cost 22 to 25 *scudi* – all amounts that a labourer would have to work for six months or even a year to earn.

Fortunately, there were plenty of cheap or even free shows in Rome. Romans, like most Mediterranean people, lived most of their lives out of doors, relaxing or working on their doorsteps, or coming into or out of the churches, or meeting at the *osterie* for food and drink. But above all, they met at the markets of the city – *piazze* in every neighbourhood where portable benches and tables were set up for selling fruits and vegetables, treats, clothing new and used, and every possible type of household goods. The papal government imposed rigid controls to keep prices within the reach of the people, but the results were often disappointing. Merchants either manipulated the quality or weight of goods (despite horrifying if seldom applied penalties like the *tratti di corda* or the galleys), or they simply wouldn't sell. In 1771, Alessandro Verri wrote to his father in Milan, 'Tell me something we are not short of. All prices are fixed, and are now too low, so that no one wants to sell.'[24]

---

22 Friz, *op. cit.*, p. 136.

23 A *scudo* was a gold or silver coin worth 100 *bajocchi*. See chapter 7 for monetary values.

24 Andrieux, *Daily Life in Papal Rome*, p. 73.

But in good years the great markets, and especially the Piazza Navona, were a veritable *cucagna*, a land of Cockagne, as this list of goods from a Roman market suggests.[25] There was:

Anise brandy old and new
Cakes and comfits [ciammellette fresche, e'l Confortino]
Oranges, lemons, figs, prunes, cherries
Leeks and radishes
Eggs, chickens, pigeons
Herbs and flowers
Cider
Tripe, sausage, fillet steaks
Frogs' legs
Pine-nuts, walnuts, hazelnuts, apples
Macaroni cooked over an open fire, to be sold by peddlers.

Tapes, pins, matches
Brooms, combs
Umbrellas, plates, pots, pans
Baskets, guitars
Women's hats and caps
Silk, cotton and fabrics
Tumblers, bottles, cups, glasses
Saddles and boots
Trunks, bags, purses
Rings, broaches, necklaces in gold and silver
Hats, caps, nightcaps
Shirts and shifts
Bird decoys
Canaries and finches and dappled mice for pets
Fans, ribbons, kerchiefs
Jackets, socks, trousers
Sauce pans, gridirons, toasting forks, skillets
Spindles and distaffs, sold by a turner
Lace and cambrick
Powder, soap, perfumed oils, scented wash-balls
Gloves
Lanterns and candlesticks by a tinsmith
Scissors, ear picks and tooth picks

Buying and selling was only part of the wonder of a market like the one at the Piazza Navona. Vendors brought customers, and customers brought acrobats and actors,

---

25 Calcott, *Three Months Passed in the Mountains North of Rome*, pp. 279-284. The scene this epic describes dates to about 1819, but the image is certainly a good deal older.

who brought more customers. Rome was full of free shows. The streets were filled with theatre the year around: even during Lent, street preachers held their audiences of sinners spellbound, and the churches were filled with elaborate and stirring sacred drama. During most of the year, the Piazza Navona and the market squares were open-air circuses. There were tight- and slack-rope walkers, 'magic ring' shows, 'magic lantern' shows, men and women who exhibited exotic animals like a mandril, a monkey and a camel. There were slight-of-hand artists, and 'scientific' exhibits such as mathematical (mechanical) figures and giants, dwarfs, and monsters – 'my niece who is of a gigantic size' or 'my son, born without arms or legs, aged nine'.[26] On the other hand, patent medicine salesmen and vendors of religious trinkets (both known as charlatans, or *ciarletani*) could always be depended on for a good show. Failing that, there were cockfights and dogfights, and at least one man who specialised in the arcane art of biting the head off a duck.

Magic lantern shows and puppet shows were especially popular. Sometimes these were offered in the streets and a hat was passed; more elaborate shows took place in rented lofts or rickety wooden buildings, for an admission price of a few *bajocchi*. The dialect poet Belli wrote about going to the Fiano (the best-known theatre for puppet shows): One went to enjoy the puppets in the early evening, when the *Vemmaria* sounded (the Ave Maria, or evening Angelus, at the first hour of the night), and then to the tavern for a meal. 'They have noses and eyes and hands just like ours', the viewer noted with wonder, and their casts of characters included the most famous of the Roman masques – Harlequin and Rugantino,[27] the Stutterer and the Doctor and the patent-medicine seller (*il Ciarletano*).

Corea Amphitheatre

On summer evenings, from the feast of St Peter (late June) until the end of the season, Romans went to the Corea, an amphitheatre built into the ruins of the ancient mausoleum of Augustus. The outdoor theatre had been set up as a money-making enterprise by the Marchese Corea, head of a Portuguese noble family. It was managed, as was the custom, by impresarios who committed to providing a season of entertainment in the hope of making a profit. Romans compared the Corea to the ancient Coliseum, and it specialised in the sort of outdoor spectacles one might have found in that venerable venue.

The August feast of the Assumption (later the emperor would appropriate this as the Feast of St Napoleon) marked the start of the bullfighting season at the Corea, a sport that combined the Portuguese tradition of non-lethal matches with their opposite, the savage medieval sport of bull-baiting. In the opening ceremonies, bull-fighters went to Macarese to select and test the bulls, which were then brought to the Porta del Popolo at night. People gathered along the streets for the parade – noblemen came out on horseback, accompanied by servants in livery carrying

---

26 The archives are full of *suppliche,* or applications to put on shows of all sorts.

27 Ruggantino, the most Roman of the *commedia dell'arte* characters, the arrogant one, first appeared towards the end of the eighteenth century dressed as a *sbirro* or policeman, with a two-cornered hat and a red jacket in the French style, and buckled shoes. See Verdone, *Le maschere romane,* pp. 36–39.

Dealing with bulls.

torches. In the arena, the bull was brought to a fever pitch of frustrated rage by various means, the most intriguing of which involved a man inside a padded wicker basket that was covered, and decorated, by a painted canvas. The basket-man leaped about taunting the bull, then retreated inside his shell to be tossed and rolled around the arena, more or less safe. Mannequins were sometimes dangled from ropes to egg the bull on to more ferocity. Bullfighters darted in and out, enraging the animal with jabs from sharp sticks or knives with coloured ribbons attached. The more daring grabbed the animal's horns, cowboy-style, and tried to drag it to the ground.

Famous fighters included Filippo Mazzoli, called Mazzoletta; a young man from Terni called Cinicella;[28] and Luigetto la Merla, evocatively called lo Zoppo, (the lame one). Lo Zoppo specialized in riding the animal three times around the arena, with spurs. The public especially admired any jouster who could light the little firecrackers that were tied to the bull's horns and tail, and place a gilt cardboard star on its head, winning the prize of 30 or 40 *scudi*.

Bulls and cattle were a source of endless fascination. Until the first municipal slaughterhouse was set up (in 1825), cattle were driven through the streets to the various butcher shops. Large crowds would gather to watch or help with what they called the *capate* – butting of heads. Bolder souls would get close to the cattle, shouting and hitting them, and driving them mad with alarm and fear, setting them dashing along the three roads leading out from the Piazza del Popolo (Ripetta, the Corso, and the Via Babbuino), in a sort of weekly Pamplona. There are reports of stampeding animals breaking into the church of San Lorenzo in Lucina, knocking down confessionals and overturning benches. Youths of Trastevere or Monti, or cowherds from Regola near the broken bridge, turned themselves into *toreros* for the day, indulging in the very dangerous sport of chasing the animals through the streets and into the courtyards.

---

28 As in Belli's sonnet 'La ggiostra a Ggorea', November 1831. See Rendina, *Roma di Belli*, pp. 34 and 44.

In 1804 Romans were entertained with a new sort of horse-race: horses with jockeys. A company of Englishmen, 'who race in this fashion' gave demonstrations at the Corea.[29] Even more eccentric amusements were available, and balloon ascensions could always be counted upon to sell tickets. Lady balloonists were popular, as in October 1811, when a Frenchwoman attempted a flight in honour of the birth of the King of Rome. Unfortunately, she ended up in the Tiber. As Fortunati reported, 'luckily there was a boat there which saved her, otherwise Madame would have drowned with her balloon.' Two months later, she tried again, taking off from the Piazza Navona. This time the balloon 'rose to a great height, and at about the 22nd hour [two hours before sunset] it came down in the plains of the *paese* of Tagliacozzo.'[30]

The craze for balloon flights had struck Rome in 1783, imported from France where this scientific enterprise provided all the thrills of the bull fights, with almost as much chance of dismemberment and death, along with the comforting assurance that this was, after all, science. The following year, no fewer than 13 amateur balloonists in Rome attempted flight; alas, all of them crashed.[31] In the autumn of 1813, the Corea management sponsored a truly spectacular aerodynamic feat, immortalised by Fortunati under the heading of 'Flying Buffalo!' Someone tried to send up 'a live buffalo and man on horseback. It worked very well, but then the ring broke, and the buffalo, the man, and the horse were all killed.' Fortunati does not mention any fatalities among the onlookers.[32]

Another, rather more tame, favourite amusement was promenading to the accompaniment of an orchestra. At a certain point in the evening, the centre of the arena exploded into the 'Bengal lights', one of the ever-popular fireworks displays. Such artistic fireworks displays and social occasions were put on during summer nights from the day after the feast of St Peter until the end of September.[33]

Public Houses and Coffee Houses

Taverns were the preferred retreat of the *popolo*, and there were many of them: one estimate is that there were almost 1,000 taverns in the city, or one for every 150 or so inhabitants, mostly concentrated in the central wards. There were no fewer than 10 in the Piazza Navona. Some of the taverns, especially the more rural ones, consisted of a hovel with a piece of board for a counter. Others were simply outdoor stalls with a few rough tables and chairs.

---

29 Fortunati, *op. cit.*, 9 January 1804.

30 Fortunati, *op. cit.*, 24 October and 22 December 1811.

31 Fiorini, *Catalogo delle Feste*, p. 212.

32 Fortunati, *op. cit.*, 19 September 1813.

33 Someone wrote on a print by Thomas: 'Non vi di danno ne danze ne giuochi ne rinfreschi: non si fa che passeggaire al suono di una musica che una grande orchestra esegue fino al momento in cui si tirano piccoli fuochi d'artificio piazzati al centro dell'arena e che vengono chimati *Fochetti*. Lo stabilimento e diretto da un'impresa; le porte si aprono all'avemaria e si chiudono alle tre di notte, quando il pubblico se ne va.' (There was no dancing or refreshments, people walked around the arena to the sound of music from a large orchestra, until the small fireworks, called *fochetti*, were set off in the centre of the arena. The establishment was run by an impresario; it opened at the Angelus and closed at the third hour of the night, when the public left.)

Bartolomeo Pinelli, *er pittor di Trastevere,* was the quintessential tavern artist. He made dozens if not hundreds of studies of life, love and amusements at the indoor and outdoor hostelries in and around his city. As a young man, after getting himself thrown out of his patron Levizzani's house, he spent a considerable time living rough and sleeping in tavern yards, paying his way with pornographic drawings to entertain the waiters and the customers. His tavern pictures often include a familiar sign, some version of which must have been exhibited in every tavern in the history of humanity. The standard Roman one seems to have been a painted rooster, with the words under it: 'When this rooster crows, then I'll offer credit.'

The staple of the *osterie* was local wine, the rough *vino romanesco,* produced in the hundreds of large and small vineyards in and around the city. The large vineyards were mostly owned by wealthy families or institutions like religious orders, and worked by hired labour. Other vineyards were not much more than garden plots, worked by families who drank half or more of their own produce. [34]

A somewhat superior sort of wine came from the *castelli romani,* the hill towns that surrounded Rome. Most of these were light white wines, and foreigners tended to prefer them (especially the wine of Orvieto). These more expensive wines were brought into town by wine carters, a daring and hardy group of men whose job was of very high status and often passed down from father to son (baby boys of wine carter families were baptised in water mixed with bran and wine). The luxury class of wine, the *vini navigati,* came from abroad, from Sicily or Corsica or even France. These wines had a high alcohol content, and were mostly enjoyed by the wealthy.

On average, Romans drank a good deal of wine, at least 2 hectolitres each in a year per person. They drank less aquivit (a sort of gin), but they were fond enough of that to support a whole class of wandering vendors who sold it by the glass in the streets at night. Aquivit was also sold in taverns, along with non-alcoholic concoctions made from citrus juices, vinegar, slightly fermented grains, or herbs. Few if any Romans drank beer. Some rich and or foreign people drank tea, but it was a taste more or less confined to the upper classes.

Taverns and Games

Favourite tavern games were *morro* and *passatella* – games that seem to have been designed to inspire fights, which often enough ended in fatalities. One diarist noted two killings on one day in two separate fights over games of *passatella,*[35] a drinking game of amazing complexity with a strong conspiratorial element. Some see its origins in the biblical story of the miracle of the wedding feast at Cana, where vats of water were turned into the best of wine, and brought to the master of the feast for distributing. There is a mad sort of logic in Romans taking a biblical parable and making a tavern game out of it, but the game, and the idea, is probably older than Christianity. Basically, a group of men and women club together to buy wine; one of them, the *conte,* has the right to name a *padrone* (boss) and a *sottopadrone* (deputy) who then make all sorts of

---

34 Gross reports that there were 172 vineyards in two Trastevere parishes alone (Santa Maria in Trastevere, and Santa Cecilia), almost all of them worked by hired peasant labour. Gross, *op. cit.,* p. 172.
35 Fiorani, *Riti, ceremonie, feste e vita popolare,* p. 284.

arcane and sometimes secret rules about who can drink, and how much; who can't drink at all; and who has to drink until he is falling down drunk. As the evening wore along, the likelihood of fighting rose exponentially, until it was a virtual certainty. Given the Roman habit of carrying knives or stiletto-shaped hairpins, the wonder is that any tavern evening ended without a death or two. Zanazzo mentions a friendly version of *pasatella*, but it is difficult to see how the game could be tamed.[36]

The other favourite tavern game was *morra*, a game with military overtones that is at least as old as the Roman legions. In its simpler form, the right hand, in a fist, was raised up to the level of the face then lowered rapidly, showing one to five fingers. At the same time, both players shouted out what they guessed the total number that would be made by adding the fingers shown (between zero and 10 with one hand or, using both hands, between zero and 20). The game required lightning reflexes, strong nerves, quick thinking, a sense for probabilities, and a knack for psychology, and the faster it was played, the better. Of course, quarrels were almost certain to occur.

There were hundreds of other games, games involving cards, or balls (like *bocce* or *ruzzola*), or swings, or dice, or counters, or nothing but the human mind; games that stressed muscle or hand-eye coordination, or keen wit. Many if not most of the games were good ways to gamble and get into fights.[37] Improvised poetry, declaimed to the tune of the mandolin, was another competitive sport, especially enjoyed at the great rural feasts of the autumn [see chapter 5].

The complexity of these games and pastimes is striking. They required fast and intricate thinking, and their main point seems to have been to reward *furbezza*, the cunning that had such a high survival value in the pre-modern world. Romans may not have worked in any Anglo-Saxon sense, but they certainly loved to be *busy*.

Coffee Houses

Coffee houses were the news centres of the day, where gossip spread like the *mal aria* (bad air) and was as difficult to suppress, where the latest *bon mot* from Pasquino was shared and copied out while the government (papal or imperial, it didn't matter) squirmed. There was the original, and still thriving, Caffè Veneziano, founded in 1725 and named for its Venetian founder. Located at the angle of a palace looking into the Piazza Sciarra, the café consisted of three shops connected together by archways broken through the walls and facing a fourth shop looking towards the Via del Caravita. It had two small rooms, one looking to the street and one in the back of the building. The *aquafresco* that it advertised was not cold water, or even fresh water, but rather a sort of vinegar that had been distilled there since 1725.

There were 10 or more other coffee houses, including the Caffè degli Specchi (of the mirrors), the Caffè Greco, the *Petracchi* café, and others known only by the street where they were found, or the building nearby, like Benedetti's 'café at Montecitorio'. Men of similar opinions tended to gather in one café or another. Benedetti reports

36 Zanazzo, *Tradizioni popolari*, II, p. 388.
37 The folk poet Gioachino Belli, who wrote in the generation immediately after Napoleon, celebrated these games in his sonnets, games like *calabraghe, bazzica, zecchinetto*, and the people who played *a boccia, ar piccolo, a piastrella, a more, a mora, a palla, a marroncino, a cavacedio, a tuzzi, a ghiringhella …'*

that in 1799 '…the urban guards, who are mostly fanatics … began to make arrests and requisitions. One of their favourite happy hunting grounds for traitors was that very café at Montecitorio, which has been especially mentioned for its illuminations when King Ferdinand entered Rome …'[38]

Closely related to the coffee houses were the inns, especially the inns frequented by foreigners. Rome, always a tourist city, long had a reputation for hospitality. In the sixteenth century, there were 113 *alberghi* or lodging houses; in the seventeenth, the number fell to 96, and by the end of the eighteenth century it was down to 75, but in the first years of the nineteenth century it was back up to 89. This number was supplemented by private lodging places, official or not – tourists rented villas, apartments, houses, rooms and even single beds.[39]

The literature of the eighteenth-century Grand Tour is full of accounts of inns. Winckelmann 'who had a weakness for broccoli in vinegar washed down by a bottle of Orvieto', invited his friends to a sort of *table d'hôte*, the first of its kind, at the inn owned by the cooks Franz and Robert Röstler. The famous Albergo dell'Orso, in view of Castel Sant'Angelo, was already in decline. Another old inn was the Albergo del Montone near the Pantheon. Roman inns had a well-deserved reputation for sleaziness, but by the end of the century some nice places were becoming available, in the style of the Germans or the French. There were German lodging houses near the Spanish Steps, one in the Via Condotti run by a man named Brendel and another in the same area (that is, the area of the Spanish Steps), run by Gottschwar. Most of the French *alberghi* were in the same area – the *locanda* of Monsieur Pio, near the Salita di San Sebastianello; the inn of Madama Stuarda located at the foot of the great stairway of the Trinità dei Monti (the Spanish Steps); and the Scuffiarina, known to Casanova, run by Anna Maria Lafont. The best, in the opinion of De Brosses, was an eating place called the Monte d'Oro (he sent his friend Neully a recipe for pudding from this one). A more modest French *alberghetto* was run by Monsieur Damont.[40]

Foreigners or artists or men of one political persuasion or another met in one or another of the many inns, lodging houses, coffee houses or taverns. There was the Dell'Arco, on the Corso, where the *decani* (employees of the cardinals) met to gossip; or the café of the English, on the Piazza di Spagna, where the *litterati* met and the tour guides congregated looking for business. German artists gathered at the Cafe delle Nocchie, run by Apollonia Nocchia, the widow of the painter Labruzzi, and her three sisters, Maria, Rosalia and Vincenza. The Germans, who couldn't pronounce their family name, called them 'noctuae', or night owls.

Picnics and Country Matters

Swimming in the Tiber
In the summer, Romans loved to swim in the Tiber, and had from time immemorial. Every year the Governor of Rome issued a proclamation to the effect that men were

---

38 Silvagni, *op. cit.,* I, p. 338, Benedetti diary, July 1799.
39 See also Friz, 'La popolazione', pp. 27–28.
40 Brigante Colonna, *Roma Napoleonica*, pp. 90–96.

not to bathe or swim, or go into the river for any other reason, without underwear; and in the neighbourhood of monasteries and convents, there would be no bathing, swimming, etc, even *with* underwear.[41] Women weren't supposed to swim or splash in fountains or in the Tiber at all, not even accompanied, on pain of 'penalties appropriate to their station'.

The imperial administration allowed women to swim or bathe, but under close police regulation, and in buildings erected for that purpose.[42] 'Bathing places for women shall be established, separate and at a distance from those for men, and to be reached by different paths from those of the men. Men are not to go to the women's bathing places, nor women to the men's.' Entrance fees were set relatively low, at five *bajocchi* (a quarter of a franc), though not so low, of course, as simply jumping into the river. People were not to bathe in the river itself, but only in 'enclosed and covered' bathing places; and it was still illegal to show oneself naked outside the bathing places. The structures were to be taken down in the autumn, at the end of what the government decided would be the bathing season.

The 'Poor Man's Villa'

Outings to the botanical gardens (the *Orto Botanico*) on the Janiculum were popular in sunny weather, when large numbers of people would spend the day playing cards or the *tombola* (a wheel of fortune gambling device). See-saws or swings were strung up for the little children, or for nubile girls who showed their ankles and flirted as they swung. Vendors sold *rosicarelle* (munchies, treats): pass-the-time peas, hardboiled eggs, carob fruit, chestnuts, *ciambelle* (rings of baked or fried dough), and honey-sucks. In the afternoon, after a meal on the grass, young people would dance the *saltarello* to the music of the *calascione* in twos or in fours, to the rhythm of tambourines and castanets.

The leaping Roman *saltarello* was a courtship ritual dance. The steps were small and rhythmic, emphasised by quick movements of the breast and shoulders, while the women waved an apron with one hand, or held it up in front with both hands. The dancers moved in tight circles, jumping on alternate feet. The leaps were athletic: the higher the leap, the more fertile the marriage, or the harvest. The French artist Thomas described the popular dance like this:

It is a complete scene of a declaration of love. Jumping and turning the one around the other, the dancers each express the passion they pretend to have, the wish to be attractive, joy or pleasure, jealousy and hope; at the end the dancer puts a knee to the ground so as to move his beloved, who starts moving toward him as she dances; when she bows and smiles, as if to ask for a kiss, the lover leaps up triumphant and another few lively steps conclude the pantomime. ... [A]s soon as one of the dancers is tired he retreats into the crowd and is instantly replaced by another; in this way men and women may extend the saltarello as long as they want ...[43]

---

41 Friz, *op. cit.*, pp. 137-8.
42 Regulations were issued by the General Director of Police, Olivieri; for example the one on 1 July 1810.
43 See Thomas, *op. cit.*, plate LVI, fn. 2. and chapter 5 for the Testaccio celebrations.

The nobility and the rich also indulged in music and dancing, and enjoyed much the same sort of outings as the *popolo*. But in the fine houses and theatres, the music tended to be of a more formal nature, and the dancing borrowed a good deal from international fashions.

Romans did not give dinner parties (though they were willing enough to attend them when foreigners did); the normal Roman social gathering among the propertied classes was the private *accademia* or the *conversazione*. These were traditionally held at specific hours: the *prima sera* gatherings, less formal and less grand, began at the first hour of the night, marked by the evening Ave Maria. Two hours later, the *seconda sera* receptions began in the great households, formal gatherings held in chilly marble rooms hung with paintings and draped with silks and velvets, with flowers and ornaments. When Cardinal de Bernis was the French ambassador, before the revolution, he held famous *conversazioni* on Tuesdays and on Saturdays, where he provided luxury and clever conversation and music. What the gatherings did not provide was food, or places to sit down. In the balmy days before the invasion, noble retainers sometimes circulated offering ices and sweetmeats; afterwards, the pickings were so lean that often they served nothing at all, not even sweetened water.

Less exalted households held gatherings dedicated to conversation, or dancing, or music. At mid-century the artist Cavaliere Ghezzi had regularly hosted a musical academy at which amateur and professional guests entertained one another with singing and instruments. What both the grand and less imposing *accademie* and *conversazioni* had in common was the love of cards and gambling, and few entertainments were possible without one or the other or both, despite laws attempting to curb them.

It was a very old custom for the Roman nobility to hold open house at certain times of year. On Sundays in October, the Borghese opened their villa at the Piazza di Siena for public entertainments that included *alberi della cucagna* (trees or posts decorated with good things to eat, which had to be climbed in competition to get at them), balloon flights, displays of elephants and other exotic animals, and chariot and horse races. On the lakes, there were boats with singers and instrumentalists; sometimes, people were allowed to hunt the ducks.

The Minor Arts

Whether or not eighteenth-century Rome had retained its status as the art centre of Europe, it was certainly a major centre for what were known as the minor arts: decoration, adornment, spectacle, souvenirs and knick-knacks. As such, it supported a large number of artists and artisans of all sorts. There were several perfectly obvious reasons for this. Rome, as a great Renaissance city, had perfected the art of civic and sacred spectacle; Rome, as the centre of Catholic Christendom, was full of churches, chapels and shrines that needed embellishment and patrons willing to pay for the best; Rome, as the great tourist destination of the eighteenth century, was a magnet for wealthy foreigners who wanted something nice to take home as a memento. In addition, Rome, as a pilgrim destination, was full of less prosperous but even more earnest foreigners who, along with many Romans, provided an endless market for devotional objects.

The tapestry factory at San Michele was state-run and trained skilled workers to make the great hangings that furnished and decorated the churches and palaces of the city. Like most projects of this sort in Rome, it was only marginally successful.

The goldsmiths and silversmiths of Rome were the heirs of Cellini and, like Cellini, most of them were not Romans. The goldsmith Luigi Valadier (father of the more famous architect) had a profitable sideline in miniature reproductions of antique statues and temples until he died in 1785.

There were potters and potteries that produced everything from cheap household wares decorated with a dab of paint or a *bas relief* squiggle or two, to fine porcelain and biscuitware made by men like Filippo Coccunos, who sold triumphal arches, pyramids and obelisks for the tourist trade. In 1785, Giuseppe Volpato, 'a prominent engraver and friend of Hamilton, Canova, and Angelica Kauffman', opened a factory that offered porcelain reproductions.

Portraits were favourite souvenirs, and most tourists tried to take home at least a sketch if not a finished oil. In quality, they ranged from life-sized masterpieces to caricature sketches on the backs of scraps of paper. The artists at the national academies supplemented their income by trying their hands at these – the most famous was Ingres. These academy artists tended to look down on portraits and yearned instead to make monumental History Art; but portraits paid the bills.

Really wealthy and important foreigners could invest in statuary, either portrait, or classical-style, or – if one were a Bonaparte – a combination of both, like Canova's monumental Napoleon as Mars the Peacemaker, or his immortal image of the lovely Pauline Bonaparte Borghese as Venus Victrix [see chapter 10].

Pilgrims favoured rosaries, crosses and crucifixes, little paintings of saints and martyrs (gruesome martyrdoms were much admired), blessed medals and cameos, and little statues of patron saints or figures from the *presepio* or manger scene like the ones that were sold by men like Bartolomeo Pinelli's father. Roman printers and engravers made charming and imaginative calling cards (*carte di visita*), business cards and book plates.

A whole new art industry sprang up towards the end of the eighteenth century, producing small bronze copies of classical statuary and famous buildings. Men like Francesco Righetti, the leading figure in this craft, and his close competitor Giovanni Zoffoli produced these to sell to middle and lower income tourists. Mrs Eaton admired the work of 'Hopmartin – a remarkably ingenious German – [who] executes models in bronze of the Triumphal Arches, Columns, Ruins, Ancient Vases, etc of Rome. He has executed a bronze model of Trajan's pillar, with the whole of the bas-reliefs accurately copied – an extraordinary work.'

Antiques and Jewellery

Other tourist items included antiquities of three sorts: real, badly faked and well faked. Eighteenth-century popes made laws against exporting antiquities without a licence, but in a city with an inept government and hopeless police force on one side, and hungry antiquarians and tourists with money to burn on the other, there was not much of a contest. The making of cameos and medallions provided any number of Roman and German gem-cutters with a good income. The respected artist Camuccini was the director of a factory that produced copies of famous paintings in micro-mosaic. Making pictures out of tiny chips of coloured stone was something of a Roman speciality. The Napoleonic Museum in Rome has a necklace, earrings, and broach set that belonged to Napoleon's sister Caroline, onetime Queen of Naples. The set consists of 30 tiny pictures, each showing a different detailed scene of country life and costume, complete with farm implements, dogs and furniture.

Roman women of all classes liked jewellery and ornaments, and brought them out for special occasions – and Roman popular culture provided plenty of these, from carnival and the October feasts, to weddings and christenings, to the feasts in honour of the local parish saint or one's own particular name-sake saint.[44]

Even the poorest girl boasted brightly coloured ribbons and combs to dress her hair, and it was the rare Roman who couldn't find a few silver pins to stick into the knot of hair at the back of her neck or the top of her head. The pins had names, according to the shape of the head. The *manufica* was a pin head shaped like a clenched fist with the thumb inserted between the index and middle finger – a very rude gesture indeed. The hairpins, famously, did double duty as stilettos when necessary. And the *manufica* would seem to have been especially appropriate for that purpose.

Sumptuary Laws
Sumptuary laws, in Rome as everywhere, limited ostentatious dress to the nobility – the idea was almost certainly to prevent social confusion. Clothing in the pre-modern world was an essential part of a man's or woman's identity. It said where you came from, and whether you were single or married, what sort of work you did, your age, your associations, your status, a whole array of facts that placed you securely in the Great Chain of Being. Wearing the clothing appropriate to another social order or – heaven forbid! – gender was a form of counterfeiting, an almost Dantesque sin of fraud. Being cut loose from all that could be a dizzying and unpleasant experience, and people, especially in the rural districts, clung to it well into the twentieth century. One of the most disturbing effects of the French revolution – abetted certainly by the soaring prosperity that industrialisation would bring – was to shatter the certainties that clothing once provided.

Sumptuary laws hung on in Rome as late as 1824, when an Edict on the Clothing of Women threatened fines and 'temporal penalties' (as opposed to spiritual ones, which could be as severe as the threat of excommunication) in the case of 'immodest and shameful dress' designed to arouse the indignation of decent folk.[45] Women were especially warned against clothing that, although it seemed to cover them, in fact was either tight, and thus revealed their figure, or clinging, thus revealing the shape of their legs. Showing or accentuating bosoms was not a problem – as one might expect in a culture where breast-feeding to the age of three or even four was unremarkable. Feminine legs and bottoms, on the other hand, were strictly private affairs. The ferocious penalties were promised not only to the offending women, but also to the 'fathers, husbands, employers or other heads of household who allow, or connive with, their women' to dress immodestly. It was all, of course, quite hopeless. And, like many Roman laws that promised the most savage of repressions, it was probably a dead letter from the

---

44 Cited in Ochiuzzi, *op. cit.*, p. 140.
45 'Edict on Women's Clothing' 1824, cited in *Il Museo di Rome in Trastevere,* p. 135.

start. When the Allies took the city and put an end to the Ridiculous Republic, they issued an order that priests should return to black clerical garb and that women should be 'decently dressed and covered', especially in church.[46] The order was unenforceable. Diarists noted glumly that scandalous, licentious, and disrespectful behaviour had become so common that after a while people simply closed their eyes to it. As Benedetti wrote in September 1798, just before the Republic's fall: 'When one sees young girls go about the streets of Rome dressed like Venus, one learns not to be squeamish.'[47]

Indeed, during the Republic, the *abbate* Benedetti had had a great deal to say about the new styles of clothing, and little of it was complimentary:

Two days ago people here began to dress in the French fashion. The three-cornered hats were exchanged for two-cornered ones, and pig-tails were cut off, and many are to be seen hanging against the walls of the city. It is well for me that I did not wear one. Coats are red or sky-blue; waistcoats, sky-blue or red. The knee-breeches have been lengthened until they fall over the shoes. Ladies have left off their high head-dresses and replaced them by turbans, and they have also done away with hoops, and now their skirts cling tightly around their legs. The prince has word from Naples that the king has issued an edict against this style of dress. Has he?[48]

Cutting off queues was probably less a sartorial statement in favour of the new government, than a protective measure. Clothing made a powerful statement, and could be not only incendiary but also hazardous to one's health, as proponents of revolution in Naples would soon discover to their regret: men who had cut their hair short and put on modern clothes found themselves pursued and killed by angry mobs. It was said that men who had cut their hair short took to wearing fake pig-tails. The mobs yanked on the queues of people suspected of revolutionary sentiments, and woe betided the man whose hair came away in the hand.

Later in the year, Benedetti described the formal attire of the new government:

The consuls were in gala carriages, escorted by the new Roman cavalry. They wore their state robes of black, lined with red, and trimmed with gold, black cocked hats, with tricolour plume on the top, and black boots. The ministers were also present, in black cloaks lined with red, black tunics and trousers, trimmed with red. They had hats like the consuls, but were distinguished from them in having a gold seal hung around the neck by a red and white ribbon. The senators had red cloaks, black tunics and trousers, and black caps with gold bands around them; the tribunes word red mantles and violet tunics and trousers, and their caps were like those of the senators, but without the gold bands. And thus the governing body of senators, tribunes, consuls, ministers, judicial commissioners, ediles, and questori *appeared more or less in masquerade attire.[49]*

The people in general did not face any such inconveniences, and continued to wear pretty much what they had always worn.

46 Fortunati, *op. cit.*, 9 October 1799.
47 Silvagni, *op. cit.*, I, 319 et seq.
48 *Ibid*, 24 March 1798.
49 *Ibid*, 26 September 1798.

CHAPTER FIVE
THE TURNING YEAR

It is appropriate that, in a city where clock time shifted with the changing hours of light and dark,[1] the year began with a moveable feast. Easter, the culmination and the beginning of the liturgical year, was tied to the ancient lunar calendar. It could occur on any Sunday between 22 March and 25 April, with the precise date determined by a complex set of astronomical observations.[2] The great feasts – Easter, Pentecost, Christmas, Epiphany, Lent, Easter and so on again – followed one another in annual cycles. Some, like Pentecost and Lent, moved with the date of Easter; others, like Christmas and Epiphany, were tied to calendar dates.

Some feasts celebrated events in the life of Jesus or his mother (like the baptism of Jesus, or the Annunciation/incarnation, or the Assumption of the Virgin); others were occasioned by celestial attributes (like the feasts of Our Lady of Divine Love or Our Lady of Mercy). Saints' days were omnipresent – every day was some saint's day, to be celebrated semi-privately (as a name day or the day of a patron of one's craft or guild or condition in life), or locally (every parish, district, and municipality had its saint or saints), or city-wide (for popular saints like Filippo Neri, Luigi Gonzaga and Charles Borromeo, special favourites of the young women; or city patrons like saints Peter and Paul; or powerful saints like St John or St Joseph). There were more frankly secular celebrations, too, like the harvest festival of the *ottobrate,* or the carnival that fell between Christmas and Lent. When the French arrived, they cut the festival days to the bare bones. This was certainly a practical step in terms of economics and productivity, but Romans resented it.

The many festivals were great favourites of artists and tourists, who have left us any number of colourful accounts. Among the most charming visual representations are those by Bartolomeo Pinelli, who knew them from the inside, and a series of watercolours by Antoine Jean-Baptiste Thomas, who spent 1817-18 in Rome at the French Academy and saw it all in one year.[3]

---

1   Roman time was counted on a 24-hour basis, beginning half an hour after sunset, which changed every day.
2   Simply stated, Easter is the first Sunday after the first ecclesiastical (though not necessarily precisely the first astronomical) full moon that occurs on or after the vernal equinox, which is set at 21 March.
3   See Rosetti, *La Roma di Bartolomeo Pinelli,* and Thomas, *Un an à Rome.*

Spring

Lent led to Holy Week, the commemoration of Christ's passion and death, and Holy Week culminated in the great spring celebration of Easter. The ceremonies began with the blessing and distribution of palm fronds on the Sunday before Easter, commemorating Jesus' triumphal entry into Jerusalem just before his death. Rome filled with pilgrims and with the curious. Barefoot and gaunt third order Franciscans poured into the city cheek by jowl with sceptical French scholars and English tourists agog to observe the near-pagan rituals of the papists. Mrs Eaton noted, on Palm Sunday 1817, that 'every hotel and lodging is full even to overflowing, with curious heretics; every church is full of devout Romans [she seems to have meant Roman Catholics].'[4]

Mrs Eaton was amused by the popish mumbo jumbo of Palm Sunday, but attended all of the ceremonies in the spirit of the anthropologist, and duly reported on what she saw:

The papal carriage made all of plate glass, within which Pius VII continuously blessed the crowd with 'a twirl of three fingers which are typical of the Father, the Son, and the Holy Ghost; the last being represented by the little finger';

The pope distributing dowries of 50 crowns each to young women, who did not, however, march in procession, probably because 'now that his finances are reduced, the number is necessarily more limited';

The pope dressed in scarlet and gold; the cardinals first in under-robes of violet, then 'in the most splendid vestments which had the appearance of being made of carved gold';

The blessing of the palms, as 'two palm branches of seven or eight feet in length, were brought to the pope who, after raising over them a cloud of incense, bestowed his benediction upon them';

A procession that she admits would have been impressive in St Peter's but, as it was held in the room off the Sistine chapel, lost its effect 'from the crowding and squeezing';

The reading of the Passion, followed by 'the usual genuflections, and tinkling of little bells, and dressings, and undressings, and walking up and down the steps of the altar, and bustling about …'

Mrs Eaton's cynicism notwithstanding, during Holy Week, Rome assumed an air of solemnity and mourning. Drums were muffled and papal troops carried their arms reversed, as at a funeral. Women dressed in black; jewellery and bright clothing were set aside. For this one week, boys ran from door to door, pounding on each with a hammer, to announce the times for the mid-day and evening Angelus – the bells, that marked the time during the rest of the year, could not be rung. [5] In the Sistine chapel, the *Tenebrae*, or shadows, liturgy lasted for four hours, as the lights were extinguished one by one to the reading of Scripture and singing of appropriate psalms.

Holy Week ended with the *triduum*, Holy Thursday, Good Friday and Holy Saturday, before exploding into the gluttonous joy of Easter. On Holy Thursday, the

---

4   Eaton, *op. cit.*, II, p. 244.
5   Zanazzo, *op. cit.*, p. 188.

pope officiated at the ceremony of the washing of the feet at St Peter's, and in every hospital and hospice of the city ladies and gentlemen competed for the honour of washing the feet of the poorest of the poor, and serving their supper. If carnival was a symbolic reversal of the social order, so was Holy Thursday.

On Good Friday the Passion and Crucifixion of Jesus were celebrated with austerity and with tears, especially at the Coliseum where pilgrims followed, barefoot, as the pope led them in the prayers of the Stations of the Cross.

Holy Saturday saw a series of popular rituals, all more or less connected with death and renewal. This was a day for ruthless cleaning. In the streets, the *scacciaragnaro*, whose speciality was cleaning out spider-webs, went around calling out 'Clean your houses, ladies …!' All worn out household items were discarded on that day, and anything that would make a lot of noise when it was broken – crockery, pots, plates, cups – was saved up especially for Holy Saturday. Pots and bowls were turned upside down over small charges of gunpowder, and blown to smithereens, to the cheers and shrieks of children. Guns were shot off to add to the pandemonium. In the evening, monks and priests came laden with holy water to bless the newly scoured homes.

In the churches there were special services. For Holy Saturday of 1797, the Oratorio of Caravita offered a live representation of the crucifixion, with 'lugubrious decorations and most tender music.'[6]

Then came the preparations for the great meal that would end the Lenten fast. Pork butchers, sausage makers, and vendors of cheese and butter turned artists and architects. Butter and ricotta were transformed into edible statues and statuary groups that looked like alabaster, with classical and biblical themes. Temples and palaces and columns and cornices were constructed of sausage and hams and cuts of pork, while mosaics and pavements were made of cheese and prosciutto and sparkling white intestines, all decorated with gold paper and lemons and rosemary and laurel leaves. By candle light and lantern light, the shops became a wonderland where the redemption of mankind was celebrated with the greatest joy that early modern man could imagine: wallowing in endless halls and vats of rich and delicious food. Paradise and the Land of Cockaigne overlapped.

On Holy Saturday the city began to tremble with the anticipation of resurrection and new life. At nightfall, the long ceremonies began. The candles, water and holy oils to be used in the coming year were blessed. The new fire was struck with a new flint in the dark church. Then the great pascal candle was lit, and the light spread to every corner of the building in ripples as it passed from candle to candle, hand to hand. Long readings from the Jewish scriptures and the New Testament traced salvation history, ending with the death and resurrection of Jesus. Finally, at midnight, all the bells of the city rang, the orchestras and choirs exploded into music, and everything burst into light and noise to celebrate the return of new life from the grave.

At home, the housewives prepared the great celebratory feast. This featured a huge cake of cheese and eggs, and a roast lamb, in memory of the paschal meal. The pope's Easter dinner was a lamb that had been selected and specially blessed on 21 January, the feast of the virgin martyr St Agnes (her name means 'lamb').

---

6   *Catalogo delle Feste* p. 254.

On 25 March, the feast of the Annunciation, dowries were distributed in the church of the Minerva to virgins who could use them either to marry, or to enter convents. As always in papal Rome, this relatively simple ceremony was played out on the public stage. The streets leading to the church were lined with soldiers with flowers or branches in their hats, while the windows and balconies overlooking the street were draped with yellow or red tapestries.

Summer

The first month of summer brought a number of important festivals, including the feast of Divine Love and the ancient summer festival of St John. June culminated with the illuminations and fireworks of the feast of the two patrons of the city, saints Peter and Paul.

The feast of Divine Love (*Divino Amore*) was celebrated on the Monday after Pentecost (50 days after Easter Sunday, between mid-May and mid-June).[7] Women saved money throughout the year to spend on a celebration of the Madonna of Divine Love, patroness of laundresses. When the day came, they would process to a shrine about twelve kilometres outside the city, down the Ardeatine road. Their hair and their hats were decorated with flowers, small pictures of the Madonna, bright ribbons and feathers, along with the artificial flowers called *tremolanti* (tremblers) that quivered when they moved because they were attached to thin, silvered wires.[8]

After Mass in honour of the Virgin, the pilgrims and their men went for lunch in the hill town of Albano. One of Bartolomeo Pinelli's illustrations shows a group of men and women gathered around a table at the tavern of the *Carciofolo*,[9] or artichoke (a popular song compared girls to artichokes: hard to get into, but tender and tasty inside). Their clothing identifies them as *minenti*, the wives and daughters of prosperous artisans and merchants. The central figure is a woman who stands between two tables, one arm raised in the classic position for declaiming: she is improvising a poem in honour of the occasion, a working class Corilla in an open air tavern Arcadia. When the eating and drinking, flirting and declaiming, praying and dancing, were finished, the highlight of the festival came: the break-neck carriage race back to the city.

---

7   Zanazzo, *op. cit.*, I, pp. 230–2. 'We'd go the day after [Easter], in the old days. In the morning, the women would get into carriages and go out for coffee, then they'd go out the San Giovanni gate. When they got there, they'd go to Mass and enjoy all the great miracles the Madonna would work – like lame men throwing their crutches away and walking, or possessed girls who vomited out the devil … then they'd go for a meal, and they'd cover their heads and their breasts and their hair, and even the horses, with flowers – *tremolanti* and roses. They they'd get in the carriages and go to Albano, and they'd have lunch and drink a lot of good wine, and they'd sing *ritornelli* … They would drive the carriages so fast that there was always a lot of trouble, carriages turned over and people hurt or even killed. When they got back to Rome, they would have ice cream …. Then the next Sunday, with the money they had left over, every *festarola* [a woman who took part in the festivities] would take another carriage ride down the Corso and have another outing outside the gates. They would all put their money together and the woman who kept it was called the *cassarola* (the cashier).'

8   Biagi et al, *Museo di Roma*, p. 99.

9   The harpists and singers from Abruzzi who plied the streets of Rome were called *carciofolari*, probably from the same song.

Corpus Domini (12 June) was the occasion for a week of city-wide celebrations as each Roman parish took its turn processing through the streets, with pride of place given to the confraternities who marched unmasked, with their finest banners flying. The confraternities were followed by virgins swathed in white, who received dowries; and by children, some dressed like little priests, others with angel wings. The child who had won the catechism competition to take the title of 'Emperor of Christian Doctrine' marched alone, in his finest clothes, with his medal proudly displayed.

The feast of St Anthony of Padua (13 June) included a procession honouring strawberries and strawberry pickers. In Thomas' illustration, 16 men struggle to carry a life-size wax statue of the popular saint who holds the infant Jesus in his arms, all inside a great gold lattice-work *macchina* lit by candles. A week later, 21 June, was the feast of the Jesuit founder Ignatius Loyola. The Jesuit order was suppressed for the best part of half a century, but their institutions and churches remained (often manned by former members of the order). Almost immediately after the fall of Napoleon, the pope re-instituted the Jesuit order. The day was especially marked at the church of St Ignazio, with illuminations and concerts.

The feast of St John, with its excursions outside the Porta del Popolo, marked the middle of summer. Roman women had a well-earned reputation for holding their own in taverns, but the feast of St John, like the October festival, was a special occasion for drinking. St John's Day was also the day for feasting on snails, called *vigne* because they were collected from the grape vines by boys who sold them in the city. John the Baptist was best known as the man who baptised Jesus, so this was the day when it was traditional to name godparents, men and women who stood as sponsors for a child and were thereafter considered important members of the family. A godfather was traditionally called a 'St John'.

The midsummer festival was, however, much older than Christianity, and it continued to carry darker and more ancient traditions. St John's eve was also called the Night of the Witches, and Romans had a lively and complex relationship with witches and witchcraft. This was the best day to buy a charm to protect one from the evil eye. It also was a day for rituals to identify one's future mate [see chapter 4].

The entire city was lit up for the 29–30 June feasts of saints Peter and Paul, the twin patrons of the city. The great bronze statue of St Peter at the basilica that bears his name was robed in scarlet silk shot with gold, crowned with a jewel-encrusted tiara, and illuminated by gold candelabra. In the evening the crypts and subterranean chapels under the basilica were open to the public.

In 1803, when Pius VII reigned in his city before the second French occupation, the day began with a Mass celebrated by the pope and his court. At sunset came the Vespers, sung by the vicar of the basilica. Then, as darkness fell, the city sprang into light with 'torches, firepots, lanterns and burning casks' at great palaces and ordinary homes alike.

Next came one of the most astonishing spectacles afforded by the pre-electrification world, and one that surely cannot be matched by mere electricity. This was the famous illumination of the dome and cross of St Peter's, first with the soft glow of paper lanterns and then, as three bells sounded (for the third hour of the night), the entire dome, cross, balconies, colonnade and facade, sprang into brilliant light as *festaioli* sprang down on ropes wielding torches to their right and left, to light the fire pots and send a sudden ripple of flame across the entire surface.[10]

One hour after the cupola flared into light, the great fireworks display began at the Castel Sant'Angelo. The deafening roar of the fireworks was supplemented by artillery, as the *girandola* lit up the great bronze angel and reflected in reds, oranges and yellows in the Tiber below. In June 1795, on the eve of invasion and revolution, preparations for the *girandola* came alarmingly close to blowing up most of the Vatican and the Borgo quarter, Sistine chapel, Michelangelo and all (a crack in the wall of the chapel is still visible). Fortunati reports the rumour that the explosion was caused by an anti-papal conspiracy gone wrong, but it seems more likely that it was simply an accident.[11]

July
25 July featured processions in honour of the Confraternity of St Anne, patroness of the *palafrenieri* or grooms (the word originally meant squires, attendants of knights). All along the route, windows were draped with tapestries, and when the image of their saintly patroness passed over the Ponte Sant' Angelo it was saluted by all the guns of the Castello – in Rome, gunpowder seems to have retained its original, Chinese, purpose: making loud noises to attract the attention of celestial beings. Thomas described this event in some detail, as a typical example of processions in Italy.[12] First came two grenadiers and drummers, followed by standard-bearers, lantern-bearers and a large group of valets in full livery. After them came more drummers, and the great banner of the confraternity, carried by men decked out with ribbons and followed by the confraternity members and penitents. One of the penitents (who paid cash for the privilege) struggled under the weight of a processional cross (during the Mass that ended the ceremony he would kneel and attempt to balance the cross in his teeth). After the penitents came another cross, carried under a fringed canopy. A military band followed the confraternity members, and after the military band came virgins, and little boys dressed as priests. Then, in order: the mace-bearer; the master of ceremonies for the event; a choir, with instrumentalists; a reliquary of St Anne, carried by a priest, a bishop, or even a cardinal. Papal grooms dressed in red followed the reliquary. Finally there was a large platform, carved in wood and gilded, carried by 24 porters, and on the platform two wax figures dressed as St Anne and her daughter, the Virgin Mary.

For the Festival of the Tree Trunk in Trastevere on 16 July, a wooden statue of the Madonna del Carmine was taken in procession through the streets.[13] Young men vied for the honour of carrying the heavy crucifix, the 'Tronco' (tree trunk) and the standard, and of carrying the wooden platform on which the statue was exhibited. The proceedings involved a great deal of masculine display, feminine admiration and frequent stops for liquid refreshment.[14]

---

10 *Catalogo delle Feste* p. 267, and Biagi et al. *Museo di Roma in Trastevere*, p. 105. The *girandola* tradition probably began in 1480 to celebrate the anniversary of Sixtus IV's election.
11 Fortunati, *op. cit.,* 28 June 1795.
12 Thomas, *op. cit.,* p. 31.
13 Rossetti, *I bulli di Roma*, pp. 21–22.
14 This festival has blended into the modern Trastevere 'festa di Noiantri'.

August and September

August was (and still is) holiday time, the time of *ferr'agosto*. On the fifteenth of the month, the feast of the Assumption, all of the street-corner shrines were illuminated, along with the houses near them. On a less pacific note, the Assumption also marked the start of the bullfighting season at the Corea amphitheatre.

Coincidentally, mid-August was also the feast day of an obscure Egyptian hermit and perhaps martyr. His name did not appear in the universal calendar of saints but he was well enough known, in Corsica at least, that the second son of the Buonaparte family was named for him. After Napoleon became emperor in 1804, he ordered that the feast of St Napoleon be made a holy day of obligation (when Catholics are obliged to celebrate by going to Mass) in France, and special lessons on his life and martyrdom were introduced into the official prayer book of the Church. When Rome came under imperial command in 1809, efforts were made to replace the Assumption there with the feast of St Napoleon, but they met with little success outside of official circles, despite considerable expenditure.

On weekends and feast days during August, the drains in the great fountains of the Piazza Navona were stopped, with the result that the entire piazza was flooded to a depth of two or three feet. Carriages and horseback riders splashed about in the water, while boys dived for coins and the ladies and gentlemen who lived in the houses around the square looked on from the windows.

Late on mid-summer afternoons, professional athletes put on handball matches in an arena near the Four Fountains on the Quirinal. These games were extremely popular, and several artists have left us pictures of the players. They wore studded armbands that look less like athletic equipment and more like a particularly vicious sort of medieval armour, akin to the spiked mace or the iron maiden. The studs were, in fact, wood rather than metal – but given the level of casual violence in Roman life, handball looks like yet another invitation to disaster.

The *coccomeri*, or watermelons, arrived in mid-summer, and every square in the city had vendors who set up tall display steps decorated with wet greenery to keep the sweet, red fruit cool. There was a summer 'watermelon festival' which was banned after 1870 because too many people drowned diving for melons, or were caught in the wheels of the mills that lined the Tiber.

August and September were dedicated to the Madonna and on Sundays there were special feasts for the local *madonelle* – the Madonna of Purity, the Madonna of Grace, of Good Counsel, of Sorrows, of the Annunciation, of the Immaculate Conception; Madonna with the Child Jesus, Madonna Enthroned, Madonna of Divine Love or Mother of the Redeemer; Madonna of the Valley, or the Orchard, or the Arch or the Oaks. Each parish or neighbourhood had its own sacred image and its own festival in her honour. These were marked by the usual drapery and illuminations of nearby houses; by music that could vary from a few neighbours or passers-by singing hymns or litanies alone or with a lute or guitar, to full orchestras and choirs; and by distributions of food and wine; and always there were fireworks, depending on the wealth or the vanity of the sponsoring individual, family, or corporation.[15]

---

15 Aslan, *Le Madonelle.*

On the evening of the feast of the birth of the Virgin (8 September), street preachers set up impromptu vigils and appealed for contrition and repentance.[16] The missionaries were usually accompanied by robed and masked penitents who held a large crucifix, painted in realistic and gruesome colours. Other penitents stood around the crucifix with lanterns. The preachers exhorted their listeners from platforms covered with tapestries, encouraging the penitent and pointing out for scorn those who seemed to resist. When a large enough number had gathered and been brought to tears by the impassioned pleas of the preacher, they were led into a nearby church where he heard their confessions and then led them in prayer.

October
October is the month of harvest and vintage, the month of the *ottobrate*. For Romans, every Thursday, Sunday and feast day in October was an excuse to pile onto open public conveyances called *carrettelle* to go to Monte Testaccio, where they ate, drank, danced the *saltarella* and came back in the condition that Stendhal described: 'they sang, they waved their arms about, and everyone was drunk, men and women.'[17]

The *carrettelle* were open, barrel-shaped vehicles, more cart than carriage, looking rather like Cinderella's pumpkin-coach, and all decorated with ribbons, bells and flowers. Three women sat up high in the back, striking tambourines and singing suggestive songs; in the carriage proper up to six women sang along with the refrain; and high up in the post of honour next to the driver sat the prettiest, her ankle-length skirts blowing in the wind (the drivers always drove too fast) showing her bright stockings. Women of any class, however economically strait, managed to get finery for the festival days, even if every *bajocco* had to be squeezed, even if the vital household goods had to take the familiar trek to the Monte di Pietà to finance the earrings, the necklace, the gay striped scarf or the brilliant feather to top her hat.

The traditional destinations for the outing were the gardens belonging to the princely Borghese family,[18] or country inns of Monte Testaccio (from the Latin *testae*, shards).[19] These inns – often no more than rough benches and tables set out under the trees – served wine that had been stored in the cool grottos in the hill made of amphora shards.

Romans didn't have to go as far as Testaccio or the Borghese gardens to enjoy the fine October weather, and they didn't have to spend even the few coins that the rough wine and simple food laid on by the open-air inns cost. Any arch or doorway would do to set up a *canofiena* or a *cantalena*, a sort of improvised swing or see-saw made

---

16 Thomas, *op. cit.,* p. 36.

17 *L'Ottobrata: Una Festa Romana,* the catalogue for a 1990 exhibit, edited by Giovanna Bonasegale, offers an extensive look at this festival. Stendhal's comments were made in 1827, but earlier and later visitors alike describe similar scenes.

18 The Borghese gardens were traditionally open to the public, but when Camillo Borghese married Pauline Bonaparte they went to live in Florence, and the gardens were closed. It was only after Camillo's death that his brother and heir, Francesco, extended the gardens to the Porta del Popolo and greatly improved them, and again opened the gardens to the people (as they remain today).

19 Testaccio is an artificial hill made up of shards of broken amphorae (the ancient equivalent of the packing case) that piled up over the centuries from the Tiber-side *emporius,* the great Roman wholesale market where oil, grain and goods from all over the empire came ashore.

up of a simple plank supported by ropes. Like much of popular life, it could be made into an occasion for flirting. Pinelli's drawings show girls who have set the *canofiena* swinging in a wide arch (every child knows how to do that with coordinated movements of the knees). The girls are laughing, singing or chanting to the rhythm of a tambourine, while the young men cluster around, hoping that a gust of wind will lift the skirts even higher than the motion of the swing has already done.

November

The sensual delights of the harvest festival were quickly followed by the reminder that death inevitably follows life, as sorrow follows joy and joy follows sorrow. During the Octave of the Dead in November, long lines of people waited to go through the crypt of the church of Santa Maria dell'Orazione e Morte in Via Giulia. This was the base for a confraternity whose members specialised in burying and praying for the anonymous dead found in the countryside. In November, members of the confraternity collected alms while visitors got an edifying thrill out of the lighting and decorations made of human bones, and the *sacre rappresentazioni* (mystery plays or *tableaux*).

In 1801, the Confraternity of Prayer and Death featured an allegory of original sin. Adam and Eve were seated on one of the slopes of the artificial mountain, with a sarcophagus between them to remind anyone who might have forgotten that death had entered the world with these two original sinners. On top of the mountain stood the Tree of Life, with the serpent twined around its trunk and the skeletal figure of death at its base.[20]

The representation for 1802 featured another mountain, this time Mount Purgatory. The top of the mountain opened up into three arches, through which one could see a great crowd of penitent souls in the flames. One of the souls was shown in the act of being fished out of the flames by a cherub. Taking the purged sinner by the arm, the cherub gestured towards the heavens in sign that she was now on the way to her eternal reward, thanks to the prayers of good folk like those in attendance. On top of the mountain stood the figure of Justice, with her scales and her sword, while the whole edifice was outlined with candelabras.

Another favourite November venue was the cemetery attached to the hospital of the Santo Spirito. Thomas described the usual burial procedure there:

Every evening at half an hour after sunset, those who have died in the hospital of Santo Spirito in Trastevere are taken to the cemetery by confraternity members dedicated to this corporal act of mercy. They walk slowly through the district, chanting in a monotone, 'Long live the Cross'. At the cemetery, there are 21 graves for adults and three for children. The graves are opened in turn, and the naked dead are lowered by chains, while the priests recite litanies and make the circuit of the stations painted on the walls.

During the Octave of the Dead the cemetery was the setting for devout *tableaux vivantes* (or, more accurately, *tableaux mortes*). Some consisted of edifying scenes

---

20 *Catalogo delle Feste*, p. 264.

from Scripture or the lives of the saints, featuring appropriately dressed wax figures and great attention to realistic detail (especially blood). In 1813 there was a famous Last Judgement played out at the cemetery, with painted scenes of hellfire in the foreground. A wax angel floated on high, on the point of sounding the Last Trumpet, and the recently dead, draped artistically around the open graves, took the parts of those on the point of being resurrected.

According to ancient custom, beans were used to honour the dead, and given or tossed over the shoulder in a ritual to placate those spirits who might want to annoy the living. By the seventh century, the Church had begun to institutionalise and Christianise many of these customs. In Rome, 2 November was commemorated with *fava* beans in all sorts of guises – convents and monasteries passed out plates of them to the poor; fasting monks broke their fast with mashed bean soups and beans in broth; lovers sent little packs of candied beans to one another, or as treats for children. More elaborate confections of candied beans could be bought from the vendors who filled the Piazza del Pasquino, near the Piazza Navona.

Christmas and Epiphany[21]

Christmas at Ara Coeli
Romans started celebrating Christmas on 4 December when the feast of St Barbara, patroness of cannoneers, was announced (as one might expect) by a fusillade from the Castel Sant'Angelo. On 8 December, the feast of the Conception of the Virgin Mary, a great procession descended the high, shallow stairs leading from the Ara Coeli to the capitol. Hundreds of Capuchin monks and white hooded and robed penitents marched slowly in two rows, carrying crosses, lanterns and confraternity banners. Behind them, escorted by papal troops in their most gorgeous uniforms, came the statue of the Virgin herself, carried on the shoulders of 20 men.

The Presepios
The start of the Christmas season was the signal for people to assemble their manger scenes. Every household with any pretensions to decency had some sort of *presepio*, where at least the baby Jesus and his Mother could accept the family's devotions. The larger and more prosperous households could dedicate an entire room to re-creating the scene at Bethlehem, complete with mountains, hills, lakes and palm tree forests. The potential cast of characters was immense and could include the Holy Family themselves, of course, plus the shepherds and kings, and the standard animals: donkey, camels, oxen and an infinite number of sheep, lambs, and the occasional goat. Dogs and cats could also appear. Fishermen and farmers could come with the shepherds, bringing the tools of their trade. Townspeople, too, flocked to the scene, carpenters and bakers and blacksmiths, weavers and spinners, and women with baskets of fruit or eggs; innkeepers and exotic travellers, and Roman soldiers and Biblical figures (even Herod was known to put in an appearance); musicians (human and/or angelic), oriental potentates, battalions of saints, prophets and sibyls. And perched majestically on

---

21 Much of this from Rossetti, *La Roma di Bartolomeo Pinelli*, pp. 135–141 and Thomas, *op. cit.*, pp. 43–4.

rooftops or kneeling devoutly by the manger or swooping joyously overhead with or without celebratory banners, were the choirs of angels. Every church had an altar set aside for a manger. By the beginning of Advent, an altar would be blocked off by draperies or scaffolding, and behind it mysterious scufflings and thumps and squeaks would hint at the marvels being arranged. Rivalry among churches and orders could be intense. The Jesuits were particularly skilled at making these theatrical displays. On Christmas Eve, the scene would be unveiled for the delight of the faithful. Throughout the Christmas season (which lasted until Epiphany) people would make the rounds of the *presepios*, admiring and comparing, and taking notes for next year. Thomas describes these as little theatres, often made like 'optics', with scenes receding into the distance at the back, mountains or fields, and especially towns, sometimes seen through an open 'window' at the rear of the scene.

The most famous of the *presepios* was the one at Ara Coeli, which featured the miraculous *bambino*. There life-sized wax or wooden figures surrounded the baby, first among them the Virgin, gorgeous in laces and cloth of gold and jewels ('in her best blue satin dress and her topaz necklace', according to the staunchly Protestant Mrs Eaton).

Crowds flocked to see all of the manger scenes in the various churches – it remains a popular Roman Christmas outing – and at Ara Coeli the visit included preaching by children. Boys and girls alike, from all stations and classes, were hoisted one by one up onto a nearby altar to deliver their little sermons. Thomas reports that the sermons usually began with this verse: 'Tonight, at midnight, between the donkey and the ox, a beautiful baby is born, all fresh and dear, who is called the Christ.' (*Sta notte, a mezza notte, tra l'asino e il bove, e nato un bel bambino, ben fresco e ben carino, il quale Cristo si chiama.*)

The *bambino* of Ara Coeli is[22] an olive-wood figure carved, it is said, from an olive tree on Gethsemene in Jerusalem by a Franciscan before the fifteenth century, when it first appeared in Rome. At 60 cm, it is somewhat larger than the average newborn. The figure was painted miraculously, in response to the Franciscan's prayers. When Romans fell ill beyond the feeble powers of medicine, they called for the blessing of the *bambino*, and the little figure was carried to them in his own sumptuous carriage. If the patient recovered the baby Jesus was given the credit, and rich *ex voto* gifts were showered on the *bambino*. When the French troops arrived in 1798 they considered it their revolutionary duty to despoil this tiny representative of theocratic tyranny of his gold, silks and precious stones. They were, it was believed, on the point of adding the olive-wood infant to their fuel supply when a certain Severino Patriarca rescued him and took him to the nuns of San Cosimato in Trastevere, who hid him until it was safe to return him to his manger on the following Christmas.[23]

The Pifferari

The *pifferari*, or bagpipers, usually worked in pairs, one piper and one flutist, who also sang. They trooped from the Abruzzi into Rome to serenade the Madonnas of

---

22 Or was – the figure was stolen late in the twentieth century and has not, to the author's knowledge, reappeared.
23 Pocino, *Le curiosità di Roma*, pp. 40–42.

the street-side shrines every Christmas and were supported by not-so-voluntary donations of locals, who gave them small amounts of money for playing their novenas (nine-day series of songs). They not only kept people awake (Madame Vigée-Lebrun was especially tormented by them), they were also prone to insert bawdy, satirical verses into their hymns. An especially favoured topic was the questioning of the virtue of the wives of citizens who had failed to subsidise the concerts.[24]

Mrs Eaton reports being wakened out of a feverish sleep by the sound of bagpipes, which she describes as 'a horrible disturbance'. On finding that they were serenading the Madonna, she noted that 'if the Virgin has any ear for music, she must be deafened by this piece of their courtesy'. Mrs Eaton did condescend to approve of the music of the *carciofolari*, the harpers, which she found 'simple, very peculiar, perhaps very ancient, and certainly very sweet', but other than the pipers and the harpers, she heard 'no street music in Rome'. Presumably, the playing of the lute and guitar, the singing and the tambourine, did not qualify, or maybe she never spent enough time among the *popolo* to hear any of it.[25]

Even the more tolerant Stendhal found it difficult to appreciate the music of the pipers:

It has been 15 days since the pifferari [...] have been waking us up at 4 in the morning. It's enough to make a man hate music. They are rough countrymen covered in goat skin, who descend from the mountains of Abruzzi and come to Rome to serenade the Madonnas. They arrive 15 days before Christmas and leave 15 days after: they get two paoli for a nine-day serenade, evening and morning. Anyone who wants to be admired by his neighbours, and not be accused of liberalism by the parish priest, pays for a couple of these serenades.

If it was extortion, it was profitable. Pipers could take as much as 100 *scudi* home to Abruzzi after a season's serenading.

Epiphany

Romans did not celebrate New Years' day except as a day when valets and workers solicited year-end tips. The first day of January was part of the Christmas season, which reached its climax on Epiphany, or Twelfth-night, 6 January. (The first 12 days of the year, of which Epiphany marked the middle, were considered especially meaningful, relating to the 12 months of the year.)

Epiphany was the last day for viewing the *presepios*. At Santa Maria in Ara Coeli, the miraculous *bambino* was taken from the manger and returned to his customary altar in a splendid procession that made its way up and down the steep stairs leading from the Capitol not once, but three times. At the head of the stairs, the city and the assembled crowd were blessed three times with the Holy Infant. All the windows of the surrounding houses, as was always the case on festivals and special occasions, were decorated with scarlet draperies fringed with gold or silver.

Epiphany was also the day for giving engagement rings.[26]

---

24 See also Biagi et al. *Museo di Roma in Trastevere*, p. 48.
25 Eaton, *op. cit.*, II, p. 325.
26 Biagi et al. *op. cit.*, p. 91.

During the days leading up to Epiphany, culminating in the day itself, there was a great children's fair held at the Piazza Sant'Eustachio, near the Pantheon, as well as the usual markets and entertainments in the Piazza Navona. The main attraction was the *befana*, a hag dressed in black, usually played by a man. The *befana* brought (and still brings) stockings stuffed with almonds, oranges, nectarines, dried figs and sweets to good children, and a stick with which to beat the bad ones. The wife of the Old Year, she was both a witch (Romans were terrified of witches) and a good fairy – in common with all women, you could never be quite sure about the *befana*.[27] Sometimes the *befana* sported two fake legs, with which she pretended to dance, leap, and do the splits. Mrs Eaton says that the children were terrified as well as hopeful, and always left out a portion of their supper, 'lest she should eat them up'.

Blessing of the Horses

The 17 January is the feast of St Anthony, protector of flocks and domestic animals. His feast day was one of the first possible dates for the start of carnival, and was also a day associated with the slaughter of pigs, which was a carnival activity. St Anthony was honoured by the blessing of the horses. Great households starting with those of the pope, the cardinals, and the nobles, brought their horses to be blessed; so did everyone else, especially people like carters who depended on the animals for their livelihood. By the end of the eighteenth century, the horses had been joined by a rich variety of working animals and pets.

Mrs Eaton attended the blessing and considered it to be 'one of the most ridiculous scenes I have ever witnessed, even in this country' – the streets were thronged with 'multitudes of horses, mules, asses, oxen, cows, sheep, goats and dogs' all decorated with ribbons and finery, and all brought by a fine variety of owners and drivers, from the 'well-dressed in very handsome equipages' to rough countrymen and families of the *popolo*. While the blessing was normally for horses, it was 'equally efficacious, and equally bestowed, upon all quadrupeds', so that there was 'scarcely a brute in Rome, or the neighbourhood' that had not been blessed.

Carnival

Carnival time in Rome, the period when it was legal for the theatres to remain open, began with Epiphany (or slightly earlier, in years when Lent came early), but the public celebrations reached their climax in the octave, or eight days, before Ash Wednesday. On Saturday the cobble-stones of the Corso were covered in sand, and the palaces that lined the long, elegant street were draped in rich fabrics. Scaffolding and stands with seats were erected, and those too were covered in festive drapery. When the bell announcing the start of carnival rang, a large number of *sbirri* attempted to keep the traffic in order while the carriages lined up for the opening cortege. (The police were also there to discourage pickpockets, and inappropriately dressed maskers – that is, maskers in satirical outfits representing clerics.) Once the opening procession was over, the carnival was officially declared open, and

---

27 'Befana' is almost certainly a corruption of 'Epifania', or Epiphany. The stockings she carries are a potent symbol of the female: *Farsi tirare la calzetta* (to pull down her stocking) means to deflower.

sanctioned pandemonium reigned. Everyone wore some sort of costume or at least the hint of a costume – Mrs Eaton noted that 'the proportion of masques here is far greater than at Naples …'. Cross-dressing was popular, and girls liked to dress up in country costumes or as 'Jewesses, because then they may accost whom they please without any breach of decorum.'[28] The most popular costumes were the figures from the traditional *commedia dell'arte*, especially the clowns.[29]

Thomas gives us this account:

Maskers may not take to the streets until after the hour of the morning office in the churches. At 20 hours (one hour after midday) the bell of the Capitol gives the signal for pleasure. This famous clock, which has been sounded for extraordinary circumstances, like the death of a pope or his election, advises maskers that they may go out in public. At this signal, troops gather along the Piazza del Popolo, shape up and, to the sound of music, line up along the Corso to the Piazza Venezia; from there, different detachments block the entrance to the roads leading from the Corso; it is a unique spectacle that presents itself along this road at 22 hours and a half (3:30 in France); everything is animated, everything breathes pleasure; a masked ball is often less attractive, and the intrigues there could not be more piquant. The pavement of the Palazzo Ruspoli is frequented by good society, and chairs can be rented there for a high price. It is along this part of the Corso that the funniest and most playful scenes take place. Then, little by little, the Corso fills with people and carriages; it becomes the meeting place for all of Rome. All along are stands and boxes, covered by tapestry; the windows of the houses and above all the loges of the palaces are ornamented with tapestries and draperies trimmed with fringe, which give the street a festive air. The carriages go in two opposite directions; those of the Roman princes, pulled by six horses, having the sole right to go between them. … Cavalcades are forbidden; they would be difficult to do without danger to the crowd. Some dragoons necessary for good order are the only horsemen who can remain on the Corso; and they move only with infinite caution.

Among the disguises, one finds a large number of peasants from the Roman States, brilliant with […] gold and silver and ribbons of all colours; clowns and pierrots, whose dress is most flattering for women; madmen dressed in chemises; Jewesses always armed with pins, which they use to attach bits of fabric or ribbon to clothing, sometimes with the intention of reclaiming them at a ball later; gardeners carrying a sort of flexible ladder by means of which they send letters or flowers to ladies on their balconies; clowns, many of them with people tied to the cord they use for a belt […] The ladies often wear little panniers filled with flowers and candies which they offer to their acquaintances.…

Carnival also meant, as it had in ancient Rome, the public execution of justice. Capital executions were relatively rare in the city by the end of the eighteenth century, but when there was at least one death sentence handed down during the year,

---

28 Eaton, *op. cit.*, II, p. 318.

29 However, when the Neapolitans occupied Rome during the carnival of 1800 the Neapolitan governor gave a public ball at the Aliberti theatre which was to be free to all maskers *except* those masked as *commedia* figures like Harlequin, Punch, Pantalone, Dr Brighella, and so on. Maybe he was just tired of them.

execution was often delayed until carnival time. Lacking that, there were the institutions of the *cavaletto*, and the *somaro*. Thomas:

Usually carnival in Rome is preceded by an execution. When this does not happen, in certain quarters of the city there is a parade of one or more condemned to the galleys. The guilty one is placed on an ass (somaro); his feet are tied with a cord under the belly of the animal; a collar of strong leather is placed around his neck to make him hold his head up high; his hands are tied behind his back; his chest is covered with a board on which is written his name, his crime, and his sentence; around him are hung the tools he used in robbery, and the objects he stole, evidence used in convicting him. The ass is led through the streets by an executioner; another opens the way, holding in his hand the nerf-de-boeuf with which one beats those condemned to the cavaletto. The executioner walks behind the guilty man; if there are several somari following the first, they are led by men taken from among the people, covered with the habit of penitents, made of sack cloth.

Carnival licence never went quite over the edge, the chaos was always of the sort that could be called back. Some jokes were licit, some were not, and anyone who forgot where the line lay was reminded by the fact that the *cavaletto* platform was generally in plain sight during this season. 'Obscenity' was never permitted, though this was a flexible concept and things of a scatological nature that could be done at carnival might curl the hair of a more delicate generation. Cross-class, cross-gender, and even cross-generational mockery could reach a high pitch, but overt political criticism of the current regime was not permitted. As Thomas observed in 1818:

The morning of the first day of carnival the scaffold is erected in a place near a place of amusement. … at night, fiaccoli [torches or fire pots] are placed at each end of the cavalletto. On the scaffold is a sort of prie-dieu with stocks secured by a vice, and the arms and legs of the penitent are secured, with his back and kidneys to the executioner. He, armed with a nerf-de-boeuf, lays on the number of blows prescribed … The magistrate, charged by the police, can condemn and execute [that is, whip] on the spot anyone who has disturbed the peace, or insulted a woman. Followed by a dragoon, he goes by horse up and down the Corso all the time of masking.

(Thomas quickly reassures his audience that foreigners who disturb the peace are not subject to this rough and ready justice. Instead, they are taken to prison until their ambassador can come and retrieve them.)

The Corso was packed with carriages, riding up and down with their costumed passengers, driven by coachmen dressed like women, picking up 'men' (that is, women dressed as men) from the crowd. Mock battles raged, with whitewashed bits of *pozzolana* called *confetti* for ammunition (at one time the missiles had actually been bits of candy, as the name suggests). Thomas:

The confetti are thrown from carriage to carriage, and from the balconies of the palaces. Often a masque will accost you and offer you confetti, or throw it at you. From this has come the other custom of throwing confetti made with [tufa] and as hard as bits of plaster. The battles with confetti *are very pleasant; after using up their ammunition, the victor and vanquished are often whiter than the walls. If some persons take it to excess, the games which disturb the peace are forbidden.*

These scenes of pleasure and folly last until it is time for the horse race. At 23 hours, on the Piazza Venezia, two boxes are placed, corresponding to two others placed at the Piazza del Popolo. This is the signal to stop any more carriages from entering the Corso. Half an hour later, the same signal is given to tell the remaining carriages to leave; this is done in less than three minutes, the carriages being obliged to take the first roads they meet to their right. ... Then the balconies, the windows, the sidewalks, the streets are filled with the crowd, and everyone waits for a new signal.

The highlight of each day was the race of the *barberi*, riderless arab horses that were urged along the Corso from the Porta del Popolo – as if the screaming crowds were not enough to terrify them – by lead balls with spikes attached to their harness, devices that bounced as they ran and made them run faster. Disasters were frequent – in 1801 the horses collided with a picket of Neapolitan cavalry – but the race horses that stayed on their feet kept running until they reached the Palazzo San Marco at the end of the Corso, where they were stopped by padded barriers and recaptured by grooms dressed in carnival finery. The owner of the winning horse received an ornate banner, the *palio*, which he draped across the back of the victorious animal. He also received a prize of money, but since he was expected to treat the city to free wine, bread and meat in celebration of his win, the race rarely produced any financial gain for the owner.

The public confusion came to an end each day at the sound of the Angelus at sundown, when people retired to more orderly entertainments – elegant balls and private suppers at the city's theatres, *festini* or little festivals in the homes of the rich, and family and neighbourhood groups who gathered at homes or taverns or theatres for more or less private parties. There was a sort of democracy on the Corso, with every masker equal to every other, but in the evenings people divided into groups. Masking and costumes continued, but lost some of their satirical edge, in favour of spectacle and luxury.

Carnival was interrupted by the first French occupation, and only gradually revived after the first restoration of 1800. By 1805, however, it was back in the grandest of grand styles, when Prince Chigi and his friends put together a spectacular float. The float was 'shaped like a chariot, in the antique style, drawn by four superb horses, magnificently ornamented.' On it was a famous allegorical scene, 'The gods in council about the marriage of Psyche', with the costumes of the gods and goddesses taken from Raphael's famous mural in the Farnesina. Since the classical deities in the painting were very scantily dressed if at all, the princesses and marchesas and duchesses who took their parts wore flesh-coloured silk with flowers and jewels arranged in strategic positions.[30] The party of gods was preceded by another float on which nymphs, shepherds and satyrs played musical instruments to create the proper atmosphere.

The weather that year was dreadful, cold and windy, and flooding threatened to turn the Piazza del Popolo and the Corso into lakes. But that did not discourage the

---

30 As described in Silvagni, *op. cit.*, II, p. 21.

nobles from repeating the triumph on Monday, with the floats rearranged to represent the marriage of Psyche. The first float carried the musicians, as before; the second carried the gods of Olympus and the bride and groom, Psyche and Cupid; while the third showed the wedding banquet, with a table (a gift from Prince Borghese to Prince Chigi) loaded with sweets, fruit and confections, all ornamented with coral.

The last event of carnival was the dangerous game of extinguishing the lights, the *moccoletti*. Like all of carnival, and much entertainment in general, the fun ran very close to violence. It was not for nothing that the event was forbidden in 1790, as the French revolution began, or that the Roman carnival finally ended in the twentieth century when Red Brigade terrorists distorted ritual violence into an unromantic reality.

The game began this way: as soon as evening fell, the lights began to appear: crystal lamps inside one carriage, glowing coloured paper lanterns casting a pale light in another; little rows of tiny candles outlining vehicles and windows; firepots on balconies, tapers in hands and on hat bands and atop elaborate coiffeures. At some point, someone began the shout of 'Sia ammazzata!' – 'Let them be murdered! – anyone who does not have a *moccolo*, let them die a horrible death!' This was, of course, the signal for every man, woman and child, cardinal or beggar, Roman or stranger, prince or lackey, to defend his own *moccolo* and put out his neighbour's. A child was perfectly within his rights to blow out his father's candle while shouting, 'Sia ammazzato il signor padre!', servants launched full-scale attacks on employers with the cry of 'May the princess (or prince) be butchered!'. Carnival covered it all. Devices for protecting one's light could be elaborate; athletic young men, unencumbered by anachronistic Freudian scruples, carried their candles on top of poles two or three stories high; others had pyramids with multiple candles in lattice-guarded frames.

Theatre

As soon as the Christmas octave was over the carnival season began, and the theatres of Rome opened for their brief but much anticipated seasons.

Most Italian cities by the end of the eighteenth century had theatres which had been built or at least subsidised by the government or by a consortium of nobles. In Rome, this was not the case: the popes rarely approved of theatre, and even when they did, they certainly did not feel it their duty to provide secular entertainment for the population. As a result theatre, whether musical or not, had a precarious existence in the Rome of the popes. Each year, impresarios decided whether or not to invest in attempting to provide a season; some years, only one or two of the city's seven theatres found an impresario. Even when open, theatres were subject to strict regulations (theatres could not be identifiable from the outside, for example); they were allowed to open only during brief periods after Christmas and sometimes for short autumn seasons; and theatrical personnel were subject to a general official hostility. Disturbances in the vicinity of theatres were particularly frowned upon, and savage penalties ranging from the *tratti di corda* to the galleys were threatened (if not always delivered) against carriage drivers who raced one another to the theatre, or against ticket scalpers, or people who tried to buy tickets outside regulation opening hours for the box office, or – above all – against partisans of a particular actor or singer who indulged in loud and unruly applause or booing.

Managing a theatre in Rome was a good way to bankrupt oneself. There were so many things that could go wrong. A performer might not appear, or might fail to please, or might fly into a temper and give the police an excuse to shut down the show. Rival theatres might lure the limited custom away – tickets to the formal theatres were very expensive, and only a small proportion of Romans could afford them. Even if nothing else went wrong, a spell of bad weather, or an earthquake or flood, or the death of a prominent person, could mean the sudden closure of all theatres, with no recourse. Few popes were as benevolent as Pius VI who, when the threat of invasion closed the theatres of Rome, reimbursed the impresarios out of the Apostolic Cameral budget.

All of this helps to explain why, by the end of the century, opera in Rome was generally considered to be execrable. But there was one other major factor: women were still banned from the stage in Rome. This meant that many of the roles were sung, as they had been in earlier centuries, by a group of performers known euphemistically as *musici*, or, more bluntly, *castrati*.

But this by no means indicates that theatricality was lacking in Rome, or that performers – especially musicians – found it hard to earn a living. On the contrary, the city was full of music. But it was music in the churches and at the great church events. Cardinals and great nobles supported choirs and choir soloists, as did the major churches of the city. The papal chapel choir, the most renowned choir in Europe since the sixteenth century, remained a magnet for the best male singers, at least for those who had failed to scale the dizzy heights of operatic fame.

A survey of the 14 *rioni* at the end of the eighteenth century indicates the number of theatrical venues of various types that could be found in each: Monti, three; Trevi, 14; Colonna, eight; Campo Marzio, 13; Ponte, seven; Parione, 12; Regola, four; San Eustachio, four; Pigna, eight; Campitelli, four; Sant'Angelo, one; Ripa, none; Trastevere, two; and Borgo, eight,[31] for a total of 88. Most of these were rooms where puppet shows might be put on, or strange animals or malformed people could be displayed. There were only a few formal theatres, but still there were more than most cities of the size could boast. After Rome ceased to be a papal city and was instead, for a time, the 'second city of the empire', a report was sent to Paris, presenting the arguments for building new theatres in the city:[32]

There are many theatres in Rome, and most of them are large, such as the Aliberti, Tordinona, Argentina, Valle, Capranica, Pace, and Pallacorda. The Aliberti, called 'delle Dame', is extremely large, and could hold 5,000 people; it is used for Opera Seria...[33] Less large are the Argentina and Tordinona, called the Teatro d'Apollo, but more elegant. The Valle is smaller but of a shape that is very pleasing to the ladies, who love to be seen by everyone. The Capranica theatre, for its structure and for the general infelicity of the complex, deserves to be burned. The same goes for the Pace and Pallacorda, except that these are more acceptable, and are an outlet for those who love the theatre but can't spend a lot of money.
None of these theatres belong to the state, but are all owned by individuals.

---

31 Cairo, 'Luoghi scenici nella Roma del Settecento'.

32 LaPadula, *Rome e la regione*, p. 131.

33 Formal, rather old-fashioned serious operas written according to strict guidelines and rules: the characters must adhere to the Greek tragic model, and be good and noble but with a tragic flaw; the classical unities had to be observed; all violence must take place off-stage, etc..

The number was deemed to be sufficient, and the project of building more was dropped from the financial plan of 27 July 1811.

A few years after the imperial period, Thomas had this to say about Roman theatres:

There are eight theatres active in Rome, which are: the Argentina, for grand opera and ballet; Valle, for comic operas and comedies; Aliberti, for masked balls; Tordinona, where the clown comedies have the Neapolitan pulcinella, *but they also play tragedies there; the Capranica, which offers bloody dramas and farces; the Pace, little comedies for the people, also featuring* pulcinella; *the Palacorda is a large theatre for marionettes; the Granari has dramas for the common people; and finally there are two other little theatres for* burrattini *[puppets], which are very popular and which often offer better works than the larger theatres; several shows are offered each evening.*

Before the box office opens, men stand at a little distance from the theatre with lighted torches; they often call out to passers-by and encourage them to come in.

While theatres were popular and well patronised, they were anything but cheap, but there were other ways to amuse oneself if one lacked the money to go to the theatre. One highly amusing activity was to stand around theatres and watch the show as the actors, and the rich patrons, processed in and displayed their fine clothing in the streets and in the foyer. One could have dances at home, or in storage rooms or even stables. Permits were required, of course, and had to be applied for with the appropriate *suppliche*. A typical permit allowed 'the applicant to hold, in the place indicated in his request, a gathering for dancing among friends, on the understanding that the place will be inspected and approved by the architect, and that the stated gathering will be free with no admission or other charges, that no one will wear masks covering their faces, and that there will be no signs on the outside of the building to indicate that a dance is being given there.'[34]

On the Brink of Spring

Lent
Carnival ended abruptly at midnight on Fat Tuesday, and the Lenten season of penance began, but the entertainment (or at least, the distractions from everyday life) did not so much end as change form. Instead of dancing and masking, with theatres draped in scarlet and gold, there were the even more gripping dramas of death and the Last Things, in churches draped with black and silver. As in November, the church of Santa Maria dell'Orazione e Morte presented *tableaux* with the centrepieces of unarticulated bones arranged in fantastic and artistic patterns. Impassioned preachers were highly valued for their ability to reduce a congregation to tears.

Penance and Repentance
During Lent the fasting regulations, strict enough during the rest of the year, became draconian. The wide Roman diet was reduced down to *ceci* (chick peas), *maritozzi*

---

34 Biagi, *Il carnivale del popolo*, pp. 26–27.

(lenten buns made with flour, oil and candied fruit or raisins, topped with a sugar frosting) and *baccalà* (dried salted cod). No eggs, no cheese and no meat without special dispensation. But Romans often found ways to enjoy even the fasting regulations. In Zanazzo's collection of traditions we learn that:

In my day, all the toffs [piani and piane, men and women who dress civilly, that is, not in traditional clothes] and all the minenti in Rome went to St Peter's every Friday in March; they said it was to hear the preaching, and they chatted and flirted and ate maritozzi.

An allegorical mock-heroic epic called 'the Battle between Meat-Eating and Fasting' explains the limits of fasting. Plenty's battalions of pork, sausage, beef and lamb struggle against Fasting's troops of shrimp and dried figs, nuts and apples, trout, pike and eels.[35] Fasting is on the point of winning the day when Christmas, allied with Meat-Eating, steps in to give the carnivorous party the victory. Fasting only manages to gain control of the 40 days of Lent, and two days each week (Friday and Saturday, or sometimes Wednesday).

Folk poet Belli, who wrote about everything in Roman life, wrote a sonnet on the Edict for the Observance of Lent (issued each year): 'At Mass, the curate read out the paper that explains everything: lunch is destroyed, but you can have some oil in the evening; no pork at all – and that means no salami or *prosciutto*. For breakfast, you can have a little wine and some bread, nothing that will break the fast. Then he said that all Christian men and women should give up sin and say their prayers …'[36]

When urging and encouragement did not do the trick, the Roman state – which was, after all, a classic theocracy – could fall back on the law to enforce the rules. Stendhal recounts the story of a Roman butcher who was sentenced to prison for selling meat on a Friday.[37]

Every Catholic was obliged to go to confession and receive the sacraments at least once a year, and at Easter that time ran out for those who had not yet done so. Priests in each parish were required to be certain that each of their parishioners had made his 'Easter duties' and to submit a list of those who had failed to do so. The list was published, and those who remained on it were formally excommunicated unless and until they complied.[38] One parish priest is quoted (accurately or not, is hard to say) as having his own way of dealing with any potential problem:

Personally, I never have a list to send in, but if I have warned a parishioner in private or publicly summoned him and he still neglects his duty, I have him sent to prison. I kept one inside for six weeks last year and he communicated in the end.

---

35 Lancialotti, *Feste tradizionali*, pp. 429-30.

36 *Ibid*, p. 435.

37 *Ibid*, pp. 436 and 438–9.

38 Andrieux, *Daily Life*, p. 122.

Mid-Lent Relaxation

The 40 days of Lent were not continual – each Sunday was a feast day, when fasting could be forgotten. In many parts of Italy, on the first or second Sunday of Lent, it was the custom to fill a pot – a *pignatta* – with sweets, and with bits of coal wrapped in silver paper, so you could not tell which you had until you opened it.[39]

But even that break was not enough for eighteenth-century Romans, and there was a popular tradition of the *mezza quaresima*, 'half-way through Lent'. In some ways this was a mini-carnival, with practical jokes, chaos and over-eating.

The Thursday that lay exactly in the middle of Lent was the time for this symbolically gruesome mini-carnival, a day off fasting. People would make an effigy of old woman out of rags, dried figs, dried fruit, and other Lenten foods; she represented Fasting. She was carried in a *sedia gestatoria* to the Cow Field (that is, the Forum), where she was set up on a sort of throne in the middle of the ruins. There, she was cut in half, to show that Lent was half over. Half the food went for the party, the other half the *popolo* fought over, in a chaotic scramble like a *cucagna*.[40]

Lent was also a time for music. There was a rota of churches in which one could go for the Stations of the Cross, and in each of these there were sermons and orchestral concerts of appropriate music. In private homes, this was a time for musical academies, which offered both sacred and profane music in a semi-private venue, to which respectable visitors were usually welcome.

40 Hours' Devotion

The 40 Hours' devotion[41] moved from church to church through the year, starting and ending at St Peter's basilica on the first Sunday of Advent (the pre-Christmas penitential season).[42] For 40 hours, day and night, there were prayers, the offices of the hours were sung, and congregations gathered for adoration. At night, the Company of the Holy Sacrament made sure that the Host was never left along.

Because this was Rome, presentation was important, and the *macchine* that were erected were reviewed in the official journal, *Chracas*, along with theatre reviews, court news and international events.

So, on 14 August 1801, the work of the architect Filippo Niccoletti (who seems to have made a speciality of these displays) was part of the devotions at the church of San Silvestro on the Quirinal hill. *Chracas* notes that the church was 'gracefully decorated', with a 'lovely *macchina* representing a temple', the work of an engraver, a gilder, a painter, and a draper, or *apparatore* (all named). Over the temple was a statue representing Triumphant Faith, and the entire *macchina* was lighted by 'many candelabras, which created the most beautiful sight for the many

---

39 The game is almost identical to the Mexican game of the *piñata*. A child was blindfolded and given a heavy stick with which to hit the pot until it shattered, and the contents scattered on the floor. However, in Rome (as in Mexico) the game was more generally associated with Christmas. Lancialotti, pp. 442–3.

40 Lancialotti, *op. cit.*, pp. 435–6.

41 The number 40 reflects the number of years the Israelites spent in the wilderness, and the number of days that Jesus passed in the desert before beginning his public ministry. These devotions were particularly popular with the devout during carnival, as a sort of counter-demonstration.

42 Andrieux, *op. cit.*, p. 129..

spectators'.[43] On 20 February 1803 the church of Gesù featured a 'majestic *macchina*' (also by Nicoletti) with the entire edifice surrounded by a pyramid of lights, topped by a great crown, from which cascaded flowers and gold-fringed damasks to make a backdrop for the temple.[44] On the last day of 1805, the famous architect Nicoletti's work was once again featured at San Silvestro when, under his direction, the altar was decorated with a variety of lamp stands and candelabras. In the evening, motets were sung by 'the most celebrated professors of music' who also accompanied the three Masses of the three days, at the end of which a procession led by a military band brought the Sacrament to the Quirinal.[45]

This sort of devotion struck the French as above and beyond the call of piety, and they were quick to suspect regular participants of disaffection. On 7 April 1811, the Ministry of Police in Paris was informed that the young Marchese Giovanni Naro Patrizi and a group of other nobles and prelates had formed a most suspicious cabal. Under the name of the '40 Hours' Union', they assembled some 400 men who each paid 8 *bajocchi* (22 *sous*) in dues, and met to pray all night in the churches designated for the 40 Hours' devotion. In addition to Patrizi, the 'conspirators' included Prince Doria, counts Ercolani and Simonetti, and Cavaliere Don Giacomo Giustiniani, who had headed the Governing Council that ruled Rome in the brief time when Ferdinand of Naples had occupied the city in 1799.[46]

Preaching in the Coliseum

Preaching in the Coliseum was an important part of this counter-carnival religiosity. The Coliseum, like much of ancient Rome, had been incorporated into the life of Christian Rome as the place where many martyrs had met their deaths. The devout met there to pray, especially following the Stations of the Cross, which recalled events of the passion and death of Jesus, and the intrusion of the archaeologists was resented as yet another example of radical irreligion.

After the fall of Napoleon and the Restoration, Cardinal Fesch, Napoleon's uncle, took to mysticism, and especially to the devotion of the Stations of the Cross. He founded a confraternity dedicated to that practice, and became its president, while the Princess Gabrielli became the head of the women's section of the group. Each Friday, they met at the Coliseum to follow the Stations, with Cardinal Fesch barefoot and wearing penitential garments over his cardinal's robes, followed prominently by Napoleon's mother, and humbly by Anna Maria Taigi.

St Joseph's Day

The feast day of St Joseph, on 19 March, fell during Lent and offered the faithful yet another opportunity to break the austerity of the season with a celebration of food and family. While Sicilians built (and still build) altars piled high with Lenten

---

43 Fiorani, *op. cit.*, p. 263.

44 *Ibid*, pp. 266-7. Nicoletti seems to have used the same *macchina* with variations.

45 *Ibid*, p. 271.

46 Report to the Minister of Police in Paris from Raffin, Secretary General. Cited by the Marchesa Maddalena Patrizi in her *Memorie di famiglia*.

dishes (no meat), in Rome St Joseph's day was the feast of the fryers: men and women with portable grills and frying pans set up shop around the city to sell fried fish, fritters and doughnuts on tables decked with flowers, ribbons, and sonnets in honour of the saint; candles and mirrors were hung in the laurel trees set up in pots along the pavements.

The rigours of Lent, even when lightened somewhat with Sundays and mid-Lent festivities, and the special delight of St Joseph's Day, nevertheless became almost unendurable as the days lengthened and spring – and Easter – drew near again.

A common enough sight: a desperate woman begs for help for a sleeping, or sick, child.

CHAPTER SIX
SORROWS

It is sometimes difficult to tell the difference between joys and sorrows. There are delights in repentance, joys in satire, satisfactions in Lent, and solemn pleasures to be found in a really good funeral. And there is no doubt that eighteenth-century Romans enjoyed things that set the teeth of reasonable people on edge: rock fighting and bull baiting, to give only two examples. The Roman rituals of November are surely related to the esoteric pleasure that many get from being frightened out of their wits by horror stories. Who could resist dark and gloomy scenes lit by flickering torches or candles reflecting fitfully off the chalk white of (real) human bones? Or a representation of the Last Trumpet that featured the (real) recently deceased in the role of the soon-to-be-resurrected?

But man is born to trouble as the sparks fly upwards, and Romans, if they considered themselves happy and were never bored, were also remarkably miserable. While the poverty of the average Roman was probably no worse than that of the poor in Paris or London, it was aggravated by the fact that there was no middle class worth mentioning. Despite the fact that Rome had a population much too small for its area, it also had a chronic housing shortage. Almost half of the available space within the walls was taken up with fields, vineyards, orchards and gardens. Much of what remained was filled by great squares and churches, convents and noble houses, to say nothing of ruins.

Virtually every traveller noted, more or less indignantly, that the city was filthy. Rome stank. There were few to no street cleaners; herds, packs and flocks of large and small animals wandered more or less at will; and people insisted on using streets and courtyards as public conveniences. And, of course, in the summer months the stench of decaying flesh filled churches and seeped out into the surrounding streets.[1]

Even after the French administrators had done their best, Mrs Eaton described the Pantheon as:

---

[1] Martorelli, *Dissertazione sopra gli odori di Roma*; a contemporary essay on the city's smells.

... sunk in the dirtiest part of Modern Rome; and the unfortunate spectator, who comes with a mind filled with enthusiasm to gaze upon this monument of the taste and magnificence of antiquity, finds himself surrounded by all that is most revolting to the senses, distracted by an incessant uproar, pestered with a crowd of clamorous beggars in the congregated filth of every description that covers the slippery pavement ..."[2]

She, and most other visitors, complained of the 'disgusting dirt', 'filthy odours and foul puddles', the 'beggarly hovels' inhabited by 'the loathsome living objects that crawl about the marble pavements'.

Most travellers before the Napoleonic period and after the Restoration laid blame for the misery of Rome at the feet of its government, and it is true that many of their rulers were elderly, generally benevolent, often reform-minded and utterly incompetent at the task of ruling a state. On the other hand, it is also true that attempts at economic or social reform were met with outrage. Travellers were unanimous in their opinion that Romans, for all their quick wit and undeniable charm, didn't like to take orders and didn't like to engage in gainful employment.

Thomas Aquinas reportedly observed that human beings generally get the government they deserve, and by extension, the society they deserve. Whether they deserved it or not, before the Napoleonic occupation Romans lived in a world that was liturgically about one third sombre gloom, a world where dirt and poverty were normal, and death – brought on by childbirth or disease or medical care or the ever-present casual or institutional violence – was never far away.

Then the French arrived, sowed the seeds of modernity, and made it worse.

'The doctor is like the executioner: you pay him to kill you'[3]

Death was a familiar companion in Rome. One normally died at home, was carried from home to the nearby parish church and, until the French arrived with their modern ideas of sanitation, one was buried under the floor of the church or in a nearby burial ground. The city was no more healthy a place to live than any other city of its size, time, and latitude, which is to say, a large percentage of babies died, it was easy to get sick there, and the best medical care was as likely to kill the patient as to cure him.

In Europe, the medical profession saw great changes between the eighteenth and nineteenth centuries, as procedures other than bleeding and enemas came into general use, along with new medicines that were almost as effective as the herbal preparations most pharmacists used, and sometimes even better.[4] Unfortunately, while all of this was taking place elsewhere, medicine in Rome was not doing well.[5] A hundred years earlier, hospitals in the papal capital had been the best in the world,

---

2 Eaton, *op. cit.*, I, pp. 251–60.

3 Zanazzo, *op. cit.*, I, p. 69: 'Er médico é ccomé ér bùjà. se pagu per àooo' ommazzati' It was customary for the person being executed to tip the executioner, symbolically forgiving him, and in practical terms, encouraging him to dispatch one in as neat and painless a fashion as possible.

4 Gross, *op. cit.*, p. 205 et seq.

5 For the politics of the medical profession see Donato, 'Alcune ipotesi sulla borghesia delle professioni e la repubblica del 1798–99: Il caso dei medici del S. Spirito in Sassia.'

but it had been losing ground for a century. By the time of Napoleon, Rome had lost its position as a capital for medical care, despite its many hospitals (appropriate for a Christian city), capable of tending some 3,500 sick people at a time and employing some 400 persons in various roles.[6]

'Medicine', according to Mrs Eaton, 'is not considered the profession of a gentleman and is most injudiciously despised.' As a result it was pursued by 'men of low birth, limited means, and dubious reputation.' Physicians were not, however, at the very bottom of the medical pecking order. While herbalists and pharmacists were superior to physicians, physicians could at least look down on surgeons, as they had done for centuries.[7]

It was probably frustration with this situation that drove a disproportionate number of physicians to support the republic in 1798. Consuls of the short-lived Roman Republic included Liborio Angelucci, Giuseppe De Mattheis, Giuseppe Flaiani; tribunes included Angelo Cocchi, Giuseppe Martelli (later minister of the interior), Pietro Paolucci, Marco Placidi, Camillo Romiti, and Camillo Corona – physicians all.

The people could also turn to the patent-medicine vendors who gathered in the market squares, the *ciarlatani* (who required a permit before they were allowed to sell their wares). Visiting physicians from other parts of Italy or Europe sometimes arrived to offer their services temporarily, like the French oculist, Professor Duchelard, who inserted this notice in the newspaper on 15 August 1807:[8]

Professor Duchelard, Oculist at many hospitals in France, has come to Rome. This oculist has a special method of operating on cataracts. It takes no longer than a minute to restore vision to the blind. He performs this operation on poor beggars at no cost, for charity, and on others according to their state. He has lodgings at the inn of M. Damont, on Croce street, near the Piazza di Spagna, and he will be there for 15 days.

Diseases

Infectious diseases in Rome included the old scourge of malaria – more prevalent in the nearby countryside but not uncommon in the city – along with typhoid, and recurrent cycles of smallpox, as well as whooping cough and scarlet fever. There were acute infections of the digestive tract (enteritis, dysentery, diarrhoea – Pope Pius VII suffered from these) and of the respiratory tract (bronchitis, pneumonia, various forms of tuberculosis, and the less dire but still irksome upper and lower lung congestions and sinus troubles). Many were afflicted with the horribly unpleasant but not often immediately fatal stones (gall or kidney). Other conditions calling for medical intervention were cancers and skin diseases, whose sufferers were collectively called *rognoso*, a general term that now means itchy or

---

6 Donato, *op. cit.*, p. 13, cites Tournon, *Etudes statistiques.*
7 Physicians, who saw themselves as intellectuals and philosophers, had long despised surgeons, whom they regarded as workmen. This remained true in Rome despite the fact that practical improvements in treatment pioneered by surgeons – diet, ventilation, cleanliness – were resulting in dramatically improved survival rates for surgical patients compared to medical patients.
8 *Diario di Roma*, 15 August 1807.

scabby. Venereal disease, the so-called 'celtic disease', was far from unknown. One of Rome's many special hospitals, San Giacomo degli Incurabili (St James of the Incurables), was set aside for treating it.

Something the doctors called apoplexy carried off considerable numbers, as did heart attacks. These were much feared. Romans at the time of Napoleon considered sudden death to be the greatest possible catastrophe, since it did not allow one time to prepare for eternity and thus have a better chance at avoiding damnation.

Hospitals

Rome had many hospitals, some among the oldest and most distinguished in Europe. The largest, and one of the oldest, of the Roman hospitals was Santo Spirito, the hospital of the Holy Spirit, which had been established as a foundling hospital in 1198. By the nineteenth century, this was the city's primary fever hospital but it continued to serve as a shelter for abandoned children, and for old people with no where else to go. It had beds for up to 2,000 patients and probably treated 10,000 or so a year. It had a medical staff of 150, including eight doctors, four surgeons, 32 students, one pharmacist and six student pharmacists, plus a *cicoriaro* (herbalist, specialist in greens).

Mortality rates in Santo Spirito ranged from the total (the few unlucky enough to contract hydrophobia were doomed to a certain and horrible death) to the high (tuberculosis eventually killed almost 85% of its sufferers) to the surprisingly low (almost 80% of surgery and wound patients recovered).

Several other Roman hospitals specialised. Skin diseases were the speciality of one of the Trastevere hospitals, San Gallicano, where they enjoyed a spectacular cure rate of between 80% to 90%. Santa Maria della Consolazione in Trastevere took in surgery cases and cases of wounds and bruising, which was convenient in one of the more violent of the Roman districts. Trinità dei Pellegrini (the hospital of the Trinity, for Pilgrims) was set up in the sixteenth century as a hospice, but by the eighteenth century it had become a full-fledged convalescent hospital, one of the first in Europe. After patients were discharged from other hospitals, they could go to Trinità dei Pellegrini for two or three days of good food and rest. San Rocco was the lying-in hospital, used (but not exclusively) by the very poor or by women who wanted to conceal their pregnancy. Most babies were delivered at home, by midwives, though by the end of the eighteenth century there were three courses in obstetrics in Rome, at the Sapienza, at Santo Spirito and at San Rocco.

Pharmacies and Pharmacists

Pharmacists and herbalists (and by this time, there was a clear difference between the two) were more highly respected than physicians, and certainly more respected than surgeons. The problem with the pharmacists and herbalists was that their professional organisation was in effect a guild (the Noble Guild of Chemists, and before that, of *Aromatari*) – and guilds were considered to be the sworn enemies of modern efficiency. In the 1700s the papal government (like most European governments) had been trying to break the guilds, but it would not be until the French arrived that the job was completed. Pius VII did manage to incorporate pharmacists into the university system, and in 1808 he established the first professorship in practical pharmacy.[9]

The French occupation and Napoleonic period transformed the pharmacy business. After investigating the reform of the pharmacy profession, the *Consulta* [see chapter 8] came to terms with the residual guild nature of the trade. In 1809 the first real school of pharmacy was entrusted to the Former Guild of Chemists, which had been suppressed with the other guilds.[10] The new school was divided into two courses, one of theory and one of practice, with an examination consisting of nine chemical and pharmaceutical operations. With the return of the papal government the courses in pharmacy were assumed directly by the Sapienza. In 1815 there were 30 degrees granted in pharmacy; in 1816 there were 71, and by 1817, only two years after the second restoration, 87 degrees were awarded.

Romans considered access to medicine to be a basic right, whether or not one could pay for it. For centuries, medical compounds had been made and distributed by members of religious orders, who by law were to provide medication free, on demand. Virtually every hospital had a pharmacy, and for centuries the popes had tried to make home care for the poor available.[11] Part of the papal home-help network for the sick poor of Rome was a system of clinics and free pharmacies. There were 10 of these, selected by competition among the shops in each district, distributed through the *rioni*. Each had a physician and a surgeon. In addition, there were about 60 public pharmacies, located in the various charitable institutions, many of them associated with the monasteries of regular orders such as the Carmelites, Capuchins, Jesuits and Benedictines. Meanwhile, charlatans and street performers were advertising the miracles of their goods (the term charlatan had not yet taken on its meaning as trickster or fake).

Medical care, in Rome as elsewhere, was still a combination of purging and bleeding, with hideously unpleasant variations such as 'cupping'. As late as the middle of the eighteenth century, medical doctors, even very eminent ones, were prescribing the ingestion of human feces. At least one highly respected French doctor recommended it as an excellent laxative and also most useful for sore throats, epilepsy and some forms of fever. A paste of powdered stools and honey was highly prized; it was called the 'golden plaster' (*empiastro aurea*) and was rubbed on sores and carbuncles. Fresh cow dung mixed with vinegar was, apparently, good for scrofula, boils, swellings and tumours.

Proverbs and Folk Remedies
The *popolo* in general, and everyone's grandmother in particular, had their own ideas about what to do about physical problems.[12] These could range from the perfectly reasonable (keep warm and drink plenty of liquids) to the grotesque if effective (brushing teeth with warm urine was sure to keep them white). The remedies, as they had been since the beginning of time, were a mixture of herbalism, common sense, tradition, plus a strong dose of superstition and appeals to a higher realm.

9   Biagi et al. *op. cit.,* pp. 38–9.
10 See Kolega's 'Speziali, spagirici, droghieri e ciarlatani'.
11 *Ibid,* p. 333.
12 See Zanazzo, *op. cit.,* pp. 7–86 and Gross, *op. cit.,* pp. 202–13.

A sovereign general remedy could be prepared by taking lamp oil (the sort used before sacred images), and various mixtures of herbs, according to the ailment. These might include stinging nettle, sage, camomile, henbane, various types of mint, wild lettuce, thyme, elderberries, hemp flowers, rue, myrtle, barley or bran.[13] Remedies for sore eyes included salving them with soft fresh cheese or beaten egg, or boiled argol laced with lemon juice, or the oldest remedy of all – piercing the ears and inserting gold earrings.

Chilblains could be bathed in hot urine before going to bed. Or, if you preferred, you could use a paste of cooked mallow or sage, crushed garlic, or boiled honey, or chickpea meal heated up in tallow or suet.

Garlic was sovereign against biliousness.

A spring tonic could be made from the juice of crushed chicory, or water in which greens like endives or watercress had been boiled.

People who desired beautiful white teeth could polish them with pulverised charcoal or cigar ash, or bicarbonate. Or, as mentioned above, give them the warm urine treatment.

Constipation, then as now, called for prunes.

For aching bones, you could cover the entire body with sambuco leaves, then with a wool blanket, until the subject broke into a sweat. Or more simply, you could just cover the afflicted area with the skin of a cat or a rabbit or a lamb.

Roman folk language was full of proverbs relating to health:[14]

Love, itching, and coughing don't go together.
Fat is beautiful.
Water makes your eyes pretty.
Anyone born in March is crazy.
Cold feet, hot head.
In a house without sunshine, the doctor will always be there.
Appetite is a good sign (but) Watch out if the sick person asks for wine.
Rice makes good blood.
Meat makes meat; wine makes blood; greens make shit (which, in the case of constipation, was considered a good thing).

Taking the Waters

Aqua Acetosa, a mineral spring on the banks of the Tiber a few miles north of Rome (near the Milvian bridge), was recommended by respectable physicians and visited by great crowds of Romans who spent the day there or went to fill up bottles to bring home for their own use or to sell in the street. The acidic waters were said to be beneficial for headaches, neuralgic pain, chest disease, asthma, all forms of skin disease, dysentery, diarrhoea, cholera, scurvy, dropsy, inflammation of the urinary tract, diabetes, and stones (both kidney and gall).[15]

---

13 Biagi et al. *op. cit.*, pp. 38–9.
14 Zanazzo, *op. cit.*, I, pp. 82–86.
15 The claims were not as wild as they sound. Their high sulphur content made the waters a cheap and quite effective antiseptic.

The waters at the town of Albula had been popular since classical times, when they were called the Aqua Albulae. Like many health springs, they were milky with sulphurated hydrogen, and they also contained borax and sulphate of soda.

Miraculous Cures

The waters were by and large free, as were miraculous cures (though a contribution was always appreciated). Every disease, as well as every moral flaw and personality disorder, had a patron saint who could be addressed directly in petition for a cure. This was more or less a private affair between the petitioner and the saint, although a church, monastery, convent, or confraternity dedicated to the appropriate patron could be and often was called upon for backup.

Some religious institutions developed reputations for being good intermediaries for miraculous cures. Santa Maria in Campo Marzo, for instance, was known for the supernatural assistance its inmates could offer in the case of scrofula or malarial fevers. But most altars, shrines and chapels had their component of *ex voto* offerings, given in thanks for miraculous rescues and cures. The *bambino* of Ara Coeli was highly regarded as a last resort for the mortally ill.

Clerics and lay people with reputations for sanctity could also be asked for help. Anna Maria Taigi, later beatified, was regarded as a holy woman for most of her life, and was famous for several high-profile cures. Cardinal Barberini and the Queen of Etruria both credited her with miraculously curing their illnesses, and numerous more ordinary Romans asked for and received cures of cancers and other diseases. When Benedict Joseph Labbré died in 1783, his funeral was a mob scene as Romans of every class and status pushed forward in an attempt to secure some relic of the holy man, relics that were regarded as at least potentially miraculous.

Death and Funerals

Before the French occupied Rome and began to make plans for burying the dead in cemeteries outside the city gates, Romans were normally buried within the city, either in churches or in cemeteries associated with parishes, convents or hospitals. There were rules against burials inside the city's churches, but they were regularly ignored and in many churches one could hardly avoid noticing the smell as former parishioners followed the way of all flesh.

Funerals swung between the extremely elaborate, and the minimal. Family members did not attend them, and many observers state that the family did not even attend the death-bed, leaving that to the priests. Thomas left a detailed record of the public ceremonies of death. He noted the custom of carrying the dead through the streets:

... with the face, hands and feet visible. The corpse is not hidden unless it is hideous to see, and has begun to decompose. A crucifix is placed on the chest; children and young people have a crown of flowers placed at their feet. Except for the clergy, who always assist at burials, often orphans make up the only accompaniment for a child.[16]

16 The family of the dead child paid a small sum to the orphans for their participation. Thomas, plates V, XVIII, XIX and XX.

Many Romans were buried with the assistance of members of confraternities dedicated to that act of charity. Thomas shows the hooded, white-robed men going in procession to the deceased's parish church to collect the bier and the clergy, then going in procession to the dead man's home to collect the corpse. On their way, every man, 'including drivers, and servants behind the carriages' removed his hat and bowed.

At the home, they placed the body on the bier, and processed back to the church:

They line up in silence in the street, and set out in strict order: first the condottiere, *then the confraternity members, the clergy, the cross-bearer (during Lent, the cross is veiled), then the bier escorted by six brothers carrying wax candles. The candle-bearers are generally accompanied by poor men who carry cardboard cones in which they catch the dripping wax; after the service, they return the wax to the confraternity. From time to time during the walk, the* porte-faix *in charge of the bier gives the signal for a pause – that is, the recitation of a Hail Mary. When the rest is over, the signal to begin again is 'Deo Gratias'.*

At the church, the catafalque was arranged with the feet of the dead man towards the altar unless he had been a priest, in which case his head would be towards the altar.

Wax candles are distributed to the confraternity members who kneel, in two rows, on either side of the corpse. After prayers, they leave. The crucifix, and sometimes some of the clothing, of the dead man is removed, a rosary is placed around his arm and he is buried either in a tomb or in a common pit under the paving.

Mrs Eaton, as one might expect, had a less sympathetic impression of Roman funerals.[17] After seeing one, she noted that she had never seen such 'long and lugubrious' funeral processions as those provided for the rich members of the middle class in Rome. Nobles, and the poor, did not indulge in them. But when 'a rich shopkeeper' or one of his relatives died, 'Rome is filled with the funeral train'. She was shocked and dismayed (it was very easy to shock and dismay Charlotte Eaton) by the fact that the corpse was painted and dressed up as if he or she were on the way to a ball, and carried through the city on an open bier, followed by great crowds of men she took to be monks of different orders, but who were probably confraternity members 'chanting the slow and solemn service for the dead'. The whole thing, she opined, must have 'an effect on people's nerves that is far from agreeable'. She seems to have misunderstood Romans and their fondness for the dramatic.

Noble funerals she found just as disagreeable. These were conducted not on foot but in carriages, with the coffin poking out a window and four priests (one at each corner) who 'chant the service as fast as ever they can, the lighted tapers they carry in their hand twinkling and dropping about as they go.'

There was, she was told, the general belief among the people that when a cardinal dies, he carries with him to heaven anyone who dies in the time between his own death and his funeral: 'a very convenient mode of being smuggled into heaven.'

---

17 Eaton, *op. cit.,* II, p. 352 et seq.

When a man fell in a Roman knife fight, the conflict was over ... unless he got up again.

Bulli *and Bandits*

Disease was by no means the only hazard to life and limb: Romans were quite capable of dispatching or maiming one another with no help at all from nature. The *bullo* was, in the Roman dialect, the word to describe a big, violent, dashing, athletic, arrogant, courageous, imposing, generous, swaggering young man, touchy about his honour, a man of his word, vain about his looks and his outfits, irresistible to women and given to acting before thinking.[18] He was the winner of the race, the best fighter, dancer, gambler, drinker. A man defined by status, not by money; an individual, not a gang member. He wore his long hair tied back in a net, an elegant and short velvet jacket draped across his shoulders or over one arm, a feather in his cap, a multi-coloured sash, short trousers tied at the knee, red stockings and shoes with buckles large enough to tap on the ground as he walked. The *ciuffo*, or forelock, was almost a part of the *bullo*'s armory. Like the brigands of Spanish-ruled Lombardy, the *bullo*'s typical gesture was a toss of the head to get the hair out of his eyes. (Wearing hair that came down below the eyebrows had been punishable by a hefty fine in seventeenth-century Milan.)

He turns up in the ancient Roman comedies of Plautus as *miles gloriosus*, the quintessential soldier; in the commedia dell'arte as the Captain. *Bulli* could be found in all classes, but especially in the popular classes in the districts of Trastevere and Monti. He explains the otherwise inexplicable *sassolate* in the Cow Field (otherwise, the Forum), which were semi-private wars between *bulli* from rival districts. The weapon of choice was the sling-shot, using rocks or chunks of marble for artillery and the velvet jacket or heavy cloak wrapped around the arm and shoulder as shield. They chose the Forum for a number of reasons – it recalled the splendours of ancient Rome,

---

18 See Rossetti, *I bulli di Roma.*

and the *bulli* saw themselves as heirs of the soldiers of Rome; it was more or less neutral territory, lying neither in Trastevere nor in Monti (nor, for that matter, in the Borgo or Ponto districts). It was conveniently full of rocks and bits of marble and so offered plenty of ammunition and plenty of cover behind the piles of stone and the columns and arches. More practically, it was close to the hospital of the Consolazione.

Battles went on until dawn, or until the lookout shouted '*al fuoco*' (to the fireside, or home). At that point the combatants and the crowd of enthusiastic onlookers grabbed their wounded or dead, and ran for it. The papal authorities made some feeble efforts to stop the *sassolate*, but with little success; the French, more ruthless, outlawed them and used cavalry to make it stick (more or less).[19]

The *bulli* had a code of honour as complicated and as strict as any Spanish knight (even his style of knife-fighting was Spanish). Few murders in Rome were premeditated or carried out by treachery. The usual murder occurred when two men quarrelled over a game or a woman, or some obscure point of honour. Words were exchanged; jackets wrapped around the left arm, Spanish style; and knives were drawn. If one man had a knife and the other did not, honour required that the fight wait until he was provided with one. When a man fell, the fight was over, unless he got up again. If the fallen man were unable to get up, the victor departed while the loser (presumed to be the one in the wrong) was taken to the nearest hospital that dealt with injuries. If the man lived, he was expected to forgive, and that put an end to it. If he died, the *sbirri* might take an interest, but they would be unlikely to get any cooperation. A more real danger was vengeance by the dead man's family or friends. If that threatened, the killer had two choices: he could take refuge in a place of sanctuary – and these were never difficult to find – until the trouble blew over, or he could join the bandits.

Bandits had been a problem in the Roman countryside since classical times, and the problem always got worse in times of trouble. By the end of the eighteenth century, the popes had by and large decided on a live-and-let-live policy with these outlaws. During the French period, the game was much more serious, with military efforts to stamp out the bandit gangs. This resulted in a great deal of carnage and confusion, but not in any substantial reduction in the numbers or violence of the brigands.

According to Madelin, the bandit gangs grew for a number of reasons. Many recruits were deserters and draft-dodgers. Some bandit gangs moved north from the Kingdom of Naples, driven out by General Manhès in the employ of the new king Murat. In Sicily, the British recruited bandits, armed them, and dropped them off along the unguarded beaches near Rome to harass the French. Most bandits near Rome, however, were native to the area. Many were *bulli*, surprised and outraged by the French tendency to prosecute the crimes of honour that had previously been either overlooked, or praised. Convicts at Civitavecchia, also surprised and outraged to find that they were supposed to behave like prisoners, took themselves off to join the bandits. To make matters more difficult, the priests who used to denounce them now looked on brigands as allies in their enmity to the French who had driven out the pope. Officers of the papal police and gendarmerie joined the bands in the mountains, and led the resistance.

---

19 Rossetti compares the rock fights to Sunday afternoon football matches, a safety valve for proud, violent people.

· Bandits seize a fashionably-dressed hostage to be held for ransom ... one hopes.

When Pius VII was restored to his throne in 1814, he immediately faced an enormous bandit problem. There were two ways to approach it, by severity or by clemency, and he tried both.

Thomas noted that the bandits around Rome lived relatively settled lives, having houses, fields and flocks that they left under the care of their wives when they went to 'work'. They generally preferred to get money without shedding blood, if they could easily avoid it. They simply snatched people and held them for ransom. Of course, if the ransom was not forthcoming, the hostage was killed with no further ado.[20]

When Mrs Eaton was in Rome, the government had offered amnesty to any bandits who agreed to lay down their arms and submit to a period six months of imprisonment, after which they were to be free, and presumably reformed, men. This provided the occasion for an exciting outing for the ladies of the city, as she reports:

People flock to see them as if they were wild beasts. We went a few days ago, and I intend to repeat my visit, for their appearance and manners are beyond description. We found them amusing themselves in a large open court, apparently enjoying the novelty of their situation and the notice they attracted. They are a very fine looking set of men – fine limbs, fine features, fine flashing dark eyes and hair, and bright brown complexions.

Their air and deportment is free and independent, expressing undaunted confidence and fearless resolution ... Their dresses were very rich and picturesque. One of them had a magnificent embroidered scarf twisted round him, which he laughed as he said he had taken from a lady. The captain boasted of having killed 18 men with his own hand. His wife was with him: she is only 19, and the most beautiful creature I think I ever beheld.

---

20 Thomas, *op. cit.*,comment on plate XXXIX.

Mrs Eaton noted that upon her return to England, she heard that the government 'had not kept faith' with the bandits, and that they were still in prison. This was typical. Policy swung between laxity and ferocity, much as the law in Rome had always done. Later in the struggle with the bandits, the papal government decided to raze an entire town, known to be a hideout for several gangs. However, they permitted Gaspare del Bufalo to go up to the town and appeal to the inhabitants. They promised to reform, and nothing more was said about levelling the place.

Law and Order: Savage Penalties, Easy Pardons
The French arrived in Rome in 1796, and again in 1809, as the armies of light and justice, prepared to rescue a people plunged into what they were sure was medieval darkness and despair. How could it be otherwise, priest-ridden as they were, and subject to horrific tortures and savage penalties. (The reputation has been an enduring one – see Puccini's *Tosca*.) But the reality they found was rather different, though certainly not more modern. The legal system in Rome, even more than in most pre-revolutionary states, consisted of a tangle of laws administered through an even greater tangle of courts (there were dozens of different ones, all more or less independent), all with competing claims to jurisdiction. Even the dreaded Inquisition was more or less toothless. Rome suffered less from high-handed tyranny than from gridlock, and legal cases could, and usually did, spend years or even decades wandering about from one jurisdiction to the next.[21]

If the court system was a chaotic mess, the Roman prison system was one of the best in Europe. Papal prisons had been among the first to separate accused persons from convicted criminals, and to house prisoners in separate cells. Given the fact that the Gospels had put visiting and seeing to the needs of prisoners right up there with feeding the hungry and tending the sick as qualifications for getting to heaven, it is not surprising to find that the city was filled with confraternities and religious organisations whose chosen work was to provide for the needs of prisoners.

The Roman police force, on the other hand, was worse than its court system. In common with many old regime states (including England) the police were either soldiers, or an *ad hoc* group of thugs who worked not for the state, but for the various courts, and were barely distinguishable from the criminals they pursued. They were called *sbirri*, and to call someone a *sbirro* is still an insult in the Italian language. The Roman *sbirro* was immortalised as a *commedia dell'arte* character, Rugantino, who is scruffy, dogged and an object of contempt and abuse.

Torture and imprisonment
One reason the *sbirri* were so despised had to do with their involvement in torture, which was part of the judicial system in Rome as in other old regime states. When Pius VII gained temporary control of his city in 1800 he set up a commission to study the judicial system and make recommendations for improving it, but judicial torture would remain legal in Rome until 1831. By 1800, however, torture

---

21 See Nicassio, *Tosca's Rome*, pp. 101–13.

had been strictly limited for almost half a century; prisoners could, and did, bring successful lawsuits against torturers who exceeded the legal limits. After 1753 the only legal forms of torture were a sleep deprivation technique called the *sveglia*, and the *tratti di corda*, or 'jerks of the rope'. The *tratti di corda* were more often a part of a sentence than a way of encouraging confessions.[22] Typically, three *tratti di corda* was the standard sentence for violations of public order, a category that could include ticket scalping, reckless driving, or going over the line with carnival celebrations. The procedure took place in public, just as capital executions did, and for the same reasons. The scaffold for the *corda* stood near the Campo dei Fiori, but there was a portable machine that could be taken to places like the Corso, for the carnival.

The machine of the *corda* consisted of ropes and pulleys. The subject of the exercise had his hands tied behind his back and was hoisted up to a height of between seven and 10 metres. He was then dropped, putting great strain on the back and shoulder muscles, and sometimes dislocating the arms.

Men who received prison sentences of more than a few months usually served them in what were called the galleys. However, this was not a Ben Hur experience; the galleys have been called 'a dangerous example of punishment that was no punishment.'[23] There was no rowing involved, as the papal state had virtually no navy, and in any case convicts were rarely required to work. The *galleotti* were taken to Civitavecchia, where they were fed and housed rather better than their guards and were free to wander about the town doing odd jobs, selling knick-knacks, or stealing. Few bothered to escape, as it was easy to get a remission of their sentence, and in any case, the prison month was calculated at 20 days.

Women represented only a tiny fraction of the convict population, and could serve their sentences as involuntary residents of convents, where they were treated no worse than the voluntary residents.

Capital punishment

Romans were famous for their quick tempers and sudden recourse to weapons. According to travellers' tales – and illustrations – every man had a knife tucked into the sash around his waist, every woman's hair was pinned with a stiletto. This was something of a romantic exaggeration, but it was nearer to the truth than one might imagine. In his magisterial collection of popular attitudes and traditions, Giggi Zanazzo recorded a man who remembered that

… for the Romans of my day, the knife was everything, it was life. You kept it in your pocket along with the rosary, every now and then you checked to be sure it was there, and caressed it like a treasure. For them, the knife was a friend who never left you, at night or in the day, at night under your pillow, in the daytime, in your pocket. From time to time you took it out, opened it, polished it, sharpened it, even kissed it.[24]

---

22 See Nicassio, *op. cit.*, pp. 106–109 for a discussion of judicial torture in papal Rome.

23 Gross, *op. cit.*, p. 230.

24 Rossetti, *op. cit.*, p. 36, citing Zanazzo's *Tradizioni popolari*.

The natural result of the marriage of attitude and opportunity was a staggering murder rate. According to a French agent in Rome in 1797, every day that summer three or four people died from stab wounds; the 11-year reign of Clement XIII (1758–69) saw (according to Silvagni) 10,000 murders, or about two and a half a day. The average rate for the eighteenth century probably lay somewhere between two to three murders a day, with many taking place during carnival – truly appalling for a city with a population of under 150,000.

With so many murders, one might expect a fair number of executions. In fact, by the time the republic arrived in 1798, there was seldom more than one execution a year, and by no means all of these were for murder. The execution rate increased dramatically with the arrival of the revolution. There had been only 20 executions in the Papal States between 1777 and 1797; 89 men were executed between 1798 and 1799, the vast majority (more than 83%) for political crimes. This was a veritable reign of terror, albeit a small one when compared to the death rate in Paris in the 1790s.[25]

The executioner of Rome during the Napoleonic period was Giuseppe Bugatti, who held that job from 1796 until he was forced to retire in 1864 after he dropped a head off the scaffold. Bugatti, in his memoirs, reports that between 1796 and 1808 he executed 105 people. By no means all of these were murderers (one was more likely to be hanged for a crime against property than for a simple street killing), and by no means all murderers were hanged.

One of the major reasons for the appalling murder rate was the fact that the criminal justice system in Rome was notoriously inefficient and unreliable. The multiple layers of courts were a tangled mess where cases dragged out for decades; the police – the infamous *sbirri* – were unpopular, badly paid, and corrupt; and even if a killer were arrested, tried and convicted, he could even at the last possible moment appeal to some cardinal or ambassador for mercy, and as likely as not be pardoned.

In popular opinion, justice was a personal affair between the injured and offending parties, and the winner (since God was just) was probably in the right. Despite famous cases, like that of the great artist and art critic Winckelmann (who was apparently murdered by a boy he had picked up for the night), foreigners and tourists were rarely bothered.

By far the most common means of execution was hanging. In some cases, after the criminal was hanged, his throat was slit. Another method (used in fewer than 20% of executions) was a procedure that looked – and sounded – worse, but in fact was relatively painless. The process was called *mazzolato e squartato* – hammered and quartered (but it had been a long time since there had been any quartering involved, live or dead). The seated criminal was dispatched with a hammer blow to the head, and once he was determined to be dead, his throat was slit. In cases of violent crimes (often with convicted bandits), the head or hands, or both, were cut off and displayed at the site of the crime.[26]

The scientific new guillotine was not introduced in the city of Rome until the end of 1813, though it had been used in the Roman states since 1810. Giuseppe Dugatti approved of it as a labour saving device, calling it a 'new edifice for the cutting off of heads'.

25 Formica, 'Vigilanza urbana e ordine pubblico a Roma (1798-99)', p.45.
26 Gross, *op. cit.*, p. 229.

Romans considered the street and tavern killings as a private matter between the parties involved. Pre-meditated murders and multiple murders were quite another thing, even if they involved the murder of an unfaithful wife caught *in flagrante*. In October 1806 a prosperous middle-aged butcher, Gioacchino (called Bernardino) Rinaldi was executed near his place of business for the murder of his pretty young wife, Giacinta, and her lover, a boy who worked in the shop with them.[27] When an anonymous letter tipped him off about their affair, the husband had pretended to leave, but hid himself and waited for his suspicions to be confirmed. Rinaldi saw the blond, blue-eyed shop boy pull the door closed and lock it; he waited for five minutes, then burst in to find the guilty pair locked in one another's arms. Snatching up one of his butchering knives, he almost severed the boy's head, then began to stab his wife in the breast and in the stomach. Her screams brought the neighbours, who found the victims in a pool of blood. Rinaldi might indeed have got away with killing the lovers, but he also deliberately killed the unborn child his wife was carrying – an unborn child who turned out to be two children, twins. At the trial, he expressed no remorse. He was sentenced to an appropriately gruesome death. Stoic and refusing religious consolation, he was killed by a blow to the head with a hammer, and his throat was slit.

One of the great frustrations of rationalists in papal Rome was the uncertainty of punishment. It was altogether too difficult to capture criminals, and once captured and sentenced, it was even more difficult to be sure that the sentence was carried out. Not only could any passing cardinal or ambassador pardon the prisoner, but the Confraternity of St John the Beheaded had the privilege of setting one condemned prisoner free each year. This had been granted to them by Paul III in 1540, when condemned prisoners were in greater supply. By the eighteenth century, they were rarer, but the tradition continued into the nineteenth century.

Each year the confraternity sent three brothers to comb through the prisons of Rome for potential beneficiaries. They were to read through the trial records and make a full report of the crime and their circumstances. In order to qualify for the confraternity's pardon, the prisoner must have made peace with the offended parties, and received their forgiveness.

Once a suitable convict had been selected, the confraternity members went to the prison in a torch-lit procession and presented the chosen man (condemned criminals were usually men) with a torch and a red robe. The prisoner prostrated himself before the crucifix and was crowned with wreath of silvered olive leaves. Then they all processed back to confraternity headquarters, while the brothers intoned the *Te Deum*. After a Mass that ended at dawn, the liberated prisoner was the guest at a banquet and was sent on his way, with a bit of money if he needed it.[28]

The French Complicate Matters
Fixing Rome, as the French would find, was a thankless task. One of the first things the French and their liberal supporters did was to outlaw the use of torture. This was

---

27 Rendina, *Mastro Titta, il boja di Roma*, pp. 36–40.
28 Maes, *op. cit.*, III, p. 107.

a typical Enlightenment thing to do, following the advice of Cesare Beccaria, who in his famous work *On Crimes and Punishments* had argued that not only was torture abhorrent, it was also inefficient and counter-productive.[29] Unfortunately, the faith of the new rulers in Beccaria did not extend to taking his advice on capital punishment, which the Enlightened jurist also condemned. Under the Ridiculous Republic, as we have seen, the execution rate increased dramatically.

When Rome became part of the imperial system in 1809, the prohibitions against torture and the relative frequency of capital punishment continued as the Napoleonic Code was applied. The French were enormously proud of this code, which was a triumph of reasonable, liberal, humane and efficient law. Unfortunately, as we will see in chapter 8, all of these virtues did not serve to make the new system popular in Rome or the Roman states.

The new regime had little better luck in trying to fix the economy. What was wrong was fairly obvious: the medieval Christian system of charity and control of the economy had to go, as clear-thinking and generally sympathetic bureaucrats like Camille de Tournon realised. Unfortunately, when the safety nets that Romans saw as their right were removed, the short term result was usually disaster.

The papal government, for example, regularly bought grain at the market price, and sold it a lower price, as a means of social control.[30] Only a revolutionary regime could attempt to break that uneconomic circle, and the republic tried it. The result was food riots. In February 1799 'about 50 women went to the Grand Edils' office, demanding bread for themselves and for their children, and surrounded the building.' In March, a 'not indifferent' riot among 'the Monticiane, Trasteverine, ... and *popolante*' forced the edils to back down.

Conscription

Throughout the empire, the only thing that was more resented than heavy taxes was conscription. The imperial wars required manpower and the day was long past when French volunteers could supply enough of that. If the mothers of Rome thought that their sons might be exempt, they were soon disabused of the illusion. On 30 April 1810, less than a year after Rome was transmuted from the capital of Christendom to the second city of the empire, Camille de Tournon announced that men born in 1789 were 'called to the honour of serving in the armies of the Great Napoleon.'[31] They were directed to the mayors of their villages or the local police commissioner, and from there were to be sent to fight in the wars of an empire that was officially at peace: in Spain, in Portugal, and two years later, in Russia.

By 1813, after the disaster in Russia, the net of the draft was cast to include men between the ages of 19 and 60. Fortunati records an episode that took place on 13 January 1813. General Miollis was making what was intended to be an inspiring speech to a miserable group of conscripts (the ones that could be caught, and had not yet escaped) outside Santa Maria sopra Minerva. When encouraged to shout, 'Long

---

29 Beccaria also argued against the death penalty, to less effect. *On Crimes and Punishment*, chapter 28.

30 Formica, 'La legislazione annonaria e le rivolte per il pane nel 1798-99,' pp. 191–211.

31 *Journal du Capitole*, 30 April 1810, n. 52; cited by Madelin, *op. cit.*, p. 302.

live the emperor' they responded by muttering, 'We don't want to go to war', and 'Damn the emperor'.[32]

De Tournon, who seems to have been an optimist by nature, put the best face on it; 20 years later, he still believed that Romans had been touched very lightly by conscription. But in his memoirs, he recounts an episode where the distraught mothers of Rome broke into his office to plead for their sons. He admitted that all he could do was to smile politely, back up rapidly and run for his carriage.[33]

Most conscripts and potential conscripts either fled immediately to the hills, or they deserted along the routes north. There were 235 who set out from Rome for Orleans and the army on 1 August. Of those, 120 arrived at the frontier. The rest had melted away along the journey, most to join the bandits in the hills.[34]

Others avoided service any way they could. They mutilated themselves, knocking out their front teeth (needed to bite cartridges), or damaging their index fingers. Still others avoided service by getting married, which automatically put them at the end of the queue. There was, it was said, a rash of young men marrying old women.[35]

Pasquino

The contempt for the law exhibited by Romans was probably related to the contempt for authority in general that they entertained. Most eighteenth-century visitors were surprised by the freedom of speech in Rome, from the puppet plays and balladeers who worked elaborate and stinging satires into their shows, to the venerable institution of Pasquino and the talking statues. There are a number of these 'talking statues', who traditionally spoke for the Romans, by means of anonymous critiques that were posted on them. The witty and appropriate pasquinades quickly spread through the city. Only rarely did the government try to track down the author, and it was even more rare that such an attempt succeeded. The statues, in effect, provided a sort of free speech alley, and Romans took full advantage of their opportunity.

Pasquino, the most famous and popular of the talking statues, was a mangled classical torso located near the Piazza Navona at the corner of the Palazzo Braschi. The practice of posting anonymous notes, the so-called pasquinades, took their name from him. He had several partners, and would sometimes engage in conversations with them. One was Marforio, another classical figure, perhaps a river god, perhaps a reclining banqueter, who is now located at the Capitoline museum; another was the classical figure known as 'Abate Luigi'. Madama Lucrezia sometimes chipped in; she was a Renaissance female bust at the church of San Marco at the Piazza Venezia. Other participants could include a fountain figure called the *Facchino* (porter); *Babuino* (the baboon), who is probably an image of Silenus, a mythological figure who looks like a full wineskin; and *Scannabecchi,* a portrait of the famous Albanian prince known as Skanderbeg.[36]

---

32 Fortunati, *op. cit.,* 13 January 1813.
33 Madelin, *op. cit.,* p. 307.
34 *Ibid,* p. 308.
35 Grab's 'Army, State, and Society' is very informative on conscription throughout Italy.
36 Biagi et al, *op. cit.,* pp. 69-75.

No one was exalted enough to escape the attentions of Pasquino and his companions. During the papal periods, the popes and their relatives were always favourite targets, so in the imperial period it is not surprising to find that the French in general, and Napoleon in particular, took their place in the pillory.[37] A favourite technique was to elaborate on the letters of the emperor's name, preferably in ecclesiastical Latin, to lend a learned and pious air:

Non
Amat
Populos
Omnes
Leges
Evertit
Omna
Nostra
Eripit[38]

Or

Nenimi
Amicus,
Protector
Omnium latronum,
Leo ferox,
Ecclesiae
Oppressor
Neronis
Emulator[39]

The imperial family came in for its own share of brutal satire. Even Madame Mère, a rigorously moral old lady who lived in Rome briefly during her son's reign, and found a home there after his fall, was not immune, as in the following:

Livia die all'Impero	*Sapere si desia*
Un mostro e fu Tiberio;	*Il pessimo qual sia.*
Agrippina Nerone,	*Il problema è elegante,*
Letizia Napoleone.	*Si scioglie in un istante:*
Fra li germi infelici	*Dal terno il piu briccone*
Di queste meretrici	*Egli è Napoleone.*[40]

---

37 See Rendina, *Pasquino*, and Romano, *La satira nella Roma napoleonica.*

38 Loosely translated: He doesn't love the people; he [overturns] all the laws, he steals everything we have.

39 Friend of no one, protector of all thieves, fierce lion, oppressor of the Church, imitator of Nero.

40 Livia gave the empire a monster, Tiberias; Agrippina, Nero, Letizia, Napoleon. Among the miserable seed of these whores, how can we decide which is the worst? It's an elegant problem, but it can be solved in an instant of the *terno*: the worst scoundrel is Napoleon.

The infant King of Rome did not escape, as in an abusive little poem that spoke of 'crowning a little bastard' (*un bastardello a incoronar si fa*). Romans especially resented imperial attempts to force them to rejoice at his birth. During the celebrations, those who went to St Peter's basilica found little packets made up of paper wrapped around the next to smallest coin, a *bajocco*. Written on the outside were the words '*Te Deum con bajocco*', a Te Deum for a penny.

Public Order

Thomas, writing in 1819, noted that street crime had been greatly reduced by the French laws that prohibited concealed weapons, and punished violators with the public humiliation of the *cavaletto*. Under the Roman republic of 1798–99, when state violence had overshadowed private violence, republicans had introduced measures designed to bring the unruly Roman populace under state control, and this would eventually reduce the crime rate. Romans bitterly resented measures designed to shine lights down unlit streets and to number houses. But the republic and then the empire considered such measures to be essential if the government was to exert any control over the people. And when the popes returned in 1815, they too recognised how valuable it was to be able to see what was going on, and identify and locate people more easily. The unpopular systems remained, and public order benefited in the long run. If nothing else, the French system had demonstrated the inefficiency and the injustice of the old, inept system of public order.

Finances

Both the republic and the imperial administrators tried bravely to make some sense of the chaotic finances of the Roman state and both failed. This was inevitable, given the brief length of time each was in power, along with the really dreadful state of papal finances. For the problems, and attempts to solve them, see chapters 7 and 8.

Alms to a begging brother or hermit became part of Rome's extensive social welfare network.

CHAPTER SEVEN
MONEY, SCHOOL AND WORK

Much (though not all) of the misery of Rome before the coming of the French can be laid at the feet of an outdated economic system; in Rome, price controls strangled any possibility of an effective market. Add to that the lavish distribution of both private and public charity, the profound contempt many Romans felt for steady work, and the assumption that money is the root of all evil, and we have the recipe for economic disaster.

The contempt for money ran through the population. The ecclesiastical government plunged into whatever projects seemed appropriate, from building palaces for papal nephews to building hospitals for the poor, confident that the faithful Catholics of the world beyond Rome would pitch in to cover any debt. The nobles, as nobles, were not supposed to lower themselves by worrying about money, and they didn't. And the *popolo*, like the nobles, refused to lower themselves by worrying about money: they were, after all, citizens of Rome and Christians who expected, and generally got, alms to cover their basic expenses.

It has even been reported that Roman money proclaimed itself contemptible, with didactic mottos like: 'I am like filth, I am the root of all evil'; 'Redeem yourself with charity'; 'Covet not silver and gold, nor set your heart upon them'; and 'If you look for salvation, do not love me'.[1]

Papal money was based on the decimal system long before the reforms of the French revolution. The basic unit was the silver *paolo*. Five *paoli* made one gold *scudo*. Ten copper *bajocchi* made one *paolo*, and five copper *quattrini* made one *bajocco*. Coins from other states also circulated more or less freely in Rome. Some of these had similar names but different values, others had different names but similar values – the Florentine *zecchino*, the *carlin* of Naples, the *ducat* of Venice. In addition to gold, silver and copper coins, there was a stable system of paper currency, based on two banking institutions: the Monte di Pietà, which ran the state pawn shops, and the Holy Spirit bank. Money printed by these two institutions circulated freely

---

1 Andrieux, *Papal Rome*, pp. 70–1.

throughout the Papal States, and were exchanged at close to face value.[2] In fact, before the end of the century it was very difficult to turn the notes into hard cash, but this didn't bother Romans, who considered it to be as good as gold within the confines of the state. It has been suggested that it was the dependability and stability of the paper money of the popes that gave John Law his ultimately disastrous idea for system of paper money in France (otherwise known as the Mississippi Bubble debacle).

It is very difficult to estimate spending power of money in Rome once the period of French dominance began. Inflation and shortages were rampant. The revolutionaries, and especially the Napoleonic bureaucrats, were justifiably appalled at the outmoded papal system, and promptly dismantled it. Unfortunately, they were not able to put anything like a reliable system in its place, either because they did not have the time, or because they had underestimated to complexity of the problems. Prices, cut loose from government regulation, soared. As if that were not enough, the economy suffered from the ordinary disasters of war: fighting in the countryside disrupted the work of peasants and harvests were slender or non-existent. Anything that had to be imported from the other Italian states either rose in price, or didn't get through at all because of war or the ever-present bandits. And Napoleon's attempt to impose the Continental System, banning all imports from or exports to England, played havoc with an already staggering economy by putting much of the trade into the unreliable hands of smugglers. All of this was made even worse by the fact that, even before the wars began, the papal state imported three times as much as it exported.[3]

Financially, the Roman state was in permanent crisis during the revolutionary period, until by the time Camille de Tournon took over the value of the paper money was more or less illusory. On 10 August 1810, the Napoleonic government set up a commission to resolve the problem of reimbursing the holders of the enormous public debt. Two years later, in a fiscal manoeuvre that even de Tournon admitted he did not understand, the debt was slashed even further, solving the problem on paper but devastating the investors who had held the promissory notes on the debt.[4]

The main sources of income for the papal government had been the money that flowed in from the Catholic populations of the world. The revolution put a stop to most if not all of that. There were few other sources. Romans were not used to paying much in the way of taxes (they paid far less tax than did Parisians). Some money came from state monopolies on tobacco and *aquivit*, and there were indirect taxes like the *quattrino* on each pound of meat sold, plus the highly lucrative state-directed lottery [see chapter 4]. The republican and later the imperial governments could, and did, add confiscations to the pot, but even taking the entire properties of recalcitrant nobles like the Patrizi family did not come anywhere near balancing the budget.

---

2   Gross, *op. cit.*, pp. 144–50.

3   *Ibid*, p 88.

4   Readers interested in the fiscal details of this plan, and the reasons why the debt got so badly out of hand, are referred to Hanns Gross, *Rome in the Eighteenth Century*, especially to pages 116 to 151. Gross suggests that it was not simply mismanagement that brought the papal government to such a sorry pass (though the criminal mismanagement of Cardinal Coscia during the reign of Benedict XIII from 1724 to 1730 certainly didn't help). It was a combination of drastically reduced income from the rest of the Catholic world, lack of a firm fiscal policy and a stagnant economy.

Making Ends Meet

The wealthy family might have an income of 10,000 *scudi* a year. Friz and Gross estimate that a Roman family of four had to bring in about 15 *scudi* a month (that is, 180 a year) to maintain a healthy diet. Giuseppe Bugatti, the executioner of Rome, was paid 15 *scudi* a month plus housing allowance and an additional 60 *scudi* during the year as a supplement. A head coachman in a noble house might make 16 *scudi*, butlers and chamberlains about eight, only slightly more than ordinary servants who took in six or seven *scudi* a month. Professionals did not do much better. The legal agent at the Farnese palace in 1741 had a wage of six *scudi*, while the household doctor, and the house surgeon, of Cardinal Orsini were each paid a princely 12.50 *scudi* per month. Clearly, ends did not meet.

Fortunately, employees did not have to depend entirely on hard cash for their food and household expenses. For one thing, most salaries came with perquisites – payments in kind of bread, wine and firewood and (at least according to De Brosses,) anything else they could get their hands on. A state employee like the executioner Bugatti could get free housing, and extra payments (most people got bonuses at major feast days like Easter, Assumption and Christmas). Workers were also experts at extracting tips from any and all. Many Romans grew some of their own food (the city was full of fields and vineyards), or had relatives in the nearby countryside or within the walls who did so, and there were many and varied charitable institutions that distributed food to the hungry. Also, it is important to remember that these salaries were the official, reported earnings: Romans, like many people around the world then as now, earned much of their income on the 'underground' economy, buying and selling, doing small jobs, or straightforward begging. Travellers reported that virtually everyone in Rome begged (in the revolutionary chaos, it was even reported that ladies of the high nobility did some genteel panhandling), and none of the mendicants seemed in the least ashamed of it.

Still, the figures are grim. When we examine the average prices of foodstuffs it appears that Roman families with incomes above the magic 15 *scudi* a month spent between 80% and 90% of their money on food alone. This left between 3% and 7% for clothing (and Romans, as we have seen, loved fine clothes), 4% to 6% for shelter, with maybe 7% left over for other expenses and for savings. The figures for people with less than 15 *scudi* were even worse: 95% of their money had to go for food.

Giuseppe Barberi, a noted architect, Jacobin enthusiast, amateur caricaturist, and father of nine children, was constantly moaning about money. In October 1793, suffering from both physical and financial troubles, he wrote: 'I'm in danger of having a debt of 1,600 *lire* foreclosed; and I can't pee.' Later that year, it got worse: his house burned down, and '... in two days I have to pay 160 *zecchini*, and I don't have a *quattrino*.'[5]

Barberi had good reason to worry. Civil debtors made up more than half of Rome's prison population, despite the difficulty involved in getting such cases through the complicated court system.[6]

---

5   Nicassio, 'The Unfortunate Giuseppe Barberi'. Barberi's casual mixing of Florentine, Venetian and Roman monetary systems – *lire, zecchini, quattrini* – suggests the complex interlocking nature of the pre-modern economy of Rome.

6   Gross, *op. cit.*, pp. 201–2.

Weights and Measures
The Roman *scudo* was a decimal-based coin – in fact, the idea of decimal divisions in the coinage goes back to ancient times. A tenth of a *scudo* was the *favolo*, a one-hundredth of a *scudo* was a *bajocco*, a two-hundredth was a *mezzo bajocco* and a five-hundredth was a *quattrino*.

If this decimalization looked modern and rational, the systems of weights and measures was anything but reasonable. Like the rest of the Roman state, it was individualistic and eccentric – in a word, it was medieval. The actual value of the pound or the ounce or the barrel or the mug could, and did, vary depending on where it was found and the specific historical traditions of that place. In the eighteenth century, the measures for two of the most basic necessities of life, oil and wine, were wildly eccentric: there were 179 different measures for wine, and 167 different measures for oil.[7]

Education

Primary Education
Ordinary Roman children had rather more opportunity for education than children anywhere else; but few of them were either willing or able to take much advantage of it, either because they were poor, or because teachers were rigid and unpleasant (this was more the style of the day than a personality defect), or because the potential students had little interest in formal intellectual activities. Most people believed that virtue and spiritual endeavours were much more important than formal learning. This was reinforced by the fact that the ordinary Roman did not need much education to succeed at the sort of life he usually chose, and in any case the ever-present security net of easy charity was always there to catch the weak (or at least, it was there until the French administration snatched it out from under them). And, too, the quick Roman intellect found much more congenial exercise in games and the puzzles of everyday life than it found in schoolwork, which at the time was highly formal and not obviously of much practical use, beyond the advantages of basic literacy.

Rome did have a universal system of free primary education, the first in Europe. However, it seems likely that, although it was available to all, most of the students were middle class boys.[8] Nevertheless it is worth noting that someone like Anna Maria Taigi, daughter of a particularly unsuccessful couple of servants, was sent to school and had some success there. At the age of 13 she was sent to what one of her biographers calls a 'workshop' – probably a hospice for poor girls where they were taught a trade. She learned to read, but probably not to write (these were taught separately, and even girls who went to school did not usually learn to write much more than their names).

Anna Maria's children were sent to school, but she insisted that they not be educated above their station: 'she wished the boys on reaching a certain age to learn

---

7   Bovi, 'Pesi e misure nello Stato Pontificio nel XVIII secolo', in *L'Ottobrata: Una Festa Romana*, pp. 22–24.
8   Gross, *op. cit.*, pp. 232–43.

a trade suited to their condition, that they might be useful and good men instead of burdens to society. She placed them in workshops which she had ascertained to be conducted in a good spirit.' 'As for the girls, she sent them to school, taking care that they should be accompanied by persons on whom she could rely.' When one of her daughters showed a talent for singing, she was discouraged from developing it for fear that she would be led to the theatre, and from the theatre to a life of leisure and pride, and perhaps even to vice.[9]

There were *scuole regionarie*, state-sponsored primary schools located throughout the city where boys could learn some reading, writing and arithmetic plus the rudiments of Latin grammar and (in some cases) French. In the early part of the eighteenth century there were 126 masters for boys' schools, scattered over 53 parishes. The teachers were named by the city authorities, but not paid by them; instead, they collected a small sum from each of their students. The teachers were supposed to be examined for competence by a board of professors from the Roman College and other institutions, but by the end of the eighteenth century this was not often done.

By the eighteenth century there were many private schools, schools run by religious orders, and what Giuntella calls *scuolette* (mini-schools) for the education of the children of the people.[10] The schools run by lay men and women did not enjoy a good reputation. The teachers there tended to be either men who had failed to make a success of any other job (including the clergy), or widows who took to teaching as a last resort in poverty. Schools run by the religious were much more successful: their teachers were there because they felt a vocational call to the work, and their orders saw to it that they were at least minimally trained.

The Scolopians started the first of the free schools for the children of the *popolo* in 1597. By the end of the eighteenth century, members of this order tended to be sympathetic to modern, liberal ideas and many of them cooperated with the republic of 1798–99 and with the empire. The Piarist order followed the work of Giuseppe Calasanzio, a Spaniard who had set up school in a small room in Trastevere in the late sixteenth century, then moved to San Pantaleone. His methods were to encourage competition and emulation among his students, rather than the almost universal system of beating learning into reluctant scholars. By the eighteenth century, San Pantaleone had become a large teacher-training institute, with more than 1,000 students. A second, smaller Piarist school was San Lorenzo in the Borgo district, where 150 boys studied.

Another order, the Fathers of Christian Doctrine (called the *Dottrinari*), had two schools with some 300 students in all: 200 at Santa Maria in Monticelli, and another hundred in Trastevere, at Sant'Agata. The Brethren of Christian Schools, with the piquant name of the *ignorantelli* ('the ignorant ones', a nickname that was later changed to the *carissimi*, 'the very dear ones') ran free schools for poor boys, with government assistance.

The Maestre Pie (the 'pious, or dutiful, schoolmistresses') of an order founded by Rosa Venerini, and the Fillippini (the Sante Maestre, or 'holy schoolmistresses') offered schooling to girls. They taught the basics of reading, plus 'feminine work' and

9   Thompson, ed., *The life of the Venerable Anna Maria Taigi*.
10   Giuntella, *Roma nel Settecento*, p. 119 et seq.

catechism to girls between seven and 14. Anna Maria Gianetti studied with the Filippini for a while, and later supplemented the family income by winding silk; after her marriage to Domenico Taigi, she sewed and at one point, when he had lost his job with the Chigi family due to the disruptions of revolution, she made and sold ladies' shoes.[11] Other girls' schools were run by the Ursulines, an order founded by St Angela Merici for the specific purpose of educating women. The Ursuline theory was that the best way to reform society was to influence the girls who would grow up to be the mothers of families. Girls were usually taught reading (but not writing) and catechism, plus household skills and skills that would enable them to get a job, usually in the textile industry or tailoring.

There were two schools in the ghetto for Jewish boys, run by the Jewish community. One taught the basics (reading, writing, arithmetic) plus Hebrew and scripture to all boys, whether or not they could pay: every morning, a collection was taken up in the community to cover the expenses of the poor boys. There was also a rabbinical school, to train young men to become rabbis.

It is hard to say how wide-spread literacy was in Rome at the time, but the evidence suggests that while many men could sign their names, they could do little else, and most women of the popular classes could not even do that. It is not surprising that the public letter writer was an important figure in Roman life, and did a brisk business. This was the sort of job – like many others – that Romans were content to leave to foreigners. It was generally agreed that foreigners, unlucky creatures that they were, had to make up for not being Roman by finding some other justification for their existence, like making money. Letter writers could make a great deal of money. Most of them came from the Marche or Umbria, worked in Rome for a few years, then retired with a nice bankroll to live like gentlemen.

The letter writers set up their rough desks in Piazza Montanara, where the day-labourers gathered, or the Campo dei Fiori, where one of the great markets was held, and offered their services for two or three *bajocchi*, reading letters to illiterate recipients, and writing appropriately-worded replies. Much of their trade had to do with love letters, but many illiterate country people came to look for help from the letter writer in dealing with authority figures. They brought with them eggs, or a pair of lambs, to pay the letter writer, who acted as secretary, counsellor, lawyer and adviser: a man who 'spoke the language' (literally and figuratively) of the lawyers, the priests, the learned, the bosses.

Catechism Classes
Most parishes in the city held religion classes where children (usually boys) memorised parts of the sixteenth-century catechism of St Robert Bellarmine. Giggi Zanazzo places the call to Christian Doctrine lessons among the most characteristic sounds of the Roman street:

On Sunday afternoons, an hour before the explanation of the catechism begins in the churches, the parish priest used to send a cleric around the parish, accompanied by some

---

11 Salotti, *La Beata Anna Maria Taigi*, pp. 15–19.

boys who rang little bells and called out together: 'Fathers and mothers, send your children to Christian Doctrine lessons; whoever doesn't will have to answer to God.' Then there would be a great ringing of little bells, and the cry would start over.[12]

Proficiency in learning the catechism carried a lot of prestige. Every year an Emperor of Christian Doctrine, the winner of a city-wide competition, was appointed and given pride of place in processions like that in honour of St Anne [see chapter 5]. At Christmas time, children were encouraged to display their learning by giving little sermons in front of the manger scenes, especially at the Ara Coeli, where they would be hoisted up onto an altar by their friends or parents, to deliver their discourses.

Colleges and Seminaries
The Nolli map of 1748 identifies 24 colleges and seminaries in the city. Some of these were institutions for training clergy, and others were colleges in the modern sense, boarding schools for young men from good families in Rome and from outside the state.[13] The Clementina (founded by Clement VII in 1596) had a student body made up of the nobility, and taught everything from reading and writing to theology and jurisprudence. Famous alumni included a pope, numerous cardinals, 'a dozen doges of Genoa and one of Venice', and a prince-archbishop. The Nazarene was a close competitor to the Clementina, and its alumni included famous literary figures like Alessandro Verri, Francesco Algarotti, and the poet Paradisi. As a school for young gentlemen, it included fencing, elocution, dancing and music along with its usual curriculum. Madelin says it had 18 professors in 1809.

The Ecclesiastical Academy accepted only 20 students, all of them noble and all of them destined for careers in the church. The College of the Propaganda Fide, as its name suggests, was a training school for missionaries, teaching boys from oriental lands to return to their homes and spread Christianity. It was most famous for its printing press, which printed books in almost 20 languages, including some that used exotic scripts.

The energetic Jesuits ran no fewer than eight schools in Rome, including 'national' colleges where clergy were trained to go out and combat Protestantism in their homelands, places like Scotland, Ireland and England. They also ran the Greek college, as well as the German and Maronite colleges. The jewel in the Jesuit crown was the Roman College. Its library was one of the most famous in Italy. After 1553, the Roman College got the right to grant doctorates, and quickly became a newer, more modern, and more attractive alternative to the Sapienza. The Roman College never got the right to grant doctorates in law, so the Sapienza held on to its primacy in that field despite the generally acknowledged fact that its courses were pretty much useless.

The student body of the Roman College was around 2,000; the facilities were three times larger than those of the Sapienza. After the suppression of the Jesuits, the Roman College was merged with the Roman Seminary (the Jesuit seminary that trained the upper clergy of Rome) and both of these were managed by a committee of three cardinals. The Jesuit professors were fired, but it proved impossible to replace them

12 Zanazzo, *op. cit.*, II, p. 425.
13 Gross, *op. cit.*, pp. 232-43.

with qualified men, and many of them were re-hired.[14] Even after the Jesuits were suppressed, most of the colleges kept up the Jesuit tradition of theatre, and students put on elaborate productions of classical plays and operas deemed to be morally uplifting.

University Education

The University of Rome in effect consisted of two colleges, the Sapienza, and the Roman College. The oldest by far was the Sapienza (the word means wisdom), which dated to the thirteenth or fourteenth century, depending on whether one relies on tradition or strict documentation. Like all primal western universities, its original reason for being was the teaching of the Queen of Sciences, theology, along with other elements of the Trivium and Quadrivium. At the end of the eighteenth century the university consisted of five faculties: medicine (which included botany and chemistry); philosophy (which included mathematics and physics); theology, or 'sacred science'; languages (Greek, Latin, Hebrew, Syriac-Chaldean and Arabic); and law (with chairs in civil, criminal and church law).

Despite occasional attempts at reform the curriculum was far from modern (with the possible exception of medicine), and as early as the end of the seventeenth century there was a serious proposal to close the Sapienza down and turn the facilities over to the Scalopian fathers as a school for poor children. The pope, Innocent XII, approved of the idea but one of the law professors used his influence with some cardinals and got it shelved. This is interesting on several counts: it demonstrates rather nicely why and how it was extremely difficult to put through any structural reforms in Rome, and it introduces the Scalopian fathers, who would by and large have the reputation as liberals who supported much of the change brought by the French a century later.

In 1773-4, the Sapienza had only 180 university students. Of these, 125 were studying law (the course, though still hopelessly old fashioned, was a sure track to success in the papal administration) and 19 were preparing for medical careers. Despite the energetic push for reform by popes like Benedict XIV, the institution remained moribund. In addition to being old-fashioned, the Sapienza had another problem, and that was the competition from the newer, and more modern, Jesuit college, the Roman College. This problem was solved in 1773 when the Jesuit order was suppressed and they were pushed out of their Roman College. As a result, more students turned to the Sapienza: philosophy students increased from 10 to 39, while the number of medical students almost tripled from 24 to 73.

There were major universities in other cities within the Papal States, most notably in Bologna, and in Perugia. The imperial functionary Norvins (who had something to say about almost everything) praised the college in Perugia: 'with its collections of natural history, chemistry and physics, its laboratory and its studios for painting and sculpture, there is not a city in France that would not be honoured to have such an institution.'[15] It would come in handy. One of the jobs of the *Consulta* was to establish an imperial university. They simply changed the name of the university at Perugia, and declared it to be the required *Université Napoléon*.

---

14 Gross, *op. cit.*, p. 236, fn 3.
15 Norvins, 22 September 1812, F 7 6531; Madelin, *op. cit.*, p. 87.

The public letter writer was a valuable ally in business as well as in affairs of the heart.

Training

Formal schooling had little to do with earning a living, unless one were in the legal or medical professions, and even there a sort of apprenticeship was the actual process whereby one figured out what had to be done and how to do it. Mrs Eaton noticed that a physician in Rome 'sets up for himself, and all have a train of young pupils who … are taught to kill according to their master's recipe.'

Technical training was offered in the shelters for orphans, foundlings, and the poor, where inmates were trained in some art or craft that would ideally enable them to earn a living. In practice, this was usually one of the cloth trades.

A school for deaf-mutes was set up in 1794 by the lawyer Pasquale di Pietro.

Most of the work of Rome was carried out in workshops set up by artisans and employing a few apprentices in the old guild system. In addition to the guilds, many of the Roman confraternities were also craft or guild associations. When a group failed to gain recognition as a formal guild, they had the option of joining together as a confraternity and setting up rules that would, in effect, function like a guild. By the time the French arrived, there were between 92 and 130 guilds or craft associations (depending on whether or not we count the confraternities). While the guilds protected the individual members, by the eighteenth century most economic theorists agreed that they curbed initiative and put road blocks in the way of newer, more efficient methods of production and distribution (this was, of course, what they had been specifically designed to do). The 1798–99 republic did not have the time to do much about such economic problems but the year after Pius VII arrived to take over his city in 1800, he suppressed most of the guilds in order to remove obstacles to the development of manufacturing.[16]

---

16 Parisi has produced a detailed study of one sector of the economy in 'Mercanti e lavoranti della lana a roma alla fine del 1700'.

Each corporation or guild had its cardinal protector. Among them were several popes: Clement XII was protector of *speziali* (grocers and druggists); Clement XIII, blacksmiths, secondhand dealers and wine merchants; Pius VI, innkeepers.

All of this served to constrict trade and generally slow down the economy, and when the French arrived they summarily ended the entire guild system. When Pius VII took his state back in 1814, he did not revive the guilds.

Work[17]

In the late eighteenth and early nineteenth centuries – that is, just before, during and immediately after the Napoleonic occupation – scholars have estimated that more than half of the inhabitants of Rome were state employees or their dependants.[18] Given the fact that Napoleonic statisticians estimated that more than half of Romans were unemployed, this leaves precious little room for anyone else.

Many Romans worked as servants, employed either by people almost as poor as themselves (like the Taigi family), or in the great houses of the cardinals and princes. The great majority of Roman domestic servants did not live in the houses where they worked. Although Romans considered jobs in great houses to be tickets to prosperity, in fact there was little or no job security to be had in such positions. On the other hand, given the experience of Charles de Brosses at the French ambassador's banquet, it seem that Roman servants knew how to take care of themselves.

The Church was a major employer, and by no means all of its employees were clerics.[19] Cardinals were technically princes, and were expected to keep up princely households, whether or not they wanted to live luxurious lifestyles. They employed large numbers of house servants, grooms, drivers, and cooks. They sponsored pubic entertainments, starting with their elevation to office when they were expected to entertain the entire city, and continuing throughout their careers. These public entertainments were the life support of the minor arts in Rome, from singers and

---

17 For recent studies on this subject, particularly the various trades and economic and professional entities in republican and, later, Napoleonic Rome, see Corbo, 'L'insegnamento artistico a Roma nei primi anni della Restaurazione'; Del Frate, 'La formazione dei giuristi nella Roma Napoleonica: la facolta di giurisprudenza della Sapienza.' [law training at the Sapienza]; Donato, 'Alcune ipotesi sulla borghesia delle professioni e la repubblica del 1798-99: Il caso dei medici del S. Spirito in Sassia' [physicians and the bourgeoisie in the republic]; Friz, *Burocrati e soldati dello Stato pontificio (1800-1870)* [bureaucrats and soldiers]; Gallo, 'I visconti, una famiglia romana al servizio ai papi, della repubblica, e di Napoleone.' [the activities of the Visconti family, which included a famous archaeologist among their number]; Kolega, 'Speziali, spagirici, droghieri e ciarlatani.'[chemists, druggists and the sellers of patent medicines]; Palazzolo, 'I provvedimenti sull'editoria nel periodo Napoleonico tra immobilismo e segnali di rinnovamento' [the publishing industry in the Napoleonic period]; Palazzolo, 'Una Dinistea di stampaori: I DeRomanis nella Roma dei Papi' [a Roman dynasty of printers]; Piccialuti, 'Istituzioni napoleoniche a Roma: i depots de mendicite' [beggars and vagrants]; Santoro, 'Il ruolo dei giudici di pace' [the justices of the peace]; Travaglini, 'Dalla corporazione al gruppo professionale: I rigattieri nell'ottocento pontificio' [the junk dealers of late eighteenth-century Rome].

18 Friz's work *Burocrati e soldati*, xvii, pp. 1–2, p. 17, is important here and cites both Madelin, *op. cit.*, and Andrieux, *op. cit.*.

19 *Ibid.*

musicians, to those who constructed the celebratory *macchine*, to those who carted the wine or prepared the food.

The prelature, the effective government of Rome, was another church-connected but not exactly clerical line of work. It consisted (according to de Tournon) of some 200 to 250 men, plus the cardinals who technically were their employers. The prelature was open to 'young men of good family, and to men who have made their mark in other professions ...' They were, he says, 'neither *abbés* nor laymen – too lay to be *abbés*, and too much the *abbé* to be laymen.'

A young Roman of moderately good family but small fortune who did not enter the employment of the Church in some fashion or other had a narrow range of career choices open to him if he wished to remain in Rome. He might choose to enter the army as an officer in the papal army. As a military force, the army was small and ineffective, but it was an army commission that provided security and a relatively high status. Or he might go with one of the liberal professions, as a physician or a lawyer (though neither of these paid terribly well, and physicians garnered little respect). Scholars and antiquarians could make a good living if they were good at it and not overly burdened with scruples. They mainly worked as tour guides and could make large amounts of money acting as middlemen for rich foreigners who wanted to buy antiquities, no questions asked. Another possible career was that of courtier. If he had the skill, there were positions in the arts, from architect or painter to musician or decorator. The occasional noble owned a theatre or a manufactory, and the great route to prosperity for the miniscule middle class was shop-keeping.

The Arts

As we noted in chapter 5, Rome supported a large number of men and women in the minor arts of decorating, weaving, jewellery making, fireworks and the constructing of the great celebratory *macchine* that filled the churches and piazzas of the city. In addition there were the great and famous artists like Canova, Thorvaldsen, Wicar and Camuccini, and communities of foreign artists from the German states, France, Denmark, England and many others flocked to draw inspiration from the well-springs of western civilisation.

Shop-keeping

A Case Study: Booksellers and Printers[20]

Booksellers and printers gathered around the Piazza Navona, and occupied an important niche in the Roman economy as well as in Roman culture. For obvious reasons, they were a topic of much interest to anyone trying to govern the city. While revolutionaries criticised the deplorable censorship of the popes, they themselves kept a close eye on anything that was printed and distributed.

Among the most notable of the Roman printers and booksellers were the deRomanis family, who sold, and sometimes printed, books near the Piazza Navona under the popes, the republic, the emperor, and again under the popes. Mariano

---

20 Palazzolo, Maria Iolanda. 'Una dinastia de stampatori nella Roma dei papi.'

deRomanis, head of the firm during the revolutionary period, bought whole private libraries of prelates and nobles, and sold them in his shop, a common practice with book dealers of the time. Most of his clients were clerics of one sort or another, which probably explains why he scrupulously obeyed papal regulations – he sold books on the Index, but they were marked with an asterisk that noted that 'these would not be sold to those who did not show the appropriate licence'.

By 1808 (when Pius VII was still technically in charge of Rome, but the French had for all intents and purposes occupied the city), the deRomanis catalogue was full of prohibited books, along with Greek and Latin titles, and no indication of limit on their sale. The deRomanis catalogues became progressively fuller as the years passed. They began to specialise, in theology and philosophy on the one hand, and in 'solid volumes of classical Latin and Greek' on the other. They also seem to have become a 'privileged connection' between German publishers of books on law and theology, and Roman readers.

The imperial administration was especially friendly to book dealers 'who enjoyed their particular interest and direct subventions on the part of the *Consulta Straordinaria*.' Mariano deRomanis had taken an active part in the republic of 1798–99, holding the post of First Grand Edil and Administrator of the *bollo* (tax stamps) and, for a very brief time, minister of the interior. As Sala noted in his diary, ' ... one must say that the choice of a bookseller and a lawyer [makes for] most interesting grand edils!'[21]

When deRomanis became minister of the interior, Sala has this to say: 'They've finally chosen as minister of the interior the bookseller deRomanis, one of the administrators of the *bollo*, no one can deny his character as an honest man.'[22] His reputation for honesty probably allowed him to survive the changes from pope to republic to pope to empire and back to pope again.

In imperial Rome, among the goodies dispensed by the *Consulta*, deRomanis got the right to publish official Acts and government documents, thus guaranteeing an income in the darkest of times. With 1810, the activities of the publishing firm of deRomanis and Sons increased. He had a good press, with imitation Bodoniana typeface (sign of a neoclassical taste) along with an established shop.

When Napoleon fell and Rome welcomed the pope back, the house of deRomanis continued on with hardly a blink. In 1815, he began the publication of an edition of Dante's *Divine Comedy*, a revised version of the 1791 Fulgoni text, with corrections and explanatory notes. Filippo deRomanis, who inherited the firm with his brother Nicola, would become a major literary figure in his own right, and published the first works of the Trastevere dialect poet, Gioacchino Belli.

A Case History: Patent Medicines[23]
Samaritan's Balm was a popular medicinal mixture based on camphor, and was also sold as a plaster. In 1750, the widow Margherita Toscani and her sons Filippo and Domenico got a licence to produce and sell the balm in Rome at their shop near the

21 Sala, *Diario romano*, II, pp. 139–40.
22 *Ibid*, III, p. 99.
23 Kolega, *op. cit.*

Piazza Barbarini. When Margherita and Filippo died, the business was carried on by Domenico and his niece, Caterina, daughter of Filippo. In order to continue the business in 1791 Gaspere Romei, Caterina's son, applied to the Physicians Guild (the Collegio Medico) for a licence to make and sell the balm under the proprietary name of GioDomenico Toscani. Domenico and his nephew after him paid 20 *scudi* a year for the permit.

Samaritan's Balm was well known in Italy and abroad. While he was alive, GioDomenico had succeeded in keeping the private licence to make it, at least in Rome. There were other Samaritan's Balms, as in Venice; in Rome, another man, Pietro Pichi Lazzarini, druggist at the Due Macelli, sold his own Samaritan's Balm which was similar to that sold by Toscani. Toscani tried to have Pichi arrested, and failed; but he did make him stop selling his product under the name of Samaritan's Balm.

In 1796 GioDomenico died and the shop passed to Caterina, who by this time was quite expert in making and selling the balm; while her son Gaspare was a minor, the shop was managed by her husband Vincenzo. However, Caterina was unable to defend the patent, and lost it after she separated from Vincenzo, on the grounds that he was violent. She attempted to run the shop alone, but on their first inspection, the Collegio Medico attempted to stop her from doing this. In a petition to the pope, Caterina asked permission to continue to keep the shop open, until the majority of her son. Permission was given but in 1806 Caterina was unable to pay the 20 *scudi* licence fee; soon, having rented the shop to others, she was considering selling it because she was reduced to poverty.

Manufacturers and Factories

From time to time the papal government took a direct hand in promoting industry, as with the famous cotton factory in the baths of Diocletian [see below]. The theory was that such enterprises would provide jobs for some of the hoards of unemployed and unemployable Romans. However, in the case of the cotton factory, the managers found themselves forced to hire foreign workers (from other Italian areas, mostly), since they couldn't find, or claimed they couldn't find, Romans willing and able to take the jobs.

There were three main areas for industrial activity in Rome. These were: building construction and repair; animal products (such as wool, leather and sheep gut); and enterprises associated with artists, spectacles, and entertainment, which also included spin-offs from classical archaeology, including the workmen who carried away the debris as well as the antiquarians and artists who made their livings selling, explaining, or otherwise impressing tourists with remnants of ancient glory.

Although they were a small part of the economy, there were real industries starting up in the city. There were tanners, and manufacturers of beaver hats and silk hats (highly regarded throughout Italy and the world), and the manufacture of white and embroidered gloves. The Pozzi concern made artificial pearls. By the end of the eighteenth century the 20 or more small factories engaged in making strings for musical instruments out of sheep gut had merged into one big business, the firm of

Pica-Tofanini and Company located in the Piazza di Napoli.[24] The business went into decline, and by 1810 there were only 25 employees at Pica-Tofanini and the two other string factories, though Mrs Eaton reports that the owner of the large factory at least was prominent in the social scene in 1819: 'there is a weekly *academia* of music given in Rome by a man who made a fortune by selling fiddle strings. Notwithstanding his plebian origins, his concerts are attended by most of the Roman nobility.' Romans also manufactured pianos, and were quite famous for the wind instruments made by Domenico Biglioni in the Via dei Banchi Vechi.

Commercial facilities for spinning wool, silk, cotton and linen were located in the large shelter of San Michele at Ripa in Trastevere, and smaller facilities located in the training schools where women and girls were taught to spin, and there were a number of small private spinning businesses. There were 11 spinning machines in the city in 1785, and in 1811 some 12,000 Romans were reported to be working at jobs associated with the making of linen fabric.[25] At the same time, most Roman women of the popular classes, like women since the beginning of civilisation, spun thread at home in their spare moments, using the traditional tools of distaff and spindle. In 1809 there were 34 factories making some sort of woollen cloth, using 456 looms; the calico factories operated by the state at Termini were famous. The state set up schools of spinning, and charitable institutions that sheltered orphan or 'endangered girls' almost always trained them in spinning and cloth work. Silk was always an attractive industry, and Rome underwrote the making of silk fabric, silk thread, silk stockings, and mixed silk and cotton cloth.[26]

Other industrial, or proto-industrial, production involved the tobacco works at San Cosimato. In San Pietro in Montorio, on the Janiculum hill above Trastevere, a Signor Giovan Antonio Sampieri established a factory for making wire out of iron, copper and brass, using power from the Aqua Paola. The waters of this aqueduct and fountain were also used to power several other small factories, and water mills along the Tiber powered machines that milled not only grain but also tobacco and paints. They were also used in tanning.[27] Another busy field of activity was the manufacture of rope from locally grown hemp. During the Napoleonic period, Rome and the nearby city of Viterbo had 120 rope-makers between them.

Perhaps the oddest industrial project was the idea of setting up a large factory for manufacturing cotton cloth in the baths of Diocletian in 1774. This never worked, perhaps because cotton does not grow well in the climate and soils of the Roman States. The factory never managed to compete with foreign manufacturers who could make the same or better cloth for half the price, even including shipping. The directors hired convicts, partly as a rehabilitation measure but mostly to save on labour costs, and were then plagued with pilfering. Taking on two Swiss experts as directors didn't help: the skilled silk workers revolted when the Swiss tried to make them work factory-style. By 1794 the Apostolic Chamber was desperate to get the white elephant off their hands, and

---

24 Gross, *op. cit.*, pp. 98–99.
25 Giuntella, *Roma nel Settecento*, p. 79, citing Del Pane, *Lo stato pontificio e il movimento riformatore del Settecento* p. 447.
26 Gross, *op. cit.*, p. 107.
27 Giuntella, *op. cit.*, and Gross, *op. cit.*, p. 91.

were delighted to lease it to a consortium including the banker Torlonia. But Torlonia and his friends had no better luck and opted out of their contract in 1801. When de Tournon took over as prefect in 1810, he tried to revive the works, but by 1812 the attempt was dead, and the baths of Diocletian returned to their archaeological serenity.

Vendors and Independent Workers
Romans preferred work that kept them out of doors, didn't require much in the way of education and made them subject to no one. They were by choice butchers, sailors, fishermen, carters, porters at the Ripa, tanners, salt-sellers. They also took naturally to selling small items on the streets (few had the capital to open shops). They fried and sold fritters, fish, fruits and vegetables, chickens.

Carters[28]
Wine carters had a high-status among the *popolo* both because it was important to the joyful side of life, and because it was hard and dangerous work. Most of the carters were from the districts of Trastevere, Monti or Regolo, and it was a typical job for the *bulli,* giving as it did plenty of opportunity for swaggering and for working to one's own timetable. The job was often passed down from father to son, in which case the little potential carter was 'baptised' to the work in a vat of water mixed with cereal and wine. They were a daring group who worked hard and took enormous risks, bringing wine to and from the *castelli romani,* the hill towns. To do this, they had to cross the malarial swamps of the *campagna* with its wolves and bandits. They went alone or in caravans, driving slowly all night long (to avoid damaging the wine), dozing while the single horse followed the trail unguided, and a small dog sat on the seat beside them, ready to give the alarm. Carters wore leather leggings fastened with buckles when they ventured out of town, with a heavy woollen cape and a tall cone-shaped hat decorated with coloured ribbons for good luck. Cart and horse were decorated with heavy, jingling bells. The carters wore gold earrings and gold watches with long chains, and small kegs of their own personal stock that hung beside their cart, or could be detached and carried away. Their carts had huge wheels, open loading platforms, and a sort of shelter called a *forcina,* made of sheepskin. They could carry 500 or so litres of wine, in barrels of 60 or 70 litres each, all strapped on to the back of the cart by means of an ingenious system of ropes, tightened with a windlass turned by two stout sticks, called *tortori.* The sticks also did duty as wheel-stops, or weapons, in case of brigands or wolves, or any other good opportunity for a fight.

Flocks and Vineyards
A large percentage of the Roman *popolo* worked in the fields within the city walls, or in the vineyards within or just beyond the gates. They would drive their flocks and herds to pasture in the ruins of classical Rome, and in the evening bring them back. As a result, the streets and lanes of Rome were filled not only with the dirt and clutter of urban life, but also with a rich layer of residue left by sheep, goats, cattle, horses, donkeys, turkeys and buffalo.

---

28 Pinelli's drawings, and the commentaries of Rossetti and others, are a key source on Rome's workers..

Women (and most Roman women worked) did similar work, especially cooking and selling food and bringing small items to market. They made chair-seats and brooms, they were weavers and laundresses. Among the most common work, women (called *lavanare*) sorted through grain, kernel by kernel, to separate it from impurities left over from threshing (where it was trampled by oxen or donkeys, or beaten with sticks, then sieved and put into sacks). Like most hand work, this was done in groups, with songs and story telling, while the young men hung around keeping them company and flirting.

Women also worked in the vineyards, harvesting or pruning the vines. This work was usually accompanied by songs, stories, jokes and the sort of behaviour that would not have been tolerated at other times of year. Even now there are dialect words related to the vintage, like *vignetta*, for a funny and preferably spicy story (it came into English as 'vignette'). At harvest time, the *mozzatrice* came back into the city from the vineyards 'wearing their best jewellery and ornaments, accompanied by their lovers, … singing and dancing' with musicians who were paid by the owner of the vineyard.[29]

In the City
The port of Ripa, where boats and barges brought goods to and from Fiumicino and Rome, was a busy one and employed hundreds of artisans, porters and small businessmen. Just beyond the Porta Portese was a dockyard, and this too employed many men. A lot of men made their livelihoods as wandering vendors. Shops were tiny, dark and narrow, and most people spent the greatest part of their time outdoors.

Different trades were typical of different areas: scrap dealers at Monte Giordano; gold-beaters in the Fico alley, watch-makers at the Piazza Capranica, mattress-makers at San Pantaleo, dealers in wine and in wood – wood for burning, and wood for building, casks, tables, boats – at Ripetta and Ripa and as far as the Piazza Nicosia. Rosary-makers between Tor Sanguigna and Panico, makers of ladies shoes in the Via dei Pianellari, tinkers at the Piazza Navona, soap-makers in the Via dei Pastini, papersellers, notaries, copyists, booksellers between Pasquino and the Chiesa Nuova, and the Governo Veccchio road; jewellers at the Via del Pellegrino, hat-makers in the Via dei Cappellari, sellers of chickens in the Piazza della Cancelleria to the Piazza della Valle, furriers in the Via dei Vaccinari, sellers of cloth and of clothing in the Via dei Giubbonari, nail-makers in the Via dei Chiavari.

Every neighbourhood and piazza had its barbers and butchers.

Then there were the comb-makers, the lute-makers, the rope-makers, basin-makers and vase-makers, who gave the names of their trades to the streets where they worked.

At Piazza Navona there were the sellers of old books, of old iron, and also the

29 Anonymous author of the *Quadro attuale della città di Roma. Osservazioni imparziali d'un viaggiatore republ. [Current picture of the city of Rome. Impartial observations by a republican traveller]*, Milan, Year II, xix, xx, cited in Giuntella, *Roma nel Settecento*, p. 60.

storytellers (*cantastorie*) and sellers of patent medicines who worked on Thursdays, when the greens, fruit and cereal market was open. The sellers of blankets were in the Via della Dogana Vecchia. At the Via del Paradiso, where the legume market was, there were inns for the muleteers. Others inns and hotels for merchants and foreigners were at the Via dell'Orso and around the Piazza di Spagna.

Artisans included the armourers at the Campo dei Fiori, where the makers of cross-bows had once worked. At the same place were sellers of horses, mules, and donkeys, sellers of hay and of fodder, and of old clothes. At the Piazza della Padella was a command post for the *sbirri*, at Piazza Giudea pawned items were sold, at Pasquino there were storytellers, at Madonna dei Monti there was a factory for making needles and every Saturday there was a food market there. Food for Rome came from the nearby countryside, from the vineyards and the farms and herds, but also from the Tiber: at Ripa Grande there were stores selling wine, salami, fruit, greens, and other goods that came by sea, on barges pulled by buffalo.

Vendors

There were more than 200 different kinds of vendors, many from outside the city of Rome. Zanazzo collected some 246 different vendors' cries, and Bartolomeo Pinelli left us with hundreds of visual images from the streets of his day:

... the *scarfarottaro*, with a bag full of shoes, slippers and boots.

... the *anticajaro*, who sold bits of archaeological finds and arrowheads and little stones dug up in one of the ancient fora (mostly trash).

... some people earned a precarious living as human alarm clocks, the 'night-time wakers-up' – who specialised in calling travellers for early departures, or as 'fire-lighters' who went around the ghetto offering to light fires for Jews who couldn't work on the Sabbath, calling out *Chi appicia? Chi appicia?* (who needs a light?).

... the *figurinaio* who sold dolls and little figures for *presepios*, like the ones Pinelli's father made

... and the *numeratari* or *riffaroli*, who sold tickets for raffles: 'There's only one left! Who wants it? Who would like this pretty little hen?' (the prizes were usually chickens or ducks).

... the *sticcalegna*, who walked around with an axe on his shoulders, looking for someone who wanted wood cut.

... the *crescioni*, who sold diuretics and stimulants, 'to make fresh piss'.

... the *lanternonari* sold lamps made of coloured paper, with pictures of saints and the Madonna, appropriate to whatever vigil was coming up; the lanterns would be placed in windows in honour of the feast.

... the *cenciaroli* (rag-sellers), street-sweepers, knife-grinders and sellers of images and dolls shaped like saints who sold their wares on the steps of churches.

... the *scacciaragnaro* went around in the week before Holy Week, when people were doing their Easter housecleaning calling out 'Clean your houses, ladies ...!'.

... the *aquacetosari* went about in a cart drawn by a donkey or a mule, selling flasks of Aqua Acetosa (mineral water from a spring near Rome).

... the *fusaglieri*, sold *lupina* and also sold 'big green flies' collected on sambuca flowers. Children bought them, tied strings around their legs, and flew them like kites.

Most vendors came from outside Rome, from Abruzzi, the Ciociaria, the Marche. Thus the seller of wooden utensils came from Abruzzi; sellers of calendars or almanacs usually came from the Marche. At Easter and Epiphany the toy-sellers came around, and on the feast of St John (also called the Night of the Witches) vendors sold charms to protect one from witches and from the evil eye.

Men, and sometimes women, walked the streets of Rome selling umbrellas, and boiled chestnuts, oil lamps, greens and *gramigna*, matches, and so many other things.

Food
Romans often bought their food pre-prepared at simple street booths and tables, or from itinerant vendors
    ... the *mosciarellari* who sold dried chestnuts from Friuli or Camerino.
    ... the *brustolinari* sold toasted dried squash seeds.
    ... at night the *aquavittaro* walked through the streets with his tray offering dry loop-shaped biscuits and shots of gin to wash them down with.
    ... the *tripparolo* balanced a large tray on his head and sold the left-overs from butchering the pigs – the tripe, feet, and heads.
    ... the *capraro* brought his goats into town and milked them on the spot for customers who brought their own jugs and watched carefully to be sure they weren't cheated.
    ... farmers from Abruzzi or Ciociaria drove in flocks of live turkeys.
    ... in the spring, men on horseback brought in large baskets in which they carried the new lambs to sell to the butchers.
    ... the watermelon sellers with their stands that looked like stage sets, and their colourful patter that was half of their stock in trade.
    ... the men and women who sold fried fish and fritters and doughnuts, in the Piazza Navona or outside the gates on St Joseph's Day in March.
    ... the *gioncataro*, who brought his soft, newly made cheese in from the countryside wrapped in leaves and kept in a basket that he carried with his shepherd's crook.
    ... you could buy live snails on long sticks, and ices, mulberries and hot rice balls filled with cheese, dried chestnuts and salted, roasted squash seeds.
    Butchers collected animals at the Cow Field and slaughtered them in the streets outside their shops.
    Ordinary people did not bake their own bread, only the palaces or institutions that distributed bread to the poor baked their own; people bought the staff of life from bakers, who were subject to strict and detailed laws about content, weight, and even shape.
    ... the *melacottaro*, who sold cooked apples, or the *peracottaro*, who went about in the early summer evenings with his cooked pears, improvising verses in praise of his marvellous fruit: 'I saw them put the sugar in, good pears, hot, hot, hot ...'.

As familiar a sight in Rome then as now were the elderly women who set out food for cats in the Pantheon or the Piazza Argentina. At the turn of the nineteenth century, food for cats and dogs was peddled by a very humble sort of vendor, the *carnacciaro*

(Belli defined the *carnacciaro* as a 'wandering seller of rotten meat for cat food'). He found his best customers in the convents, where nuns were notoriously fond of cats. The vendors were also known to steal fine cats and sell them to people who were in the market for an elegant pet (again, nuns).

The *carnacciaro* had a characteristic whistle as his call, and was usually followed by a mewing cortege of cats. From time to time, he took his big knife and cut off a chunk of meat, gratis, as a sort of advert. This was an extremely humble occupation, picking up scraps of rotten meat from butchers, or from road-kills, and selling it for pet food.

French guns pointing at the papal residence on Monte Cavallo, June 1809.

CHAPTER EIGHT
THE NEW REGIME

Love may be essential to any modern understanding of tragedy. If so, what happened in Rome in the seven years between 1808 and 1815 was certainly a tragedy. Napoleon loved Rome like a bridegroom; Rome did not love Napoleon. The affair progressed from courtship to rape and ended, as such affairs must end, in mutual destruction.

On 10 June 1809, the ancient city of Rome passed from independence as the seat of empire and the seat of the Church, to the ambiguous status of an imperial city, associated and then amalgamated with France. The best men that Napoleon had to offer came to restore the ancient city, to embellish the existing city and to create a modern one. They had talent. They had incentive (the emperor was not an easy taskmaster). They had, at least in theory, plenty of money. They had a population that, if it did not welcome them, was at least cowed. They worked like Hercules. And they failed.

If Napoleon and the pope parted on good terms after the imperial coronation in December of 1804 – and it seems that they did – the honeymoon would last little more than the traditional month. Early the next year, the emperor travelled to Milan to be crowned King of Italy under the ominous title of *Rex Totius Italiae* – King of all Italy.[1] While the emperor and king was happy to leave the pope as head of the Church, he was determined that that Church would have to be the willing handmaiden of the state in civil affairs. Unfortunately, Napoleon and Pius differed on the definition of civil affairs. For Napoleon, when there was a conflict between the Church and the State, whether it was a matter of blockade or divorce, it was the State that must have the final word. By the end of 1805 there were a whole string of conflicts between the new Charlemagne and his strangely uncooperative pope.

---

1 The motto appeared on a medal struck for the coronation.

That summer, the emperor was annoyed by his youngest brother Jerome's quixotic American marriage, to a Protestant (worse, a commoner). It was the pope's clear duty to annul the pretended marriage, or approve a divorce. The pope declined.

An imperial catechism was being prepared, informing citizens that 'to honour and serve our emperor is to honour and serve God himself.' It was the pope's duty to approve the catechism. The pope declined.

A new feast day was proclaimed, the feast of the hitherto obscure St Napoleon. The new feast was to displace the mid-August feast of the Annunciation. It was the pope's duty to approve. The pope declined.

The English continued to threaten the empire, their ships continued to call openly at the ports in the Papal States; British nationals remained in Rome, protected by the pope; the emperor's own defiant brother Lucien was living in Rome. It was the duty of every subject king in the empire to condemn the enemies of their emperor. The pope declined.

By 1806, Napoleon was writing to his ambassador in Rome (Uncle/Cardinal Fesch) that the pope was behaving like a 'lunatic'. 'I expect the pope to accommodate his conduct to my requirements. If he behaves well, I shall make no outward changes; if not, I shall reduce him to the status of bishop of Rome …'

In July, when Cardinal Fesch proved unable to secure the pope's cooperation, he was recalled and replaced by a layman, a Monsieur Alquier. When Fesch introduced Alquier, the pope informed him that if the emperor threatened the independence of Rome, the pope would 'use the temporal and spiritual means which God has placed in our hands' – in other words, excommunication. Fesch remonstrated. The usually gentle Pius shouted him down.

The following year, to enforce the continent-wide blockade against English trade that he had proclaimed, Napoleon sent troops from the Kingdom of Italy to occupy the eastern provinces of the Papal States.By January 1808 General Miollis was on his way south, and on the second day of February he occupied the Castel Sant'Angelo. The pope, it was reported, was only with difficulty dissuaded from barring Miollis' entry into the Castello with his own body, defying that urbane and generally sympathetic commander to strike him down with his sword.

After February 1808 Pius VII was technically still a monarch, but all of the Papal States were now occupied by imperial troops. The pope withdrew to the Quirinal palace, a virtual prisoner, and sent a message to the emperor. 'You may tell them at Paris', he informed the departing ambassador Alquier, 'that they may hack me to pieces, that they may skin me alive, but always I shall say no …'

Diplomatic relations were severed. Alquier returned to Paris to inform the court that there was no hope of bending this pope, who had seemed so pliant and meek, to the imperial will. 'You do not know this man,' he told them.[2]

The Carnival that Was Not

In the battle for control of Rome, Miollis had all the troops, but Pius had all the moral authority. When Miollis, a generous and genial host, gave parties, the pope let it be known among the clergy that it was not appropriate for them to socialise with his

2   Anderson, *Pope Pius VII*, p. 66.

jailer; and the clergy did not attend. Some nobles did, either because they were sympathetic to the French cause or because, lacking the 'vocation of martyrdom', they had a horror of making waves.

As early as November, General Miollis realised that there was likely to be trouble with the coming carnival, if the pope forbade the celebrations (which he was clearly likely to do).[3] The general took steps. On 6 November, Benedetti reports that

... there has been a great disturbance today in the Casa Radanini. The sbirri *surrounded it, as though it was besieged, and for what? To seize the trappings of the horses that run in the carnival races, which are kept there.*

Despite the general's best efforts, 1809 turned out to be the year when they gave a carnival and nobody came. On 17 December 1808 the French commander issued a notice, stating that carnival would take place as usual, with the usual amusements. Craftsmen, costume-makers and other interested parties were to make preparations. On the following day, another notice appeared from the prisoner in the Quirinal. Far from authorising the carnival, he urged the faithful to follow the example of the first Christians: Peter is in chains; the Church should be at prayer.

The French took this as an open declaration of war. They forcibly seized the decorations; they commissioned Pietro Piranesi, son of the famous engraver and an enthusiastic francophile, to organise the great affair. They built platforms for the spectators and requisitioned horses for the racing; they opened the theatres and decked them out for the usual carnival balls; they ordered that the costume shops be opened, and spread sand and roped off the streets to contain the crowds ... and nobody came. On the Corso, there were the horses, and there were the French. But the shops closed in protest, and the people, unmasked, turned their backs. At General Miollis' carnival ball, the only Roman family to accept his invitation were the Borghese – and at least half of them (the half designated by family policy to remain loyal to the pope) no doubt stayed at home.

Pasquino was moved to some of his finest quips. There were one-liners:

Bears dance when you beat them, men don't.
You can force a man to weep, but not to laugh.
There was a race [the traditional climax of carnival]. *Who won? The pope.*

... and little rhyming couplets:

Avremo il carneval: oh cosa bella!
I francesi faran da pulcinella!

Voi, Sestili e Piranesi, come amici dei francesi,
Domandate al generale se gli piace il Carnevale! [4]

---

3   This would not be an unprecedented move. Carnivals could be, and often enough were, cancelled or curtailed in hard times.

4   We'll have a carnival: how lovely! The French will be the clowns! You, Sestili and Piranesi, as friends of the French, Ask the general if he likes the carnival!

To add insult to injury, a few days after the end of the carnival that was not, came the anniversary of the election of Pius VII. Without orders, the entire city of Rome was illuminated in celebration.

A police report informed Paris that 'the pope rules more here with his little finger than we do with bayonets.'

By no means all Romans hated the new regime. A pro-French minority included representatives from all classes. From the liberal clergy came men like the Scuole Pie priests, educators who believed in modernism and enlightenment, and who saw no real contradiction between Christianity and the new politics of democracy. Indeed, when Barnaba Chiaramonti (later Pius VII) was Bishop of Imola he had belonged to that group. It almost cost him the papacy: many cardinals were most reluctant to crown a man they saw as soft on democracy. A few members of the upper clergy – up to and even including the pope – had long been frustrated in their desire to modernise the economy (doing away with guilds, for instance) or the city (numbering houses, lighting the streets). Some clerics – and this group did not include the pope – felt that the temporal power of the papacy was a hindrance, not a help, to the spiritual responsibilities of the Church. The great nobility of Rome included members who were willing, for one reason and another, to make themselves pleasant to the new rulers; some, like members of the Chigi family, or Duke Bonelli-Pio, or the Cesarini-Sforza, had long cherished liberal ideas. Others, like the Braschi pope's nephews, leaned whichever way the wind blew.

Members of the secular middle class felt the same frustrations that their fellows had long felt in Europe. To many of them, it seemed like good common sense to clean up the law codes (they had read their Beccaria), open jobs to talent rather than tie opportunity up in the complicated knots of family and class. Medical doctors were cramped by religious prohibitions. And in Rome, the non-clerical middle classes shared one enormous frustration with the aristocracy: both were excluded from government or administration.

The great bulk of the *popolo* resented any attempts at change, but some – like the artist Pinelli – felt curbed and confined by the laws of religious government, and looked with some hope to the new liberty. And, of course, there were men and women in all classes who kept a keen eye open to see which side would best butter their bread.

But even with these exceptions, most Romans preferred the devil they knew and bitterly resented the intrusion of strangers. The French, they believed, were atheists and tyrants. Romans were suspicious of any measures, no matter how reasonable or benevolent, they tried to introduce. Worse, when the French came, prices went up, supplies went down, people went hungry, the poor were expected to work, and their sons were expected to fight.

Whatever objections they might have had to papal government (and they had many), by comparison to the French the pope looked like a loving father. When he defied the emperor, Romans felt that he was defending his family. When he was kidnapped and sent away, Romans considered him a martyr. When his supporters were expelled, expropriated, scorned and dragged away literally in chains, Romans felt they had been plunged back to the dawn of Christianity, or to the chaos that would usher in the end of the world. When the Stations of the Cross were removed from the Coliseum to accommodate the archaeologists, many Romans wondered if the lions would soon put in a return appearance.

'Plotting by the Court of Naples'

Napoleon had never been enthusiastic about Joachim Murat's marriage to his sister Caroline, but they made an effective couple, and the dashing general's star rose steadily. According to some reports, he first came to Rome in 1801, shortly after the battle of Marengo had put Italy in Napoleon's pocket. At that point he asked Napoleon for permission to occupy the Castel Sant'Angelo, and it took all Cardinal Consalvi's diplomacy, plus half a million in cash, to dissuade him. After sister-in-law Pauline became the Princess Borghese in 1803, Murat was a frequent visitor, and his appetite for Rome grew.

In June of 1808 – that is, some four months after Miollis had been sent to occupy, but not rule, Rome – Murat and Caroline became their majesties the King and Queen of Naples. (They replaced Napoleon's older brother Joseph and his wife Julie, who were moved from Naples to the far more important and difficult throne of Spain.) On his way to Naples, Murat stopped at the Palazzo Farnese, and installed his Corsican police chief, Salicetti, to run the Neapolitan agents in Rome (if the word 'dashing' was coined to describe Murat, the word 'wily' was made for his police chief). Whether it was his plan, or Caroline's, the Murats set about playing a complex diplomatic game. They intimated to the papal chancellor Cardinal Consalvi that they were shocked by Napoleon's treatment of the papal court. They worked hard to win over the most influential Roman nobles – the Doria, the Colonna, the Pallavicini. On Murat's urging, these nobles petitioned Paris to the effect that, should the condition of Rome change, it should be united to Naples. (Eugene wrote in the margin of the petition: 'plotting by the court of Naples' (*intrighi del gabbinetto napoletano*).

At the same time King Murat was urging Napoleon to authorise him to use Neapolitan troops to seize the city and depose the pope – all in the name of the emperor, of course. In December, in one of a series of urgent but fawning letters, he wrote to Napoleon:

How long will Your Majesty put up with the audacity of that fanatical ingrate [the pope]? Let Your Majesty only give me the authorisation, and his [Pius'] reign will come to a quick end. Rome will be at your feet![5]

Murat had every reason to hope that his new Kingdom of Naples would be extended to include Rome and the Roman States that lay just across his border at Gaëta. General Miollis, who had been in the city for almost a year, had accomplished nothing, was inept to the point of treason – or so Murat charged. The Civic Guard [that is, Roman supporters of the French], 'abandoned by Miollis', looked to Naples for their salvation. In December, while Miollis was trying to see that a carnival took place (and that was of central importance), Murat was pursuing his own plans.

5   Murat to the emperor, 9 December 1808, Archives de la Guerre, Armée du Naples, 1808-1809; cited by Madelin, *op. cit.*, p. 197.

He failed. Miollis and the members of the *Consulta* reached Rome late on 9 June, and the next day Miollis put an end to two governments at once: the ancient rule of the popes, and the still-born rule of Murat's Naples. But this would not, as we will see, be the end of the Murat family hopes.

Rome: Imperial City, 10 June 1809

At dawn on 10 June 1809, the bridges that joined Trastevere and the Borgo to the city of Rome were occupied by French infantry of the 101st regiment of the Line, their strength supplemented by cannon from the 2nd Artillery regiment.[6] Anyone who tried to cross the river from those potentially troublesome districts was turned back or arrested.

General Miollis, who for 18 months had been in actual command of Rome by force of military occupation, had returned to his residence on the Piazza di Spagna from the north, where he had gone for orders. Salicetti, Murat's minister of police, hurried in before dawn from Albano to the Farnese palace. At 8.00, a Neapolitan regiment moved to reinforce the men guarding the Ponte Sisto, the bridge that led directly from Trastevere to the heart of the city.

At 9.00, two cannon shots boomed from the Castel Sant'Angelo: every man, woman and child in Rome knew that was a signal that could not be ignored. At 10.00, the papal flag was slowly lowered from the battlements and, as 100 cannon shots were fired to underline the momentous import, the French imperial tricolour – red, white and blue, topped with the eagle – rose to take its place.

Heavy carriages with coachmen and lackeys in French livery rolled from Miollis' residence at the Piazza di Spagna to the Farnese palace. They carried the members of the new government, the *Consulta* appointed to transform Rome from a backward theocratic state, to its new glory as the second city of the Western Empire. The patricians of Rome hurried to the Farnese to learn what the new order would mean for them. Salicetti, who seems to have dexterously shifted sides, informed them of the facts of life in his blunt Corsican Italian: 'Society', he said, 'is divided into hammers, and nails. If you refuse to become hammers – you will be nails.'[7] While the patricians were alternately coaxed and bullied, the *popolo* hurried to the Capitol, the heart of the city and seat of its government.

At 11.00, as the last cannon shots from the fortress died away, a group of officers appeared at the Capitol; a herald stepped forward to read the proclamation making Rome a free imperial city. Then a brilliant procession formed up, led by cavalry men of the 4th *Chasseurs*, their equipage jingling as their horses danced and the hooves struck sparks from the paving stones. The procession halted three times along the Corso that led to the northern gate at the Piazza del Popolo: once at the Piazza Venezia, once halfway along the way, at the Piazza Colonna; and finally at the Piazza del Popolo itself. The mounted herald, dressed in red and gold (the colours of the city of Rome), stopped to read from the parchment: 'From our Imperial Camp at Vienna, this 17th of May 1809 …'[8]

6   For a vivid description of the day's activities, see Madelin, *op. cit.*, pp. 19–26.
7   General Pepe, *Mémoires*, p. 109, as reported by Madelin.
8   Correspondance de Napoléon, 17 May 1809, 15219.

The edict appeared on 'enormous placards' on the walls of Rome:

Romans, the will of the greatest of heroes has reunited you with the greatest of states. It is fitting that the first people of the earth should share the benefits of their laws and the honour of their name with those who, in another age, preceded them along the triumphal way. ...

You become part of the Empire, after the sacrifices needed to create it have already been made; you are called to triumph without having had to share the danger. In joining you to his empire, Napoleon the Great wants only the glory of giving you, after so many centuries of oblivion, a fate more worthy of your ancient destiny...

[there followed more mundane paragraphs, which caught the eye of Fortunati, below. The proclamation ends with an oratorical flourish:]

... How sweet, oh Romans! is the future that awaits you, for which the Consulta *has been charged with preparing the basis.*

Romans! By seconding our efforts you will bring sooner, and make easier for us, the good which we have the duty and the intention of doing for you.

With these tortured and bombastic, but tragically sincere, phrases the representatives of the Grand Nation informed the Romans of their happy destiny.

Francesco Fortunati, who copied everything into his diary, reported his version of the proclamation. Stripped of the rhetoric, for Fortunati the proclamation promised: French law, the continuation of the city as head of the Church, restoration of the ancient monuments, patronage for the arts and economic assistance.[9]

The Consulta

In 1808, when General Miollis arrived to occupy the city, there were 21 departments of Roman government (called 'congregations'), which looked after matters like the Inquisition, Apostolic Visitation, 'Good Government', Bishops' Residences, Clerical Immunity, Waters and Marshes, the Propagation of the Faith, the Index, Sacred Rites and the Economy. It was, as Camille de Tournon would later advise his emperor, 'a real Tower of Babel, a confusion of tongues.' It was impossible to tell the difference between the civil and the ecclesiastical, so that the Water Board as well as the Committee for Good Government were both completely entangled with the Church.

---

9   Fortunati, *Diario* 10 June 1809. 'Our government has been changed from papal to French government, by an imperial proclamation from Vienna, which included things like: "Romans you are not conquered but united, fellow citizens not servants, not only will the strength of the empire be yours, but her laws will also become yours, the same laws that have made France peaceful and happy within, and respected and feared without,... You will lose nothing that is already yours." ... "Rome will continue to be the visible head of the Church, and the Vatican will be decorously assisted." ... "religion, made more pure, will have even greater splendour." ... "Equal care will be given to the monuments of your ancient patrimony and glory; the Arts, daughters of genius, will under the reign of the Great Emperor, will no longer have to go begging." ... "Romans, this is the future that awaits you, which the Extraordinary Committee has the duty of preparing the basis." ... "We will guarantee your public debt; animate your agriculture and arts ... etc, etc" It was signed by Saliceti and Janet, Miolllis as governor and president; and for the Committee, Balbo.'

A cardinal, in theory answerable only to the pope, headed each section of government. But the pope was absorbed in Church matters, and most of his time was taken up with elaborate and demanding religious ceremonies, so he had no real idea of what was going on around him. As a result the cardinals who headed the various congregations decided matters for themselves. Or rather, the prelates made the decisions for the cardinals. Prelates, however, were also busy with their own business, and their secretaries made the decisions for them. 'And very often', de Tournon concluded, 'women make the decisions for everyone.'[10]

This was completely unacceptable in the clear, bright, masculine world of the new empire. In the place of this medieval confusion, Napoleon appointed a *Consulta* to help Rome make the transition from papal capital, to the capital of a new world empire, and from an absolute monarchy to a constitutional (but arguably just as absolute) government.[11] The *Consulta*, as it eventually shaped up, was to be headed by General Miollis as acting Governor General and President; the Baron Joseph Marie de Gérando, a devout Catholic; Laurent-Marie Janet, the fiscal agent; del Pozzo, in charge of justice; and Count Cesare Balbo, secretary (with scruples).

Antoine Cristophe Salicetti, Murat's Corsican chief of police, was also an early member of the *Consulta*. He co-signed the first 21 edicts of the *Consulta* as King Murat's representative in Rome. He may have been put on the *Consulta* because Napoleon believed he had had a falling out with Murat, but, whatever the reason, in June Salicetti took up residence at the Farnese palace. His sudden death six months later after dining at the home of Maghera, his replacement as chief of police in Naples, gave rise to inevitable stories about poison.

The Men of the Consulta
One of Murat's agents described the men of the *Consulta* to his king, shortly after they took office:

Count-General Miollis is well regarded as a soldier, but people complain that he does not have the head for organising a government; his principles make him see the Patriots as devoted to the government, but he is wrong because they abuse this title. The general is incapable of disloyalty, but they say he sometimes gives in to the charms of Venus.

Imperial count, general of the army, head of the *Consulta*, and governor general of the Roman States, Sextius Alexandre François Miollis' given names made him a particularly appropriate choice for commander in Rome – two classical, and the third suggesting the Renaissance French monarchy that patronised, and fed on, Italy. The sixteenth child of a provincial noble family of Aix, Miollis was on his way to a military career by the time the revolution began in 1789, with the regimental rank of captain of infantry. He had fought against the British on the side of the American colonists,

10 ASR-MGGF, cass. 1. Letter sent by the emperor to Gaudin, Minister of Finances, (17 May 1809). As cited by Costanzo, 'Tournon e l'assechement des marins pontines', in *Camille de Tournon, Prefect de la Rome Napoléonienne* p.31.
11 Is it merely a coincidence that the word *Consulta* recalls the consular government of the Roman republic, or is it rather a reflection of how deep Rome is embedded in the languages descended from Latin?

and was injured fighting at the battle of Yorktown; the wound disfigured his face and he tried to hide it with a luxuriant moustache. A tall, thin, somewhat stooped man, he had joined the revolution with enthusiasm and rose quickly in rank, and in 1797 was the military governor of Mantua after the French besieged and took the city. He did well in Mantua, and then went on to rule in Ferrara (where he had the ashes of the poet Ariosto moved to the university with great pomp and splendour) and at Verona (where he restored the Roman arena, thus earning the future good will of people who like to combine tourism with a taste for spectacular operatic productions). He had a good reputation as an honest, cultivated and amiable man, and a good governor, though he tended to trust the pro-French Italians (Madelin called him a 'natural optimist' who lacked the cynicism necessary for a true politician) and had a weakness for beautiful women. At least at the start he had his reservations about Bonaparte: in 1802 he declined to vote in the referendum that made Napoleon First Consul for Life, and instead of delivering the expected speech in praise of Bonaparte switched at the last minute to a speech extolling George Washington. But he served as governor general of the Roman States from 1808 to the fall of Napoleon in 1814, and remained doggedly loyal to the empire even after Rome was occupied by Murat's Neapolitans, preferring to take refuge in the Castel Sant'Angelo with the loyal troops rather than surrender. Even more than most cultivated Frenchmen, he loved Rome and spent a great deal of his own money on beautifying the city, and patronising science and the arts. A great admirer of Canova, he brought the great sculptor – who had little reason to love Napoleon – into the imperial restoration and antiquarian projects. He wrote verse under the Arcadian name of Amarilii Etrusca (an imperfect anagram of his own names, as was traditional). He also gave really good parties.[12]

M. de Gérando has a good reputation [Murat's agent continued], *the way he conducts his administration is admirable, he is moderate and inclined to the good. The good reputation he made in Tuscany is reinforced in Rome, which finds the opinion of the Tuscans to be most accurate.*

The 'amiable, always smiling' Baron Joseph Marie de Gérando was an effective blend of the eighteenth-century polymath (he was knowledgeable about mathematics, administration, history, philosophy both natural and intellectual, education and what we would now call anthropology). He was a good friend of Madame de Staël, and something of a Rousseau-ist (in that he believed in the natural goodness of man). His study of philosophy brought on a crisis of religious faith, but he emerged more or less unscathed and was regarded as a sympathetic friend in Catholic Rome. He had had a hot time of it in the early, radical days of the revolution. He fled Lyons after being implicated in counter-revolutionary riots, and lived the life of an émigré, first in Switzerland and then in Naples (where he wrote some memoirs piquantly titled, 'My Neapolitan Nights' [*Mes nuits de Naples*]). Napoleon, however, recognised talent when he saw it, and cultivated the brilliant and eclectic baron as an invaluable

---

12 Nardi, *Napoleone e Roma* p. 90.

ally among the intellectual circle known as the 'ideologues', and made him an important leader among the administrative shock troops sent to Italy in the wake of the conquest. After sorting out Lombardy, Tuscany and Rome, Gérando went on to the Council of State in Paris in 1810. The fall of Napoleon was by no means the end of his career, and he went on to establish the study of administration at the Sorbonne. In Rome, he lived in the Palazzo Corsini with his 'excellent' Alsatian wife, and was generally regarded as a cheerful, optimistic reformer and a reliable servant of the empire. He was an early advocate of the science and philosophy of administration, and a *devoté* of the study of history ('The secret of the future is in the past', and 'the history of nations is the first study of the law-maker. The history of thought must be the first study of the philosopher'). Among his life work, in addition to ground-breaking works on administration, we find studies of philology and language, of 'special education' (on the education of those deaf-mute from birth), and an investigation of methods to follow in the study of savages. The last two might have been particularly relevant to the creation, *ex nihilo*, of a new Roman state.

The author of the anonymous report to Murat observed that:

M. Jeannet [sic] has severe principles, but he finds himself in a difficult position because he is in charge of finances; sometimes one must pay in good will what one cannot pay in money.

The 'money man' of the *Consulta*, Baron Laurent-Marie Janet was a provincial lawyer before 1789, and he seems to have remained a typical middle-level bureaucrat, immersed in the details, hardworking, determined, careful and not very likeable. Miollis was afraid of him, and Madelin dismissed him as 'hard to the point of cruelty, with a mediocre education, and always quarrelling with his colleagues,' especially with Gérando.[13] He treated Rome like a conquered province (which, of course, it was). He was universally disliked, but didn't mind a bit; he belonged body and soul to the emperor, and his skills as a finance officer were unquestionable. After the restoration, even Consalvi (who had no reason to admire anything French) kept his fiscal arrangements in place with little or no change.

He had only one friend on the *Consulta* (or, for that matter, outside it), and that was Fernando del Pozzo, who was in charge of setting up the judicial machinery. Del Pozzo had extensive legal experience, and was widely considered a leading expert on Roman law, but the people of Rome hated him from the start for the simple reason that he was a Piedmontese and (of course) he filled up his administration with his fellow countrymen. Like Janet, he was something of a martinet: even the police, it was said, thought he was too strict. But also like Janet, he was very good at his job, and quickly organised the courts into an efficient and well-administered system. He wrote extensively and published works in Italian, French and even in English ('Catholicism in Austria') and died in 1843 on the losing side of the national debate, a supporter of Austrian rule in Italy.

The fifth member of the first *Consulta* was another man from Piedmont, the much more likeable young Count Cesare Balbo. He was the secretary of the group,

---

13 Madelin, *op. cit.*, p. 218.

and had no real talent, or responsibility, for administration. He had entered the imperial service over the disapproval of his family and despite his own qualms, and when the 'war against God' began (that is, priests and officeholders began to be arrested for failing to take the loyalty oath) he reproached himself for not having the courage to join them [see chapter 9]. Balbo was to have a long career as an Italian patriot and historian, but at this phase of his career he worked hard, kept his nose clean, and was in general a nice young man, if somewhat too religious for the taste of Janet ('he needs to gain a lot of experience' was Janet's judgement – 'and lose some scruples'). General Radet, too, thought him too inclined to follow his conscience, but then General Radet (who would kidnap the pope) knew all about suppressing one's scruples when the job required it.

General Radet may indeed be considered as a sixth member of the governing body of Rome, although he never served on the *Consulta*. Sent to Rome to organise the gendarmerie, he considered himself the equal of Miollis and the only man of action among the top administrators. Madelin, who had access to a lot of documentation, considered Radet to be 'bizarre, and extremely eccentric', bombastic, unreliable, contradictory and too likely to get involved in plots. He directed the kidnapping of the pope, to the point of smashing down doors himself with a hatchet, but in later days he claimed to have been the pope's pious protector. He liked to discuss theology with bishops, and, as head of the gendarmerie, wrote up a circular for police spies on the nature and attributes of God. He also wrote hymns to the Blessed Virgin, but that did not stop him from courting the wife of another general, or from buying up (under assumed names) monastic property that he had, in his official capacity, confiscated.

The Work of the Consulta

The *Consulta* was commissioned to do two things, which were not always in agreement. On the one hand, they were to set up a government by which the second city could be ruled as an integral part of the empire; on the other they were to transform Rome in the image of its new ruler.[14] So, one of their first acts was to create an arts council that consisted of superstars ... most of whom declined to cooperate. This was, unfortunately, symbolic of much of the imperial experience. On paper, it was magnificent; in reality, it left little behind it beyond the Pincio gardens, and some minor archaeological works.

Their more practical commissions bore more obvious fruit. Late in 1809, emblematically and literally, the *Consulta* decreed that there should be light. Fortunati, without comment, noted that the lights went on in Rome. By law.

16 November – An order has been given that after the first hour of the night [half an hour after sunset], *the bell at Monte Citorio would ring for a quarter of an hour, so that all vehicles and carriages would put on lights. At the second hour, the bell would ring for another 15 minutes, giving the signal that pedestrians too had to carry lights. Not obeying this rule would be punished.*[15]

---

14 Abstracted from Nardi, *Consulta strordinaria per gli stati Romani (1809-1810)*, pp 16–34.
15 Fortunati, *op. cit.,* 16 November 1809.

How could anyone object to such rational and obviously beneficial reforms? But Romans did, as they objected to numbering houses, or improving the postal system (all the better to spy on one's private mail, was the general opinion). Undeterred, the talented and energetic men of the *Consulta* set about making the new state.

Romans were to immediately stop using their barbaric old methods of telling time, following the motions of the sun and the changing hours. Instead, time (like Rome) was to conform to the rational rules of the empire, in two never-changing twelve-hour periods that would meet when the sun was directly overhead. On the other hand, perhaps as a concession, Romans were to be allowed to continue to use their own language. Of course, anyone who wanted to have dealings with the government better know French.

Reconstructing – or perhaps, constructing – the modern Rome was an enormous and a complex task. Just the bare outline of their work makes exhausting reading. Within a year (as it happened, it took a year and a half), three or four men were expected to identify, and deal with, the following tasks.

New civil courts were to replace the typically old regime tangle that, in Rome, was even worse than usual. The *Consulta*'s decrees dealt even with the minutiae of what judges were to wear, making sure imperial decrees were printed and distributed to the appropriate parties, defining parameters of authority among the various bodies and personnel, and thousands of other details.

A new prison system would replace what were the best run, and most humane, prisons on the continent. There were new rules about what prisoners should wear and eat; when wine might be distributed (only in case of contagious disease); pay scales were set for guards, physicians and chaplains; procedures for inspections, for sentencing, and for the release of prisoners who had served their time were determined.

Commissions were established for antiquities, for beautification of the city, for architecture and the arts; consultants for agriculture, industry, commerce, and manufacturing were identified as were men who were to advise on the administration of hospices, hospitals, charitable institutions; other consultants were to evaluate and otherwise care for works of art confiscated from various sources, and look after confiscated properties (including all the papal palaces and hundreds of religious institutions); and provisions were made for selecting and paying employees.

Pensions, assistance, and indemnities for retired or terminated employees and their dependants, were to be determined and put into effect.

Other structures were created to deal with the administration of the *Consulta* itself, and with the more than 800 municipalities within the two departments of the Roman state, establishing departments and prefectures, systems of criminal justice, law codes and provisions for the civil government of Rome (personnel, duties, pay, offices, etc), posts, the organisation of the notaries and their archives. How the territory of the state was to be divided, and who was in charge of what; upkeep of the property of foreign monarchs and states in Rome (which included paying expenses for visiting members of the court of Naples, and the cost for lighting up St Peter's and the Piazza di Spagna for gala visits); and winding down and cancelling the functions of the papal government, the old municipalities, and the feudal properties and nobles.

Then there came financial and economic matters, like commerce and industry, taxes, state properties, agriculture, waters and forests, the Monte di Pietà (see below), coins and money (they brought in a new machine for minting coins), and the lottery (much beloved of Romans and Italians in general), with related matters such as the dowries funded by the lottery.

Then they had to deal with new institutions and new definitions for religious entities, public assistance, and public health – matters that under the old system had been the provenance of the Church, but now that Church personnel were public employees, it all came under the control of the government. This included convents and monasteries, parish churches, cemeteries, distributions of food, clothing, and dowries, and an infinity of other topics.

Then came little matters like the police and the military; public works (roads, bridges, gates, rivers, canals and the enormous, eternal question of what to do about the Pontine Marshes.

Archives had to be established, to deal with the mountains of paper records that would be generated in the future as well as the material that Rome still held, despite the wholesale export of much of it to Paris (old archives like that of the Jesuits, and new archives for the new imperial institutions), to say nothing of a government printing office to generate even more documents.

In the all-important field of culture and the fine arts, there were entities to be created to oversee festivals, starting with the most important, and newest, festival, that of St Napoleon (which had been moved to 15 August to nudge aside the Madonna), but also including other important new events like the anniversary of the coronation on 2 December and the 22 April anniversary of the imperial wedding, plus old matters like theatres and fireworks and, of course, carnival.

The *Consulta* was also to set up schools and academies (all with personnel to be selected and paid); bodies whose duty it would be to support, select, and exhibit art; and they could not overlook the critical area of antiquities (which must have a section all to themselves).

The Archaeologists

When Napoleon went to Egypt in 1798, he brought with him shiploads of scholars, scientists, and artists to study the eternally fascinating ancient civilisation, and thus took the first step in scientific archaeology. It would be unreasonable to expect him to resist the attractions of an even more important ancient civilisation in Rome. Unfortunately, while ancient Egypt lay more or less undisturbed under the sands of Egypt, Rome had not so conveniently died and been buried but rather had served as the seed-bed for a Catholic civilisation that was still (in the French view) clogging up the area of the Seven Hills.

The archaeologists were to be primarily responsible for two major projects, and several less spectacular but equally demanding ones. These were the excavation and renovation of the Coliseum (which was functioning as a religious site with its Stations of the Cross and hermitage), and the Forum (used primarily as a storage area, a place to hold cattle, and a venue for inter-district rock fights).

They were to create a Rotunda Square outside the Pantheon, now mostly hidden behind a fish market and (until the flood of 1806 destroyed it), a bakery; this, like the creation of all the new squares, would entail demolishing the encroaching buildings.

The Capitol Garden was to be a public promenade which would incorporate a sort of archaeological park with the most important monuments in and around the Forum. These would include the baths of Titus, the arch of Titus, the temple of Venus and Rome, the basilica of Maxentius, the temple of Antoninus and Faustina, the temple of Domitian, all the way to the Coliseum, the Capitol and the Palatine.[16] This could be extended to the Tiber by means of the temples of Vesta and of Fortuna Virile, and the arch of Janus.

The archaeologists were also to oversee the cleaning up the theatre of Marcellus (the Orsini palace had incorporated parts of the theatre, and other parts were intertwined with houses and apartments) and the Octavia gate (the entrance to the ghetto, and almost completely hidden behind a fish market and old buildings).

Modern City Projects
In their work of creating a modern, efficient new city where papal Rome stood, the men of the *Consulta* were to:

... turn the Lateran palace into a hospice for beggars (not a new idea, but one that the revolution had embraced with enthusiasm, for confining the poor);

... create two large, modern cemeteries outside the city, to replace burial within churches or neighbourhoods;

... create central markets, slaughterhouses, and stockyards;

... create open piazzas around Trajan's column, the Pantheon (getting rid of the offending fish market) and the Trevi fountain;

... enlarge, beautify and otherwise transform the area around the Porta and Piazza del Popolo, to create a Garden of the Great Caesar;

... simplify and enlarge the square outside the Quirinal palace, as appropriate for an imperial residence;

... cut two great connecting boulevards through the city, one from St Peter's basilica to the Castel Sant'Angelo, and the other from the new imperial palace on the Quirinal to the Coliseum.

... create a series of promenades, primary among them the Garden of the Great Caesar around the Porta del Popolo;

... widen the street that led through the Borgo from Castel Sant'Angelo to St Peter's.

The plan, as de Tournon wrote to the emperor, was this:

On arriving from France, your Majesty will enter through the Porta del Popolo and proceed along the fine street of the Corso, which will be extended to the Forum, passing under the arches of Septimus and of Titus, enter the capital and the temple of Antoninus, and by this proceed to Your palace by a great street cut through one of the most densely populated quarters.[17]

---

16 In effect, much of the area that would have been included in the great imperial palace design by Perosini.
17 Letter from Paris, 28 August 1811, enclosing a plan, no doubt by Sterne, annotated by de Tournon. Archives Nationales, Paris, F20 102.

The temple of Jupiter in 1809 and 1813 - before and after the French-sponsored archaeological works.

The New Arts and Sciences

The new regime intended, among other things, the complete reorganisation of the sciences and arts of the new imperial city. One of the first steps would be to create an imperial university, with a completely new, and entirely secular, faculty, all based on the latest French models. Young Romans would learn their classics, and at the same time would learn that it was only under Napoleon the Great that their ancient state rose again, as part of 'the French empire, the only worthy successor of the ancient Roman empire'. Unfortunately, the only result of this new education system was to paper over the old system and add new paint, without changing much. The *Consulta* could report to Napoleon, at the end of their tenure in December 1810, that there was indeed an imperial university – but it was merely the old university in Perugia, re-named the *Université Napoléon*.

The *Consulta* none the less did manage some real reforms to the education system. These included the creation of a new meteorological observatory and a new laboratory at the Roman College; enlarging the almost defunct botanical gardens; reorganising the libraries that the state had acquired when they dissolved the religious corporations. They also decreed that the Vatican library must receive a copy of every book published after 1811.

Despite, or maybe because of, the ravages caused by the treaty of Tolentino, the *Consulta* tried to ban the export of the artistic and antiquarian treasures of Rome. This was an exercise in closing the barn door after the horse has been stolen, but none the less an admirable idea. But it would be in Paris that the artistic restoration of Rome would be planned. Canova, called to his famous breakfast visit with Napoleon in the autumn of 1809, returned to Rome virtual dictator of the arts.

Napoleon's dream was to create a new, imperial, academy in Rome, with its seat in the former monastery and church of Ara Coeli, the medieval edifice that rose above the Capitol. Napoleon hoped to use Canova to create this new academy to demonstrate the new imperial mastery over the arts, in the same way that Louis XIV had used the French Academy to emphasise and publicise the cultural dominance of France in the previous century. The new body, headed by Canova, was to have departments of painting, drawing, sculpture, architecture, mythology, anatomy and geometry. Decreed in May of 1812, the new academy never got the chance to fill the role Napoleon had planned for it. Canova was frequently in dispute with Martial Daru, the intendant (and would-be dramatist) given the task of supervising how the money was spent. Canova, however, remained the most prestigious and the most successful figure in the arts in Rome. He later earned the papal title of Marchese d'Ischia for his work in securing the return of at least some of the artistic and cultural masterpieces that had been looted and sent to Paris.

There was a parallel attempt to create an academy of literature, building on a renewed and revitalised Arcadian Academy. But even with the enthusiastic and expert cooperation of de Gérando, this attempt was doomed from the start.

There was to be a new school of music, designed to restore Rome to her status as chief city for ecclesiastical music. (We know that her reputation as an opera city had long since dissipated; everyone agreed that opera in Rome was the worst in Europe.) The obvious choice for director of the new school was the great Zingarelli, despite the obvious fact that he was a papal supporter who showed no enthusiasm for the new order. When the loyalty oath was introduced in 1810, no one tried to make Zingarelli take it, on the understanding that he would refuse and thus rob the empire of an exceptionally useful, if unenthusiastic, servant. No one tried to make Canova take the oath, either. And Canova's loyalty to Rome, and to his native state of Venice, would finally triumph.

Zingarelli was also to become the head of an imperial chapel choir that would absorb the students of the new music school. There were to be eight professors of music, in addition to the director Zingarelli (with a salary of 2,400 *livres* a year). The organist would earn the respectable salary of 1,200 *livres*, and the first and second rank sopranos, contraltos, tenors and basses would be paid 1,200 and 800 *livres* respectively. From this group would be drawn the singers required for the 'solemnities at the chapel of St Peter's, at San Giovanni in Laterno, Santa Maria Maggiore, Santa Maria in Trastevere, San Paolo fuori le Mura.' The imperial chapel would provide the *Te Deum*s that would glorify the heroic accomplishments of the emperor. Unfortunately, it was on precisely the question of a *Te Deum* to glorify an accomplishment of the emperor – specifically, his ability to father a legitimate son – that Zingarelli, and the whole project of an imperial chapel choir, would come to grief.

Finally, there was to be a new and enlarged school to produce a uniquely Roman art form, the great mosaics. The head of this enterprise was to be Vincenzo Camuccini, considered to be the finest living landscape painter in Italy (Mrs. Eaton agreed that he proabably was) in addition to being a highly accomplished painter of neoclassical historical subjects. Like the school of music, little came of the plans.

Canova.   Camille de Tournon.

The Law

Among the enlightened reforms on which Napoleon most prided himself was his reform of the law. The *Code Napoléon* was precisely the sort of thing that a modern, enlightened ruler was supposed to bring to his grateful people – a rational codification that would eliminate the conflicting and overlapping laws and jurisdictions that had made old regime law such a tangled mess. Romans, their emperor proudly announced, were to enjoy the same 'laws that have made France peaceful and happy within, and respected and feared without.' Unfortunately, from the papal point of view there was a large fly in that legal ointment: the state was bound and determined to assume control of every part of the citizen's life, including those parts of life that the Church considered her own special province. There was an even larger and more difficult problem: Gallicanism, the movement that defended the independence of the national churches, threatened to transform the new Catholicism into an ornate variety of Protestantism. In terms of authority, the chapter of Paris declared that the 'head of the state was not subject in any of his acts to the head of the Church; the Church was instead subject to the emperor, and bound to obey all of the laws.'[18]

Camille de Tournon, 'my youngest and best prefect'

The man in the unhappy position of intermediary between Romans and their voracious emperor was the 30-year-old prefect, Camille de Tournon. Madelin describes him as 'a gentleman by character as well as by birth', a man who loved Rome and was loved in return, fond of good paintings and fine horses, and always ready to look on the bright side. His official portraits reveal a surprisingly gawky, shy-looking man, young for his years, dark haired, red-faced, his head two sizes too small for his body. His dark eyebrows are raised, making him look worried, so that he seems to ask

---

18 Silvagni, *op. cit.*, II, pp. 223–5, after the Napoleonic decree of 25 February 1811.

our pardon for intruding on our gaze. He is not wearing his official, French finery, heavy with gold braid. Wrapped in his dark cloak, he looks less like a successful bureaucrat than like a Roman, or an artist (he was in fact a skilled amateur).

Efficient, intelligent, and humane, in August 1811 minister of the interior Montalivet called him his 'youngest and best prefect'. De Tournon admired, deplored, analysed, worked incessantly, and did his best in an impossible situation. Named prefect in September 1810, he arrived in Rome two months later, with his heart 'palpitating with emotion' to set foot on this 'sacred soil'. Next day, he wrote to his mother giving his first impressions:

It is with a lively emotion that I set foot in this city, for so many centuries the object of veneration by the whole world; as a simple traveller, I could not see it in a disinterested manner. The appearance of its ruins and of the desert which surrounds it fills the soul with a singular melancholy. May I be so happy as to be able to plant some seeds of prosperity in this soil which is so poetic, but so wretched.

He took frequent trips from Rome to the surrounding areas and towns, keeping meticulous notes – walking, sensitive to the feel and the look of the countryside but not blinded by the romance of his own impressions. His was the eye of the conscientious administrator, systematically surveying the domain for which he was to be responsible. He did his best, and his best was very good, but it would not be good enough. In June 1811, Camille de Tournon returned to France to report to the emperor, and marry Adele de Pancemont. The marriage was a success; the meeting with the emperor went badly. By this time Napoleon was keenly aware that Rome was the city where things were going worst for the empire. De Tournon was the first functionary from Rome to arrive in the imperial presence since the priests, 'in open revolt', began to agitate the people and kept the ungrateful city far from the embrace of its benefactor.

The lawyers of Rome had for the second time refused the oath. Enraged, Napoleon told de Tournon: 'Tell them clearly, Monsieur, tell them that I owe them nothing, that I owe them only death.' He grew even more angry, added some words between his teeth, then broke off and curtly gestured for the prefect of Rome to leave.[19] De Tournon went back to Rome, with his charming new wife, and tried to make the best of things. Towards the end of the year, he sent a doggedly optimistic report to the emperor:[20]

On Brigandage: I can assure your majesty, speaking politically, the country is perfectly tranquil and under the wise and prudent direction of General Miollis it cannot give the least worry. It is only necessary to avoid occupying the spirits with religious affairs.

De Tournon attempted, ever so delicately, to warn the emperor to stop his war with the clergy, secular as well as regular. The prefect, like some members of the *Consulta*, was sympathetic to Catholicism.

---

19 Madelin, *op. cit.*, p. 511.
20 *Rapport sur rome et les États Romains*, a report probably sent to Napoleon some time in late 1811. Archives Nationales de Paris, AF iv, 1715, Chap. II, 3ere Cahier. See Lemmi, "Roma nell'Impero Napoleonico".

On conscription: *It is very new, but imposed with the greatest ease, the Romans make soldiers capable of the greatest enthusiasm.*

De Tournon would continue to believe that Romans had been coddled in the matter of conscription, which was imposed much more rigorously and harshly in other states. This did not impress Romans, who had not had to deal with conscription since the Spanish left in the seventeenth century, and had no desire to start again.

On the Roman attitude towards the French military: *The French soldiers are 'cherished and honoured by the Roman people'.*

On an individual basis the Romans did seem rather to like the French, or at least the Roman elite found the officers charming and amusing. To judge from their memoirs, the officer corps arrived expecting a delightful break from military duty, and were not disappointed.

On the people of Rome: *The Roman people are still a people set apart, and truly a people in all they have: manners, habits, affections, opinions. All is in common. 'Rome says', 'Rome believes', 'Rome hopes' ... A singular thing! Romans have a lively memory of her ancient grandeur, and have no feeling for it; it is an idea that occupies the imagination without descending to the soul.*

On the Roman nobles: de Tournon made up a list, dividing the nobility into three parts: *those who claimed descent from the ancient patrician families; those ennobled by the popes; and those ennobled most recently, by Pius VI and Pius VII.*

In his opinion, the Roman nobles were unhappy with the papal government and ready to cooperate with a new system. They had little real authority in the city run by clerics, and their only access to power was through members of their families who made it into the upper ranks of the hierarchy. They were, de Tournon believed, irked by the fact that the prelature, the only way of access to papal government, was open not only to them, but equally to nobles, and even non-nobles, throughout Italy. The result was that 'the ancient nobility has no other way of preserving itself than by attaching itself to your majesty. They know this, and are happy to take advantage of it; the young men in particular are excited about this prospect. As your majesty knows, it is among this class of nobles that we have found the most reasonable men.'

It was far too late for any of this to make any difference. And a police report sent to Napoleon dated 8 May 1810 shows an entirely different picture:

The population has already lost 30,000 inhabitants; if the emperor does not turn his eyes and his hand to it, those who know the place well are certain that in less than 10 years the city of the popes will be almost as ruined as that of the Caesars ... The gardens of the Quirinal are dry; the palace is nothing more than a deserted and crumbling monastery. The great families close their houses, either from distress or from greed; the streets are empty except for beggars ... There is so much discontent that it is impossible to predict what would happen if France experienced some setback while the lower part of Italy is denuded of troops, while the priests never stop pointing out to the people the example of the Spanish.[21]

Murat's Game Continues

On 10 November 1809, King Murat made his solemn entry into Rome via the Porta San Giovanni. He had his supporters meet him at the spa town of Albano just outside of Rome, and rode into the city in great style, with gold-trimmed uniform, yellow boots and a plumed hat. Not all Romans were impressed. That night, he got a nickname he couldn't lose: 'Il Franconi incoronato' (Franconi crowned – Franconi was a famous circus performer).

He took up residence at the Borghese palace, and received homage – though not the homage of the few cardinals in Rome, who declined to call. He reviewed the troops in St Peter's piazza, in another splendid uniform: a spencer lined with precious furs, gold galloons on his breastplate; cascades of feathers, a Turkish sabre (from his cavalry days in Egypt) and morocco leather boots – all of which only reinforced the name the Romans had given him the day before.

He visited the Castel Sant'Angelo, and hosted a gala ball at the Valle theatre that night. His Roman visit was 'a series of *feste*, of splendours, of apotheoses'.

He attended a ball hosted by Miollis at the Palazzo Doria, and the ladies were all dazzled – he was very handsome. Next day, de Tournon (who found him enchanting) took him to inspect the port of Civitavecchia. They returned to Rome for a gala dinner for 400 followed by splendid fireworks. When the crowd applauded the fireworks master, Murat thought it was for him, but gracefully acknowledged his error when he found out.

He closed his Rome visitation with calls on to the Vatican museums and Canova's studio where he admired the nearly finished statue of the emperor as Mars the Peacemaker.

Fortunati, who realised that King Murat was a figure with whom Romans would have to deal, wrote this account:

10 November 1809: The King of Naples, Gioacchino Murat, arrived in Rome, and a great number of people waited along the way he would pass, as well as a great number of soldiers who lined the way. Finally, one saw a carriage all lit up, it was that of the same King Murat dressed in a royal robe …. He and his retinue and soldiers dismounted at the Palazzo Borghese. Wherever he went through Rome, no one applauded him except for some Jacobins who were gathered in various places for that purpose. The next day there was a review of the troops in the Piazza di San Pietro. After that, they went to Sant'Angelo and toured the fort; in the evening the cupola was illuminated. That evening he went to the Valle theatre, where the king mounted the throne and a comedy in prose immediately began; when the first act was over, the first act of a musical piece was played, and after that act the king got off his throne and left and the curtain came down immediately, the people were not pleased. On the following days he went to the studio of

---

21 Archives Nationales, F7 6531, Madelin, pp. 394–95.

the famous sculptor Canova, to see all the rarities, both antique and modern. That same evening he came to the ball at the Aliberti theatre, as soon as he arrived he mounted the throne and the dance began. Afterwards, Miollis gave another ball and a dinner for him. On 17 November he left Rome for Naples.

An Imperial Marriage and the Birth of the King of Rome

Murat may have been motivated by a certain sense of urgency. In April 1810 Napoleon married his second wife, the young, plump and fertile-looking Marie Louise, daughter of the Austrian emperor. Whatever hopes Murat and Caroline were cherishing seemed to be dashed by the birth of a much more royal son of the emperor, who was given the title of King of Rome. The event, which should have been the greatest triumph of the imperial city, was a public relations disaster, despite frantic attempts to paper over the cracks. The new regime had taken a special interest in salvaging at least the appearance of cooperation with and respect for the Church, and had been particularly frustrated at their failure to force Bishop Atenasio, the vice regent of Rome, to have *Te Deum*s sung in St Peter's basilica in celebration of various imperial festivities. With the birth of the King of Rome, Atenasio finally agreed to authorise a *Te Deum*, and a glittering officialdom gathered for the singular event. According to the reports of Norvins, however, many of the priests rounded up for the occasion simply refused to attend. Worse, on the very morning of the *Te Deum*, the pious maestro Zingarelli ('the fanatical imbecile!') also refused to have anything to do with the celebration. The police were sent to bring him to the cathedral, but nothing saved the *Te Deum*: the singers ('animals!') refused to sing. Zingarelli and his recalcitrant choir were arrested, and the maestro was sent first to the Castel Sant'Angelo, and then to Paris. Napoleon, who liked Zingarelli's music, did nothing worse than commission a new piece from the maestro.[22] The official *Journal du Capitole*, undeterred by the reality noted by the imperial police, reported that the affair had been marked by 'numerous clergy, much excellent music, which took on an even more august character in the immense and richly decorated cathedral.'

Artists from Ingres to Bartolomeo Pinelli ground out celebratory images for the birth of the Napoleonic heir (one of Pinelli's less inspired ones showed the infant crawling out of a helmet). Miollis and de Tournon hosted lavish entertainments, and the theatres featured the usual spectacles including an allegorical ballet in which the gods presented the new-born hero to a Rome personified by the beautiful Pauline Bonaparte Borghese. The Apollo theatre offered an old opera by Hasse, *Romolo ed Erisilia* (Romulus and Erisilia, or the Sabine Women), that dated from 1765. Like most of the mandatory celebrations, this struck a sour note: Romans were not in the least bit interested in old operas, nor were they impressed by the transparent allegory (Romulus was supposed to represent the magnanimous Napoleon, Marie Louise the devoted mother Erisilia).[23]

---

22 Madelin, *op. cit., p.* 424. Norvins report of 10 June 1811, F7 6531, and notes on the Norvins report by de Savery, F7 6536.
23 Cesare, *I Romani e la nascita del Re di Roma,* p. 84. The opera was performed on 26 July 1811.

Madame Blanchard.

The misadventures of Madame Brancal, the celebrated *paracadutista*, may be emblematic of the whole episode. Madame Blanchard (Fortunati misspells her name and notes that she was Jewish) planned a balloon ascension from the Corea Amphitheatre, in order to celebrate the royal birth. It did not go well. She did not make the attempt until October, and when she did, the balloon failed to gain enough height to go over the housetops, and instead ended up in the Tiber. Fortunati notes, somewhat snippily, that 'fortunately there was a boat there which saved her; otherwise Madama would have drowned, along with her balloon.' But Madame Blanchard was a hard woman to discourage (she would be killed in a crash in 1819): On 22 December she tried again, this time lifting off from the Piazza Navona. She stayed aloft for about an hour, and came down safely outside the city.

Romans let Pasquino speak for them: 'the little bastard', the talking statue observed, 'has been crowned'. Napoleon's very real affection towards the city had its limits, and this was most certainly one of them. At the best of times the emperor's sense of humour was a bit rudimentary – he liked to wad up bits of bread and throw them at people across the dinner table. He most certainly did not appreciate *pasquinades*. Napoleon never understood the tradition of Pasquino, and tried to put an end to it, but that only made matters worse. 'Rome', he complained indignantly, 'has become a theatre for defamation, a headquarters for libel!'[24]

In 1811, the government increased their efforts to punish those who posted *pasquinades*, or at the very least, to get rid of the offensive barbs before they could circulate. It was useless. In the dark of night, or under cover of a passing crowd in a busy piazza, a satirical verse or a joke would appear, posted on one of the traditional talking statues. They were removed as quickly as they were found, but – *samisdat*-like – they were copied and passed from hand to hand in coffee houses and taverns and parlours.

The infant whose birth had caused all of the brouhaha, the 'Eaglet', was destined to have a short and sad life. He was a child of two when his father was first defeated, and barely four when the desperate gamble of Waterloo failed. The emperor hoped that the victorious Allies would recognise his son and establish a regency in his name – a not unreasonable hope, given the fact that the boy's mother was an Austrian archduchess and his grandfather, the Emperor of Austria. However, the Allies had no intention of providing a potential rallying point for disgruntled Bonapartists. The little boy, who was never strong, was hundled off to the court at Vienna. There he was raised by a series of tutors and kept in more or less splendid confinement, while his mother turned her plump hand to ruling the Duchy of Parma and Guastella, with the help of her chief of police and lover, Count Neipperg.

---

24 Romano, *La Satira*, p. 17, after Radet.

Isolated and melancholy, the boy who would have been Napoleon II, died of tuberculosis in 1832, at the age of 21, 11 years after his father had died on St Helena, of stomach cancer, or arsenic poisoning, or neither, or both. The emperor had hoped to leave the boy the gift of the Western World, with its crown jewel, Rome, presented on a red cushion; instead, he left him an elegant game of *Ombre*, its pieces handpainted on ivory, a game that had helped him pass the time while he waited to die on St Helena. The boy never received it. One of his few friends, Antonio Prokesch, donated the game to the Napoleonic museum in Rome.

The Debacle, 1812

On 24 November 1812, the military bulletins announced a great victory: Napoleon had entered Moscow. A *Te Deum* was ordered at St Peter's and Romans, as usual, declined to participate (this, like the other celebrations performed on order, was attended by 'four cats' and whatever French officials could be mustered). Romans might have shown more enthusiasm had they realised that this victory was in fact the harbinger of a disaster that would ultimately destroy the empire.

Napoleon did not give up easily, however. He hurried back to Paris (leaving his Grand Army to die in Russia, as he had abandoned his army in Egypt in 1799) and tried furiously to mend fences. This included a desperate plan for raising of a new army from the dregs his conscription boards had left behind, plus a plan for announcing a new concordat, to demonstrate to the world that he had the full backing of the Holy Father. Pius was still at Fontainebleau, where he had been brought earlier to await the imperial pleasure.

Kidnapping Pius VII was reduced to comic opera when a kidnapper fell of a ladder.

CHAPTER NINE
THE EMPIRE VERSUS GOD

In certain circles, Napoleon has always attracted thoughts of the Anti-Christ and the Apocalypse. This was true as early as 1798, when he left Italy to invade Egypt, and when, in the following year, he campaigned in Palestine it seemed even more likely that he might be stirring ancient and dangerous waters. French revolutionary persecution of Christians in general and Catholic clergy in particular had already led many to think in apocalyptic terms. In 1804, when the representative of revolution declared himself not only king, but emperor, some braced themselves for the worst. In 1806 the emperor invited Jewish leaders to convene a Sanhedrin in Paris, the first since the Roman conquest. According to Jewish law, only the Messiah could convene a new Sanhedrin: was Napoleon claiming that title? And if he were, who could possibly doubt his identity as the Anti-Christ, usurping the work of Christ? His promise to rebuild the temple of Solomon in Jerusalem was, if possible, even more inflammatory. The new imperial catechism of 1806 clearly stated that duty to the emperor was the same as duty to God, and condemned to eternal damnation those who failed to honour and obey their emperor – even more evidence of Anti-Christ-like usurpation. And who could fail to notice that his very name, Napoleon, could pass for a transliteration of the name of Apoliel, the Angel of the Bottomless Pit?

Romans looking for evidence of the imminent apocalypse did not lack for clues. As the years passed, there would be more. On 10 May 1810 the madonnas began to move their eyes again: an image of the Virgin at Civitavecchia was reported to open and close her eyes; by the end of the year, several of the street-side shrine images were convicted of demonstrating anti-imperial sentiments and were confiscated and removed. In June of that year, an invasion of grasshoppers destroyed the crops; in June of the following year, the crucifix in the Coliseum was reported to have been mutilated, an act of blasphemy that Romans were quick to blame on the French. On 1 September 1811, there was a meteor. Earthquakes during the carnival of 1811 and in March of 1812 added to the portents. And on 21 March 1812, lightning struck the entrance to the Quirinal palace, already being prepared for a visit from the emperor (a visit that would never come).

Posting the Bull of Excommunication.

Consumatum est: *The Excommunication*

On the morning of 10 June, at the Quirinal palace, Pius VII and his closest advisor Cardinal Pacca heard the cannon shots that announced the transfer of Rome from papal rule to imperial rule. They exchanged looks and (according to the cardinal's memoirs) both whispered, '*consumatum est*' – it is finished. Neither was surprised. For 18 months, the empire and the papacy had confronted one another in Rome. Miollis, urbane and humane, may have hoped for a gradual and peaceful resolution, but the two major players, the emperor and the pope, both understood that they had reached a place where no more compromise was possible. The pope went to his desk and signed the formal protest that had already been prepared. Then, after a brief hesitation, he signed another, much more explosive document, one that had been drawn up some time earlier to be used in case the pope were deposed or abducted. It was an order of excommunication for those who cooperated with the expropriation of the Papal States. Napoleon was not mentioned by name, but there was no doubt that he was first among the expropriators.

Cardinal Pacca later remembered that Pius had then turned to him and urged, 'but take care those carrying out your instructions be not discovered, for they would certainly be condemned to death, and I should be inconsolable.' Late on the afternoon of 10 June the Bull of Excommunication was posted on the doors of the major basilicas, in full daylight, by messengers who melted, un-remarked and un-denounced, back into the mass of people coming to vespers services.[1]

Secretaries and street cleaners, police and couriers, Romans in any way involved with the civil administration refused to carry on working until they knew if it applied to them. In the meeting rooms of the *Consulta* itself, Cesare Balbo felt the first

---

1   Anderson, pp. 68–9, from Pacca's memoirs.

stirrings of guilt. Pius had special instructions issued to confessors and parish priests so people would know who might incur excommunication and who might safely continue in his work.

This sequence of events was the culmination of years of misunderstanding and anger. On one side, there was a self-made emperor who believed himself to be a true friend to the Church – and Pius, at the end of the story, would say that Napoleon's defence of the Church in 1801 was 'Christian and heroic'. But the emperor was adamant that the pope had to support his policy against the enemies of the empire, specifically, against England. On the other side was a small, frail-looking churchman for whom there was no 'Emperor of Rome'. Whatever else he was willing to negotiate, he would die rather than surrender his rule over Rome, which he considered the last guarantor of the independence of the Church.

Napoleon had made a policy decision to abandon the revolutionary antagonism to the Church. There were many possible reasons for this. For one thing, it was impractical: to fight against religion *per se* was a useless expenditure of energy, people would cling to their old ideas, and making martyrs would only encourage others to follow them. Besides, what harm would it do? Religion could help guarantee order, especially if it could be used to support the state. In fact, after Napoleon decided to restore the monarchy (by making himself emperor) the Church was precisely the partner he needed.

He assumed that Pius, who seemed gentle and tractable, would cooperate. In exchange for his cooperation, Napoleon was willing, even eager, to offer his protection to the Church, to demand piety from his people, and to make any number of arrangements that would be to the advantage of a pliant clergy.

In return, the Church was expected to play its part. The secularisation of the law was to continue without opposition, and to spread from France through the empire. Popes, bishops and priests were to accept the Civil Code that put family law, for instance, entirely in secular hands, including the granting of divorce.

The pope was to surrender his temporal authority to the empire, which undertook to provide all the protection necessary – against everyone but the emperor. In matters the empire saw as secular, the pope was to act as a loyal subject. So that, for instance, when Napoleon decided to impose a total ban on trade with England, he expected the pope to enforce it in the Papal States. When the emperor decided that his name-day (15 August) should replace or at least overshadow the Assumption of the Virgin, he was not only shoving aside one of the most popular feasts on the calendar, he was also insisting that the state should be able to proclaim a feast day without reference to the Church. So an obscure Egyptian confessor and martyr whose name might have been Neapolo or Neopolo, was catapulted to temporary glory.

The pope's position was that his temporal power, as an independent sovereign, was essential if he were to maintain the neutrality that he had to have as ruler, not of a single state, but of the universal Church. As a member of the Napoleonic confederation, he judged that he would be in a worse position than the popes at Avignon had been during the fourteenth century, the period known as the babylonian captivity of the Church.

Pius was a very small man, so small that when he was elected, none of the new vestments fit. Three sets had been prepared – large, medium and small. But even the small had to be pinned up for the initial ceremonies. The papal white slippers had to be stuffed with straw before they would stay on his feet. Calm, conciliatory, with a quiet sense of self-deprecatory humour, he was absolutely intractable once he had reached a decision. Lefebvre, the French *chargé d'affairs* in Rome, described him this way:

The pope is not a man whom one may hope to persuade by persistent argument; he is firm and immovable in his attitude. Once he has made up his mind anything you say to him to change it will fail to persuade him. He does not prevent you from speaking, but after you have finished he lowers his head onto his breast and allows you to go without replying.[2]

He was also a man capable of startling outbursts of rage. When General Miollis sent troops to arrest Cardinal Pacca, Pius burst into the room, his hair literally standing on end (so Pacca reports). Defying the astonished soldiers, he took the cardinal by the hand and escorted him back to 'share my prison' in the papal apartments.

Will no one rid me of this troublesome pope?
When Napoleon learned about the excommunication, he was furious. The pope, he said, was 'a dangerous madman who must be restrained'. Murat believed that he had finally received the orders he wanted, and lost no time in passing them on to General Miollis, and to the commander of the gendarmerie in Rome, General Etienne Radet.[3]

The deceptively frail Pius by now believed that he would probably die on the scaffold; the idea of martyrdom was not unattractive. He was a prisoner in his residence on the Quirinal hill, though no one had actually moved to arrest him. He had his Swiss guards and his household, including the bull-necked and uncompromising Cardinal Pacca – a short, powerfully built, capable man, known as the toughest of the cardinals. The pope also had a printing press, and the Roman clergy and most of the population were his eyes, ears and hands throughout the city.

Across the street from the Quirinal palace were the French troops and the French cannon, aimed at his study window. No one thought they were there to shoot. They were there to make a statement. By July, the city was already being transformed by the presence and actions of the *Consulta*, and by the enthusiastic young prefect, Camille de Tournon. One of their first steps had been to form a local militia, the Civic Guard (this was always among the first acts of a new revolutionary state), but they had met with a stone wall of passive resistance.

In order to form the Civic Guard, the new government turned to the men who had always acted as the interface between state and people: the parish priests. They needed two lists: one of men who might be drafted to join the force, and another of men rich enough to buy themselves out of being thus constrained. In late June, the following notices were sent to each parish in Rome:

---

2   Hales, *The Emperor and the Pope*, p. 95.
3   It is beyond irony to learn that General Radet, organiser of the Italian gendarmerie and man in charge of kidnapping Pius VII, was also the man who, in June of 1791, had attempted to rescue Louis XVI after the fleeing king and his family had been captured at Varennes.

21 June 1809
You are requested to send me, within 48 hours, a correct list of all the citizens in your parish between the ages of 18 and 60, who will be liable for service in the Civic Guard. C. Gaetano Gerardini, Director of Police.

22 June 1809
It is the express wish of His Holiness that all parish priests will excuse themselves from giving a list of their parishioners between the ages of 18 and 60, asked for by the police, with civility but firmness. The Cardinal Vicar.

23 June 1809
Parish priests should inform their flocks that no one can serve in the proposed Civic Guard, either as efficient or as contributory [that is, by joining or by paying not to join] without doing violence to his conscience. The Secretariat of the Vicar General.

The French and their supporters were, in fact, in a precarious position. For all the imperial pomp and glory, there were no more than 500 imperial troops on the ground, and sometimes as few as 300, including about 100 gendarmes commanded by the dashing, impetuous General Radet (of whom more later). In Naples and in parts of the north, the population had risen up to butcher the people they considered invaders. Nothing of the sort had happened in Rome, but if the pope were to appear at his balcony and call for a crusade, who could tell what the result might be?

Meanwhile, as the pope baulked at becoming the vassal of the new emperor of the West, the emperor was having problems in two regions that were, more than any other part of Europe, Catholic. In the east, Poland was absorbing much of his attention. In Spain, guerrilla warfare, with all of its attendant horrors, was being invented. In both of these countries, it was essential (from the point of view of the common people, at least) that Napoleon be on the right side of the Church.

The emperor, who had just defeated Austria at the battle of Wagram, was rapidly running out of patience. After the excommunication, he had called the pope a 'dangerous lunatic'. In letters to Murat he wrote, 'If the pope, contrary to the spirit of his age and of the Gospels, preaches revolt and wishes to take advantage of the immunity of his house for printing circulars, he will have to be arrested.' In the same letter, he noted the examples of Philip the Fair (the French king who had had one pope kidnapped and brought another to Avignon), and Charles V (the emperor who had presided over the brutal sack of Rome in 1527).

On the sultry night of 5–6 July, Cardinal Pacca noted that there were more patrols than usual, and kept watch through most of the short mid-summer night.[4] Towards dawn, he retired, but was soon awakened by the news that the palace was under attack. One party had put up ladders and had been attempting to climb in by the windows when a man fell, and his cry alerted the household. Another group were scaling the garden walls, while the main party approached across the roof from the Dateria.

---

4   Elie,.*La curieuse vie de General Radet.*

PopePius VII and his adviser, Cardinal Pacca, were arrested on 6 July 1809.

They seem to have been an ill-assorted band. Except for General Radet and his officers, there were only three members of the recently-organised militia, the Civic Guard. The rest represented a wide range of ranks and occupations, from priests, employees of the curia, and aristocrats, through to professionals and artisans, to cops, peasants, a jailbird, and an escaped prisoner from the Castel Sant'Angelo. Pietro Piranesi, son of the famous engraver and designer of the failed carnival, was there. So were the following: a notary's boy; two surveyors, uncle and nephew; a tinsmith, a silversmith, and a couple of brick layers; a bank cashier; a hatter; a gun-maker; a bookseller; the son of a gravedigger; three locksmiths (for obvious reasons), two pork butchers and a lamb butcher (not, one hopes, for professional purposes); a coachman; the son of a man who ran the Bastone Madonne coffee house near San Lorenzo in Lucina; a man who ran an inn at the Barcaccia in the Piazza di Spagna; an ex-porter at the Apostolic palace who had been fired for stealing; and someone nicknamed 'the little mule' who fell off the ladder and broke his leg (it was his shouting that alerted the cardinal). Finally, there were three *sbirri*, two *festaroli* who had been drafted because they owned a couple of tall ladders, and a woman named Diana from Ceccano, who seems to have been a sort of armed secretary – she 'wrote the questions and answers with paper and ink, and was armed with a sabre and a sword.'[5]

Pacca hurried to alert the pope, who rose and dressed in his white official robes; together, they went to the audience room and waited as the doors were battered down

---

5   Silvagni, *op. cit.*, III, pp. 87–122.

one by one. Finally, at dawn, the pope ordered the door to the audience hall unlocked, and admitted the raiding party. General Radet stepped forward, still panting and sweating from the exertion of breaking down the doors with an axe. He later reported that it had all seemed 'splendid' until that moment; face to face with the pope, he felt like a little boy at his first communion.

Whatever qualms the general may or may not have felt, the pope and Cardinal Pacca were given a few minutes to pack before they were taken directly to the waiting closed carriage. They brought their breviaries and rosaries, and the Sacrament in a ciborium. No one remembered a change of underwear. The pope was 67, and subject to digestive problems; it was a sweltering July day. As the carriage rolled along the bumpy road north, the two prisoners looked in their pockets: they had a total of 35 *bajocchi* between them, about enough to buy a dozen eggs at pre-inflation prices. Radet reports that he was puzzled when they started to laugh; when they shared the joke with him, he was even more puzzled.

Did the emperor order the kidnapping? He denied it; Miollis' letters and Radet's memoirs make it plain that they believed that was what Napoleon wanted. In any case, the emperor accepted the *fait accompli*, and had the prisoners taken to Savona. Pacca was sent on to the fortress at Fenestrelle; Pius remained in the palace at Savona until Napoleon, after having lost Russia, brought him to Fontainebleau.

Whether or not he had ordered the kidnapping, Napoleon was obviously still furious with the recalcitrant cleric. When Pius wrote to remonstrate with Napoleon about the coup in Rome, the emperor wrote a letter to the minister for public worship, which was to be read aloud to the prisoner at Savona:

His Majesty does not judge it fitting to reply to the pope's personal letter. He will write when he is satisfied with him ... The emperor was pleased to scorn the said criminal and ridiculous document [the Bull of Excommunication] *...*

His Majesty pities the pope's ignorance .... As the pope is not sufficiently enlightened by the Holy Spirit, why does he not resign? For he is evidently incapable of distinguishing dogma from the essentials of religion ... If [he] *is unable to understand this fairly obvious distinction, easy enough for a young seminarian, let him come down from the Pontifical Chair and make way for a man of better sense and comprehension.*[6]

Closing the Convents and Monasteries
Napoleon decided in 1809 and 1810 to declare war on the institutional Church in Rome, which he now saw as ungrateful and obstructionist.[7] To begin with, he would clear out the convents and monasteries of the regular orders – that is, religious societies whose work was not in the world, under the command of their local bishops, but rather according to a rule (or *regula*) of a founder, like Dominic or Francis or Clare of Assisi. In doing this, he was following the Enlightenment dictum that, while some clerics served socially useful purposes as educators, nurses, or parish clergy, regular clerics were nothing but parasites, taking up space and money and

6   Anderson, *op. cit.*, pp. 119–20.
7   Madelin, *op. cit.*, pp. 316–329.

contributing nothing tangible to the improvement of the world. This was a policy adopted by, among others, Joseph II of Austria, or the grand dukes of Tuscany.

After Pius VII had proved himself stubborn and uncooperative, Napoleon, in his role of Enlightened Absolutist, did not hesitate to take the clergy in hand. The Roman clergy, for their part, remained passively hostile and uncooperative.

De Tournon and the *Consulta* were, it seems, appalled. They had realised that the monasteries and convents would be closed – French law now insisted on this point throughout the empire – but they had hoped to have five or six years in which to carry out the policy gradually. Now, they were unable to do much more than close their eyes when monks and nuns took their personal property with them, or try to keep orders intact in a few isolated cases.[8] In some cases, they also closed their eyes when monks, now wearing civilian clothes, simply moved back into the monasteries from which they had been expelled.

The imperial war against God (which was how the Romans saw it) was laid out like a military campaign. Napoleon made sure that he had a sufficient number of soldiers and police to enforce his decisions. Then he ordered his representatives to restructure the Church in Rome and the Roman territories, reducing the numbers across the board. First, a loyalty oath would be required of all secular clergy; if they refused, they would be summarily arrested and deported. The 43 Roman parishes would be reduced to 20, with appropriate cuts in personnel. One curé was considered sufficient to serve the needs of towns of 5,000 and fewer inhabitants. Monks were to be sent back to the towns they came from, with a small pension (to be funded by confiscated church property – there was an elegant symmetry to the plan).

A decree of 17 April 1810 dissolved all regular religious corporations, to take effect within 15 days. Agents hurried from monastery to monastery, making lists of names and inventories of property and putting seals on doors and windows. The men offered little resistance in the face of military force. The women were another story. In convent after convent in Rome, they barred and locked their doors and windows. On the night of 14–15 June, the military took the convents by assault, one by one, breaking down the doors and throwing the ladies out into the streets. The people of Rome were outraged: clearly the days of Nero and Diocletian had returned, and if anyone doubted it, there were the new martyrs visible on every street corner, begging for their bread. At the end, some 10,000 monks were dispossessed in the Roman states alone, and the same was true throughout Napoleonic Italy. They were highly visible. It was a very bad idea.

Even worse was the decision to enforce the loyalty oath.

The Oath

The matter was perfectly simple and reasonable in the emperor's opinion. Under the terms of the concordat of 1801, the parish clergy were state employees; even regular clergy received a pension from the empire. True, the concordat as agreed had applied only to France; but the emperor had unilaterally decided expand it to the empire as a

---

8   Among these, the nursing order of the Fatebenefratelli, and the teaching priest and brothers of the Scuole Pie.

whole. If he paid them, he reasoned, at the very least the emperor should be assured of their loyalty. They were ordered to sign the oath, and submit it as a legal document.

In the pope's opinion, the matter was equally simple: by occupying Rome, the emperor had forfeited any claim he might have on the Church. The primary loyalty of the clergy, and of the people of Rome for that matter, was to their legitimate sovereign, Pius VII.

The irresistible force and the immovable object confronted one another, and the people were caught between.

The problem with the oath was that it demanded that the signer swear hatred of all monarchs other than the emperor, 'without restriction and without modification'. This legally obliged the clerics to swear hatred to the pope, whom most regarded as their legitimate sovereign, and whom all regarded as a monarch within the meaning of the oath. Sometimes those administering the oath would allow clerics to sign a version that did not include the offensive paragraph, which would be written in later. This jesuitical manoeuvre could soothe the consciences of some clerics, and some administrators, but it was acceptable neither to the pope, nor to the emperor.

Napoleon seems to have been honestly amazed that large numbers of clerics refused the oath and went more or less cheerfully to prison; while those who did swear were ashamed and insisted that they did so with mental reservations, and recanted as soon as they dared. The entire business was fatal to the morale of many who would have otherwise supported the new regime. Cesare Balbo, the *Consulta* member afflicted by scruples, was appalled by the spectacle of the passive but powerful resistance that some of the clergy demonstrated. Some 30 years later, he wrote in his autobiography:

I was made even more ashamed than ever by the improving demonstration of strength given by these priests. I began to suspect that these, so despised, might be the strongest men in Italy, or the only strong men in Italy. Perhaps if I had had this salutary example earlier, even I would have known how to imitate them. ... With the pope absent, authority fell on the cardinals: those whom they discovered, they took away; but another was quickly substituted; then another and another, until either the secret was better kept, or the powerful became tired – they couldn't send them all away. ... As for me, I did as little as possible and refused any greater office that was offered; and sought to distract myself with diversions, which in this Rome, holy in name but too often perverted in fact, I never failed to find.

At the end of 1810 the *Consulta* wrapped up their mission. That mission had already failed, as everyone but perhaps de Tournon and Napoleon realised. Balbo was eager to escape a charge that divorced him from full communion with the Church.

Three times, Pius VII forbade clerics to take the oath: first on 22 May 1808, then on 22 June 1809, a few days after Rome had been declared an imperial city and the emperor was excommunicated; and finally on 13 March 1810, from his confinement at Savona.[9] Most canons and more than 200 priests refused to sign, and were deported. The oath was then extended to civic officials, and 50 mayors resigned.

---

9   Spina, *Nuovi documenti*, fn 1.

There was a bright side to the refusals, at least for the bureaucrats. By 1810, steps were being taken to reduce the number of Roman bishops, first from 32 to 23, later to 13, and finally to 5. When bishops, and canons, refused to take the oath, they simply facilitated the process of winnowing down the upper clergy. In fact Janet, the money man of the *Consulta*, worried that not enough bishops would refuse the oath, but Radet was able to reassure him, and in fact most bishops refused, and were removed from their posts and, in some cases, deported.

After the bishops, it was the turn of the parish priests.

In the district of Trasimène (formerly and latterly known as Umbria), Prefect Roederer was outraged when his valuable general secretary felt himself obliged to go to confession during Lent of 1810, and was told that he could not receive absolution so long as he continued to work for the French. The secretary handed in his resignation; the Prefect of Trasimène went through the roof. 'If the countryside is not in open revolt, it's not the fault of the priests!' Clergy refused the sacraments to anyone who worked for the French, and the people threatened them and considered them to be enemies of religion.

Of the 12 Umbrian bishops, nine refused the oath, some in a manner that outraged Roederer even further: the Bishop of Todi 'spoke only of resignation and his desire to be martyred', while the Bishop of Orvieto made a joke of the whole thing and abandoned his office with unseemly joviality.

In Rome, at first the amiable and sympathetic de Tournon seemed to have better luck. He told the bishops that they were free to add written reservations in the blank space under their signatures – reservations that were then snipped off, while the signed oaths were forwarded to the *Consulta*. Ten Roman bishops signed, writing that they 'reserved the rights of the Church and the Papacy [*Sainte-Siège*]'. It almost worked, until Roederer blew the whistle.[10] Still, de Tournon ended up with six signed oaths from his bishops. The lower clergy were quite another matter. By the end of July 1810, 216 parish priests from the Tiber *département* (aka Rome) and 154 from Trasimène (aka Umbria) had refused to take the oath. Obeying the instructions and following the example of their sovereign, now a prisoner at Savona, the non-juring bishops and priests allowed themselves to be arrested without resisting (though sometimes gendarmes had to be used to clear a way through the infuriated crowds, who felt no obligation to be docile).

Napoleon was annoyed but, at first, satisfied. The priests and bishops were behaving in an absurd and fanatical manner, and deserved everything they got. There were, after all, far too many clerics in Rome, even after those not native to the city had been deported. Let them thin themselves out, then – the stubborn ones could be interned or imprisoned in France. By the end of May, the trains of deportees began to head for the newly constructed camps, surrounded by squares of gendarmes. They were hailed along the way as martyrs, and people – even people who had formerly been impatient with the theocracy of Rome – knelt by the roadsides to ask for their blessing. By October bishops, canons and parish priests who had at first signed loyalty oaths began to retract them, and joined in the parade. At about the same time,

10 *Mémoires de Tournon* cited by Madelin, *op. cit.*,p. 336-7.

the closing of the monasteries was complete, and monks and nuns now appeared as very visible – and very well supported – beggars in the streets. Romans, exaggerating just a bit, felt that they had returned to the days of the pagan emperors. Ignoring the officially sanctioned parish priests, the faithful sought out the monks who had been expelled and found them living in miserable quarters, wearing borrowed civilian clothing, and basking in the happy light of popular sanctity.

By 1811, Napoleon's love for Rome was rapidly developing into the hatred that only a rejected suitor can feel. He referred to Rome as 'the one city that gives scandal to the empire'. In March, Rome refused to rejoice in the birth of an imperial son; in May, the emperor ordered a census of the sons of the Roman nobility. The results of that survey would create an even deeper chasm between the emperor and his subjects.

On 10 April 1812, the Council of State meeting at St Cloud discussed the imperial order to confiscate the goods of those who refused the loyalty oath. Papers of the sitting were later given to Cardinal Consalvi and published in his memoirs. When some at the meeting suggested that it would be unjust to confiscate the family property of those accused of disloyalty, they were quickly overruled. Napoleon himself commented that, 'children almost always have the same opinions as their father. … This won't be the only time when the family finds itself ruined because of the bad behaviour of its head.' … 'It would be cowardly of the state to allow men to accept the benefits of the state while refusing to swear loyalty.' Weakness would only encourage defiance, the emperor knew: 'Now they make a joke of it, they go home and laugh [at us]!' Pasquino's barbs were driving the emperor towards irrational rage, and Russia beckoned.

The result of the sitting of the Council of State was the decree of 4 May 1812, which was posted in Rome on the 23rd. Those who refused to take the oath of loyalty were declared 'felons, outside the protection of the law.' They were to be arrested, brought before a military tribunal and, if they continued to refuse, their goods were to be confiscated and they themselves imprisoned.[11]

Lawyers who would not swear loyalty must be deported, within 24 hours. The Roman priests sent to prisons in Parma and Bologna were judged to be too near Rome where, thanks to the benevolence of the inhabitants, they were well treated; 600 of them were to be transported to Corsica, 150 of them immediately.

Priests, who had already been forbidden to wear clerical clothing in public, were now ordered not to move about without a security card showing that they had taken the oath. In Corsica, some of the curia lawyers, or *curiali,* were put in irons. Others were transported to prison in irons, like violent criminals. In Rome, de Tournon was distraught but saw no way to interpose himself between his city and his emperor that would accomplish anything but his own destruction. Miollis, reluctant but determined to do his duty, prepared to carry out his orders.

In Rome, a pious and charitable young woman, Elisabetta Canori-Mora (she would be declared a saint in 1994), passed a girl begging on the street. Signora Canori-Mora had her own troubles – the mother of four children, she had an unfaithful and abusive husband and, although she was of a moderately prosperous family, she was on the point

---

11 Madelin, *op. cit., p.* 520; Decree of 4 May 1812, *Bulletin des Lois,* 4th series, vol XVI, number 7982.

of beggary in a city where so many were newly reduced to misery.[12] Still, something about the girl called her back, and she brought her home to give what little help she could. The girl, she discovered, was the daughter of one of the *curiali* who had lost their jobs and their property for refusing to take the loyalty oath. Her father had had a stroke, and was unable to move, so he had not been sent to prison. They had no furniture – the daughter slept on the bare floor, her father had a little straw. She was, she sobbed, on the point of suicide … or worse: there were men who would help a pretty, desperate girl, for a price. Elisabetta did something rather unusual for a Roman – she sent to verify the girl's story. On learning that it was true, she found a way to arrange for assistance.

The Experiences of a Deported Confessor
Father (later Monsignor) Giuseppe Canali worked as a confessor, an employee of the S. Penetenzieria. Since he was neither a canon nor a parish priest, he had not technically been liable to the oath in the early days. However, after the May edict of 1812, virtually all priests, along with virtually all civil employees, were required to swear loyalty to the regime or face severe penalties, including confiscation of their property, a declaration of 'civil death' (that is, outlawry), and indefinite imprisonment. Monsignor Canali, who died in 1851, left a lively account of his arrest and imprisonment for his nephews.[13]

The evening of 2 June 1812, returning home, I found a note calling me to the residence of the director general of police, Maumbritton, at the Palazzo Rinuccini. I immediately realised that my hour had come. I left my home to go immediately to my friend Padre Stracchini, and was surprised to learn that he had received a similar invitation, along with his friend Fr Mariano Ferraris. We decided therefore to go together.

The three men spent the evening like conspirators, making sure that certain 'most secret matters' were passed on to a fellow cleric who did not seem in immediate danger of deportation, and making arrangements for another priest to pick up the 'secret correspondence with the Tribunal' (Imperial paranoia seems to have been well founded):

In the morning I rose carefully, and took care of various small matters to be sent to me in case I was not able to return home, and then I parted with my aunts and my sister. I encouraged them, but inside I felt my heart break, especially as I reflected on the total desolation in which I was leaving them.

While he was finishing up some of the small matters, three men came to ask him whether or not they could accept jobs that required them to take the oath. They left, he says, 'persuaded and edified'. After a 'good cup of chocolate' with his friends Stracchini and Ferraris, they proceeded to the police headquarters.

---

12 Elisabetta Canori-Mora's *Diario* is available on the internet at www.intratext.com/X/1TA1070.htm She, like many in her day, included apocalyptic prophecies in her writings.
13 Canali, G. 'Memorie di un prete romano deportato al temo di Napoleone'.

[W]e were brought in separately, one by one. After two others, I went in also, and found the Signor director general lying down on a sofa, all serious and gloomy, while three other commissioners or secretaries were seated around a little table. I remained standing, and they asked me my name, surname and homeland … They then asked me my occupation and I replied that I was a priest … At these words this one muttered through his teeth, 'Penitenzieria [confessor] at San Girolamo'. He then added, 'You are a troublemaking priest and an enemy of the oath.'

Father Canali tried to dodge the issue of the oath, saying that it could hardly prove his loyalty, since he could easily lie, and arguing that since he was neither a canon nor a parish priest, he didn't see that he was legally bound to take it. The police were not impressed. He must sign the oath.

I replied calmly that if this were absolutely required of me, I would have to tell him that I could not oblige him. … 'So it seems', he exclaimed, 'that the things of heaven and of earth cannot come together.' 'Not always', I agreed. Then he stopped tormenting me.

When all of the accused had been interviewed, with much the same result, they were all ordered to prison at the Castel Sant'Angelo. There followed a bizarre little exchange. The police were determined that the priests should go to prison by carriage, rather than create a public spectacle by walking. The priests said they were happy enough to walk, with chains or without them. The police agent insisted that they had to ride, and they had to pay for it. The priests, obviously enjoying making the man feel ridiculous, said that they didn't have any money, since all their goods had been confiscated. Flustered, he went back for further instructions.

The employee left, but came back after a little while all resolute and said, the Signor Direttore *most definitely wanted us to go by carriage.*
　　'The Signor Direttore', *I replied …, 'will have to pay for it himself, because we will not pay for the carriages.' He had nothing more to say, so I was silent, and the carriages, in sum, were not paid.*
　　…And so about an hour after mid-day, in the habit of an abbate *… and having in my pocket as my entire capital 75* bajocchi, *I entered with my companions into Castel Sant'Angelo.*

Prisoners in the Castello

At the Castello, Canali found himself under the care of a couple of old friends, the guard and his wife, Marianna. They greeted him and his companions with great distress, and allowed him to pick out the nicest cell:

This spot was at the top of the main tower, over the room called the Treasury; it consists of a spacious room, on the side dominated by the Angel, and held up by four columns, and beside it are two rooms, between the west and the north, that look out on St Peter's … It was a dry place, clean and airy. … A fine thing for a prisoner to pick out his own prison!

Next, they sent out for a late Roman supper.

'Marianna', we said to our new hostess, 'we're too late to have food sent in today, we don't feel like fasting, do you suppose we could do something about that?' … I suggested that she make up a plate of macaroni and send for some quarters of suckling lamb from the Fontanelle di Banchi, and a little fruit, and that would be enough. The poor woman set to it willingly and soon it was all arranged, and so we ate cheerfully for the first time in our new lodgings. The Signori Francesi [French gentlemen] *don't much like our macaroni and, knowing its reputation as a* piatto d'allegria [cheap dish], *they take it for an insult if you offer it to them.*

As was normal for the time, the prisoners were responsible for arranging their own food, furniture and clothing, and their families soon sent in mattresses and, for Canali, a little library of his favourite books.

That night we slept very nicely on our mattresses on the floor, which made Fr Ferraris, who got all tangled up, complain, 'I don't know how to do this! I've always climbed up to go to bed, and now I have to climb down!'

Within a week there were more than 70 priests in the Castello, and like all internees they set up their own little government. They structured the days' work, prayer and exercise, and kept watch for the inevitable government spies, appointing a shrewd parish priest from the town of Velletri as 'minister of police' (he found and expelled three spies among them).

People sent them food and money, and a group of pious women of the people appointed themselves to bring them cool water every day ('a real refrigerator for us, both because the weather was very hot and also because the water in the Castello was not very nice'). The monastery of Santa Cecilia sent them gifts of lemons, along with sweets, and wine, and fruit ('I became an excellent butler, I learned to make coffee and chocolate for a crowd marvellously well, and my lemonade was stupendous'). When the government tried to put a stop to this by cutting off all visitors, the wife of the commander of the fortress interceded for the prisoners, and once again people of all classes poured into the Castello, their handkerchiefs filled with little gifts, until the authorities again put a stop to it ('otherwise the Castello would have become a shop and we would have been able to support ourselves by selling things').

Keeping up morale was an important duty. They 'sang and told stories' and every morning Canali got a big laugh with the following prayer, recited loudly:

My God, if Napoleon makes me die of privation and fatigue I will be patient, I am here for love of you, but I promise you that I absolutely refuse to die of feeling sorry for myself!

Whether he needed the money, or whether he was just being cheeky, Canali actually sent a friend to Prefect de Tournon to ask him to send his monthly government pension. De Tournon, who couldn't afford to see the humour in the situation, informed the friend that the emperor did not pay his enemies. Canali was philosophical: 'He's right, I said, laughing, and thought no more of it.'

For the first few days of their confinement, the priests were allowed to say Mass, but that privilege was soon withdrawn. This policy seems to have been a sort of psychological warfare – when Giovanni Patrizi was sent to the Fenestrelle prison, he was refused the opportunity to hear Mass or take communion for two years, and this caused him great distress.

After a little more than a month in the Castel Sant'Angelo, they were informed that they were to be sent to an unknown destination. Eventually Canali and his companions were among the 'hard cases' sent to prison in Corsica. Before the game was over, they would be held in irons, and some of them would die.

The Golden Levy

The Patrizi

The Patrizi were members of the oldest of the Roman nobility, though not necessarily the most eminent or the richest. Pious and cultivated, they numbered among their friends men like the papal chancellor Cardinal Consalvi, and the famous Venetian sculptor Antonio Canova. Canova, a pretentiously unpretentious genius,[14] lived abstemiously, slept little, ate sparingly (usually a peasant-style dish of polenta and small game birds), but in the evenings he liked to visit the homes of particular friends. His 'favourite houses of call were the Patrizi and Martinetti palaces', and one or two others, where he was often a guest along with Cardinal Consalvi.[15] There they enjoyed 'the performances of classical music with which the hosts delighted their guests'. He seems to have been especially fond of the young Patrizi couple, and made Cunegonde a present of a marble head of the Madonna.

For the first 10 or 12 years, Giovanni and Cunegonde Patrizi's family lives were ordinary enough for their class and time. They lived in the Patrizi palace, across the street from the church of San Giovanni de'Fiorentini, with the groom's family, the Marchese and Marchesa Patrizi, and their still-young family (the bride's youngest sister-in-law was three). In the first seven years of their marriage they had three sons: Saverio, born in June 1797; his brother Costantino, born in Siena 4 September of the following year while the Ridiculous Republic ruled Rome; and Filippo, born in Rome on 7 April 1803. By this time, Pius VII was ruler of Rome, and First Consul Bonaparte (who had already set his star on the imperial throne) was far away in Paris.

The city was occupied for the second time in February 1808, and the following June Rome passed from the rule of the pope to the rule of the emperor of the French. The great nobles of the city were to be co-opted into the new government. Some, testing the wind and seeing which way it blew, accepted their new roles with more or less good grace. Others kept their heads down and hoped the storm would pass. Five – the princes Massimo, Altieri, Barberini and Rospigliosi, and the Marchese Patrizi – refused to participate, and were called to Paris to answer for it. At this point the new

---

14 Silvagni, *op. cit.*, III, p. 7.
15 Consalvi was Pius VII's chancellor who was forced to resign in 1808 and was replaced by Cardinal Pacca.

emperor, King of Italy, and Protector of Rome, took notice of the Patrizi family. It cannot have been a coincidence that of the five summoned to Paris, three were directly connected by marriage to the Saxon princesses, cousins of Louis XVI (two of Cunegonde's sisters were married to Prince Altieri and Prince Massimo, respectively). Their stay in Paris was tense, but they were not subjected to harsh treatment, though they remained under close supervision until April of the following year. At one point, the emperor condescended to entertain them, and took the opportunity to make a jab at Prince Massimo: 'They say you are descended from Fabius Maximus. That is not true!' In a perfectly polite aristocratic put-down, Prince Massimo brushed the attack aside. 'I can't prove it', he yawned, 'it is merely a rumour that has been around in our family for about 1,200 years.' Napoleon, who was intensely aware that the old aristocracy of Europe considered him a parvenu, must have smarted. He was not a man to overlook an insult.

He could, of course, have simply abolished the aristocracy; but he had chosen rather to co-opt them. In April 1810 the hostages returned none the worse for wear, but the emperor was by no means finished with the cousins of the dead king of France, or with their Roman families. He had made the political decision to join the monarchs of Europe, by right of conquest and by the new political coin, the will of the people. He had divorced his somewhat shady first wife Josephine and, at the same time that he sent the Roman hostages back, he married Marie Louise, daughter of the Hapsburg Emperor of Austria. He had brought the French nobility to heel, recognising their titles in return for loyalty, and diluting their ranks with his newly ennobled followers. But, the French nobility had been chastened by revolution and exile. He would have to make other arrangements for the Italian nobility. He ordered a census of the nobility of Rome, along with a list naming and describing every son of that class between eight and 12 years of age. If the older generation was uncooperative, the simple solution was to take the children and raise them up in the imperial faith.

De Tournon, in his unpublished memoirs, said that he was 'appalled by this act, which was only calculated to estrange the parents without giving any solid guarantees to France by taking possession of a few children. The policy ... was carrying us back to the most barbarous times!'[16]

At the same time, the *popolo* began to experience their own induction into the imperial faith. On 30 April 1811 the prefect announced that young men who were born in 1798 were to report for conscription. The policy towards the aristocracy would not, of course, be called conscription. It had a much more elegant name: the Golden Levy, the *leva dorata*. First came a census of the Roman upper classes. The aristocracy, carefully divided into ranks (the old patricians, the papal nobility and the recently ennobled), and the upper bourgeoisie were identified, the numbers and ages of their children noted, and their income quantified. Each rank was assigned a quota. Young nobles were to be sent to one of three schools: the School for Pages, St-Cyr or the Prytanie de la Flèche. Boys from the *haute bourgeoisie* were to be sent to the High School of Arts and Crafts at Chalons.

---

16 De Tournon, unpublished memoirs, quoted by Marchesa Maddalena Patrizi, *op. cit.*, p. 23; (Forester translation, p. 62).

The Patrizi family, duly enumerated, appeared thus on the list:

Patrizi, Xavier [Saverio]: *12 years old; family of the ancient nobility. Parents' revenues, 10,000 Roman* scudi. *Observation: in good health and of good constitution; the eldest of the children.*

   Patrizi, Philippe [Filippo]: *eight years old, brother of the above mentioned. Good health. There is another son, aged 10, who has delicate health.*

An imperial decree of 9 July 1811 identified the boys to be honoured by the call to serve their emperor. Starting on 7 August, the families were notified; on 30 August – ironically, the same day on which de Tournon announced conscription for the men born in 1789 – the Patrizi family received the news that two of their boys, Saverio and Filippo, were to proceed with all deliberate haste to the military college of La Flèche.

   Napoleon seems to have believed that he was honouring the Romans with these opportunities. He was surprised and disgusted to find that most families resisted, and besieged his prefect and his police with pleas for exemptions on the flimsiest of grounds. When a single family not only resisted, but adamantly refused, they earned his personal and unrelenting determination to crush them.

   Giovanni, the son of the Marchese Patrizi and father of the boys in question, did his best to avoid open defiance, but by October the police were running out of patience. Norvins, on instruction from the highest quarters, ordered Giovanni Patrizi to send his boys to France by 25 November, or else follow them to Paris and 'remain at the disposition of the Central Police'. In his prison diary, Giovanni remembered that he went to his wife's room when he received Norvins' message:

… my first words were, 'Well, what ought I to do?' Without hesitation she replied that we must resist to the very last, and her courage rekindled my own.

The family continued to delay and temporise, but soon the inevitable happened. As Fortunati noted in his omnipresent diary:[17]

On this night [25 November], *while the Marchese* [Giovanni] *Patrizi was at supper with his family, he was arrested by the gendarmes; they didn't even give him a quarter hour before taking him to the Castello, and after three hours they made him get into a carriage and took him to Civitavecchia. His crime was no other than that he refused to obey the order to turn over his children to be sent to school in Paris.*

The Marchese Giovanni was taken directly to the fortress prison at Civitavecchia, where he found that he soon had the company of priests and lawyers and others who had refused to take the oath of allegiance (among them, our old friend the *abbate* Benedetti). In Rome, Cunegonde was unable to prevent her sons being sent to France; leaving her 10-year-old with his grandparents, she determined to go with Saverio and Filippo, and did so. After a gruelling mid-winter journey, they reached

---

17 Fortunati, *op. cit.*, 25 November 1811.

La Flèche, where the director of the school found her a small house where she could be near her sons. She was under virtual house arrest, and required to report to the local police once a week, 'like a woman of the pavements', she lamented.

De Tournon received orders to sequester the goods of the Marchese Giovanni Patrizi. Reluctant to stir up even more resentment among the Romans, he replied that Giovanni was the son of the family and owned nothing in his own right. General Miollis, however, was of the opinion that the Patrizi resistance might spark a general revolt among the nobility, and urged the family property be seized. The recommendation was sent to the emperor, who wrote in the margin, in his own hand: 'Oui! Napoleon. St Cloud, 30 janvier 1812.'

At the same time, Giovanni Patrizi was moved from Civitavecchia, where he was quite near Rome, to the dreaded Fenestrelle prison in the mountains of northern Italy. Here he found, again, plenty of company, including a man he referred to in his letters as *Peccorella* (the lamb), or 'Bartélémy Brebis' (Bartholomew the Sheep). He was no other than Pius VII's intransigent and most un-lamb-like counsellor, Cardinal Pacca.

Giovanni and Cunegonde – or Gio [pronounced 'jo'] and Gondina as they addressed one another in their correspondence – from time to time found ways of exchanging uncensored letters. In several of them he advised her to claim that she could not cooperate with the imperial authorities for fear of what her tyrannical husband might do to her, while at the same time assuring her that he would leave it to her own good judgement to do whatever she thought best.

After reading the 'incriminating' uncensored letters (passed along by spies), the emperor ordered that Giovanni be transferred, under strong escort, from the Fenestrelle to the Chateau d'If, a rocky outpost off Marseilles, considered impregnable and escape-proof. (Alexandre Dumas, of course, later chose the Chateau d'If for his much-abused hero, Edmund Dantes, the Count of Monte Cristo.)

For many months, the family had no letters – they were consigned to a banker in Marseilles, who sent them (as he was ordered) to the emperor. One wonders what Napoleon made of this one, from Saverio to his father:

It would be a fine thing if one day or the other … we would be united …. I warn you as a precaution you should put on an iron collar so as not to be suffocated by my embraces. If I could see you, at the cost of pulling your carriage from where you are to where we are, I would be happy to do it, all by myself. My papa, I beg you to bless me.

Soon, however, Napoleon would have other matters to concern him. In May 1812, the invasion of Russia began. At the end of the following year, Francesco Patrizi dictated his last letter to his son Giovanni, still at the Chateau d'If:

Courage, then, dear son; endure all that the good God asks of you, and keep ever before your eyes the great maxim that we suffer here for only a short time while that [happiness] which awaits us is, God helping, eternal.[18]

---

18 Patrizi, *Memorie di Famiglia*, p. 265.

Francesco died in January 1814, as the Allies invaded France. It was not until the following 10 April – Easter Sunday – that Cunegonde would write a letter to her husband Giovanni that began with the words, 'Allelulia! Allelulia!' The war was over. 'My dear Gio', she wrote, 'after almost 29 months, then, we are at the point of being reunited, and reunited in a miraculous way; the Cavaliere [a family friend] is beside himself, as are we all.'

Five days later, Giovanni Patrizi wrote one word in his prison diary: *Libertà*.

The family missed one another on the road, but they were finally reunited in Rome on 22 May 1814, two days before Pius VII returned in triumph to his city. But before we reach that point, there are many other events to be considered.

Pope Pius VII returns to Rome along with other exiles.

CHAPTER TEN
RESTORATIONS

From St Helena, Napoleon had a very curious image of his relationship with Italy:

It will take me 20 years, I said in 1805, at the Council of Lyons, to create the Italian nation. 15 had sufficed; all was ready; I waited only for the birth of a second son, in order to take him to Rome, and proclaim the independence of the peninsula, from the Alps to the Ionian Sea, and from the Mediterranean to the Adriatic.

This is a very peculiar claim, given its chronological inexactitude and the fact that he seems to be saying that a second son would usurp the title of King of Rome he had already given to his first son, and then be set up as ruler of an independent Italy.

Did he despise Italians? He certainly said often enough that he did. But at the same time many felt that he had an attachment to the peninsula, and that was probably true. His family was of Genoese origin, and his French never lost its Italian inflection. His first great foreign military successes came in Italy. Above all, there was the glamour of the ancient empire that he sought to emulate. The Tuscan minister Fossombroni, put it this way:[1]

Napoleon was never free over the matter of Italy. He remained purely Italian in principles, tastes, morals and ideas, but was restrained in his preferences by his entourage. We, the Italian party, were sure to cause the secret fibres of his soul to vibrate, and the French ministers used all their art in silencing them. That is the fatal dissidence that decided the fate of Italy and paralysed Napoleon to the point of shaking his own beliefs. Whenever he set foot in Italy, all his dreams of grandeur, of the future, of

---

1   Heriot, *The French in Italy.* p. 141.

prosperity were in his heart. He breathed freely, was without constraint: in his eyes, Italy grew as if by magic. He was proud to belong to it; on its behalf he conceived the grandest hopes; he filled us with joy, but that joy was of brief duration. Back in Paris he fell once more under the influence of his ministers; Italy was for him once more a subsidiary element and no longer the cornerstone of his edifice. And he thought no more of it but as a source of men and money.

What Rome Gained and Lost

By 1815, in the 18 or so years that had passed since the treaty of Tolentino, Rome had been demoted from capital of the world to a small provincial city. She got new civic, social, financial, legal, educational, commercial, postal, penal and judicial systems. She even got a new way of telling time, a new system of weights and measures, and for a while, a whole new calendar (mercifully, when Napoleon became emperor he shelved the Republican version). All of this was administered for the most part by foreigners (which for Romans meant anyone not from Rome). Even if the new systems turned out (in time) to be far better than the ones they replaced, they were foreign, and they were by their very nature disruptive. They were also imposed with an unseemly haste. When the members of the *Consulta* went to work, they had one year (in fact, they took a year and a half) to transform the ancient city into a modern, efficient, well-oiled cog in a vast imperial system. But the foreigners were enlightened thinkers, and they saw no difficulty with this. After all, it was an article of enlightened political faith that a government and a society, like a watch, could profitably be taken apart and put back together again.

At the same time that this truly radical transformation was being attempted, the economic supports had been pulled out from under the city. Rome lived on patronage, on spectacle, and on religion. All of this was either destroyed, or profoundly changed. The bulk of the papal budget had come from contributions, or taxes, from the Catholic world. These were either cut off, or drastically curtailed, by the new political realities. The royal court (that is, the papal court) was abolished. It was to have been replaced by an even more splendid imperial court, but that never happened. Along with the royal court, the city lost the courts of some 50 cardinals, who had lived like princes whether or not they wanted to do so. She also lost the courts of foreign dignitaries and ambassadors, and the households of thousands of lesser but still relatively wealthy foreigners like the British *dilettanti* and tourists, who perforce disappeared *en masse* with the French occupation. The Roman nobility who remained – and many left the city to take up positions in other parts of the empire or retreated to their rural estates to wait out the storm – either cut back drastically on their staffs, or joined their fellow Romans in misery. Visitors after 1815 reported that the nobles had closed down their *palazzi*, or rented them out in apartments, and had stopped even the most rudimentary entertaining. One anonymous source even reports that he saw a distressed nobleman standing in line at a bakery to buy bread, having no servant to send.[2] While our modern democratic hearts may not bleed for the nobleman, they should certainly bleed for the unemployed servant.

---

2   Wiseman, *The Last Four Popes*, p. 59.

Thousands of domestics, secretaries, hairdressers, tailors, dressmakers, artists, artisans and gentleman attendants to formerly wealthy ladies were suddenly cut off from their livelihoods. The butchers, bakers and candlestick makers who had once done business with these unfortunates suffered from a ripple effect, and were often plunged into distress themselves. And all of this happened at precisely the same time that the elaborate net of public and private charity that had once supported such unfortunates disappeared. When the Chigi left for Paris, Domenico Taigi lost his job. Anna Maria, already heavily burdened with the care of her children and her parents, took to making and selling ladies' shoes.

To all this, we must add the more or less serious distress caused by (a) the looting of works of art and scholarship that Romans had considered their communal property, (b) the sudden and drastic curtailment in religious festivals and feast days, and (c) the arrest and deportation of their sovereign, as well as of many of their physical, psychological and support staff.

Finally, and most fatal of all, the new imperial system never had time to do anything more than disrupt the status quo in Italy. The entire revolutionary experience lasted for only 18 years. The Napoleonic rule of Rome began in the summer of 1809, and while it did not officially end until May of 1814 when the pope re-claimed his capital, it was effectively over by the end of 1812, when news of the Russian disaster spread.

Meetings at Fontainebleau

Napoleon hurried back from Russia, determined to salvage his empire from the destruction that now stared him in the face. He set about creating a new Grand Army from the old men, young boys and semi-invalids who remained in civilian life. Then he went to Fontainebleau where Pius VII, brought from Savona, waited.

There are many accounts of the negotiations at Fontainebleau in 1813, the six days during which Napoleon, alone with the pope, alternately cajoled and bullied him to force him to sign the agreement that would be published as a new concordat. One popular story had it that the emperor broke a set of Sèvres porcelain and struck the pope, and the pope responded by calling the emperor a comedian. It is unlikely that much of this is true. The closest thing we have to a first hand account comes from Cardinal Pacca's memoirs. Pacca, released from the fortress of Fenestrelle, arrived at Fontainebleau after the documents had been signed. On his way, he heard that a new concordat had been signed, giving up the temporal powers and condemning the cardinals who had refused to acknowledge the emperor's second marriage. The emperor claimed the right to name all bishops in the empire except in the immediate vicinity of Rome, and the pope accepted (it was said) a civil list of two million francs.

Pacca says that he found the pope seriously ill and so distraught that he feared that he would lose his mind. Pius denied, however, that he had suffered any overt violence. Napoleon had grabbed the buttons on his soutane, a gesture that rings true – the general, and the emperor, had a habit of doing this when one of his officers annoyed him, grabbing his buttons and jerking him back and forth. The 'comedian' comment probably comes from Pius' recollection that he had observed that the negotiations had begun as a comedy and would end as a tragedy.

Whatever the truth of the new concordat was – and Pius formally disclaimed it two months later – Napoleon had indeed offered to return the Papal States, and Rome, to the rule of the pope. When Murat claimed Rome, Napoleon had decided that he would much prefer the pope, however stubborn, to his disloyal brother-in-law:[3]

The King of Naples having concluded with the coalition an alliance, one of whose objects appears to be the reunion of Rome with his own states, His Majesty the Emperor and King [of Italy] has considered that the political interests of his empire and those of the people of Rome require that he should give back the Roman States to Your Holiness. Consequently, I am authorised to sign a treaty by which peace will be re-established between the emperor and the pope.

Pius declined to sign such a treaty – what was the point of agreeing to a treaty with Napoleon, when the Allies had already marched into France and were on the point of deposing him? Napoleon had no intention of relinquishing any more of his drastically reduced store of chess pieces. The pope was to be sent back immediately to Savona (although he was told that he was going to Rome), and the cardinals who were with him at Fontainebleau were to be dispersed to various places in the French interior, away from Paris, where the invaders were obviously heading.

When the Allies closed in on Paris, Napoleon retreated to Fontainebleau with his remaining troops. There, deserted by his marshals, and even by his servants, he may have tried to commit suicide. This would have been perfectly consonant with the antique Roman cult of the empire, but if he tried, he didn't try hard enough. Napoleon had a horror of physical disfigurement, and if he wanted to die, he wanted to do it in a way that would allow his body to lie in state in an appropriately calm and heroic fashion.[4] He therefore tried to poison himself with a vial of opium, but only succeeded in making himself violently ill. Another reported plan (a very odd one, reminiscent of one of the attempts to martyr St Cecilia) was to enclose his bathtub in a tent, then stoke up the coals under it so that he would be suffocated in the steam. When this failed, he considered using his pistol to blow his brains out, but was talked out of it by his loyal general Caulaincourt.

The Patrizi Family Return Home
At the Chateau d'If on 14 April 1814, Giovanni Patrizi and his fellow prisoners looked out the tiny window that faced towards Marseilles across the bay, and saw fireworks, *feu de joie,* blazing over the city.

The sight sent us nearly mad with joy, and as soon as the guards had locked us in and gone away we began to give vent to our delight, embracing one another, dancing up and down, indulging in every wild demonstration that the unfortunate are capable of when they see that their troubles are over. I instantly brought out my whole provision of tallow candles, some 20 in all, and in the absence of candlesticks stuck them in bottles and

---

3   Hales, *op. cit.,* pp. 158–9.
4   The following stories are reported by Hales, pp. 161–2.

lighted them to celebrate the coming deliverance. My four colleagues did the same so that our dark cell looked like a brilliantly lit ballroom. Nor did we forget to turn gratefully to our Heavenly Benefactor, singing in low voices the Te Deum …

The next day, a group of officials wearing the white cockade of the Bourbons arrived with the official news – printed in a newspaper that no longer carried the imperial eagle – that the emperor had abdicated and was on the point of being exiled to the island of Elba. By night, Giovanni was in a launch for a half-hour trip to port of Marseilles, where he and his fellows were hailed as heroes by the crowd, and kissed by the women (perhaps for Gondina, who would see the diary, Gio reported that he only kissed the white-haired ones). He spent the night at the home of a man he considered a friend, who had been helping him communicate with his family, but found that the banker Carminati was mysteriously absent. He never learned that the banker had been sending his letters to the French secret service.[5]

By this time, the boys had been released from the military school at La Flèche and Cunegonde had taken them to Paris to urge her husband's freedom (and, while she was at it, to try to get back some of her late father's property). Letters went astray, and Giovanni decided to go directly to Rome, where his recently widowed mother and his now 12-year-old second son were waiting. He and a fellow former prisoner pooled their money to hire a post carriage and made their way south along roads crowded with returning deportees, exiled cardinals, boys who had gone to the hills to dodge the draft and others who had simply walked away from their units, along with hordes of people who had been keeping their heads down waiting for times to change. In Modena they found that the people had set up a free hospice for returning exiles, where they plied them with chocolate. Patrizi travelled by hired carriage, horseback, sometimes on foot, and at one point sliding down a steep snow-covered alpine incline on his backside.

He reached Rome two hours after sunset on 16 May and hurried to his home on the Piazza San Giovanni where he was welcomed by his son Costantino, his little sister Maria, and his mother Porzia. On the 22nd, the family was reunited when Cunegonde arrived with the two young veterans from military school.[6]

On 24 May Pius VII made his triumphal entrance into Rome.

Murat as Patriot

Murat, as we have seen, had long had his eye on Rome. Whether it was his idea, or Caroline's, he had certainly wanted to incorporate Rome into the Kingdom of Naples at least since 1808, and probably before. He was hardly the first Neapolitan king to covet Rome – Ferdinand had made an inept snatch at the city in 1798.

Murat had first come to Rome in 1802; in 1808, and again in 1809 he had paid state visits to the city, and (at least in the jaundiced opinion of Fortunati) had made a spectacle of himself courting the Romans with his gold-trimmed uniform, yellow

---

5   Maddalena Patrizi discovered this in the files of the Secret Police when she was working on her book based on the family adventures under Napoleon.
6   Giovanni Naro Patrizi died in January 1817 at the age of 39, but only after receiving the honour of being named Senator of Rome. Cunegonde died in 1828. Of the three boys, Savierio became a Jesuit scholar, Costantino rose to the rank of cardinal and Filippo married and became the father of several children.

boots, and a plumed hat. In fact his visit was not without effect and when, in 1813, the Roman nobles hoped to get rid of Napoleon, they turned to Murat as their protector, and the protector of the old order. On the night of 3–4 November 1813, King Murat came to Rome in strict disguise and stayed at an inn – the Hotel de Londres on the Piazza di Spagna – like a private citizen. De Tournon and Miollis met him there, and he proposed returning to Naples to get an army of 30,000. It was there they learned of Napoleon's defeat at Leipzig 14 days earlier. The King and Queen of Naples hoped to join the Allies and keep their throne, enlarged by the addition of Rome, and Metternich offered them some encouragement in this plan in a secret treaty. They were also encouraged by a petition inviting them to assume rule in Rome, a petition signed by the mayor, Duke Braschi, as well as by the dukes di Sora and Sforza-Cesarini, the princes Barberini and Chigi, and Duke Bracciano (who used to be the banker Torlonia).

On 24 January 1814 Murat arrived as a liberator. He came to the Porta S Giovanni with his ministers, his functionaries, the generals of his army, and was met by a curious if not particularly enthusiastic crowd. That evening, he received Braschi and Sforza-Cesarini in the royal box at the Argentina theatre, amid the applause of the nobility and the general indifference of the people who wanted to see the opera. He made some attempts to win over Romans, giving 13,000 *lire* to the Academy of San Marco, and enclosing the Rafael loggia at the Vatican behind glass – the only thing he did in Rome that remains visible. De Tournon refused to cooperate with him, and left the city, after selling his furniture to Torlonia and carefully packing up the notes and papers that would form the basis for his *Etude statistique*. General Miollis withdrew with the few loyal troops to the Castel Sant'Angelo where they remained under siege for 49 days. There was a period of some confusion, but in the end the victorious Allies meeting at Vienna decided that Rome should be returned to the pope, and Murat, after attempting to meet with Pius on his way to the city, was forced to withdraw.

Murat may indeed have dreamed of uniting Italy under his rule. When Napoleon escaped from Elba and returned to France for the famous Hundred Days restoration, Murat again changed sides. He joined his brother-in-law and emperor once again marching on Rome while Pius and his court fled to Florence, and then to Genoa. It was a brief triumph, but one that has had enduring echoes. Murat issued his famous proclamation of Rimini on 30 March 1815, calling on Italians to flock to his side. 'The hour has come for the high destiny of Italy to be accomplished: Providence at last calls you to be an independent nation.'[7] But his call fell on deaf ears, and his forces abandoned him at the battle of Tolentino. He escaped abroad but later returned to attempt an audacious coup. But he was captured at Pizzi and executed after a mockery of a trial on 13 October 1815. His last request was that the firing squad not aim at his face – it was said that he remembered the execution and disfigurement of the Duc d'Enghien.

After his death, his wife Caroline and his daughters were forbidden to stay in Rome. Caroline's relations with Madame Mère remained cold, though Letizia eventually invited her to stay nearby at the Palazzo Venezia. She came to Rome under the name of the Countess of Lipona (an anagram for Napoli) to visit her mother after

---

7   Proclamation of Rimini, signed Gioacchino Napoleone (Murat), issued 30 March 1815.

Murat in front of the firing squad.

the old lady broke her leg walking in the Borghese gardens, but she was not allowed to stay long. The Austrians and everyone else were still suspicious of her intentions. They most especially did not want anyone re-awakening thoughts of Italians uniting in an independent nation.

The Battaglia Affair

In the confusion of the collapse of Napoleonic power in Italy, there was another call for national unity. Felice Battaglia, a liberal cleric with an apparently flexible view of vows (his main representative in Rome was said to be his mistress), presented himself as leader of an Italian League which purported to have cells in Naples, Bologna, Rome and Milan. For a few brief but intense months, from November 1813 to February 1814, he featured prominently in official reports and correspondence. He had dealings with Murat's agents at the Palazzo Farnese in Rome, and with the English who prowled ever closer to the coasts of Italy. He was, however, captured by General Miollis' men in early December, and that was more or less the end of this particular *risorgimento*.[8] In the short period when he seemed to represent a military threat he created panic in the countryside, carrying with him a portable press on which to print incendiary posters.[9]

The statement he made when he was captured was reported:

He wished to put on the throne a man born in Italy [by which he apparently meant Murat, who was in fact born in France], *a term which included all of Italy below the Alps, which would never submit to foreign domination. He would be happy to die for so fine a cause: if he were set free, he would continue to pursue his project.*

---

8 Literally, resurgence, the term used for the nineteenth-century movement that ended in unification in 1870.
9 Madelin, *op. cit.*, pp. 620–3.

Battaglia was treated as a common bandit. He was tried by a military tribunal along with some brigands captured in the same general area, and given the rather mild sentence of deportation. Before this could be carried out, however, the wind changed again. While he was still cooling his heels in a Roman prison, Murat arrived, found him there, and sent him off under guard to Naples. He never arrived: his former accomplices may have found him an embarrassment.

Restorations and Retribution

Pius VII's return to Rome in 1814 was not the first restoration: that had come when the newly-elected pope had arrived to take possession of Rome in July 1800.[10] That first restoration had been characterised by a surprisingly mild attitude towards the so-called Jacobins, subjects who had actively and very publicly welcomed the French and then participated in the Ridiculous Republic.

Against the advice of the provisional government, the new pope had pardoned two notorious Jacobins – Prince Santacroce, who was freed from the fortress of Civitavecchia on condition he return to his estates; and the carriage-maker Saverio Pediconi, who had already been condemned to death. He even freed the two former consuls (chief executives) of the republic, Giacomo De Mattheis and Federico Zaccaleoni, and in October Cardinal Consalvi issued a pardon for everyone who had participated in the republic (the pardon only exempted those whose acts of rebellion had taken place before the fall of the papal government).

In 1800, Pius' main problem had been preventing trouble between Jacobins and anti-Jacobins, who bitterly resented them. The diarist Galimberti wrote, after the release of the ex-consuls:

The Patriots freed from prison are strutting around the city in an overbearing sort of way; you see a lot of them now, men who were in hiding before.

While being soft on Jacobins, the papal government was most insistent that anti-French insurgents from Naples not be admitted to the Papal States, and this led to the curious situation whereby pro-papal, anti-French insurgents and anti-papal, pro-French Jacobins were lumped together in the same archival file. This tendency to moderation and pardons found one of its most controversial applications in the case of Duke Pio Camillo Bonelli. Bonelli had been the only exponent of the pro-Jacobin aristocracy to be condemned to death (in the name of Ferdinand IV of Naples) for his participation in the 1798–99 Roman republic.[11] Pius cancelled the death penalty and the confiscation order, and had the duke released, whereupon Bonelli joined in the new invasions of Italy. He continued to petition for a full pardon and the right to return to Rome, and the pope finally granted this in 1806.

---

10 In a sense, 1814 was not his last restoration either – one could argue that that would come after being driven out briefly by the threat of a Neapolitan occupation in 1815.

11 See Caffiero, 'Perdono per I Giacobini, severità per gli insorgenti': La prima restaruazione pontificia.

Restoration 1814

On 24 May 1814 the pope arrived at the Milvian bridge north of Rome, to be welcomed by a two-day orgy of celebrations. His carriage was unhitched from the horses and 64 young Romans dressed in black, with powdered wigs and silver buckles on their shoes, pulled it through myrtle and laurel arches decorated with roses and past houses draped in tapestries to St Peter's, and from there up the steep hill to the Quirinal palace. The entire city was illuminated for two days and two nights, and a great bridge of boats was built across the Tiber to make it easier for the *popolo*, on foot or in carriages, to flock to the Vatican piazza. The city was filled with monumental sculptures and paintings, and some enormous unofficial satirical cartoons – one showed the pope on his throne and Bonaparte naked in the dust at his feet.

Despite the mood of the city, Pius showed no more vindictiveness on his return in 1814 than he had 14 years earlier. Most of the Roman nobles had compromised themselves with the French rule in one way or another – there were few Giovanni Patrizis among them. In the last, confused, days of French rule some had supported Murat's claims to Rome rather than petition for a return of the pope. But all was forgiven and forgotten. 'And we?', he was said to have asked a particularly worried noble, 'do you suppose that we have no fault with which to reproach ourselves?'

Unlike some of the more militant of the sovereigns who were returned to power in 1814–15, the pope showed no interest in eradicating any and all reforms that had been made by the imperial representatives – there was no throwing imported French furniture out of windows in Rome, and no closing of new roads, as was said to happen in some of the northern Italian states. Instead, Pius chose to retain much of the Napoleonic code, and his government found that they liked the idea of mandatory street-lighting, and insisting that streets be named and houses be numbered.

Other measures were not so acceptable. The Jesuit order was restored, much to the horror of liberals of every description. And the Jews, who had been made citizens by Napoleon and freed from restrictions on where they could and could not live, were required to return to the ghetto. Some of the property that had been confiscated from the regular orders was returned to them, to the discomfort of those who had paid good money to buy it. Some feudal rights were restored

However, the restoration government gratefully continued the measures the French had taken to disarm men like the *Traseverini*, who were strongly encouraged to leave their knives at home under their pillows by being arrested and publicly humiliated if they were caught with them. The papal government was also willing to accept modern improvements in executions, but only with reservations. The guillotine had been introduced in Rome on 28 February 1810, and continued in use until December 1813 (during which time the executioner of Rome, Maestro Titta, oversaw 56 decapitations). At the restoration, the papal government at first returned to the more old fashioned hanging, but by October 1816, the guillotine was back.

For a while the restored papal government retained the old regime preference for a variety of methods of execution, to suit the crime. Eventually, however, the egalitarian guillotine replaced other forms of execution, despite embarrassing incidents such as the 1864 episode when the elderly executioner (Bugatti was by then well past 80) dropped the decapitated executee's head. This caused general confusion and uproar among the bystanders, who hadn't intended to get quite so close to the event. Bugatti was retired, with a pension.

Public executions, which continued to be relatively rare, were not the only popular entertainments that the restored papacy provided to Romans. Cardinal Consalvi, now secretary of state, turned his hand to providing public celebrations and was quite good at it, as was Prince Corsini, the new Senator of Rome (there was only one at a time, a longstanding if somewhat peculiar tradition). As senator, Corsini showed a real talent for public spectacle, favouring the sort of activities that involved a great deal of free wine and ices. His fireworks' displays and illuminations were said to approach the grand Renaissance scale. On one occasion he arranged for the two basalt lions at the Capitol to spout wine for two days (the preferred mix was one white, or *bianco*, one red, or *nero*); for another event, the two fountains in the Forum did the same.

Pius VII continued to encourage archaeological explorations, as he had done before being deposed. The one exception was the Coliseum, where French engineers had been working to clear the underground corridors and chambers. Pius ordered them filled up again, which outraged scientists who accused him of obscurantism. However, in this case the pope believed that it was more important to restore the old devotion of the Stations of the Cross.

Other archaeological projects engaged his full cooperation. He continued French work at the Forum, the temples, and the Via Sacra, restored the arch of Titus, and excavated Constantine's ancient basilica, the forerunner of the modern St Peter's basilica. He ordered the clearing of the medieval clutter of buildings that still backed up against the Ara Coeli stairs. He even completed French work on the beautification of the Pincio and the piazza of the Porta del Popolo. Fortunately, he retained the services of the greatest of the Roman architects, Valadier, who had worked for him before working for the French.

Antonio Canova, who had never been enthusiastic about working for Napoleon, also returned happily to the fold. His work in securing the return of many (though not all) of the looted works of art and scholarship earned him the title of the Marchese d'Ischia.

Baron Radet

After 1809, 'the man who kidnapped the pope' (as he would henceforth be known) eventually returned to Rome where he spent a happy year. In 1810, he was made a member of the Society of Arts and Manufactures and delivered an address about the need for industrial and agricultural schools, for a school of veterinary science, and for the draining of the Pontine Marshes. He liked Rome so well he bought an establishment nearby at San Pastor. He hoped to make this his seat when he was named Baron of the Empire, but he was ordered to Hamburg and so passed out of Roman history.

In September 1814, he wrote an account of the *triste événement* of the night of 5–6 July 1809, and sent it to the pope along with a letter pleading with the Holy

Father to 'come to the aid of the honour of one of your children' by acting as his witness. He was, he said, the victim of calumnies that made him the object of 'universal animadversion'.[12]

After the restoration, the pope gave him his land at San Pastor back, taking it away from the Dominicans who had claimed it. The restored Bourbon monarchy in France had Radet imprisoned for three years but he was freed by a royal pardon, and on his return home his friend Colonel Hugo (Victor's father) wrote a nice poem about what a fine fellow he was.

He died, peacefully, in 1825 without having returned to Rome.

The Refuge of Exiles
Napoleon had a large family and, in the Italian tradition, he expected the family to provide the stable base on which he would build his dynasty. In order, the Bonaparte children were:

Joseph (Giuseppe), born 1768
Napoleon (Napolione), born 1769
Lucien (Luciano), born 1775
Elise (Maria Anna), born 1777
Louis (Luigi), born 1778
Pauline (Maria Paola), born 1780
Caroline (Maria Annunziata), born 1782
Jerome (Girolamo), the baby of the family, born 1784

For Napoleon, relatives were game pieces to be placed on strategically located thrones – Joseph in Naples and then in Spain; Caroline, with her husband Murat, in Naples; Elise, with her husband Felice Bacciochi, in the Grandduchy of Tuscany; Louis as King of Holland, Jerome as King of Westphalia. As Benedetti observed, 'he makes kings the way the pope makes monsignors.'[13]

Even in exile, Napoleon continued to think of advancing the family through his often disappointing siblings. In his memoirs (published only in the mid-twentieth century) General Bertrand remembered that the exiled emperor repeatedly stressed the roles his family must take to recoup the Bonaparte fortunes. 'The family must take over Rome by marrying into Roman princely families. ... Soon it will have popes, cardinals and papal legates among its members.'[14] Unfortunately, the family either declined to cooperate, or simply lacked the talent to fulfil such grandiose dreams.

Pasquino took a special pleasure in belittling these *parvenue* monarchs, who, in public opinion, all added up to 'Nothing' (nihil):

---

12 Reproduced in Cardinal Pacca's *Mémoires*, pp. 263–91.
13 The rank of monsignor is one step up from ordinary priest, and well below that of bishop, which is in turn below that of cardinal.
14 Count General Bertrand, *Journal du général Bertrand, Grand maréchal du palais. Cahiers de Sainte-Hélène*. Paris, 1949.

Napoleon
Iochim [Joachim Murat, King of Naples]
Hieronymus [Jerome, King of Westphalia]
Iosephus [Joseph, King of Spain]
Ludovicus [Louis, King of Holland]

And with such barbs as:

Marforio: Pasquino, why has oil got so expensive?
Pasquino: Because Napoleon needs it to fry republics and anoint kings.[15]

If Napoleon never saw Rome, his family made up for it.[16] Madame Mère, Letizia Ramolino Buonaparte, widow of the noble but improvident Carlo, came to Rome first in 1804, then returned in 1814 and finally came to stay in 1815 until she died in 1836 at the age of 87. She lived in what is now the Palazzo Bonaparte with Uncle/Cardinal Fesch, her half-brother, who had come as ambassador and then returned to take refuge there after his nephew's fall from power. Lucien, who didn't get along with Napoleon, also lived in Rome from 1804 to 1808, and returned after the fall of Napoleon (one of his descendants founded the Museo Napoleonico); Joachim Murat and his wife, Caroline visited in 1802 and made a serious attempt to take over in 1814 (she was thereafter *persona non grata*); and Napoleon's sister Pauline married Camillo Borghese and after 1814 lived in great and ostentatious luxury at the Villa Paolina in Rome until shortly before her death in 1825.

Joseph, first-born of the Bonaparte children and senior to Napoleon by one year, served as ambassador to Rome, then went on to be King of Naples and then, disastrously, King of Spain (though, to be fair, the insurgency there made it impossible for him to do much in any case). Joseph's Roman role was, however, a key one: it was Joseph, sent there in August 1797 to undermine the papal government and pave the way for a Roman republic, who would bring about the Ridiculous Republic, in a ridiculous way: a fatal accident. His other diplomatic successes were less accidental: in 1800 he negotiated a treaty with the United States, represented his brother in the peace negotiations of 1801 with Austria at Luneville, and at Amiens negotiated a treaty which resulted in a brief peace with Napoleon's implacable and eventually fatal enemy, England.

Joseph was seriously unhappy about being left out of the line of succession to the throne when Napoleon made himself emperor (Pauline, too, had been unhappy about her status), but he filled in as king where required. When Napoleon fell, Joseph went to America and stayed there for a quarter of a century before returning to die in Italy.

Lucien was the only one of the Bonaparte boys who was never given a throne, despite (or perhaps because of) the fact that he had saved Napoleon's career and

---

15 Romano, *La satira nella Roma Napoleonica*, p. 138. There was a great shortage of oil in Rome at the time, and the price had risen to an unprecedented 15 *bajocchi* for a *foglietta*.

16 Titoni, 'Napoleone, i suoi fratelli, e le loro residenze romane'.

maybe his life during the coup of 1799. A republican at heart, he quarrelled with Napoleon about politics and about his second marriage (to Alexandrine de Bleschamp, Mme. Jouberthon, a Dutch widow with a reputation), and moved to Rome in April 1804. His mother came along in solidarity, and Lucien bought the Nunez palace (later purchased by Torlonia) and settled down with his wife and his rapidly increasing family. When Rome was absorbed into the empire, they tried to flee to the United States, but were intercepted by the British navy and spent the rest of the war years first in Malta, and then in England. In 1814 he took refuge in Rome, but soon left and moved to the Villa Ruffinella near Frascati, which he hoped to transform into a sort of Mount Parnassus, with statues, grottoes and fountains on the nearby hill. This fell through, but he contented himself with cultivating the land, planting rows of myrtle trees among which to intersperse his statuary.

After 1806, his preferred place of residence was the castle of Musignano at Canino, near Viterbo. While his brother conquered and then lost Europe, Lucien dabbled in epic poetry and pursued his archaeological excavations and studies. In 1828 he published a valuable survey of his work on Etruscan artifacts, *Catalogue of Selected Etruscan Antiquities found in the Excavations of the Prince of Canino* (his papal title).

In Rome, he gave literary evenings attended by various French and Italian *litteratti*; and also attended by his charming daughter Charlotte (from his first marriage to Christine Boyer) with her French governess 'full of spirit, quite erudite, and an excellent musician'. He and Alexandrine had a large family, several of whom intermarried with the Roman aristocracy to establish a Roman branch of the Bonapartes.

Life in the countryside was not always amusing. His secretary, the painter Chatillon, tells a lively and possibly even true story about being abducted by bandits, who were under the impression that he was his employer. Once at their hideout, the bandits began to doubt his identity, especially because he didn't speak Italian well. Chatillon told them he was Bonaparte's employee, and an artist. Decaris, the bandit leader, said, 'If you're an artist, draw, and make a picture of me.' He did, and convinced the bandit that he was an artist, not a Bonaparte. The disappointed bandit agreed to exchange him for a reduced ransom, so the affair ended happily enough.

In addition to being a respectable amateur archaeologist, Lucien was something of an author, and when Napoleon abdicated he was on the point of publishing a poem on the subject of Charlemagne. This inspired him to comment, 'we have in the same family at the same time a Charlemagne about to be born, and a Charlemagne who is going into the shadows.'[17]

In Rome, Lucien bought the Palazzo Nunez, on the corner between the Via Condotti and the Via Bocca di Leone. There he built a swimming pool – he called it a *naumachia* – where he taught his wife and children to swim, and a little private theatre where they performed French tragedies.

Elise, the eldest of the Bonaparte girls, and the only one with anything like an education, was born Maria Anna in 1777. When she was nine, her father brought her to the Royal Academy at St Cyr near Paris, to be educated with the daughters of the

---

17 Romano, *op. cit.*, p. 137.

French nobility. Whatever his purpose – Carlo rarely paid much attention to the children, and especially not to the girls – it was a mixed blessing for the child. She was thoroughly miserable there. Not only was she a very insignificant member of a quite insignificant Corsican noble family, she had the Bonaparte combination of awkward self-consciousness and overriding arrogance. She was also poor. She spent only a few years at St Cyr before family finances forced her to return home, but she was there long enough to isolate her from her younger and prettier sisters, Pauline and Caroline. Her brother Napoleon later paid her the high compliment of saying that she had a 'masculine mind, a forceful character, noble qualities and outstanding intelligence', and made her Princess of Piombino and Lucca (1805) and then Granduchess of Tuscany (1809). In 1797, just as her brother began his climb to glory, she had married Felice Pasquale Bacciochi, a handsome distant relative, a Corsican boy from back home perhaps best described as insignificant. Napoleon did not fully approve, but he allowed cousin Felice to go along for the ride. When their first child, a girl, was born in June 1806 she was named Napoleona. The emperor wrote to Felice: 'My cousin, I offer my compliments on the daughter which you have given to my sister. I am pleased to hear that she is doing well. Continue to give me news of her. But please see to it that next time you give me a boy.' Eventually, he did.

After 1814 Elise, like the rest of the family, was forced to seek asylum. She ended up in Trieste, where she set up a reduced court and hired tutors for her daughter Napoleona. One of these was the maestro of her court orchestra, the renowned Farinelli. Napoleona, pretty and spoiled, eventually came to Rome, in 1823, with her husband Count Filippo Camerata.

Louis, the third Bonaparte boy, fought alongside his brother in the early days in Italy. In 1805, he was given command of the armies in Holland and within a year was crowned King of Holland. Unfortunately, he took the well-being of his new country rather more seriously than his brother had intended. In 1806, Napoleon introduced his Continental System, an attempt to prevent the continental states from dealing with the English, either buying from or selling to them. Louis, as king of a country that depended on commerce for its life, baulked. By 1810 Napoleon had had enough of fraternal stonewalling, and Louis was deposed. He spent some time in Rome in exile with Madame Mère and Lucien, but soon quarrelled with them and left. He returned, however, and was with his mother when she died. He died in Italy in 1846, before he could realise that he would have the last laugh. In 1802, much against his wishes, Louis had been forced to marry Josephine's daughter Hortense de Beauharnais. In 1852, the son of that marriage, Louis Napoleon, would become the Emperor Napoleon III.

Pauline, the most beautiful and many consider the most sympathetic of the Bonaparte girls, also had the closest ties to Rome. Like many beautiful, wilful, and sensual young girls, Pauline had a sweetness of character that made people who knew her forget about her stunning absence of any moral sense. Of all the famous women who have been labelled nymphomaniacs, Pauline may indeed have earned the title (according to her brother Jerome, she couldn't see that there was any moral difference

Canova's statue of Napoleon's sister Pauline presented her as Venus.

between infidelity and fidelity). Her enemies called her the Messalina of the empire, but she was neither vindictive nor ruthless. Her problem was that she had appalling taste in men. As a teenager she had been determined to marry a middle-aged roué, until her brother more or less forced her to marry the promising young General Leclerc. Leclerc died in Haiti, leaving her a young widow with an infant son (no one seems to have noticed when the child died a few years later). A few months after Leclerc's death Pauline decided that she wanted to marry the handsome, rich, and (briefly) amusing Roman prince Camillo Borghese.

Though she soon tired of the prince, Pauline was delighted with the Borghese family jewels and the Borghese collection of art and treasure. She set up a Roman court complete with gentlemen in waiting, pages and musicians. Her parties, her elegance, and her beauty dazzled Romans of all classes as she paraded up and down the Corso in a carriage drawn by eight white horses. Soon after her marriage, Napoleon wrote to give her good advice: 'Distinguish yourself by your sweetness and affability, your ability to get along with everyone.... Above all, accommodate yourself to the customs of the country; never despise anything, find everything beautiful, never say, "At Paris, it's better."'[18]

But she had married in haste, and the marriage went badly. Shortly after the wedding, she was quoted as saying that she would have preferred to remain a widow with 20,000 *livres* a year income, than 'be married to a eunuch'. (The slur, deserved or not, has stuck.)

Canova wanted to sculpt her as the virgin huntress Diana (a wicked bit of sarcasm on the sculptor's part), but she insisted on being represented as Venus Victrix, the Venus who won the golden apple from Paris. She had a magnificent body, whether or not Canova sculpted it from nature. When the young Chateaubriand was sent to bring her a pair of slippers that had arrived in the diplomatic pouch one morning, he

18 Letter written from his camp at Boulonge on 19 November 1803.

was admitted to the presence of the scantily clad princess, and reported that her bosom was 'an unforgettable sight'.

After the fall of Napoleon, Pauline was the only one of his siblings who did not abandon him. Always careless with money, she sold her jewellery and brought the cash to Elba, where she took up residence; encouraging and cheering up his court (he called her the Mistress of Amusements, which she was), organising balls and parties. She also encouraged him to try to get his throne back, as did Madame Mère when she learned of the plan of escape.

After Waterloo, Pauline returned to Rome. There, people blamed her for the sale of the Borghese collection (much of which had been put together by the Borghese pope, Paul V) to Napoleon. Pasquino's comment was: *Paulus fecit, Paolina disfecit* (Paul made it, Pauline unmade it).

Stendhal blamed her for what may have been an even more egregious *faux pas:* the initial failure of Rossini's *Barber of Seville* in 1816. On a blank page of his copy of a biography of Rossini (at the Primoli library), Stendhal wrote: 'The foolishness of Pauline Borghese caused the *Barber* to be whistled down. She loved the tenor [who was none other than the famous Garcia, founder of an operatic dynasty]; the tenor asked for some changes in the music; as was his custom, Rossini mocked the singer, and the singer's mistress bought a large number of tickets and had this divine music whistled.'

When she arrived in Rome as a refugee, Cardinal Fesch gave her apartments on the second floor of the Falconieri palace. She intended to move into the Borghese palace, or the palace on the Pincio, but her relationship with her husband made that impossible. She turned to the conditions of her marriage contract, and asked the pope to enforce them, asking for a pension of 40,000 Roman *ecu*. With that she bought a villa near the Porta Pia and wanted to call it the Villa Bonaparte, but Madame Letizia wouldn't allow it, so it became the Villa Paolina. She lived there for nine years, increasingly suffering with the illness that would kill her, 'which she saw coming, with a private and continual terror' (says Fernand Bac). While her health allowed, she lived in Rome 'like a little queen', holding court among her many admirers, artists, and the English tourists brought there by the Duchess of Devonshire.

When her doctors recommended she go to Florence for a change of air, she agreed, but was horrified when, on the point of leaving, she dropped her hand mirror and it shattered. 'This bad omen', Jerome reported, 'appalled her superstitious soul.' She died in Florence 9 June 1825, after a long and painful illness, which she bore with courage.

Her much abused husband, it is said, mourned her death.

Jerome, the baby of the family, caused his brother (and the pope) a great deal of annoyance by an imprudent marriage. Jerome's divorce was only one particular instance of a much bigger problem: the introduction of the Napoleonic Code in Italy. The problem with the code was that, in the modern fashion, it transferred control over the critical elements of the private lives of citizens from the Church to the state so birth, education, marriage, and death became secular events. The pope had recognised the code in France, as a *fait accompli.* Extending it into Italy, as Napoleon began to do after having himself crowned King of Italy in May 1805, was quite a different matter.

The pope was particularly concerned about divorce, which was a key part of the civil code. The emperor would take advantage of that to divest himself of Josephine (15 December 1809) and take a younger, more fertile Austrian bride (2 April 1810). The King of Rome was born 20 March 1811. It was said that, in Paris, one marriage in five ended in divorce (a statistic that would not be rivalled in the west until the twentieth century).

L'affaire Jerome, or perhaps *l'affaire Patterson*, unfolded as follows.[19] In 1803 Napoleon, in an attempt to help his 19-year-old brother grow up, had given him a commission as a naval officer and sent him off to the West Indies. Jerome made his way to the rather more amusing new United States, and there he met the daughter of a rich American banker, pretty Elizabeth Patterson, a girl who knew better than to succumb to French charms without a wedding ring on her finger. The marriage was a secret one, there were no witnesses, the groom was underage and acting without the consent of his family, and Miss Patterson suffered under the serious disadvantage of being a Protestant. It should, in all, have been a perfect sham. As Napoleon commented, 'Why, it's no more a marriage than that of two lovers who get married in a garden, "on the altar of love", in the presence of the moon and the stars. They may say they are married, but when they fall out of love they will soon discover they are not."[20]

There was, however, one large problem. As the pope would learn when he investigated, no less a cleric than the Catholic bishop of Baltimore had somehow been induced to perform the ceremony. It was irregular, it was objectionable, it was thoroughly inconvenient. But, in the eyes of the Church, it was a marriage.

Napoleon, then only First Consul, was merely annoyed when he heard about the affair. But by the time Jerome arrived back in Europe in 1805, with his pregnant bride in tow, the First Consul was emperor, and an emperor who had no intention of wasting a perfectly good brother whose marriage could be used to cement alliances, on the daughter of an American banker, however rich.

He wrote from Milan, where he was in the process of making himself King of Italy:

Monsieur Jerome has arrived at Lisbon with Mlle Patterson, his mistress. I have ordered him to come and see me, and his mistress to be shipped back again to America.

Pius' adamant (in Napoleon's eyes, stubborn) refusal to annul the marriage was incomprehensible. After all, the emperor proclaimed, Patterson was a *Protestant*. Did the pope not understand the horrid implications of such a match? Could he countenance the possibility, however remote, of a Protestant empress and a Protestant heir to the imperial throne? It seems that he could. Perhaps Pius was not completely surprised when Napoleon, having extracted an annulment from the more pliant Archbishop of Paris, immediately turned around and married Jerome to Catherine, the Protestant daughter of the King of Westphalia.

When Napoleon fell, Jerome and Catherine ceased to be King and Queen of Westphalia and Jerome eventually made his way to Rome with the rest of the family.

---

19 See Lamar, *Jerome, The War Years.*
20 Hales, *op. cit.,* p. 76.

He bought a palace on the Via Boca di Leone from Lucien. He was there when his mother died in 1836. She died, it was said, in the arms of her youngest child and her brother, Cardinal Fesch.

Jerome was the only one of the immediate family to live to see the family fortunes revived, at least temporarily, under his nephew, Louis Napoleon, Napoleon III.

Letizia Ramolino Buonaparte (Madame Mère) first came to Rome in 1804, having quarrelled with Napoleon over his treatment of his brother Lucien, and perhaps also over Napoleon's ordering the execution of the Duc d'Enghien. Her presence was commanded for the 1804 coronation, and she and Uncle Fesch left Rome for Paris, but she did not arrive until several days after the event (though Napoleon had David paint them into his famous painting). She returned to Rome after Waterloo, and remained there until her death.

Her first visit had been brief. She arrived at the end of March 1804, and Uncle Fesch wrote to Napoleon to tell him what had happened.

Your mother arrived in Rome … on Holy Saturday after a journey of 18 days without stopping either at Lyons or at Milan. She was received in the Papal States with the highest honours. At Loretto, she lodged at the papal palace.

On her arrival in Rome his Holiness invited her to participate in the Easter Mass on an equal footing with the Queen of Sardinia and the Princes of Mecklenburg, but since these honours must come after the honours to the above mentioned … I believe she will refuse on the grounds of being tired from the journey.

Yesterday I presented her at the Quirinal, along with her daughter [Pauline] … The pope spoke of his affection for you, and of the prayers he has offered for your well-being; and he said that he would be very happy to see you, and you could stay with him whenever you wished. And in fact, I had to excuse myself from him after a long conversation.

The Roman nobility, without waiting for a formal reception, came to call. The head of the Sacred College invited all of the cardinals to come and give her their respects within 24 hours. All were in a hurry, even the Neapolitans, to give these honours, reserved to sovereigns. She knew how to carry herself very well in all of these ceremonies, and I believe that Rome will be the place that suits her best. I shall do my best to see that she is happy.

She took ill, however, and left the city on 1 July for spa at Bagni di Lucca, and returned to Rome in mid-Autumn. But she left again on 14 November, and did not return until after Waterloo – when she took refuge under the protection of the pope.

Like any good Italian, Napoleon was in awe of his mother. For her part, she was much too much of a realist to give him the reverence he felt he deserved. Lucien's memoirs, at least as quoted by one *romanista,* includes this revealing conversation.[21]

Napoleon: *Speaking of mamma, Joseph must tell her to stop calling me Napolione. The name sounds bad in French. First of all, it is an Italian name. Mother should call me Bonaparte, as everyone does. But above all, not Buonaparte, which is even worse than*

---

21 Angeli, *I Bonaparte a Roma.*

Napolione. She could call me First Consul, or Consul, certainly. I would prefer that. But Napolione, always this Napolione, this gets on my nerves.

Lucien: *But Napolione – in French, Napoleon – is a fine name, at least in my view. There is something grand about it.*

Napoleon: *You think so?*

Lucien: *Something important.*

Napoleon: *You think so?*

Lucien: *Something majestic.*

Napoleon: *In fact ... but after all, because my mother pronounces it in the Italian fashion? For this reason, I have tried to make it more French, but have never succeeded. And since we're talking about it, our mother has never learned to speak French. C'est désagréable.*

Cardinal Fesch, or Giuseppe Fesch, Madama Letizia's step-brother, was born at Ajaccio on 3 January 1763. He was the son of a Swiss in the service of the Genoese Republic who had married Angela Maria Pietrasanta, widow Ramolino. They had two children, a girl who died shortly after birth, and the boy who would become a cardinal and the uncle of an emperor.

Like his half-sister, Fesch spoke French badly, and always used Italian in private. He was a short, vivacious man, with very black eyes and hair. While he was always conventionally pious, he probably entered the clergy more for family reasons than for a personal vocation, and when the revolution in France made being a cleric dangerous, he stopped dressing as a priest. When his nephew later restored the old religion, he resumed his clerical career. Napoleon, taking advantage of the Gallican liberties, had him created bishop and later cardinal, and it was as a cardinal that he first visited Rome in 1803.

When he arrived as ambassador of France, he of course attracted the attention of Pasquino, as Fortunati reported with some relish:

Marforio: Pasquino mio, what does your heart tell you about this new ambassador?

Pasquino: Bad, bad, bad: he's a Corsican, and a cardinal![22]

During his stay as cardinal and ambassador, Fesch passed on the orders he received from his nephew. First, he demanded that the pope arrest and expel the Russian legation. Then he ordered him to expel all Russian, Swedish, English and Sardinian residents from Rome, and finally informed him that he should close his ports to ships from those nations. Later, he passed on Napoleon's demand that Pius should come to Paris for his coronation, which the pope eventually did. Finally, however, Fesch failed to get the pope to agree to a divorce for Jerome, and Napoleon yanked his uncle out of the job and put in a new ambassador, Alquier.

While he lived in Rome, Fesch continually posted bulletins on the walls of his palace (this was normal procedure, of course), exaggerating Napoleon's victories (it was not for nothing that the phrase, to 'lie like a bulletin' was by then proverbial in French).

---

22 Romano, *op. cit.,* p. 139.

Pasquino and Marforio had a little exchange on this, too. In December 1805, both the Argentina and the Alibert theatres put on popular shows, and tickets were hard to get.

Pasquino asked Marforio why he hadn't gone to the theatre, and was told that he had tried, but his ticket was a forgery, it was no good. Who gave it to you? Asked Pasquino, and when he was told that it had come from Cardinal Fesch, Pasquino exclaimed that 'everyone knows that all the paper that he puts out is fake!'

Whatever his faults, no one denied Cardinal Fesch's staunchly orthodox religious views, or his courage in stating them publicly, no matter how they angered the emperor. When his nephew wanted to make him Archbishop of Paris, Fesch refused because the appointment had not been approved by the pope. Napoleon, disgusted, appointed Maury instead. When Fesch was president of the Council of Paris (1811), Pius VII asked that all of his bishops swear loyalty to the pope. Fesch was the first to do so, in a loud, clear voice that encouraged the others to follow his example.

Fesch, like Madame Mère, took refuge in Rome after the fall of Napoleon. At Cesena, in Romagna, he asked for an audience with the returning pope, which was granted. 'You will be welcome', Pius assured the emperor's uncle and mother. '… Through the centuries, Rome has been the refuge of exiles. You will be doubly welcome, as a cardinal, and as the uncle of the emperor.' This welcome was all the more grateful, as the Holy Alliance (who had defeated him) was fulminating against all family of Napoleon as enemies of public order.

Fesch and Letizia arrived in Rome the night of 12–13 March 1814, and went to the Palazzo Falconieri in Via Giulia that he had rented. There Fesch organised his life. He rose at 5.00 for common prayers, in which the entire household was required to join. At 7:30, he went to the chapel in the church that was next to his palace; then at 8.00 he went to his private chapel where he celebrated Mass. In the evening, he walked on the Janiculum or the Palatine, or went to the Coliseum, where he often mixed with the penitents making the Stations of the Cross. In the evening, he said the rosary with his secretary, and then read, or wrote, or catalogued his considerable art collection.

At the end, Fesch and Madame Mère would be unwitting participants in a bizarre plot that may have made Napoleon's last days unnecessarily wretched. At the point when the imprisoned emperor most needed help, he wrote asking that an Italian doctor and a spiritual counsellor be sent to him at St Helena. Ironically, it seems that at about this time, Cardinal Fesch and Madame Mère were falling prey to a fake mystic (hidden, like a leaf in a forest, among so many real ones), an Austrian woman who claimed to be a clairvoyant, and was probably an agent.[23] It may well have been her influence that made his mother and uncle brush aside what seemed to be (and indeed, were) his requests. They sent an unqualified physician, and an elderly and deaf priest.

Soon after her brother's death, Pauline wrote in despair of her mother and uncle:[24]

I've had much to put up with these last two years, through my uncle, mother, and Colonna letting themselves be guided by a scheming woman, a German and a spy for the Austrian court, who says the Madonna appears to her and told her the emperor is no longer there.

---

23 Decaux, p. 248 et seq.
24 July 11, 1821.

It's all the wildest nonsense! The cardinal has almost gone mad, for he openly says that the emperor is no longer at St Helena, that he has had revelations as to where he is.

Louis and I have done all we could during the past two years to eradicate the effects of this sorceress, but to no purpose. My uncle hid from us the letters and news he received from St Helena, and told us that this silence ought to be enough to convince us!

A Christian and Heroic Act

Whether or not she was later convinced that her son had left St Helena, in 1816 Napoleon's mother was near despair, and was filled with gratitude for the refuge she and her family received, when she wrote to Pius:

I am indeed the mother of all sorrows, and the one consolation I have is to know that the Holy Father forgets the past and only remembers the kindnesses he has shown to all the members of my family … Our only support comes from the papal government and we are most grateful for such good will. [25]

The following year, Pius attempted to intervene on the part of the imprisoned Napoleon, writing to Cardinal Consalvi and asking him to intercede with the prince regent in England:

Napoleon's family have made known to us through Cardinal Fesch that the craggy island of St Helena is mortally injurious to health, and that the poor exile is dying by inches. We have been deeply grieved to hear this, as no doubt you will be, for we ought both to remember that, after God, it is to him chiefly that is due the re-establishment of religion in the great Kingdom of France. The pious and courageous initiative of 1801 has made us long forget and pardon the wrongs that followed. Savona and Fontainebleau were only mistakes due to temper, or the frenzies of human ambition. The Concordat was a healing act, Christian and heroic. Napoleon's mother and family have appealed to our pity and our generosity; we think it right to respond to that appeal. We are certain that we will only be ordering you to act as you would wish to act when we instruct you to write on our behalf to the Allied sovereigns, and in particular to the Prince Regent. He is your dear and good friend, and we wish you to ask him to lighten the sufferings of so hard an exile. Nothing would give us greater joy than to have contributed to the lessening of Napoleon's hardships. He can no longer be a danger to anyone. We would not wish him to become a cause for remorse.

In the end, with or without papal intervention, nothing was done, and Napoleon the Great, emperor of the West and the new Charlemagne, lover and enemy of Rome, died on the rock of St Helena on 5 May 1821. The news did not reach Rome for many weeks. When it did, Madame Mère accepted it immediately as true. She was prostrate with grief for this, her greatest and most unfortunate child. She outlived him by almost fifteen years. She spent her last years as a semi-recluse in the Palazzo Bonaparte, surrounded by her growing family of exiles and watching the crowds on the Corso though the green venetian blinds of her loggia.

---

25 Decaux, *op. cit.*, p. 236.

The romantic remains of the Coliseum were the site of a tug of war between the archaeologists and the devout. The devout won, at least for a while.

BIBLIOGRAPHICAL ESSAY

꧁꧂

This is a book about Rome and Romans rather than a book about Napoleon, though Napoleon is the never-present but always dominant figure who overshadows it all. The history of Rome at the start of the modern period was strongly coloured for at least a century after unification by the circumstances under which the city had ceased to be a papal capital and became instead the capital of the newly, and contentiously, unified nation-state of Italy. The military conquest of Rome by Italian troops on 20 September 1870 meant that for 100 years the historiography of the city was sharply divided into those who saw papal Rome as irredeemably backward, repressive, corrupt and decadent, and those who mourned the passing of the Church's rule in Rome as the end of civility and tradition. Drawing on travel literature, members of the first school stressed the hypocrisy of the clerics, the gossip of the despised aristocracy and the brutal suppression of the rest of society – we might call it the 'Tosca school' of Roman history. The admirers of tradition on the other side formed a smaller, defensive group, papal biographers and the devout, who deplored what they saw as the absurd excesses of the revolutionaries and looked with regret at the passing of the old Rome, whatever its undeniable failings. To this mix must be added the important work of the (often anti-clerical) students of popular culture, drawing their inspiration from men like Gioacchino Belli, the revered Trastevere writer whose dialect poetry described the joys, sorrows and passions of daily life in papal Rome during the first half of the nineteenth century. In the late nineteenth and early twentieth centuries, folklorists like Costantino Maes (*Curiosità romane*, Rome, 1885) and Giggi Zanazzo (*Tradizioni popolari romane*, Rome, 1907–1910) laboured to rescue the rich but dying folk culture of papal Rome while rejecting the theocratic state that had been its cradle.

The first study of Rome in the eighteenth century was published in 1971, a century after unification, by the distinguished and aptly named Vittorio Emanuele Giuntella, whose works on the revolutionary period also remain important. The more than three decades that have followed Giuntella's *Roma nel Settecento* (Rome in the Eighteenth Century) have seen a vigorous and growing field of Roman studies that has included the scientific work published in *Roma Moderna e Contemporanea*, the wealth of new archival investigations, and a vast and impressive body of more popular publications aimed at the general reader by publishers like Newton Compton. Newton Compton not only publish the familiar red-covered books on all aspects of Roman history and life, but also a large selection of pamphlet-size booklets in their 'economical pocket-sized' paperback series (*Tascabili Economici Newton*).

Little of this work has made its way into English except in the ground-breaking synthesis of Hanns Gross who drew on the already rich Italian research into every aspect of Roman life for his *Rome in the Age of Enlightenment* (Cambridge, 1990).

Studies in English

By far the best, really the only, English-language overview of early modern Rome is Hanns Gross' *Rome in the Age of Enlightenment: The Post-Tridentine Syndrome and the Ancien Regime* (Cambridge, 1990), which deals with the city in the eighteenth century up to, but not including, the revolutionary period and presents a clear picture of the social and cultural milieu of the city which ichanged little until after unification.

Giuntella's seminal *Roma nel Settecento* (Bologna, 1971) is, of course, written in Italian, but readers not familiar with that language may still benefit from his extensive bibliographical essay (pp. 317–333), especially the section dealing with books by travellers (pp. 329–333).

The Papacy and the Empire

While it was obvious from the beginning that religious issues were near the root of much of the conflict between rulers and ruled in the revolutionary and Napoleonic periods, objective scholarly examination of the phenomenon has been rare. Michael Broers' recent (2002) monograph, *The Politics of Religion in Napoleonic Italy* is a welcome addition to this literature. While it deals with Italy as a whole, chapters 6 and 7 directly address the situation of the Church and clergy of Rome. Broers' 2001 article, "'The War against God": Napoleon, Pope Pius VII and the people of Italy, 1800-1814' in *The Historian* offers a brief and illuminating examination of the roots of the conflict between pope and emperor.

Other English-language introductions to Church-State relationships include Owen Chadwick's *The Popes and the European Revolution* (Oxford, 1981) and two works by E. E. Y. Hales: *Revolution and the Papacy* 1796–1846 (1960) and *Napoleon and the Pope* (1962). More frankly Church-orientated are *The Church in an Age of Revolution 1789–1870* (London, 1965) by Henri Daniel-Rops and Robin Anderson's *Pope Pius VII (1800–1823): His Life, His Times, and His Struggle with Napoleon* (Rockfort Il, 2000).

David Sivagni's eccentric (and questionable) essay on the period, *La corte pontificia e la società romana nel secolo XVIII e XIX* (4 vols. Rome, 1881–1885), was quickly translated into English by F. MacLaughlin and published as *Court and Society in Rome in the Eighteenth and Nineteenth Centuries* (3 vols., Boston 1887). While it is reportedly based on the diary of a curia lawyer, the Abbate Benedetti, it is vigorously anti-papal, a tone only magnified in translation.

Christopher Hibbert's *Rome, the Biography of a City* (London, 1985) devotes only one chapter to the Napoleonic period, but provides an eminently readable synopsis of generally agreed scholarship (plus several anecdotal frills) and puts the period into a context.

Graphic Representations

Art is, to some degree at least, a universal language, and interested readers can discover a great deal about papal Rome, and Rome in the Napoleonic period, in the work of two Roman artists, Bartolemeo Pinelli, and (later) Ettore Roesler Franz.

There are several excellent collections of Pinelli's work available, and his depictions of the Rome he knew and loved require no translation (though the commentary provided certainly offers invaluable insight into the art and the period). Among the best are Bartolomeo Rossetti's *La Roma di Bartolomeo Pinelli: Una città e il suo popolo attraverso feste, mestieri, ambienti e personaggi caratteristici nelle più belle incisioni del "pittor de Trastevere"* (Rome, 1985). Renato Paccini's earlier study, *Bartolomeo Pinelli e la Roma del suo Tempo* (Milan, 1935), which includes the text of the first Pinelli biography, by Oreste Raggi, published a few days after the artist's death in 1835.

The watercolours of Ettore Roesler Franz capture the last days of the old city as it was being transformed into the modern capital at the end of the nineteenth century. The catalogues of the numerous exhibits of these works are most valuable (for example, the 1995 exhibit at the Studio Ottocento in Rome). Books by De Rosa and Tertulli, Biagi and Bonfili, and by L. Jannattoni, and others, all offer good collections of Franz's work.

French artist Antoine Jean-Baptiste Thomas spent a year in Rome as a student at the French Academy immediately after the fall of Napoleon, and several years later published his collection of delightful and informative views of life in the city in *Un an à Rome et dans ses environs* (Paris, 1823, republished in Rome, 1971).

Museums and Guidebooks

The visitor to Rome interested in the Napoleonic period will find a great deal of information and entertainment in the city's excellent museums. The *Museo Napoleonico*, based on the collection of the Primoli family, Bonaparte descendants, is not to be missed. The collection includes miniatures, personal possessions and portraits of several generations of Bonapartes, starting with Madame Mère. A guidebook is available in English. The Museo di Roma in the Braschi palace offers the double pleasure of seeing a superb collection of Roman art and artefacts in the last-built of the great Roman *palazzi* – built by Pius VI for his nephew, Duke Braschi. The *Museo di Roma in Trastevere*, located in the heart of the district just off the Piazza Santa Maria in Trastevere, has painstakingly authentic re-creations of Roman scenes, taken from the work of Bartolomeo Pinelli, as well as other topical exhibits and art.

Roman museums have published guidebooks of varying quality in languages other than Italian. Readers interested in cultural history are especially directed to the substantial booklet published by the Museo di Roma in Trastevere, most of the text of which is provided in both Italian and English.

For guidebooks to Rome in general, there are any number of well-illustrated examples available, but for text it is difficult to beat Georgina Masson's 1965 classic, *The Companion Guide to Rome*. An interesting if eccentric guide to the city is the

Little Bookroom's *Guide to Rome* (New York, 2000) a collection of 'special favourites' from Fellows at the American Academy in Rome.

MONOGRAPHS

The Arts

Two excellent recent works in English are available on art and archaeology in Rome during the period. Christopher Johns' *Antonio Canova and the Politics of Patronage in Revolutionary and Napoleonic Europe* (Los Angeles, 1998) and Ronald Ridley's look at the Napoleonic efforts to discover, preserve and restore Rome's ruins, *The Eagle and the Spade: Archaeology in Rome during the Napoleonic Era* (Cambridge, 1992).

Susan Nicassio's *Tosca's Rome: The Play and the Opera in Historical Context* (Chicago, 2000) is a study of the city in the summer of 1800, when Sardou's play and Puccini's opera are set. The same author's paper, 'The Unfortunate Giuseppe Barberi and his Pictorial Diary of the Roman Republic, 1798-99' (Tallahassee, FL, 2002) deals with the Jacobin architect whose caricatures served as a virtual diary.

A related, but quite different, publication is *Tosca's Prism: Three Moments in Cultural History, 1800–1900–2000* (Boston, 2004). This is a collection of conference papers by musicologists, performers and historians, edited by Deborah Burton, Susan Nicassio, and Agostino Ziino, and connected by a common theme of Puccini's *Tosca*. Among the most useful essays relating directly to the revolutionary and Napoleonic period are 'The Protagonists and the Principal Phases of the Roman Republic of 1798 to 1799' by Marina Formica; 'The Napoleonic Legacy in Italy' by Alexander Grab; and 'Victorien Sardou and the Legend of Marengo', by William Laird Kleine-Ahlbrandt. Formica is an authority on the Roman republic and this is the only English-language translation of her work currently available.

An older, quixotic, and extremely readable study is Angus Heriot's *The French in Italy 1796–1799* (London, 1957), which deals with the entire peninsula during the *triennio Jacobino* (three Jacobin years), but includes a good treatment of Rome.

Intriguing glimpses into the lives of ordinary people can be found in investigations into the lives of men and women who gained reputations for sanctity. Such people were the subjects of exhaustive research by the Church includinginterviews with anyone who knew them. Both Albert Bessières' *Wife, Mother and Mystic (Blessed Anna Maria Taigi)* (Steven Rigby, trans. Tan, 1982, first published in French, 1952) and Thompson's nineteenth-century biography (*The Venerable Anna Maria Taigi*. London, 1873) are based on such interviews. More politically active was Gaspar del Bufalo, the son of a servant in the Altieri household who after the revolutionary period founded a new religious order, and was eventually canonised as a saint. Del Bufalo was a young man when Rome became an imperial city, and like many of his colleagues he refused to take the oath of allegiance and was arrested and deported. His prison experiences form the basis for a book by a member of St Gaspar's order, Luigi Contegiacomo, *St Gaspar's Prison Experiences, 1810-1813* (Cartegena, Ohio, 1988).

Memoirs

None of the several Roman diaries from the revolutionary period (by Fortunati, Galimberti, Sala and others) has been translated into English (and few have been published at all). One memoir that has been translated (into French) is that of Cardinal Pacca, counsellor of Pius VII who received so much praise or blame for the Pope's firmness (or intransigence). Marchesa Maria Maddalena Patrizi based much of her *Memoire di Famiglia, 1796–1815* on extensive archival researchas well as on the prison diaries of Giovanni Patrizi. Translated by Mrs Hugh Fraser as *The Patrizi Memoirs: A Roman Family under Napoleon, 1796–1815* this is primarily a didactic examination of the defiance of one deeply religious noble family.

Travel Literature
There are many fascinating collections of letters and memoirs of English-speaking travellers in Rome before and after the Napoleonic era, but the long war between France and England that began in 1793 and continued with only a brief interruption until 1815, meant that few British subjects saw Rome in those years. For general studies of such literature, see Paul Franklin Kirby, *The Grand Tour in Italy 1700–1800* (New York, 1952); George Parks, *The English Traveller to Italy* (Rome, 1954); and C. P. Brand, 'A Bibliography of Travel Books describing Italy published in England, 1800–1850' (*Italian Studies*, vol XI (1956): 108–17).

Before our Period:
Goethe's *Italian Journey* includes classic descriptions of carnival, and of the art community in the city, by the great German dramatist. Christopher Hibbert, *The Grand Tour* (New York, 1969) is an overview of tourism in Rome in the pre-revolutionary period, while Tobias Smolett's *Travels through France and Italy* (London, 1776) and James Boswell's *Boswell and the Grand Tour: Italy, Corsica, France 1765–1766* (London, n.d.) are as charming and as opinionated as one might expect (Smolett was in Rome in 1760, Boswell in 1765). Other, less literary, visitors in the 1760s included Samuel Sharp (*Letters from Italy describing the Customs and Manners of that Country* London, n.d., in Rome 1765–66), and John Moore (*A View of Society and Manners in Italy*, London, 1787, in Rome in 1777).

   Two English lady travellers visited Rome on the eve of the French invasion, and left useful recollections. These were Hester Lynch Piozzi Salusbury who visited Rome in 1784 (*Observations and Reflections made in the course of a Journey through France and Italy and Germany*, London, 1789) and Marianna Stark, who was in Rome in 1792 (*Letters from Italy, 1792 and 1798*, London, 1800).

During our Period:
Richard Duppa, a British artist, found himself in Rome when the death of General Duphot led to the invasion and revolutionising of the ancient city, and quickly he published his recollections of the events in *A Journal of the Most Remarkable occurrences that took place in Rome upon the Subversion of the Ecclesiastical Government in 1798* (London, 1799). Robert Wilson (later General Sir Robert Wilson) passed through Rome on his way to Naples during the war years, and his memoirs recount some of his adventures, in *The Life of General Sir Robert Thomas Wilson 1777-1849* (translated by Herbert Randolph as *Vita del Generale Sir Robert Wilson*, Milan, 1972).

After our Period:

Mrs Charlotte A. Eaton arrived in Rome within two years of the fall of Napoleon. She was a keen observer and wrote exhaustive and highly opinionated letters which she later published, anonymously, as *Rome in the Nineteenth Century ... a series of letters written during a residence in Rome in the years 1817 and 1818* (2 vols, New York, 1827). She was not alone. Maria Calcott, who visited the town of Poli in the Papal States, published her observations in *Three Months Passed in the Mountains North of Rome* (London, 1821).

The post-war years inspired an understandable curiosity on the part of English visitors who, along with a generation of French Romantic writers, fed the public fascination with Rome with books like William Hazlitt's *Notes of a Journey through France and Italy* [1824-5] (London, 1826), and several others including Stendhal [Henri Beyle] with works like *Roman Journal, Promenades dans Rome* and *Rome, Naples et Florence en 1817* (many of which were based on his stay in Rome during the Napoleonic period); and Chateaubriand, especially his *Lettre à M. de Fontanes sur la campagne romaine* and *Lettre à Madame Récamier pendant son ambasade à Rome*.

Popular Histories

The enduring, and somewhat misleading, image of papal Rome as gossip-ridden and permissive has been perpetuated by several charming studies of the city, and of Italy in general, which were drawn mostly from the delightful but unreliable travel literature of the eighteenth century. Most notable of these translated works are two by Maurice Andrieux, *Daily Life in Papal Rome* (translated by Mary Fritton, London, 1968) and *Rome* (translated by Charles Lam Markmann, New York, 1968), and a more general study by Maurice Vausard, *Daily Life in Eighteenth-Century Italy* (translated by Michael Heron, London, 1962).

More reliable, but still written for the popular market, is the section on Italy in Will and Ariel Durant's *The Age of Napoleon*, part of their series on the story of civilization.

Languages other than English

As one might expect most of the current work done on Rome in the eighteenth century and early nineteenth century in general, and during the age of Napoleon in particular, is being done in Italian. Multilingual readers are referred to the general bibliography, and to the footnotes, for reference to such scholarship. It would be remiss, however, not to make some mention of the major sources of information.

General Histories

The proto-history of Napoleonic Rome, and still the best (if by no means objective) overall study is by Louis Madelin, a French cleric and lover of Rome who spent many years in the French and Roman archives preparing his *La Rome de Napoleon: La domination française à Rome de 1809 à 1814* (Paris, 1906).

Among Madelin's most important sources, beyond the archives, was the work of Prefect Camille de Tournon, who rescued his papers when he fled the city in 1814, and later published his statistical studies in *Études statistiques sur Rome et la partie occidentale des états Romains* (Paris, 1831).

Giuntella's *Roma nel Settecento* (see above) is the first, and most substantial, attempt to deal with the city as a whole during the eighteenth century, but there have been several studies of the Roman republic of 1798–99, including recent work by Marina Formica and the older but still useful monograph by Antonio Cretoni, *Roma Giacobina. Storia della Repubblica Romana del 1798–99* (Rome, 1971).

For the history of popular culture in the city, the Commune of Rome has published Luciano Zangarini's *La Cultura Popolare a Roma, un itinerario bibliografico* (Rome, 1992), a bibliographical guide which identifies several hundred works on various aspects of popular culture.

Archival Studies

There are two major sources of archival materials, French and Roman. If the imperial bureaucrats failed to assimilate Rome permanently into the French imperial system, they did accomplish one thing: the archives of Paris and Rome are inextricably mixed, and anyone wishing to study the history of Rome, or indeed of Italy, cannot fail to recognise the fact that at least a part of it lies in the Archives Nationales de Paris.

In France, major sources include: the National Archives (*Archives Nationales*) (files for the Police, the Secretary of State, Departmental Administration, the administration of Religious Bodies, of Crown Goods and Public Works); the Foreign Affairs Archives (*Archives des affaires étrangères*) (for events in Rome before 1809 as seen by French representatives, including correspondence concerning Rome and Naples after 1809, and the letter-books of Baron Janet); Military Archives include records of the Army of Italy as well as of Naples, and the records of imperial administrators who were also military men, such as General Miollis.

Archivio di Stato di Roma (ASR) (State Archives of Rome)

The *Archivio di Stato* is an indispensable source for archival materials relating to the French period. Sources for the Roman republic of 1798–99 are indicated by Marina Formica in 'The Protagonists and the Principal Phases of the Roman Republic' (*Tosca's Prism*, Boston, 2004), pp. 67–81. They include the file, '*Repubblica romana del 1798–9*', the trial papers of the *Giunta di Stato*, and the always useful collection of public documents, the *Editi e bandi* along with the *Miscellanea* of political and confidential papers, and the records of individual churches and ecclesiastical bodies.

Two recent publications by the State Archives guide the researcher through some of the collections at that institution. These are Calzolari and Grantaliano, *Lo Stato pontificio tra Rivoluzione e Restaurazione: istituzioni e archivi (1798–1870)* (Rome, 2003) and Carla Nardi's inventory of the decrees issued by the *Consulta* (*Consulta straordinaria per gli Stati Romani, 1809-1810*).

The decrees to which Nardi provides a guide are perhaps the single most valuable resources for the period, along with Prefect Camille de Tournon's statistical guide.

Biblioteca Apostolica Vaticana

The *Vatican Secret* (*ie,* Private) *Archives* hold the instructions of Pius VII as well as records of the imperial administration and its relations with Rome, while the Vatican

Library (*Biblioteca Apostolica Vaticana*) holds important secondary sources like Pastor's history of the popes after the Middle Ages (*Storia dei papi dalla fine del Medio Evo*) and the manuscript journal of Father Francesco Fortunati (*Avvennimenti sotto il pontificio di Pio VII dall'anno 1775 al 1800* and *Avvenementi sotto li Pontif. Di Pio VII e Leone XII dall'Anni 1800-1828*), as well as a complete run of the official eighteenth-century *Diario di Roma*, published by Chracas.

The primary first-hand reports of the period are found in Fortunati's journal (Vatican Library), Galimberti's diary (National Library) and two published diaries from the time of the Roman republic of 1798–99 edited by Carlo Gasbarri and V. E. Giuntella (*Due diari della repubblica romana del 1798–1799*, Rome, 1958).

Documents related to the Patrizi saga include letters and reports, including reports from the secret police, in the Archives Nationales de Paris, and letters, memoirs, journals and account books in the family archives of the Patrizi, and of the counts of de Tournon

Archivio Storico del Vicariato di Roma (ASVR) (Archives of the Vicariate of Rome)
Among the most interesting documents from the papal era are the records of the exhaustive interviews held by the Church authorities during investigations into purported miracles (like the moving eyes of the images that caused such excitement in Rome on the eve of the French invasions) and the lives of men and women put forward as candidates for sainthood (the Napoleonic era produced several of these, notable but not alone among them Anna Maria Taigi, Gaspar del Bufalo, and Elisabetta Canori-Mora). Some, but by no means all, of these documents are in the Vicariate archives.

The Vicariate also has copies of notices, edicts and official pronouncements, among them such things as a collection of documents issued between 1803 and 1818, covering parts of the first and second papal restorations (Bandimenta, vol. 19).

Museo di Roma
The primary seat of the museum of Rome is in the Braschi palace, and it holds a number of fascinating records, not least the Caricatures of Giuseppe Barbari (legato XVIII and XIX, Mat. 3266 and 3267). These include, but are not limited to *Roma negli anni di influenza e dominio francese 1798-1814* (ed. Boutry, Pitocco and Travaglini, ed., Rome, 2000) and *La Rivoluzione nello Stato della Chiesa* (ed. Luigi Fiorani, Pisa-Rome, 1997).

In addition to the wealth of Roman and Vatican archives, any serious scholar must investigate the flowering of conferences, exhibitions, and museum catalogues dealing with the period.

BIBLIOGRAPHY

Manuscript Sources

Biblioteca Apostolica Vaticana
Fortunati, Vat. Lat. 10730 and 10731, 'Avvennimenti sotto il Pontificio di Pio VI, 1775-1800',
and 'Avvenementi sotto li Pontif. Di Pio VII e Leone XII Dall'Anni 1800-1828.'

Biblioteca Casanatense
'Raccolte di varie satire o pasquinate pubblicate in Roma in diversi tempi e circostanze'. MS
3934

Biblioteca Vallicelliana
Il collezione di canone Falzacappi, vols. XIII – XVI.

Museo di Roma
Mat. 3266 and 3267 Caricatures of Giuseppe Barbari, legato XVIII and XIX,
Plastici. Plastica di Roma, T. Falcetti and G. Valadier, 1826.
[The museum also has an extensive collection of prints and watercolours by Antoine Thomas as
well as a collection of contemporary clothing, numerous illustrations and a model by Valadier.]

Museo Napoleonico
1232 (Jewellery in micro-mosaic)
637 (Game of 'hombre' belonging to Napoleon)
146 (seven-stone bracelet belonging to Letizia Bonaparte)
3878 ('Murat's despair', by Pinelli)
1350 (Proclamation of Rimini, 30 March 1815)
7053 (Order for the execution of Murat, 10 October 1815)
616, 595, 612, 608, 605, 3925, 600 (designs in honour of the birth of the King of Rome, by
Bartolomeo Pinelli)

Museo di Roma Trastevere
Scenes and re-creations of Roman life after the work of Bartolomeo Pinelli.

Bibliothèque de l'Ecole Française à Rome
Thomas, A. J-B. *Un an à Rome,* Paris, 1823.

Archivio di Stato di Roma
Archiconfraternità di S. Giovanni Decollato, 1497-1870, Busta II (1772-1810).
Archiconfraternità di S. Giovanni Decollato, Giustiziati 1772-1810.
Editti e bandi, 416.

Istituzioni di beneficenza e di istruzioni, buste 2056-62 and 2070-74.
Consulta Straordinaria per gli Stati Romani.
Decreti e rapporti 51, 108, 115, 118, 128, 129, 152, 167, 359, 379, 406, 415, 447, 453, 856, 876,
908, 1259, 1260, 1618, 1679, 2029 B, 2378, 2656, 2689, 2702-2703, 2707, 2708, 2328, 3599, 3661,
3727, 3763, 3785, 4060, 4214, 4252, 4492, 4577, 4635, 4941, 5026.
Registri dei decreti 1 – 27, 1809-1810, n. 20-24, 1810.
Repubblica romana (1798-99), b. 8 fasc 43, 'Decreti del Consolato'.
Collezione di carte pubbliche, proclami, editti, ragionamenti ... tendenti a consolidare la
rigenerata Repubblica Romana, 5 vols. Rome 1798.
Collezione dei Bandi.

Biblioteca Nazionale
Antonio Galimberti, 'Memorie dell'occupazione francese in Roma dal 1798 alla fine del 1802.'
Manuscript diary, 2 vols. MSS 44 and 45 in the Victor Emanuel collection.

Archivio di Vicariato, Rome
Tragnoli, Basilio. *Diario di memorie appartenenti all'insigne basilica di S. Maria in Trastevere scritte
da Basilio Tragnoli benefiziato e cerimonista della medesima basilica dall'anno 1780 al l'anno 1814.*
in ASVR Capitol di S Maria in Trastevere, b. 19, Funzione religiose straordinarie, fasc 9, pp 88-306.

Guide to Italian materials in the National Archives of France
Peroni, Baldo, *Fonti per la storia d'Italia dal 1798 al 1815 nell'Archivio nazionale di Parigi.*
Rome, 1936.

Secondary Sources

AAVV *French Artists in Rome: Ingres to Degas, 1803-1873*, Dahesh Museum of Art, New York.
AAVV *Bibliografia Romana, 1989-1998*. Ricerche, fonti, e testi per la storia di Roma. Eimond, 2004.
AAVV *Centenario del ritorno di Pio VII alla Sede romana e festa di Maria SS. 'Auxilium
Christianorum':* 24 maggio 1814 - 24 maggio 1914.
AAVV *Berthold Thorvaldsen, Scultore Danese.* Rome, 1989.
AAVV *S. Gaspare del Bufalo e Piacenza nell'età napoleonica.* Atti del Convegno di studi,
Piacenza, Palazzo Fogliani, 9 nov 1986. Piacenza, 1987.
AAVV *Giuseppe Gioachino Belli e la Roma del suo Tempo: Mostra del centenario della morte del
Poeta (1863-1963)* Catalogue of exhibit at Palazzo Braschi, Dec 1963-Feb 1964. Rome, 1963.
AAVV *Riti, ceremonie, feste e vita del popolo nella Roma deli papi.* Bologna, 1970.
AAVV *Roma negli anni di influenza francese, 1798-1814. Rotture, continuita, innovazioni tra fine
Settecento e inizi Ottocento.* Rome, 1994.
AAV. *Il Settecento a Roma.* Rome, 1959. Catalogue of the exhibition.
Alberti, G. 'Medicina popolare minima', in *Strenna dei Romanisti.* Rome, 1953.
Amadei, E. 'L'antico Caffe Greco compie 200 anni'. *Capitolium*, XXXIV, fasc 10, 1959.
Anderson, Robin. *Pope Pius VII (1800-1823): His Life, His Times, and His Struggle with
Napoleon.* Rockford, IL, 2000.
Andrieux, Maurice. *Daily Life in Papal Rome in the Eighteenth Century.* Trans. Mary Fritton.
London, 1968.
_____ *Les Françaises à Rome.* Paris, 1968.
_____ *Rome.* Trans. Charles Lam Markmann. New York, 1968.
Angeli, Diego. *I Bonaparte a Roma.* Rome, 1938.
_____ *Roma Romantica.* Milan, 1935.
_____ *Storia Romana di Trent'anni, 1770-1800.* Rome, 1931.
Anon. 'La Roma di Napoleone.' *La Civiltà Cattolica*, 57/2, 1906.
Anon. 'La liquidazione del debito pubblico a Roma.' *La Civiltà Cattolica*, 57/3, 1906.
Anon. 'Lavori in Roma nell'epoca napoleonica. Il Palazzo di Venezia, il Pincio.' *La Civiltà
Cattolica*, 57/4, 1906.
Aquaro Graziosi, Maria Teresa. *L'Arcadia: Trecento anni di storia.* Rome, 1991.
Arcienegas, Don German. 'Simon Bolivar a Roma.' *Capitolium*, XXXIV, fasc 12, 1959.
Armando, David. 'La "Democratizzazione" di Roma nel Carteggio Chigi-Fossombroni

(gennaio-marzo 1798).' Roma Moderna e Contemporanea, 1994: 55-76.

Aslan, Sissi. Le Madonnelle. "Bancarella Romana # 22", Claudio Rendina, ed. Rome, 1994

Baldini, Antonio. 'La morra e la passatella.' Strenna dei Romanisti. Rome, 1950.

Bandini, G. Roma nel Settecento. Rome, 1930.

Barberini, Urbano. 'Un autoritratto di Bartolomeo Pinelli.' Bollettino dei musei comunali di Roma, XII 1-4, 1965.

Beaumont, Fernand. 'Napoleon et Rome: les travaux du Tibre.' Rivista Italiana di Studi Napoleonici, 1972-74, 11: 75-85.

Belli, Giuseppe Gioacchino. Tutti i sonetti romaneschi. Rome, 1972.

Bertrand, Count General. Journal du général Bertrand, Grand maréchal du palais. Cahiers de Sainte-Hélène. Paris, 1949.

Bessières, Albert, S. J. Wife, Mother and Mystic (Blessed Anna Maria Taigi). Trans. Steven Rigby, Rockfort, IL, 1982, first published in French, 1952.

Biagi, Maria Cristina. Carnevale di popolo a Roma tra il XVIII e il XIX secolo. Rome, 1997.

Biagi, Maria Cristina, Marcella Corsi, Donatella Occhiuzzi. Il Museo di Roma in Trastevere. Palombi, 2004.

_____ and S. Bonfili. Gli aquerelli di E. Roesler Franz nelle collezioni del Museo del Folklore. Rome, 1989.

Boime, Albert. Art in an Age of Bonapartism, 1800-1815. Chicago, 1990.

Bonasegale, Giovanna. L'ottobrata: Una Festa Romana. Catalogue of exhibit at the Museo del Folklore, 15 oct to 2 dec 1990. Rome, 1990.

Boyer, Ferdinand. Le monde des arts en Italie et la France de la Révolution et de l'Empire. Paris, 1969.

Blumer, M. L. 'Catalogue des peintures transportées d'Italie en France de 1796 à 1814.' Bulletin de la Société de l'Histoire de l'Art Français, 1936: 244-348.

Bonechi, Simone. 'Chiesa e Societa nell'Italia napoleonica. Rassegna di studi recenti (1989-96) e proposta di ricerca.' Cristianesimo nella Storia, 19, 1998: 297-332.

_____ 'L'impossibile restaurazione: I vescovi filonapoleonici nell'Italia francese tra "servilismo" e primato di Pietro (1801-1814).' Cristianesimo nella Storia 21 (2000): 343-381

Borghini, Gabriele. Divertimento e Penitenza nella vita popolare romana. Catalogue of an exhibit of images from the Gabinetto Comunale delle Stampe, held at the Palazzo Braschi. Rome, 1975.

Bortoccini, Fiorello. Roma nel Ottocento. Bologna, 1985.

Boutry, Philippe. 'La Roma napoleonica fra tradizione e modernità (1809-1814)', in Fiorani, Roma: La Citta del papa. Turin, 2000.

Boyer, Fernand. Le monde des arts en Italie et la France de la Révolution et de l'Empire. Études et recherches. Turin, 1970.

Broers, Michael. The Politics of Religion in Napoleonic Italy: The war against God, 1801-1814. London and New York, 2002.

_____ '"The War against God": Napoleon, Pope Pius VII and the people of Italy, 1800-1814', in The Historian, London, Spring 2001: 16-21.

Brown-Olf, Lillian. Their Name is Pius: Portraits of Five Great Modern Popes. Milwaukee, 1941.

Buratta, A. 'Il cardinale Giuseppe Antonio Sala e la visita apostolica agli ospedali di Roma.' Rivista di Storia della Chiesa in Italia, XLI, 1987.

Burton, Deborah, Susan Nicassio, and Agostino Ziino, eds. Tosca's Prism: Three Moments in Cultural History, 1800-1900-2000. Boston, 2004.

Caffiero, Marina. La Nuova era. Miti e profezie dell'Italia in rivoluzione. Geneva, 1991

_____ 'Perdono per i Giacobini, severità per gli insorgenti: La prima restaurazione pontificia.' Studi Storici. 1998, 39 (2).

Cajani, L. 'Pena di morte e tortura a Roma nel Settecento', in Criminalità e società in età moderna. Milan, 1991.

Calcott, Maria. Three Months Passed in the Mountains North of Rome. London, 1821.

Calzolari, M and E. Grantaliano. Lo Stato pontificio tra Rivoluzione e Restaurazione: istituzioni e archivi (1798-1870). Rome, 2003.

Campagnol, Isabella. 'La moda "empire" attraverso gli abiti di corte del Museo Napoleonico.' Bollettino dei musei comunali di Roma, 1996.

Canali, Giuseppe. 'Memorie di un prete romano deportato al tempo di Napoleone: Giuseppe Canali.' Civilta Cattolica, 2, 1934; 3, 1934.

Canonica, Maria Assumta. 'Un autografo di Antonio Canova al Museo Canonica.' Bollettino dei

Musei Comunali di Roma, XX, 1973.

Canonici, C. 'Il dibattito sul giuramento civico (1798-99)', in Luigi Fiorani, *Deboli Progressi della Filosofia: Rivoluzione e religione a Roma, 1789-1799*. Vol. 9 in series, *Ricerche per la storia religiosa di Roma*, 1992.

Canonici, C. 'Giuramenti, adesioni, e ritrattazioni nel periodo napoleonico e nella Restaurazione: il caso della diocesi di Sutri.' *Rivista di Storia della Chiesa in Italia*, 40, 1986.

Capograssi, Antonio. *Gli inglesi in Italia durante le Campage Napoleoniche: Lord W. Bentinck.* Bari, 1949.

Cattaneo, Massimo. 'L'Opposizione popolare al "Giacobinismo" a Roma e nello stato Pontificio.' *Studi Storici*, 1998, 39 (2).

Cattaneo, M. 'Gli Occhi di Maria sulla Rivoluzione', in *Miracoli a Roma e nello stato della Chiesa* (1796-1799), Rome, 1995.

Chadwick, Owen. *The Popes and the European Revolution.* Oxford, 1981.

Clementi, Filippo. *Il carnivale romano nelle cronache contemporanee.* Città di Castello, 1938.

Cofini, Marcello. 'Canti, soni, balli de Rom', in *Vita popolare romanesca dalla letteratura pianistica: saltarelli, tarantelle, zampognate e pifferate, serenate, barcarole e altro.* Rome, 2001.

Connolly, Owen. *The French Revolution/Napoleonic Era.* New York, 1979.

Contegiacomo, Luigi. *St Gaspar's Prison Experiences, 1810-1813.* Cartegena, Ohio, 1988.

Corsi, Marcella. 'Appunti per una cronologia delle *Scene romane* al Museo di Roma in Trastevere.' *Bollettino dei Musei Comunali*, NS 2000-2001.

Cretoni, Antonio. *Roma Giacobina. Storia della Repubblica Romana del 1798-99.* Rome, 1971.

Davis, John. *Conflict and Control: Law and Order in Nineteenth-Century Italy.* Atlantic Highlands, N. J., 1988.

Daniel-Rops, Henri. *The Church in an Age of Revolution 1789-1870.* Trans. John Warrington. London, 1965

Decaux, Alain, *Napoleon's Mother.* Trans. Len Ortzen. London, 1962. First published as *Letizia, Mère de l'Empereur*, Paris, 1959.

DeCesare, Raffaele. 'I Romani e la nascita del Re di Roma', in *Quaderni dei cultura francese*, Rome, 1996.

De Felice, Renzo. 'Gli ebrei nella repubblica romana del 1798-99.' *Rassegna storica del Risorgimento*, 11, 1953.

_____ *Aspetti e momenti della vita economica di Roma e del Lazio nei secoli XVIII e XIX.* Rome, 1965.

Del Frate, Paolo Alvizzi. 'La formazione dei giuristi nella roma napoleonica: La facolta di giurisprudenza della sapienza.' *Roma Moderna e Contemoranea*, II, 1 (1994): 91-104.

Della Paruta, Franco. *Malattia e medicina.* Vol. 7 of *Storia d'Italia.* Turin, 1984.

Dal Pane, Luigi. *Lo stato pontificio e il movimento riformatore del Settecento.* Milan, 1959.

DeRosa, P. A. and P. E. Trastulli. *Roma d'una Volta.* Rome, 1991.

_____ *Roma Sparita e dintorni negli aquarelli di Ettore Roesler Franz.* Rome, 1994.

Donakowski, Conrad. 'God in Man's Image: Religious Ritual as Mass Media during the Aufkalrung.' *Proceedings of the Consortium on Revolutionary Europe (CRE)*, 1985.

Donato, Maria Pia 'Alcune ipotesi sulla borghesia delle professioni e la repubblica del 1798-99: Il caso dei medici del S. Spirito in Sassia.' *Roma Moderna e Contemoranea*, II, 1 (1994): 11-30.

Driault, E. 'Rome et Napoléon.' *Revue des études napoléoniennes*, 1918.

Duppa, Richard. *A Journal of the Most Remarkable occurrences that took place in Rome upon the Subversion of the Ecclesiastical Government in 1798.* London, 1799.

Durant, Will and Ariel. *The Age of Napoleon. Story of Civilization*, vol. II. New York, 1980.

Eaton, Charlotte A. *Rome in the Nineteenth Century ... a series of letters written during a residence in Rome in the years 1817 and 1818.* 2 vols., published anonymously. New York, 1827.

Elie, Bernard . 'La curieuse vie du General Radet, l'homme qui a enlefe le Pape, 1762-1825.' *Revue Historique de l'Armee* 1959, 15 (3).

Faggiolo, Maurizio and Marurzio Marini. *Bartolomeo Pinelli 1781-1835 e il Suo Tempo.* Rome, 1981.

Fiorani, Luigi. *Le confraternite romane: esperienza religiosa, societa, commitenze artistica: Colloquio della fondazione Caetani, Roma, 14-15 maggio, 1982.* Rome, 1984.

_____ 'Roma, la citta del papa: Vita civile e religiosa del giubileo di Bonifacio VIII al giubileo di papa Wojtyla.' *Storia, Annali 16*, Turin, 2000.

Fiorelli, Piero. *La Tortura Giudiziaria nel diritto commune.* Giuffre, 1953.

Formica, Marina. 'Potere e popolo. Alcuni interrogativi sulla Repubblica romana giacobina.'

Studi romani 37 (1989), 3-4: 235-257.

_____ 'The Protagonists and the Principal Phases of the Roman Republic of 1798 to 1799', in *Tosca's Prism: Three Moments of Western Cultural History*. Boston, 2004, pp. 67-81.

_____ 'Vigilanza urbana e ordine pubblico a Roma (1798-1799)' in Roma Moderna e Contemporanea II, # 1 (1994): 31-54.

_____ 'Vox populi, vox dei? Meccanismi di formazione dell'opinione pubblica a Roma (1798-1799)', in *Dimensioni e problemi della ricerca storica, Rivista del Dipartimento di studi storici dal Medioevo all'età contemporanea dell'Università 'La Sapienza' di Roma*, 2 (1989): 47-81.

_____ and L Lorenzetti. *Il Misogallo romano*. Rome, Bulzoni, 1998.

Friz, Giuliano. *Consumi, tenore di vita e prezzi a Roma dal 1700 al 1900*. Rome, 1980.

_____ 'La popolazione di Roma dal 1770 al 1900.' *Archivio economico dell'unificazione italiana*, series II, vol. XIX, IRI. Rome, 1974.

_____ *Burocrati e soldati dello stato pontificio (1800-1870)*. *Archivio economico dell'unificazione italiana*, series II, vol XX, IRI. Rome, 1974.

Frutaz, Amato Pietro (ed.). *Le piante di Roma*. 3 vols. Rome, 1962.

Fusco di Ravello, A. 'Tra conservazione e ragione: la tortura giudiziaria nello Stato pontificio nel '700', *Archivio Storica romano di Storia Patria*, CVII (1984): 305-324.

Gallo, D. 'I Visconti: Una famiglia romana al servizio dei papi, della Repubblica e di Napoleone'. *Roma Moderna e Contemporanea*, II, 1, (1994): 77-90.

Giuntella, Vittorio Emanuele. *Bibliografia della Repubblica romana*. Rome, 1957.

_____ and Carlo Gasbarri. *Due Diari della Repubblica Romana del 1798-1799*. Rome, 1958.

_____ 'Gli esuli romani in Francia alla vigilia del 18 brumaio', *Archivio della Società romana di Storia Patria*, LXXVI, 1953.

_____ *La giacobbina Repubblica romana*. Rome, 1953.

_____ 'Le classe sociali della Roma giacobbina', *Rassegna storica del Risorgimento* XXXVIII, 38 (1951): 428-433.

_____ 'Roma nell'eta Napoleonica', in *Napoleone e l'Italia*, Atti del Convegno, Rome, 1973.

_____ *Roma nel Settecento*. Vol XV of *Storia di Roma*. Bologna, 1971.

Goethe, Johann Wolfgang. *Italian Journey, 1786-1788*. Trans. W. H. Auden and Elizabeth Mayer. London, 1962.

Gorani, Giuseppe, *Memoires secrets et critiques des cours, des gouvernements et des moeurs des principaux états de l'Italie*. 3 vols, Paris and Brussels, 1793.

Gorgone, Giulia. *Elisa Bonaparte: Ritratti di Famiglia*. Catalogue, Museo Napoleonico. Rome, 2004.

_____ 'Da Sant'Elena à Roma: Storia di un *jeu de l'hombre*', in 'Play, Society and Cultures in Europe and Italy between the 18th and 19th Centuries', *Rivista Napoleonica* 2/2001.

Gori Sassoli, Mario. *Della chinea e di altre 'Macchine di gioia': Apprararti architettonici per fuochi d'artificio a Roma nel Settecento*. Rome, 1994.

Grab, Alexander. 'Army, State, and Society: Conscription and Desertion in Napoleonic Italy (1802-1814)', *Journal of Modern History* 67 (1995): 24-52.

_____ 'The Napoleonic Legacy in Italy', in *Tosca's Prism: Three Moments in Western Cultural History*. Boston, 2004, pp. 3-18.

Graziosi, Maria Teresa Acquaro. *L'Arcadia, trecento anni di storia*. Rome, 1991.

Gregory, Desmond. *Napoleon's Italy*. London, 2001.

Gross, Hanns. *Rome in the Age of Enlightenment: The Post-Tridentine Syndrome and the Ancien Regime*. Cambridge, 1990.

Hales, E. E. Y. *The Emperor and the Pope*. London, 1962.

_____ *Revolution and Papacy, 1796-1846*. London, 1960.

Hartmann, Jurgen Birkedel. *Bertel Thorvaldsen: Scoltore danese, romano d'adozione*. Rome, 1971.

Hazlitt, William. *Notes of a Journey through France and Italy*. London, 1826.

Henry, Jean. 'Antonio Canova, the French Imperium, and Emerging Nationalism in Italy', *Proceedings of the Consortium on Revolutionary Europe* (1980): 82-95.

Heriot, Angus. *The French in Italy 1796-1799*. London, 1957.

Hibbert, Christopher. *The Grand Tour*. New York, 1969.

Hibbert, Christopher. *Rome, the Biography of a City*. London, 1985.

Huet, Valerie. 'Napoleon I: a new Augustus?', in *Roman Presences: Receptions of Rome in*

European Culture, 1789-1945, Catherine Edwards, ed. Cambridge, 1999, pp. 53-69.

Incisa della Rochetta, G. 'Il carnacciaro, in *Strenna dei Romanisti*. Rome, 1956.

_____ 'Un nuovo album di disegni di Bartolomeo Pinelli', *Bollettino dei Musei comunali di Roma*, XX (1973): 13-20.

_____ 'Pio VII a Palazzo Colonna', *Bollettino dei Musei Comunali di Roma*, XVI, 1969.

Indovino, Fortunato [pseudonym]. *Il vero mezzo di vincere al lotto: Nuovo lista alfabetica di tutte le voci appartenenti a visioni e sogni col loro numero*. Carla Ferrario, ed. Milan, 1989. [first published in Venice, after 1759, this is a copy of the 8th edition, Venice 1813]

Jannatoni, L. *Roma sparita negli acquarelli di Ettore Roesler Franz*. Rome, 1981.

Johns, Christopher M.S. *Antonio Canova and the Politics of Patronage in Revolutionary and Napoleonic Europe*. Los Angeles, 1998.

Kleine-Ahlbrandt, Laird William. 'Victorien Sardou and the Legend of Marengo', in *Tosca's Prism: Three Moments in Western Cultural History*. Boston 2004, pp. 94-113.

Koenig, Duane. Banditry in Napoleonic Italy.' *Proceedings of the Consortium on Revolutionary Europe*, iv (1975): 72-80.

Kolega, Alexandra. 'Speziali, spagirici, droghieri e ciarlatani. L'offerta terapeutica a Roma tra Sei e Settecento.' *Roma Moderna e Contemporanea* 6, # 3 (1998): 311-348.

Kotzebue, August von. *Travels in Italy in the Years 1804-05*. 4 vols. London, 1806.

Labat, J. B. *Voyages en Espagne et Italie*. 8 vols, Paris, 1730.

Lamar, Glenn. *Jérôme Bonaparte: The War Years, 1800-1815*. Westport, CT, 2000.

Lamartine, A. de. Letter to Mme Haste, 15 nov 1811, published in R. Doumic, *Le Correspondant*, 1908, N.S., 186 and in *Carnet de voyage*.

_____ *Les Confidences*. Paris, 1934.

_____ *Nouvelles confidences*. Paris, 1887.

_____ *Mémoires inedites*. Paris, 1881.

Lancellotti, Arturo. *Feste Tradizionali*. Milan, 1951.

LaPadula, Attilio. *Roma 1809-1814*. Rome, 1958.

_____. *Roma et la Regione nell'epoca Napoleonica*. Rome, 1969.

LaPaglia, Vincenzo. *La morte confortata: rite della paura e mentalita' religiosa a Roma nell'eta' moderna*. Biblioteca della storia sociale, 13. Rome, 1982.

Lemmi, F. 'Roma nell'Impero napoleonico.' *Archivio Storico Italiano*, LXXIII (1915): 119-142.

Lio, Anna and Giulia Gorgone. *Caricatura, satira e mito traverso le stampe popolari*. Rome, 1984.

LoSardo, E. 'Le statistiche francesi negli Stati romani.' *Rassegna degli Archivi di Stato*, XLIV, 1994.

Madelin, Louis. *La Rome de Napoleon: La domination française à Rome de 1809 à 1814. Ouvrage accompangé de deux cartes*. Paris, 1906.

Maes, C. *Curiosità romane*. Rome, 1885.

Maria Luigia. *Memoir of the Queen of Etruria, written by herself. Including an Authentic Narrative of the seizure and removal of Pope Pius VII on the 6th of July 1809*. London, 1814.

Mariotti Bianchi, Umberto. *I Molini sul Tevere. Nascita, vita e morte delle antiche mole fluviali*. Rome, 1996.

Martini, Stelio. *I negozi d'epoca a Roma*. Rome, 1996.

Martorelli, *Dissertazione sopra gli odori di Roma*. Rome, 1812.

Menozzi, D. 'L'orginazzazione della chiesa italiana in età napoleonica.' *Cristianesimo nella storia* (1993): 405-445.

McVaugh, Robert. 'A Generation Misplaced: Central European Artists in Rome, 1800-1810.' *CRE*, 1989.

Mercati, A. 'Elenchi di ecclesiastici dello stato romano deportati per rifiuto del giuramento imposto da Napoleone.' *Rivista di Storia della Chiesa in Italia*, 7, 1953,

Miller, Marian. 'The Italian Revolutions and the Musical Arena.' *CRE*, 1987.

Nardi, Carla *Napoleone e Roma: la politica della Consulta romana*. Rome, 1989.

_____ *Consulta straordinaria per gli Stati Romani (1809-1810). Inventario*. Rome, 1990.

Nicassio, Susan. 'The unfortunate Giuseppe Barberi and his pictorial diary of the Roman Republic, 1798-99.' *Consortium on Revolutionary Europe, Selected Papers* (2002): 351-359..

_____. *Tosca's Rome: The Play and the Opera in Historical Perspective*. Chicago, 2000.

Norci Cagiano de Azevedo, Letizia. *Lo specchio del viaggiatore. Scenari italiani tra Barocco e Romanticismo*. Rome, 1992.

Occhiuzzi, Donatella. 'L'abito popolare di Roma e Dintorni, nella collezione del Museo di

Roma in Trastevere.' Pre-publication essay given to the author.

Olivier, Michel. *Vivre et peindre à rome au XVIIIème siècle*. Rome, 1996.

Pacca, Bartolomeo. *Mémoires du cardinal Pacca sur la captivité du Pape Pie VII*. Trans. L. Bellaguet. Paris, 1833.

Paccini, Renato. *Bartolomeo Pinelli e la Roma del suo Tempo*. Milan, 1935.

Paglia, V. 'La morte come spettacolo', in *La Morte confortata. Riti della paura e mentalità religiosa a Roma nell'età moderna*. Rome, 1982.

Palazzolo, Maria Iolanda. 'L'Arcadia romana nel periodo napoleonico (1809-1814).' *Roma Moderna e Contemporanea*. Rome, 1993 I (3).

_____ 'Arcadia e stampatori: I De Romanis nella Roma dei Papi', in *Tre secoli di storia dell'Arcadia*. Rome, 1991.

_____ 'Banchi, botteghe, muricciuoli. Luoghi e figure del commercio del libro a Roma nel Settecento.' *Roma Moderna e Contemporanea*. 1994 II (2).

_____ *Editoria e Istituzioni a roma tra settecento e ottocento: Saggi e documenti*. Rome, 1994.

Pastor, Ludwig von. *History of the Popes from the Close of the Middle Ages, 1305-1800*. 40 vols., London, 1891-1953.

Patrizi, Marchesa Maddalena. *The Patrizi Memoirs: A Roman Family under Napoleon, 1796-1815*. Trans. Mrs Hugh Fraser, with historical introduction by J. Crawford Fraser. London, 1915.

_____ *Memorie di famiglia 1796-1815*. Rome, 1912.

_____ 'La leva dorata del 1811', in *Atti del Congresso nazionale di studi romani*, edited by G. Galassi Paluzzi. Rome (1931): 396-405.

Pietrangeli, Carlo. 'Medaglie romane per il Re di Roma.' *Bollettino dei Musei Comunali di Roma*, XVI (1969): 29-33.

Pocinio, Willy. *Le Curiosità di Roma: Storie, anedotti e segreti legati a luoghi, tradizioni e monumenti esistenti e scomparsi di una città irrepetibile*. Rome, 1985, vol 31 in series *Tradizioni italiani*.

Pommier, E. Quatrèmere de Quincy, A. C. translated as *Lo studio delle arti e il genio dell'Europa. Scritti di A.C. Quatrèmere de Quincy, e di Pio VII Chiaramonti*. Paris, 1796 (reprinted Paris, 1989).

Pratesi, Ludovico. *Le Cupole di Roma: Un'affascinante passeggiata 'a testa in su' alla scoperta delle protagoniste del paesaggio romano*. Rome, 1999.

Raggi, Oreste. *Cenni intorno alla vita ed alle opere principali di Bartolomeo Pinelli*. Rome, 1835.

Rendina, Claudio, ed.. *Mastro Titta, il boja di Roma: Le spettacolari 'giusitzie' del famoso carnefice pontificio tra cronache e storie d'appendice*. Rome, 1992.

_____ *I papi, Storia e segreti*. Rome, 1983.

_____ *Pasquino: Statua parlante. Quattro secoli di pasquinate*. Rome, 1992.

_____ *Roma di Belli: La città, i luoghi, i monumenti, le feste e gli spettacoli in 50 sonetti romaneschi del grande poeta*. Rome, 1994.

Ridley, Ronald T. *The Eagle and the Spade: Archaeology in Rome during the Napoleonic Era*. Cambridge, 1992.

Righetti, R. 'Un insigne giurista algli albori del Risorgimento. Vincenzo Bartolucci.' *Capitolium*, XXVII, 1952.

Rocciolo, D. 'Documenti sulla vita religiosa primo e durante la Repubblica romana', in Luigi Fiorani, *Deboli Progressi della Filosofia: Rivoluzione e religione a Roma, 1789-1799*. Vol. 9 in series, *Ricerche per la storia religiosa di Roma*. Rome, 1992.

Romano, Pietro. *Ottocento Romano*. Rome, 1943.

_____ *Tre secoli di vita Romana*. Rome, 1941.

_____ *La satira nella Roma napoleonica*. Rome, 1936.

Rosenberg, Martin. 'Raphael's Transfiguration and Napoleon's Cultural Politics.' *Eighteenth-Century Studies* (1985-86): 180-205.

Rossetti, Bartolomeo. *I bulli di Roma*. Rome, 1996.

_____ *La Roma di Bartolomeo Pinelli: Una città e il suo popolo attraverso feste, mestieri, ambienti e personaggi caratteristici nelle più belle incisioni del 'pittor de Trastevere'*. Rome, 1985.

Sage, Robert, ed. *The Private Diaries of Stendhal*. Garden City, NY, 1954.

Sala, G. A. *Scritti di Giuseppe Antonio Sala pubblicati sugli autografi da Giuseppe Cugnoni. Diario Romano*. Rome, 1882-1888.

Salmon, J. *An Historical Description of Ancient and Modern Rome*. London, 1800.

Saraceno, Chiara. 'Women, Family, and the Law, 1750-1942.' *Journal of Family History* Vol. 15, #4, 1990.

Sarazani, Fabrizio. *Scene e costumi di Roma e del Lazio di Bartolomeo Pinelli.* Rome, 1966.

Schneid, Frederick. 'Eugene and the Defence of Italy, 1813'. *Proceedings of the Consortium on Revolutionary Europe* (1991): 171-181

Severi, Stefania. 'I teatri di roma, dall'antichità fino a oggi', in *Quest'Italia, Collana di storia, arte e folklore.* Rome, 1989.

Seward, Desmond. *Napoleon's Family: The Notorious Bonapartes and their Ascent to the Thrones of Europe.* New York, 1986.

Shryock, Richard Harrison. *The Development of Modern Medicine; an interpretation of the social and scientific factors involved.* New York, 1936.

Silvagni, David. *La corte e la società romana nei secoli XVIII e XIX.* 4 vols., Rome, 1881-1885. Trans F. McLaughlin, *Court and Society in Rome in the Eighteenth and Nineteenth Centuries.* 3 vols., Boston, 1887.

Smolett, Tobias. *Travels through France and Italy,* London 1776.

Sofia, Francesca. '"Recueillir et mettre en order": Aspetti politica amministrative di J.M. de Gérando à Roma.' *Roma Moderna e Contemporanea,* 2, 1 (1994): 105-124.

Sonnino, Eugenio and Adriana Brasiello. 'La mortalità infantile a Roma durante la seconda dominazione francese alle base registrazioni dello "Stato Civile", in *Roma degli anni di influenza e dominio francese.* Rome, 1994, pp. 326-337.

Spina, A. 'Diario della deportazione del canonico di Albano G.B. Loberti (1810-1814).' *Studi Storici* I (1985): 21-26.

_____ 'Diario anonimo di un deportato in Corsica nell'epoca napoleonica.' *Rivista di Storia della Chiesa in Italia* 47/2, 1993.

_____ 'Nuovi documenti sulle deportazzioni napoleoniche di ecclesiastici dello Stato della Chiesa (1810-1814).' *Rivista di Storia della Chiesa in Italia* 45/1, 1990.

Spinelli, Mario. *I Santi di Roma.* Rome, 1999.

Staccioli, Paola and Stefano Nespoli. *Roma Artigiana: Attualità, storia e tradizioni dell'artigianato artistico romano.* Rome, 1996.

Staccioli, Paola. *I Briganti della Campagna Romana.* Rome, 1996.

Tamburini, E. 'La penetenziaria apostolica negli anni della occupazione napoleonica (1808-1814).' *Archivio della Societa romana di storia patria,* serie 3, vol. 27, 1973.

Thompson, Edward Healy. *The Venerable Anna Maria Taigi.* London, 1873.

Thomas, Antoine. *Un an à Rome et dans ses environs.* Paris, 1823.

Titoni, Maria Elisa. *Mito e storia nei 'Fasti di Napoleone' di Andrea Appiani.* Rome, 1986.

_____ 'Napoleone, I suoi fratelli e le loro residenze romane.' *Capitolium*(1998): 85-89.

Tournon, Camille de. *Etudes statistiques sur Rome et la partie occidentale des états Romains.* 2 vols. and atlas, Paris, 1831.

Travaglini, Carlo M. 'Dalla corporazione al gruppo professionale: I rigattieri nell'Ottocento pontificio.' *Roma Moderna e Contemporanea* IV, # 3 (1998): 427-472.

Vaussard, Maurice. *La vie quotidienne en italie au XVIIIe siecle.* Paris, 1959. Trans. Michael Aheron, *Daily Life in Eighteenth-Century Italy.* London, 1962.

Verdone, Mario. 'I Cammuccini. Alcune notizie biografiche su tre pittori.' *Strenna dei Romanisti,* XL, 1979.

_____ *Le Maschere Romane.* Rome 1997.

Verri, Alessandro. *La Repubblica Francese,* Milan, 1862.

_____ *Vicende memorabile dal 1789 al 1801.* Milan, 1858.

Weber, Eugen. *Apocalyspes: Prophecies, Cults, and Millennial Beliefs through the Ages.* Cambridge, 1999.

_____ 'Mme. De ....' *Consortium on Revolutionary Europe, Selected Papers,* 2003.

Wilson, Robert Thomas. *The Life of General Sir Robert Thomas Wilson 1777-1849.* Trans. Herbert Randolph *Vita del Generale Sir Robert Wilson.* Milan, 1972.

Woolf, Stuart. *A History of Italy, 1700-1860.* London, 1986.

Wiseman, F. N. *Recollections of the Last Four Popes.* London, 1858.

Zanazzo, Luigi (Giggi). *Canti popolari romani con un saggio dei canti del Lazio.* Turin and Rome, 1910.

_____ *Tradizioni popolari romane. Usi, costumi, e pregiudizi del popolo di Roma.* 4 vols., Rome, 1907-1910 (re-published Rome, 1994).

Zangarini, Luciano. *La Cultura Popolare a Roma, un itinerario bibliografico.* Rome, 1992.

TUTTO FINISCE